A

[signature: Philip E. Lilienthal]

■   ■   ■

B O O K

The Philip E. Lilienthal imprint
honors special books
in commemoration of a man whose work
at University of California Press from 1954 to 1979
was marked by dedication to young authors
and to high standards in the field of Asian Studies.
Friends, family, authors, and foundations have together
endowed the Lilienthal Fund, which enables UC Press
to publish under this imprint selected books
in a way that reflects the taste and judgment
of a great and beloved editor.

The Narrowing Sea

ASIA PACIFIC MODERN

Takashi Fujitani, Series Editor

The Narrowing Sea

FUKUOKA, PUSAN, AND THE RISE AND FALL
OF AN IMPERIAL REGION

Hannah Shepherd

UNIVERSITY OF CALIFORNIA PRESS

University of California Press
Oakland, California

Cataloging-in-Publication data is on file at the Library of Congress.

ISBN 978-0-520-40528-8 (cloth : alk. paper)
ISBN 978-0-520-40529-5 (pbk. : alk. paper)
ISBN 978-0-520-40530-1 (ebook)

Manufactured in the United States of America

GPSR Authorized Representative: Easy Access System Europe, Mustamäe tee 50, 10621 Tallinn, Estonia, gpsr.requests@easproject.com

34 33 32 31 30 29 28 27 26 25
10 9 8 7 6 5 4 3 2 1

The publisher and the University of California Press Foundation gratefully acknowledge the generous support of the Philip E. Lilienthal Imprint in Asian Studies, established by a major gift from Sally Lilienthal.

In memory of Carter J. Eckert, 1945–2024

"The morality of the historian is ultimately humanistic. It might be described as a fearless commitment to knowledge of the human condition in all its complexity, a factual, honest, and richly detailed exploration of the things human beings have done, why and how they have done them, and their impact on human life. When the historian renders judgment, let those judgments be made not merely with the vision of hindsight, but also from a scholarly, empathic understanding of the full temporal and psychic context of the human lives and actions being studied. One could say that the historian should aim to be no less than a Shakespeare of facts."

—CARTER J. ECKERT, "Exorcising Hegel's Ghosts: Toward a Postnationalist Historiography of Korea"

CONTENTS

ILLUSTRATIONS

MAPS

FIGURES

TABLES

ACKNOWLEDGMENTS

They say it takes a village, but having tried to make a comprehensive list of everyone whose support and wisdom has helped me reach this point, I disagree—I think it might take a city or two. What follows is an inevitably imperfect attempt to say thank you to all involved.

Sheer chance—or historical forces beyond my control—took me to Fukuoka in the first place. Thanks to the JET Programme's random assignment, I taught English at Kurume Commercial High School for two years after university. Visits to Fukuoka's Modern Asian Art museum and screenings at the Asia Focus Film Festival inspired me to study more about the city's links with Asia. Angus Lockyer's Japanese Modernity Seminar at SOAS was my Japanese historiography boot camp, and where I began to explore Fukuoka's modern history. I couldn't have afforded the tuition at SOAS without the financial support of my grandmother, Madge Booth, for which I am still so grateful. I returned to Fukuoka thanks to a Monbukagakusho (MEXT) Scholarship, which allowed me to study at Kyushu University for two years with a huge amount of freedom. In hindsight, I can see that at Kyudai, the seeds of this project were already being sown via encounters with friends and mentors who have gone on to shape it—and me as a historian—in important ways, especially Itoh Kaori, Kurihara Miwa, Lee Yoon Soo, and Professor Yamaguchi Teruomi.

Throughout the PhD process at Harvard, I was lucky to have *sempai* like Sakura Christmas, Shi-Lin Loh, and Michael Thornton, a writing group like Cookiegawa and its illustrious members, especially Andrew Campana, Billy French, Erin Hutchinson, David Porter, and Eric Schluessel, and the friendship and support of Floris van Swet and Joanna Linzer—especially in the final stages. I'm so glad to have been able to navigate through the many ups and downs of the PhD process with Charles Clavey, whose friendship continues to mean a lot to me.

This book has evolved from the doctoral dissertation I submitted at Harvard back in 2018, but it still bears the imprints, and the influence, of my academic mentors and advisors. This is even clearer to me now with several years' distance. First and foremost, my thanks must go to my advisor, Ian J. Miller. Ian gave me the necessary intellectual freedom to follow my instincts, but he has also been an invaluable source of advice and support during and after the PhD. I thank him for always believing in the importance of my project and his ability to convey this more elegantly and persuasively than I could manage at times. Andrew Gordon trained me to be attentive to questions of labor. Later, he lent his critical and astute eye to drafts of my work, and they are infinitely better for it. Carter Eckert's guidance and example in the field of colonial and post-colonial Korean history showed me what such scholarship could achieve, and what the stakes are. It is hard to put into words my feelings of loss at his passing. I am grateful to Yumi Moon and Sungik Yang for organizing such a fitting celebration of Carter's achievements upon his retirement, and for having been able to thank him in person, for everything.

Working with Neil Brenner helped to shape the early stages of this project, and his enthusiasm for my work inspired me to ask new questions about urbanization in Korea and Japan. David Howell has always been a wonderful interlocutor and source of support and advice for my work, especially its maritime side. Sunil Amrith's advice in the final stages of the dissertation, and his suggestions for the project's next steps, were the encouragement I needed. It's a real honor to now be colleagues at Yale. I must also thank my Korean teachers at Sogang University, and Jeong Hee-Jeong at Harvard, for their patience and talent for language education.

In Japan, Professor Yamaguchi Teruomi made it possible for me to return to Kyushu University as a visiting researcher for my doctoral research, and I am grateful for his continued support. Itoh Kaori has been there through thick and thin—as *sempai*, friend, drinking partner, and interlocutor. Thanks also to Mimaki Seiko for her introduction, and to Professor Asano Toyomi and Waseda University for their support of me as a visiting researcher for the final year of my PhD. Over the years I've learned a lot about Fukuoka and Japanese history from conversations with Akashi Tomonori, Arima Manabu, Matthew Augustine, Ide Maiko, Ishibashi Tomoya, Namigata Tsuyoshi, Onjō Akio, Ōtaguro Mami, and Yao Keisuke.

Fukuoka felt like home, not just a research subject, because of the many friends I'm lucky to have made there, many of whom predate this project, and in various ways inspired me to start it. Firstly, I want to thank the Ikedas—Naoko, Sawako, and the late Hirosuke—who first welcomed me into their family when I lived in Kurume from 2006 to 2008. Thanks to all the Kyudai Noh *gakubu* members in Fukuoka and in Tokyo for your continued friendship. Thanks also to my Ichiuson family—Nakamura Kyōichi sensei, Izumi Rumi, Ushijima Hikaru, Ayah Ai, and Uchida Yuki, and the extended Ichiuson network that made my research year in Fukuoka so rich and exciting. Thanks to Ikeda Mio and Hirosawa Eri for all the fun adventures around Kyushu. Special thanks must go to Ryu Youngjin for his comments at the URC workshop in 2015, and for all the advice and Pusan-Fukuoka–related discussions since. Thanks to Ryu-san for also introducing me to Egami Kenichirō, who offered me a new perspective on current Pusan-Fukuoka links. Finally, the friendship of Matsuo Miki, Tachibana Aika, and the rest of the Fukuoka Film Festival family is a large part of what made, and will continue to make, Fukuoka feel like home.

In Pusan, I cannot thank librarian and archivist at the Pusan Municipal Simin Library, Ko Yujŏng *sŏnsaengnim* enough for her warm welcome and support on my many research trips to the city. I always looked forward to my archive visits knowing that she would be there. In Seoul, my thanks go to Michael Kim at Yonsei University for sponsoring my application as a Visiting Fellow, and the Institute of Korean Studies, especially Park Eun-yeong, for their support during my stay. Thanks also to Lee Yoon Soo, who has been a constant friend since we met at Kyudai in 2010, for her friendship and advice over the years.

I am eternally grateful to the Master and Fellows of Trinity College, Cambridge, for electing me as a Title A Fellow, and to Dominic (Chai) Lieven for seeing something in my project and convincing them to do so. The three years I spent as a Junior Research Fellow at Trinity, despite the global pandemic, were very special. I'm especially thankful to the Catering, Gardening, Housekeeping, and Porters' Lodge staff for keeping those of us based in college healthy and relatively sane throughout such extraordinary circumstances. I also feel lucky to have met such wonderful friends and interlocutors in Cambridge, especially Arthur Asseraf, Anna Berman, Erik Clark, Alex Freer, Tom Hutchinson, Ailsa Keating, Aleks Reinhardt, George Roberts, Partha Shil, and Clare Walker Gore.

This book and I have benefited from the feedback of many different audiences and colleagues over the years. Thanks to the Korean history research workshop at Kyushu University, especially Morihira Masahiko and Tanaka Misato; to Yamada Misato and the Fukuoka Asian Urban Research Center; to Arima Manabu and the Fukuoka City history workshop; to Umemori Naoyuki for inviting me to speak at Waseda's inaugural Global Asia Studies seminar; to the Immigration Studies Workshop, especially Iijima Mariko and Yoshida Ryō to Catherine Phipps and the members of the "Global Meiji" workshop; to the organizers of the Yun Posun Symposium at Edinburgh University, especially Holly Stephens and Youngmi Kim; to the International History of East Asia Seminar at the University of Oxford; to the East Asia Seminar at the University of Cambridge, especially Mickey Adolphson and Barak Kushner; to Carl Nightingale and the participants at the inaugural Global Urban History Conference; to the members of the East Asian History workshop at INALCO, especially Noémi Godefroy and Alain Delissen; to Aleksandra Kobiljski and the Centre de recherches sur le Japon at EHESS; and to Sherzod Muminov and the Centre for Japanese Studies at the University of East Anglia.

Special thanks must go to the editors, organizers, and participants of two Oceanic Japan workshops, in Berlin and Cambridge, Massachusetts. Writing a chapter on the Tsushima Straits for *Oceanic Japan* and receiving feedback from such incredible colleagues in the process helped me figure out a lot. Thanks also to the audiences, my fellow panelists, commentators, and chairs at AAS Denver and Boston; to Sarah Kovner and the Columbia Modern Japan Seminar; to Seungkyung Kim for inviting me to present at Indiana University's Institute of Korean Studies; to Stanford's Center for East Asian Studies, and to Kären Wigen, Yumi Moon, and Jun Uchida for their incredibly helpful and astute feedback at a critical moment for the book; and to Partha Shil and Nora Barakat for inviting me to workshop a chapter at their Eurasian Empires workshop during my visit to Palo Alto.

At Yale, I am grateful to Lav Kanoi, Paul Sabin, and Yale's Environmental Humanities program for inviting me to talk on my work and for the questions from our fantastic students. I am also thankful to Shivi Sivaramakrishnan and Elisabeth Wood for inviting me to present a chapter at the Program on Agrarian Studies workshop, to Tom Monaghan for discussing it, and to the many faculty and students who attended and gave such excellent feedback.

This project has been made possible by the institutional and financial support of many organizations: at Harvard, the wonderful staff of the History Department, the Reischauer Institute, the Program on U.S. Japan Relations, and the Asia Center. For funding my dissertation research in Fukuoka and Seoul, my sincerest thanks go to the Akiyama Life Science Foundation, the Japan Foundation, and the Korea Foundation. Since arriving at Yale I have been incredibly lucky to be supported by the Council on East Asian Studies and the MacMillan Center, and I must thank Injoong Kim, Dylan Siegel, and Tahreem Wasti in particular.

I can't think of a better place to be working than Yale's History Department. It has been an incredible privilege to teach alongside and learn from my fellow historians of Japan, Dani Botsman and Fabian Drixler. Thanks also to the three department chairs, Joanne Meyerowitz, Alan Mikhail, and Regina Kunzel, who have guided my first four years at Yale, and to the wonderful departmental staff, without whom nothing would be possible. Denise Ho welcomed me to Yale and New Haven with generosity and warmth and is much missed. Hwansoo Kim has built a Korean studies community at Yale from the ground up, to the benefit of faculty and students alike. Valerie Hansen has shown me how to get things done. David Engerman has been a stalwart mentor and sounding board. My students, undergraduate and graduate, continue to amaze and amuse me on a daily basis. Thanks also to Yale's Japan and Korea Librarians, Haruko Nakamura and Jude Yang, for all that they do for faculty and students. Finally, I'm grateful for brilliant colleagues and friends in and beyond the department, especially Alvita Akiboh, Kyunghee Eo, Rosa van Hensbergen, Yukiko Koga, Claire Roosien, Erika Valdivieso, and Fadzilah Yahaya, for all their support and camaraderie.

When I realized that the University of California Press's Asia Pacific Modern series would be the book's perfect home, I reached out to Tak Fujitani. I'm so grateful that he saw what I was doing with the project and believed in it. My editor, Enrique Ochoa Kaup, has helped me through every step of the process. Thanks also to my developmental editor Sarah O'Brien, my indexer Florence Grant, and to Emily Park and Sharron Wood for their support and work on the book's final stages. Working with Kate Blackmer, mapmaker extraordinaire, has been one of the most enjoyable parts of putting this book together. Talking to her about these cities and seeing my ideas transformed into beautiful maps has been truly magical.

I am indebted to Michael Goebel and the two other anonymous peer reviewers, as well as the reader for the UC Press Faculty Board, whose careful comments, criticism, and feedback have all pushed me to keep making the book stronger. It is better because of them. Thanks to the support of Yale's History Department and CEAS, I was also able to hold a manuscript workshop in April of 2023. Many, many thanks to David Ambaras, Dani Botsman, Mary Lui, and Andre Schmid for their generosity—both in terms of their precious time, but also intellectually. They made the colloquium so rewarding and, dare I say it, *fun*. It was a privilege to have so many people I respect read and comment on my manuscript. Thanks to Fabian Drixler, whose comments at the eleventh hour caught some clangers, and also helped me make some crucial final edits, and to Alvita Akiboh, who was the perfect person to ask about US regional imperialism.

I am very grateful to the many librarians and archivists in Japan and Korea who made this work possible. In particular, I am grateful to Kyushu Historical Museum, to the Hitotsubashi University Institute of Economic Research, and to the Nishiyama Uzō Memorial Library for their permission to include images of their archival holdings in this book. A special thanks must also go to Lee Sooyeon, curator at Busan Art Museum, and to the family of Yang Dalsuk for letting me use his artwork as this book's cover.

Russell Burge has been a constant interlocutor and true friend throughout my PhD process and beyond. I am so grateful for all his careful comments on my work and for our conversations about Japanese and Korean urbanism, among many other things. Sakura Christmas and Michael Thornton continue to be important sounding boards and sources of moral support. I'm also incredibly lucky to have gained another academic community, of David Ambaras, Sayaka Chatani, Paula Curtis, Ethan Mark, Amy Stanley, and Chelsea Szendi Schieder, in the middle of the pandemic, and am proud of all the work we've done together, and the work still underway!

I'm grateful for the support of my friends back in the United Kingdom—whom I see far too little of these days—especially Christine Forder, Hayley Douglas, Pamela Hunt, Sophie Ivan, Hetal Patel, and Olivia Senensieb. Luckily, when you've been friends as long as we have, it doesn't seem to matter how long we go without seeing each other.

Finally, none of this would be possible or mean nearly as much without the constant love, support, and gentle mockery of my family, to whom I dedicate this book. To my mother Jane, who instilled in me a love of reading and writing; to my father Simon, who is responsible for my interest in all things maritime (except when the boat tips); and to Emma, my sister and dearest friend: This book is for the three of you.

NOTES ON TERMS

In this book, when transliterating Japanese and Korean, I use the Hepburn and McCune-Reischauer romanization systems, respectively. Exceptions are made in cases where another romanization is better established, for example, Seoul and Pyongyang. I use macrons to represent long vowels in Japanese, except in well-known place names like Tokyo and Kyushu.

For Japanese and Korean names, I follow the convention of listing the surname followed by first name. In this case, too, I use the romanization systems listed above, except when the person is better known by another romanization.

The period covered in this book was one in which multiple namings, renamings, readings, and pronunciations existed, especially for toponyms. I have tried where possible to give both Japanese and Korean readings, but for simplicity's sake I have not done this in every case. Similarly, in this book I employ the terms "Japanese" and "Korean" to refer to my historical actors' national identities, although I am aware these were not always the terms used at the time, nor how everyone would have thought of themselves.

Translations throughout are my own, unless otherwise noted.

KOREA

NORTH KYŎNGSANG

• Taegu

Ulsan •

SOUTH KYŎNGSANG

Masan •   Pusan

YŎNGDO/
MAKINOSHIMA

Kŏjedo

TSUSHIMA

• Izuhara

Tsushima

Genkainada

IKI

Fukuoka City

Shimonoseki–Pusan Ferry

Strait

NORTH

HONSHŪ
YAMAGUCHI

Shimonoseki

K Moji

Seto
Inland
Sea

FUKUOKA

C

KYUSHU

Kurume •

SAGA

ŌITA

KUMAMOTO

• Kumamoto
City

Ariake Sea

NAGASAKI

Nagasaki
City

MIYAZAKI

50 MILES
50 KILOMETERS

BLACKMER MAPS

MANCHURIA   USSR

KOREA

East Sea
Sea of Japan

JAPAN

Seoul/
Keijō

Tokyo •

Osaka

East
China Sea

Pacific Ocean

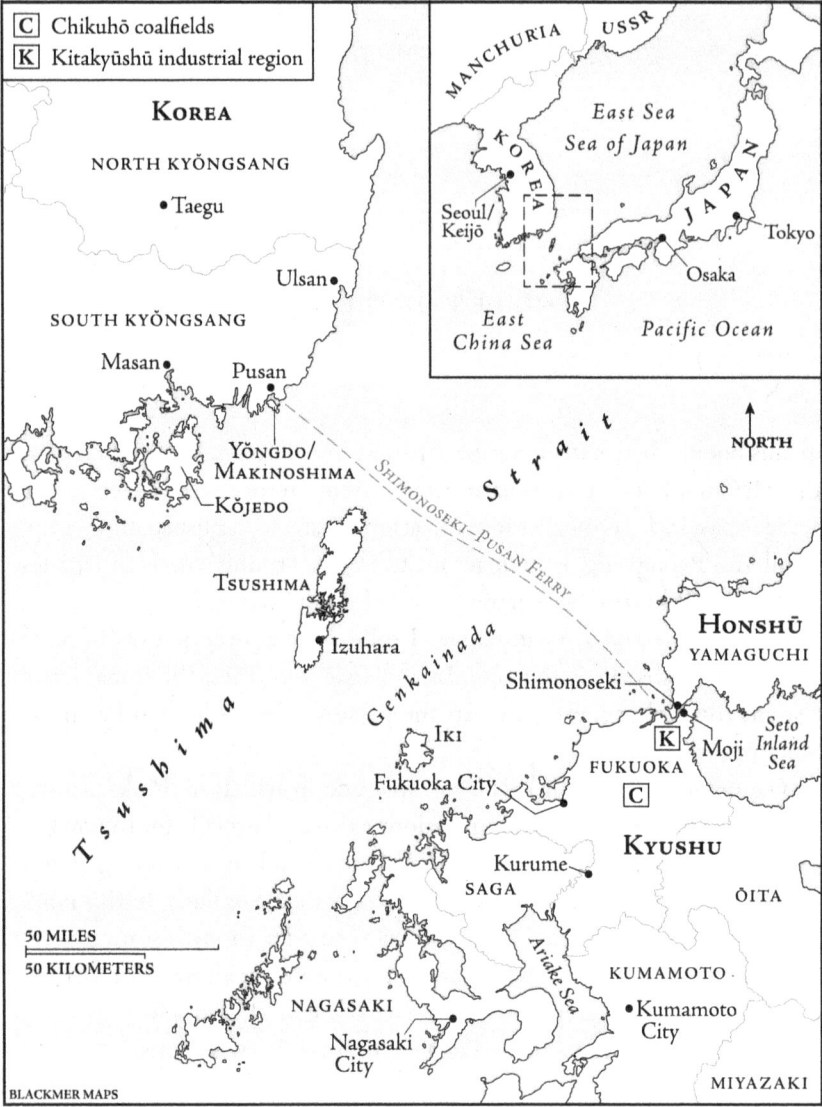

MAP 1. The Tsushima Strait region, ca. 1930. Credit: Kate Blackmer.

Introduction

IN LATE AUGUST OF 1944, Kawahara Toshio arrived back in Pusan. He had been born in the Korean port city in 1913, to parents Toyo and Ujirō, who had migrated across the Tsushima Strait in the first decade of the twentieth century, from a rural part of Fukuoka prefecture, on Japan's southern island of Kyushu (see map 1). Arriving even before Korea became a Japanese colony, Ujirō and Toyo found a city and country in flux. Pusan's harbor was full of Japanese fishing boats with a mixture of Korean and Japanese crews; its waterfront neighborhoods contained warehouses stacked with fish and marine products from the waters off Korea's northeast coast, ready for transport inland by Pusan's local *kaekchu* (merchant brokers); Korean laborers were flattening slopes with pneumatic drills, changing the city's landscape beyond recognition at the behest of the Japanese Residents' Association; there were clusters of Korean market stalls, Australian missionaries tending to the urban poor, and Japanese shopkeepers advertising their wares, calling out in the familiar dialect of back home. From the perspective of Pusan's Koreans, the Kawaharas' arrival was just one among thousands by new Japanese settlers who were relegating them to a minority in their own city.

Ujirō took advantage of the port's location as a hub to set up a coastal shipping business. He became friendly with other Fukuokans in the city's growing settler community, including Tanaka Kichinosuke, who came from a rural background similar to his own and also worked in shipping. Tanaka was a member of Pusan's Fukuoka Prefectural Association and, like Ujirō, was raising his family in Japan's colony of Korea: His daughter Chizuko had been born there in 1914.[1] The two families were joined together when Toshio and Chizuko got married in 1936.

When Toshio returned to the city in 1944, it must have looked very different from the place his parents had arrived in some four decades earlier. Pusan was now an industrialized hub of military transport between Japan and the continent. As his train pulled into the terminus, Toshio would have passed numerous factories in the growing industrial zones north of the city center. The city's waterfront had expanded out into Pusan Bay, and new piers jutted into the waters, off limits to all but military vessels and personnel. Toshio had taken the train south from Manchukuo, where he had worked since the client state's founding in 1932, because he had been called up to the Imperial Japanese Army. When the war ended in August 1945, he was stationed on Irabujima, a tiny island between Taiwan and Okinawa. Toshio made it back to Fukuoka by late December that year, while Chizuko and their son, Ken, were eventually repatriated from Huludao in Manchuria back to Fukuoka City's port of Hakata in August 1946.

In the years after the war, Toshio and his brother used what money they had managed to bring back from Pusan to set up several food stores in Fukuoka City's reemerging markets. In 1948 Toshio and Chizuko opened Fukuya, in Nakasu Market, where the city authorities had designated twenty-five storefronts for repatriates from Japan's former empire. Nakasu was the city's entertainment district, now booming again with occupation troops and women from the city's rural hinterlands trying to find any work they could. Fukuya sold all kinds of foodstuffs, from Kraft cheese to dried squid to lard—mainly wholesale, especially to Chinese restaurants.

In 1949 the Kawaharas tried offering a new delicacy, *mentaiko*, spicy, salt-preserved cod roe, which had been sold in Pusan's fish markets as *myŏngnanjot*. *Myŏngt'ae* (*Gadus chalcogrammus*; Alaska or walleye pollack) is the most used fish in Korean cuisine and provided fishermen in the colony with their biggest catches—mainly from the colder waters off the northeast coast of the peninsula.[2] It took a while for Toshio and Chizuko to get the flavor to match the taste memory of their colonial childhoods, but eventually the Kawaharas' *mentaiko* business took off.[3] Today, spicy *mentaiko* is almost as synonymous with Fukuoka City as Hakata ramen, another local dish that also emerged in the crucible of colonization, war, and its aftermath.[4]

Chizuko and Toshio's family histories are representative of a much bigger story that ties the modern histories of Fukuoka and Pusan together. But this larger history—of urbanization and colonial expansion, and how the two became connected in the growth of an imperial region spanning the Tsushima Strait—is a lot less visible in Fukuoka today than the city's famous delicacy *mentaiko*. The larger histories and memories contained within this dish have been flattened and remade into a local, consumable identity via its ubiquity as the representative Fukuoka souvenir. For Chizuko and Toshio, the taste of *mentaiko* evoked memories of colonial Pusan, whereas now, the taste takes me back to Fukuoka.

Historical connections with Asia have been central in the crafting of Fukuoka City's modern identity. When I first visited Fukuoka City Museum in the mid 2000s, the triangular relationship of Fukuoka, Asia, and Japan, and the beneficial results of the region's geography for its history and growth, were at the center of almost every display. From displays on the first-century Gold Seal from the late Han Court, to the ninth-century Kōrokan guesthouse for envoys from Tang and Silla, to the medieval Hakata merchants and their overseas trade, it was only in the final modern display that Asia was absent as a factor in the Fukuoka region's historical development.[5] Covering the years from the Meiji era (1868–1912) through to the 1950s, the final display focused on the many industrial expositions held in Fukuoka in the late nineteenth and early twentieth centuries, centering the narrative of Fukuoka's modern urban development on domestic, not international, factors. The discussion of Japan's imperial expansion into Asia and the subsequent Asia-Pacific War was limited to displays on the US firebombing of the city in June 1945, and on Hakata becoming a key "overseas repatriation port," where former settlers like Chizuko Kawahara and her son were returned after the collapse of Japan's empire. In the displays of the City Museum, Fukuoka City's growth as a modern city, between 1868 and 1945, was decoupled from Japan's rise as an empire and expansion into Asia.

It was through trying to understand *what* was missing, and *why*, from Fukuoka's modern history that led me to the research project that became this book. When I began my research I kept finding references in my sources to another port city—Pusan. I soon realized that writing a modern history of Fukuoka would be an impossible task without widening my lens. Just as maps of the expanding Japanese empire shifted westward, and moved Fukuoka from periphery to center, this widening of my focus across the straits made possible an account of Japanese empire—of imperial expansion as it was intertwined with urbanization—that spanned the border between Japan and its nearest colony, Korea, and began and ended beyond the dates of formal colonial control.

This book is the history of the rise and fall of an imperial region, centered on the cities of Fukuoka and Pusan, linked by the Tsushima Strait. In the period under discussion, we could not call these "twin" or "sister" cities, for their relationship was inherently unequal in ways such terms obscure. As seen in their different postimperial trajectories, the two cities were mismatched in several aspects. However, during the time frame of this book, they became an imperial dyad, a pairing far more advantageous to the growth of the provincial city of Fukuoka than the key port of Pusan. The winds of empire lifted Fukuoka, filled its sails, and propelled the visions of its inhabitants northwest across the Tsushima Strait. During the period covered in this book, the waters of this maritime border were narrowed by imperial projections of power, by the increasingly swift journeys across them via ferry and later airplane, and by the local networks that sought to bind Fukuoka to Pusan. However, the smoothing of these barriers to travel did not always pertain: In the opposite direction, Korean travelers were surveilled, policed, and sometimes rejected from crossing. The increasing numbers of Korean arrivals in Japan were seen not as "pioneers" but often as threats—to public safety, or to Japanese jobs. This maritime border, and the relationships between colonizers and colonized, remained unequal, and often violent.

Urban growth in Fukuoka and Pusan was defined by the interconnected processes of industrialization, imperial expansion, and colonization, and it drew these cities together even as it impelled their planners to create competing visions for their futures. In the eight decades between 1876 and 1953, wars and territorial expansion created flows of people and networks of capital and labor crossing the straits. War reparations built steel plants, powered by local coal, which brought in laborers from southern Korea as well as Kyushu. Imperial border control led to increased people trafficking across the straits, which prompted further links between authorities on either side. Pusan's urban areas were built by unemployed laborers rejected from travel across the straits. These feedback loops led the cities and their hinterlands to become more integrated, in complex and contested ways, in the rise and fall of empire. What emerged was a single, urbanizing region of Japanese imperial space containing northern Kyushu, the southeastern tip of the Korean peninsula, and the waters between them.

My focus on the imperial dyad of Fukuoka and Pusan reveals a process of urbanization that was neither smooth nor inevitable but contested and contradictory. This process created tensions between periphery and center, divided factions and interests among both colonizer and colonized, and created contradictions between the goals of territorial and economic expansion.

These dynamics produced a region of uneven and unequal geographies, with contested boundaries, centers, and margins of its own.

I refer to this process as "imperial urbanization," in opposition to the more common histories of "colonial urbanization." The term highlights connections between imperial expansion and urban growth in not just colonial but also metropolitan cities, where even histories of ports and capital cities are often subsumed within national histories of modernization, with empire as an afterthought.[6] Writing a history of the imperial dyad of Fukuoka and Pusan allows us to think about how imperial expansion propelled urbanization across and between both metropole and colony, and what new geographies and regions emerged as a result.

URBANIZATION AND EMPIRE IN JAPAN AND KOREA

My framing for this history may have come about through the serendipitous encounters with sources and consequent recalibrations that often occur during the early stages of one's research, but it was also heavily influenced by the shifts taking place in the fields of Japanese and Korean history since the late 1990s. In hindsight, my spatial reframing, to focus on both Fukuoka and Pusan, appears an almost comically simplistic response to reading, early in my graduate career, Andre Schmid's 2000 article "Colonialism and the 'Korea Problem' in the Historiography of Modern Japan." Centering my study on the Tsushima Strait region, writing on the histories of one imperial and one colonial city, was certainly a way to ensure that, as Schmid cites British historian Bernard Cohn as arguing for, "the metropole and colony [are] seen in a unitary field of analysis."[7]

In this book I use this framing first and foremost to reorient urban histories of Korea and Japan. Urban historians of both imperial Japan and colonial Korea have used the built environment and urban space, especially of the capitals of Seoul (J: Keijō) and Tokyo, as a historical source in order to "read" the city as a stage or produce typologies of Korea's colonial cities that show the spatial impact of colonization. While historical analyses of urban space foreground Korea's colonial domination, in Japan, the same methodologies produce scholarship on the emergence of urban modernity, with "imperial" elements more symbolic than material.[8] Although Japan's modern urban history cannot be separated from its rise as an empire, the heavy historiographical focus on single-city histories and the rise of modern urban culture have tended to obscure the links between Japan's overseas expansion, its industrialization, and its urbanization.[9] This connection is far clearer when viewed from the cities of Japan's former colonies. As Se-Mi Oh argues, in colonial Korea, "modernity [was] not a condition brought about by urbanization but the totality of the processes through which colonial power discursively formulated itself in the urban space."[10] By tracing the entangled histories of Pusan and Fukuoka, this book will show how Japan's urban modernity was as imperial as Korea's was colonial. By imperialism, I refer to both the formal and informal expansion of Japanese power beyond the borders of the home islands, or *naichi*. When this took the form of gaining formal control over a territory—colonization—we can refer to that internal projection of power and processes of rule as colonialism. This book shows how the urban history of Japan's imperialism was not just discursively formulated—that is, it was not just a symbolic spatial language of imperial power—but was embedded in the uneven processes of urbanization itself via the people, capital, visions, and wars that simultaneously co-constructed urban space alongside empire.

On the subject of capital, while historical scholarship has directly linked colonial Korea's rural-to-urban migration and industrialization to its embedding within Japan's imperial economy, similarly focused histories of Japan have viewed these phenomena as part of the emergence of a modern capitalist economy—one boosted by imperial wars, to be sure, but not intimately tied to military imperial expansion until the mid-1930s.[11] However, Japan's expansionism—its formal and informal imperialism across the Asia-Pacific—was a driving factor in its modern capitalist development.

In defining and discussing "capitalism" in this book, I emphasize two key spatial aspects that tied metropole and colony together. First is the sea change that David Howell talks about as creating "new relations of dependency" in Meiji-era Japan: the reorganization of the nature of production and the emergence of labor itself as the "last great commodity."[12] As I discuss more below, the buying and selling of labor power in late nineteenth-century Japan—that is, the creation of a mobile workforce—was a process that almost immediately exceeded the bounds of the nation-state, linking late Meiji Fukuoka to Hawai'i, Korea, and beyond.[13] Second, this book also traces what emerges alongside this labor market—what David Harvey calls the "urbanization of capital"—which is the investment of the surplus value of labor into the built environment for the further production and circulation of capital.[14] This book traces these key aspects of capitalism—the people who moved to sell their labor power, and the growth of the places they moved into and through—via a spatial lens to show how both these processes led to the formation of an urban region spanning colony and metropole.

In this volume my focus on the imperial dyad of Fukuoka and Pusan allows me to make three key interventions. First, as noted above, this book shifts our view of urban history beyond the metonymic spaces of capital cities to the shared *regional* impact of discourses of imperial development. By doing so, this book offers not only a particular account of a single region, but also an approach and an argument for recentering imperial expansion within understandings of urban growth and industrialization in modern Japan, as well as in its colonies. As many recent scholars have argued, Japan's emergence as a modern nation and colonial empire, like other global examples, was a mutually constituted process.[15] In this book I show how this process also led to new regional forms of urban growth.

As Kären Wigen has shown, Japan's emergence as an incipient nation with a single national core required the "making of regional peripheries."[16] However, Meiji discourses of national development via a capitalist economy and military strength—Japan's consolidation as an imperial nation—allowed for, and often relied upon, competition between these new peripheries in the expanding imperial field.[17] That is to say, while urban *planning* emerged and remained as a centralized institution throughout this period, urban *development* was tied to the local responses and visions for growth produced by boosters, bureaucrats, and local elites in urban areas across the empire, responding to geopolitical and economic shifts caused by the interconnected processes of industrialization and overseas expansion.[18] What is more, local urban development was a discourse that often transcended the metropole/colony divide. In Korea, it was a discourse shared by, and in the interests of, local landowners and business elites—both Japanese and Korean. A regional framework allows us to disaggregate "Japan" and "Korea" and think about how other factors, such as class, ideology, and local identity, shaped the nature of such "development."

Second, this study reconnects the histories of domestic and imperial migration, tracing the urbanizing movements of both Japanese and Koreans between Pusan and Fukuoka. Influenced by recent scholarship on the movement of people across the Asia-Pacific, thinking of this as *mobility* rather than migration better captures the multiple journeys many of my actors made, and the circuits of movement enabled by their networks.[19] By following rural Koreans from their villages in the Kyŏngnam region surrounding the port city of Pusan, and then across the straits to Kitakyūshū; and by following merchants and fishermen from Fukuoka's villages across to Pusan, this book shows how rural-to-urban mobility occurred along routes spanning empire and metropole and created urbanization on both sides.

Following these journeys from end to end reincorporates rural hinterlands into urban history and reveals the local causes and effects of this movement.[20] In Pusan and Fukuoka, settlers and migrants did not shape their urban environments as just "Japanese" or "Koreans" but as people entangled with specific local networks, made even more important when we consider the proximity of home and destination, and the often-continuing mobility between the two. By doing so, this volume demonstrates how the urbanization of this region was shaped not just by shared elite visions of local development, but also by the movement of non-elite Japanese and Koreans. Their journeys—whether forced, out of necessity, inspired by desire for a better life, as part of the bureaucracy of imperial control, or in the wake of war, liberation, or defeat—are the animating force of this book. While some of these movements might have been unforeseen or unplanned, they were soon absorbed into the uneven and unequal processes of imperial urbanization.

Third, focusing on historical dynamics at a regional scale sheds light on the need to widen the temporal framework beyond an imperial narrative in order to uncover and discuss the precursors to and impact of imperial expansion on patterns of mobility and urbanization.[21] I demonstrate how imperial expansion helped a provincial city like Fukuoka gain its eventual—and fleeting—prominence, but I also discuss the double-edged effects of Korea's colonization for earlier, regional imperialism across the straits. Expansion across the straits happened at different scales and in a variety of time frames: In particular, I argue that informal imperialism prior to formal colonization also had a particular regional character, and the former was not simply laying groundwork for the latter.[22] Regional imperialism, its histories and geographies, formed an initial layer, complicated by and often in tension with later formal colonization and colonial rule. These overlapping dynamics and the continuing presence of agents of regional informal imperialism would later lead to Pusan's colonial economy being tied far more closely to Japan's than the economy of the rest of the Korean peninsula. What is more, regional settler capital kept a hold on the city and hampered incursions from central Japanese capital in the 1930s. All this is to say that empire is not a simple explanatory device in *The Narrowing Sea*; rather, the book shows how easy distinctions of metropole and colony did not always dictate the nature of urbanization and urban growth across the straits.

The creation of new geographies of urbanization before and during Japan's formal colonization of Korea also had effects on postwar urbanization. Decolonization and the population movement that went with it affected urban growth across Japan and Korea. After 1945, Japan's—and to some extent Pusan's—postwar economy was still structured around war, and it grew with further conflict in East Asia. As the final chapter of this book shows, the Korean War led to the temporary reappearance of colonial-era dynamics across the straits. Furthermore, in postwar Japan the emergence of seemingly new paradigms of regional urbanization beyond the city—the rise of a Tokyo megalopolis and the girding of an industrialized Pacific Belt—had their origins in the processes that had confronted prewar planners during Japan's imperial urbanization.

HISTORICIZING PLANETARY URBANIZATION

In Japan, histories of urbanization beyond the bounded city—a centralized, delimited urban area—often begin with the late 1950s, tying the Japan case to that of Jean Gottmann's powerful "BosWash" visualization of the United States' northeast corridor, which proved the single bounded city paradigm no longer held.[23] As Jeffrey Hanes has shown, postwar Japanese urban theorists were early adopters of Gottmann's vision of a "megalopolis," which in the case of the Japanese archipelago they posited as extending from Tokyo to Osaka, and possibly reaching as far as Fukuoka in the future.[24] Jeffrey Hanes describes how, in the rush in the 1960s to theorize Japan's growing "Tōkaidō megalopolis," urban planner Takayama Eika even imagined its eventual extension beyond Fukuoka and across the Tsushima Strait, "going so far as to suggest a suboceanic railway line to Korea." Hanes sees this "mad neo-colonialist vision" as reminiscent of "the prewar impulse to Japanese imperialism on the Asian continent."[25]

In fact, those prewar impulses had already led to the rise and fall of an urbanizing region spanning the straits. In its title, *The Narrowing Sea* hints at several of the dynamics and processes of urbanization beyond the bounded city. These included material changes and connections: exploitation of fisheries that fed urban populations and fertilized rice paddies; land reclamation along the region's coastlines; and new networks of travel and communication across the straits. They also included rhetorical representations of diminishing distance that narrowed the seas and "relocated" the opposite shore.

Contemporary urban theorists like Neil Brenner and Christian Schmid refer to such dynamics as now contributing to "planetary urbanization."[26] This "urban theory without an outside" dismantles binaries such as city and country to show how, in the twenty-first century, urbanization's reach extends into all corners of the globe. It is this definition of urbanization—one in which "the non-city is no longer exterior to the urban [but] a strategically essential terrain of capitalist urbanization"—that I have borne in mind as I researched and wrote this book, and it is via combining such an understanding with the processes of imperialism and colonization that I hope to make more visible the wider causes and precursors to the planetary urbanization of the late twentieth and early twenty-first centuries.[27]

Many contemporary works on planetary urbanization have their intellectual origins in the assertion by French Marxist theorist Henri Lefebvre, in 1970, that "society has been completely urbanized."[28] In *La Révolution Urbaine,* Lefebvre plotted stages of urbanization along an axis that implicitly measured historical time as well as levels of urbanization. Lefebvre points to the historical shift to industrialization as a key driver of planetary urbanization. For him, this began with the rise of the "industrial city (often a shapeless town, a barely urban agglomeration, a conglomerate, or conurbation like the Ruhr Valley)."[29] Such "shapeless towns" and "barely urban" spaces near coal fields or on the edge of Japanese cities were the subject of much consternation in 1920s Japan.[30] Indeed, many such "urban issues" (J: *toshi mondai*) facing early twentieth-century Japanese cities—like the quickly growing and unplanned "edges" of the city, or the rise of slums—appear to us now as heralding the advent of processes of extended urbanization. Some planners attempted to ignore these realities and force the unbounded city back into the bounded "metropolitan" ideal.[31] However, as this book discusses, by the 1930s others recognized these urban spaces as a new form of urban morphology and worked to create planning paradigms, and language, to order and shape them.

While urban theorists, whether subscribers to planetary urbanization or not, have focused on the key role of capitalism in advancing modern urban growth, the importance of imperialism and imperial expansion as similarly crucial factors have been remarkably underanalyzed within urban studies.[32] Connections between the rise of global capitalism and urbanization, and the spatial dynamics linking capitalism and imperialism, have received far more attention than those between imperialism and urbanization. In urban theory, imperialism and colonization are more often used as metaphors for capitalist expansion than a lived reality that has affected urbanization across much of the globe.[33] Earlier historians of imperial cities have remarked how "ahistorical" studies of globalization treated those processes as "revolutionary and unprecedented," despite the fact that today's "global" cities have shaped and been shaped by imperialist as well as capitalist forces.[34]

In this book I want to expand our scope beyond a single city. In my study of the formation of an imperial region centered on Fukuoka and Pusan, I have been informed by Harvey's account of the role of urban politics in formulating "the geography of uneven capitalist development," and his discussion of how the geopolitical power of an urban center's ruling classes is "projected geopolitically onto other spaces."[35] Importantly, for the histories covered in this book, as well as for many other historical and contemporary cases, this projection also occurred across an uneven imperial region. I argue that in order to understand how we reached this moment of planetary urbanization, we must look to modern imperialism and the new scales of power it projected and the changes that it wrought: on human movement, resource extraction, and the rise of "operational landscapes" such as ports, shipping lanes, and industrial zones, as well as the expanded horizons of imperial visions beyond national boundaries and across regions.[36]

IMPERIAL REGIONS AND IMPERIAL HISTORY WRITING

By studying the history of metropole and empire together in a single analytical frame, this book makes interventions into the scholarship on Japanese empire and urban history, and it shows the importance of imperialism for understanding the urban theory of planetary urbanization. Furthermore, by *regionalizing* imperial history, this volume offers a new scale of study through which to connect, compare, and reassess global imperial history.[37]

This book includes within its time frame the entire lifespan of the Japanese empire (1869–1945) and the global shift from the "new imperialism" of the late nineteenth century, through the first half of the twentieth century and its world wars, before concluding in the era of global decolonization in the 1950s.[38] During this time Japan's empire was just one in a world of many imperial geographies and networks. This leads me to the question of how historians of Japan and its empire should connect or compare their focus of study to the historiographies and histories that have shaped it. Just as Japan's colonial administrators kept abreast of policies used by the French in Algeria or the English in Ireland, so historians of Japanese empire today read widely on histories and theories of other imperial regimes to inform their own writing. But only occasionally does scholarship on modern imperialism writ large make substantive engagement with histories of Japanese empire.[39] There is more work which engages with the period after Japan's imperial ambitions provoked war with the United States and its allies. However, for decades prior to Pearl Harbor, Japanese imperialism was a reality that those at the time—American and European imperialists, Asian leaders and intellectuals, as well as colonized peoples—could not ignore.[40]

Over the past few decades, historians of Japanese and U.S. imperialism have drawn connections to, and benefitted from, engagement with scholarship on European empire and postcolonial studies. However, history writing on imperial Japan and its colonies should allow us to push beyond the *incorporation* of Japanese empire into global imperial history—an action that suggests a preexisting corpus that Japan and its colonies' experiences can be slotted into—and instead to provoke new discussions, and to offer new frameworks for understanding the workings of empire.[41]

This book offers one avenue for reframing aspects of modern empire: that of regional imperialism, and the imperial region. Japan's imperialism is often described as different from that of most European empires, both for its perceived lateness in world historical time and for its colonization of lands close to home. However, while some of Japan's colonies were proximate, others were not. Japanese imperialism, like that of other modern empires, encompassed several different modalities and timelines of colonial rule. No one term applies to all of Japan's colonization efforts. Furthermore, framing this as a key difference from other empires allows one to overlook the many examples from European and American modern history where such regional colonization took place, and the colonial relationships that, although not formally declared as such, developed through long histories of "intervention."[42]

If we use a single region—rather than an entire empire or imperial relationship—as our scale of analysis, we can find many global examples that bear a resemblance to the particular imperial formation and colonial situation studied in this book. Nearly all European empires engaged in the colonization of, or projection of power over, a country separated from the metropole by only a single land or maritime border. Several different terms have been used to describe this relationship: continental imperialism, proximate colonialism, peripheral colonization.[43] A general term such as regional imperialism, however, allows us to make more links across a wider range of histories and connect the formation of these imperial regions to what came before and after.

For someone like myself, who grew up across the River Mersey from Liverpool, the history of regional empire that springs to mind most readily is that of the English colonization of Ireland and the effects this had on the Irish Sea region.[44] Over the first half of the nineteenth century, the Irish Sea became "Liverpool's private empire."[45] This regional relationship transformed Liverpool into a global hub. From a key port in the trade with Ireland to primacy in the Irish Sea area, Liverpool went on to gain control of the "emigrant trade" and trade with the British Empire in general.[46] The city itself was transformed by this relationship with "an inner and outer world": Its inner, "private" empire of Ireland supplied Liverpool with laborers, and the outer empire of America and beyond made the city's merchants and brokers rich.[47]

Elsewhere, the "colonial sea" of the Mediterranean acted as an imperial border connecting several European powers and their regional colonies. For those viewing the maritime border from the metropolitan center, their colonizing desires often manifested themselves via a rhetorical shrinking of this maritime space. Seen from Paris in the 1830s, the Mediterranean was no more than a "French Lake."[48] Fascist Italy styled its colony of Libya as the metropole's "fourth shore" (Quarta Sponda), part of a Greater Italy with all its coastlines lapped by the Mediterranean.[49] However, in all these cases, longer regional histories of migration within this space bequeathed imperialists entangled geographies of migrant groups prior to the rise of nation-states, protectorates, or colonies. In the case of Spain and Morocco, the shared history of al-Andalus and of the cities of Granada and Tetouan, separated by the "narrow river" of the Strait of Gibraltar, was mobilized first by both Spanish colonialists and then Moroccan nationalists.[50] Thus, recent work on the colonial Mediterranean, conducted with a regional scale of analysis, has pushed back against Eurocentric perspectives and simplistic binaries and chronologies of previous scholarship.[51]

Just as in Fukuoka, regional imperialism around the Mediterranean also had an impact on peripheries within the metropole: The French Midi had been at the center of France's expansion across the Mediterranean, and with decolonization it "suffered from the breakdown of the Mediterranean colonial economy and became a main target of postcolonial migration from former French colonies." Such postcolonial movements led to new calls for "internal decolonization" within the French metropole.[52] In Italy and in the Spanish enclaves of Ceuta and Melilla, the echoes of regional imperialism continue to resound in spaces of detention and border control related to the new Mediterranean migration crisis.[53] By disaggregating these different imperial regions from their empires, and by connecting their histories to each other, I hope that Japan's imperialism can be seen as less unique, while Europe's blind spots about its own imperial histories close to home can be overcome.

Recently, historians of the United States have charted its own imperialism in order to counter ideas of American exceptionalism regarding empire and nation.[54] This includes reframing the violent dispossession of land within what are now the contiguous forty-eight states as a process of "continental imperialism," fueled by the ideology of manifest destiny and the material desire to support a new industrial economy. They also highlight regional imperialism in the Caribbean, often pursued under the auspices of the Monroe Doctrine, and in the Pacific, often in pursuit of access to the fabled "China Market."[55] Though the United States would not claim Caribbean and Pacific colonies until the turn of the twentieth century, throughout the nineteenth century, US expansionists projected ideas of manifest destiny beyond the bounds of what we now understand "sea to shining sea" to represent: In eyeing Cuba, they "lusted after a third sea, the Gulf of Mexico," and in eyeing Hawaiʻi they began conceiving of the Pacific as an "American lake."[56] Indeed, this belief that the Pacific was the United States' imperial region would eventually lead it to clash with imperial Japan in the Asia-Pacific War. This reframing both connects US history to wider debates on imperialism and grounds it in a regional context, showing how its national borders today were neither inevitable, nor the complete story.

Regional empire and the imperial region were ways of understanding and mediating empire and nation for historical actors, and they are also a scale of analysis that historians can use today. For historical actors, regional networks connected their everyday to larger global shifts. For historians, analysis at the regional scale allows us to trace the earlier histories and continued echoes of imperial expansion and mobility, and also connect our particular cases with others around the globe. Studying the case of Fukuoka and Pusan, and finding other parallels, shows us that the Japanese empire is not an "outlier" because these easy contrasts do not hold: There were many European or American imperial relationships that took place on similar scales whose historical echoes continue today. My hope is that the imperial region is a new framework to better understand these relationships, their historical development, and their echoes into the present.

GEOGRAPHY AND ORGANIZATION

The sea in this book's title refers to the Tsushima Strait, the body of water that connected and divided this book's actors. The narrow straits between Japan and Korea are part of a larger body of water that separates Japan from the Asian continent, known as the Sea of Japan (J: Nihonkai) or East Sea (K: Tonghae). As the sea contains many meanings and histories, fraught debates over its naming continue to this day.[57] Similar to the case of the East Sea / Sea of Japan, there are debates and disagreements over the naming of the Tsushima Strait. On English-language maps, the eastern stretch of water between Japan and the island of Tsushima is often referred to as the Tsushima Strait, whereas the stretch between Tsushima and Korea is known as the Korea (previously Chōsen) Strait. In North and South Korea, the entire body of water is referred to by names referencing the two nations—Taehan Haehyŏp, in the south, and Chosŏn Haehyŏp in the north.[58] In Japan, however, it is called the Tsushima Kaikyō. In this book I have chosen to use the term Tsushima Strait (occasionally Straits) to suggest the body of water's multiple facets. On one hand, the term connects the waters to their local rather than national geography, with the contact zone of the island of Tsushima acting as a transferred epithet. On the other, I use its Japanese name to highlight the imperial projections of power over this ocean space that characterized its history in this period.[59]

Debates over its naming alone make clear the presence of multiple understandings and constructions of the Tsushima Strait. After all, ocean space is not a "formless void *between* societies but rather a unique and specifically constructed space *within* society."[60] Accordingly, the Tsushima Strait has multiple historical topographies, local and national. In the late thirteenth century, the waters of the strait protected Japan from invasion by Mongol forces, when "divine winds" (J: *kamikaze*) scuppered the Mongol fleet in Hakata Bay. This led to the strait developing a literary and military pedigree that has been held up as talisman and symbol of the sacred borders of the country. In a process that would be repeated many times over, the disruption of warfare also led to new regional and social geographies. After the Mongol invasions, this maritime border became a zone of interaction: The region was associated with Japanese pirates (K: *waegu*; Ch: *wokou*; J: *wakō*), whose borderless maritime activities helped to constitute a region "comprised of southern Korea, Cheju, Tsushima and northern Kyūshū," which had "a burgeoning identity different to the *nihonkoku* [Japan] of the emperor."[61] Although these pirates were of varying backgrounds, Korean and Chinese officials were keen to associate them with Japan for their own ends.[62] In Korea, this tied in to older associations of these waters with Japanese threats: In the seventh century, Silla King Munmu had ordered his tomb to be built at sea off the southeast coast of Korea in order to keep watch for Japanese marauders from beyond the grave.[63]

Along with the threat of military violence, the waters of the strait offered the lures and advantages of trade and connection. From the early fifteenth century, all of Japan's official interactions with Chosŏn Korea (1392–1897) were funneled through "Japan houses" in designated ports on the southern coast of Korea, until they were disrupted by the Imjin War, Toyotomi Hideyoshi's brutal invasions of the peninsula in 1592 and 1597.[64] When official trade diplomacy was officially restored with the new Tokugawa regime in 1607—after significant work to repair relations by those based in Tsushima and Hakata—it was far more restricted.[65]

The island of Tsushima became one of early modern Japan's gateways to the outside world, and it continued as such until the fall of the Tokugawa government in 1868, and even briefly after. Chosŏn Korea's practice of "neighborly relations" (K: *kyorin*), both diplomatic and commercial, with Japan occurred via the mediation of the Sō family on Tsushima. Tsushima domain merchants, translators, and officials, as representatives of the new Tokugawa regime, were now based in a single Japan House (K: Waegwan J: Wakan) outside the provincial capital of Tongnae, in the port of Pusan.[66] Early Tokugawa-era trade via Tsushima, licit and illicit, rose to significant levels and linked the two countries to global silver and arms trade networks.[67] After the Meiji Restoration of 1868, the new Meiji government delegated "day-to-day" operations to Tsushima officials until the unequal Kanghwa Treaty of 1876 forced open Korea's ports to trade. The end of the intermediary role of the Sō, and the replacement of the Japan House with the Japanese Legation, meant that from 1876—the moment when this book begins—"Tsushima now. . .served as a definitive border of the Japanese nation-state."[68]

As Doreen Massey and John Allen have argued, "there is no complete portrait of a region." This is because, they contend, regions can be said to "only exist in relation to particular criteria." That is to say, regions are particular "space-times"—Massey's reconceptualization of the spatial as "an ever-shifting social geometry of power and signification."[69] Taking inspiration from Massey, then, the three parts of this volume cover three distinct "space-times" of the Tsushima Strait region in order to trace its rise and fall. The portraits contained in this book have been formed through the reading and analysis of sources representing differing scales and viewpoints, which have cumulatively produced a palimpsest: This region is not one flattened field with sharp outlines, but instead the accretion of many overlapping fields and intersecting lines of urbanization and imperial expansion crisscrossing the Tsushima Straits—lines that begin and end outside the frame of formal empire.

Mirroring the many movements of the book's historical actors, the chapters' perspectives move back and forth across the Tsushima Strait. Part 1, "Watersheds," focuses on the planned and unplanned processes that led to the formation of this region—processes of urban growth, migration, and displacement—involving the movement of people from Fukuoka prefecture into Pusan and, in the opposite direction, people from southern Korea through Pusan and across the straits to northern Kyushu. Chapter 1 begins in late nineteenth-century Fukuoka, a city and prefecture that many among its elites considered in danger of peripheralization after the changes wrought upon local society by shifts in power after the Meiji Restoration (1868). It uses materials produced by these local elites, such as local newspapers the *Fukuoka Nichi Nichi Shinbun* and *Kyūshū Nippō* and Hakata Chamber of Commerce publications, to analyze the new visions of martial and mercantile expansion based on earlier tales of samurai glory in the Imjin War, which occupied the minds and galvanized the interests of former samurai and merchants alike. In contrast to these elite visions, this chapter also uses applications for travel documents (*ryoken*) from the years surrounding the Sino- and Russo-Japanese Wars, held in the Ministry of Foreign Affairs diplomatic archives. These documents help us understand the nature of the mobility and networks of rural-urban movement being created by early Japanese migrants who traveled between Fukuoka and Korea in the years prior to Korea's annexation in 1910. It then positions these networks within the wider trends of population movement fueling domestic as well as imperial urbanization in Meiji Japan.

Prior to Korea's colonization by Japan, migrants from Fukuoka, along with others predominantly from Western Japan, played an outsized role in shaping the growth of the port city of Pusan. In chapter 2 we move across the straits to view these processes of imperial urbanization from Korea, both before and after its colonization. This chapter looks at the visions of urban life and local development as shaped by "local imperialists"—those regional settlers living in Pusan and claiming it as their adopted home—and the minority of Korean elites that joined them in the city's local institutions, whether the city assembly or Pusan's chamber of commerce. It uses materials created by Pusan's Japanese Residents' Association as well as local Japanese-language newspaper the *Pusan Nippō*, along with analysis of the changing memberships of local institutions, to chart the continued grip that these self-proclaimed local elites kept on the city, even after colonization.

Among the Japanese settlers in Pusan, Fukuokans held significant positions in the city and were so numerous as to warrant two separate prefectural associations. In the final section of chapter 2, I look at the visions of those in these groups as they appeared in the publication of the Fukuoka Prefectural Association, *Fukuoka Kenjin* (*The Fukuokan*). This publication paints a portrait of a community using their cross-straits connections for the benefit of both Fukuoka and Pusan—and themselves. In contrast, I then analyze the fine-grained census materials produced by the Korea Government General in the 1930s to show how regional migration and decades of informal imperialism had created a city not only shaped by the visions of settler elites along with local landowners, but one in which working-class Japanese from the Tsushima Strait region relegated Koreans to the most precarious forms of work.

As a maritime border like the English Channel or the Mediterranean, the multiple constructions of the Tsushima Strait have depended on the experiences and desires of those depicting it.[70] In Japan, the most storied and notoriously dangerous area of the Tsushima Strait is the stretch bordering northern Kyushu, known as the Genkainada, or Genkai Sea, made famous by the Mongol invasions, and by accounts of early modern scholars traversing its rough waters to and from Nagasaki. In 1931, Osaka shipping captain Miyano Hanafumi noted how what we might call a "folk memory" of the historical waters still pertained in the modern age: "That passengers still pray to Konpira or take Jintan tablets—even on board steel ships some fifty to one hundred times bigger and faster than those one hundred–ton junks [of the past]—is a rather sad sign of our country's lingering maritime cowardice."[71] In modern, imperial Japan, the capabilities of new technology to shrink time and space were still in tension with older memories of these waters. In its modern history, travelers across the Tsushima Strait were not just at the mercy of the winds, but also at the mercy of empires and navies, traffickers and coast guards. For those without the protection of steel ships, the Genkainada—as early modern travelers had experienced it—still existed.

The arrival of Japanese settlers on the Korean peninsula led to the displacement and uprooting of Koreans and began a second round of rural-to-urban movement in the opposite direction. Chapter 3 shifts its attention to these people: Koreans from Pusan and the surrounding South Kyŏngsang province. This group formed the largest number of migrants traveling across the Tsushima Strait. Many of them went to work as manual laborers in industrializing Western Japan. Analysis of sources from municipal institutions in Pusan and Fukuoka show how, in the 1920s and '30s, authorities were brought together in their responses to the displacement, unauthorized migration, and employment of Koreans on both sides of the straits. The structures set up to control and manage these populations during this period would be repurposed in the war years and during decolonization.

The unauthorized and dangerous journeys across the straits taken by many Koreans in brokers' boats were very different from those of Japanese in the opposite direction. This maritime border was far more perilous for them than for imperial tourists in their large steamships. Mirroring the multiple cultural constructions of these dangerous waters, during the colonial period Koreans began to refer to the entire straits as Hyŏnhaet'an—the Korean pronunciation of the Japanese term Genkainada.

The final section of chapter 3 reassesses scholarship on the prewar Korean communities in industrial Fukuoka, looking at their representation in sensationalist local newspaper reports and in local government, and reframing our terms of analysis away from colonial categories of "rootlessness" or "model" minorities, to reveal the underlying regional labor networks that led Koreans from the rural hinterland around Pusan to become heavily involved in the construction of northern Kyushu's urban environments, and how these networks produced local "leaders." Finally, I show how this left Koreans in a double bind between assimilation and representation.

As Japan's empire and imperial ambitions on the Asian continent expanded, especially after the founding of Japan's client state of Manchukuo in 1932, the Tsushima Strait region became an increasingly central and important link in transportation and later military networks. Part 2 of this book, "High Tide," focuses on the intensifying development of the region's national and imperial connections in the 1930s, and how inhabitants of Fukuoka and Pusan co-opted and reacted to this. Local and national development plans for port and harbor infrastructure and transport networks—both sea and air—facilitated Japanese imperial expansion and movement across the strait and brought these port cities new prominence.

In chapter 4 the scale of perspectives on this region grows progressively larger, beginning with Tsushima ferry operators' petitions to Fukuoka city government and ending with air route maps in which geography was abstracted to colored lines on a blank page. First I outline the local demands and international catalysts for a direct ferry link between Hakata and Pusan in the wake of the Russo-Japanese War. Using local booster sources and colonial publications focused on urban development like *Korea and Architecture* (*Chōsen to Kenchiku*), I then chart the development of the two ports of Pusan and Hakata, focusing on the 1920s and '30s, which saw the largest interest and investment in the ports' expansion. The visions out from these two cities were on different levels. While Pusan's imperial elites saw the city as a global entrepôt, Fukuokans were content for the port of Hakata to be a gateway to Japan's growing empire. However, later developments in the 1930s shifted the relationship between these two cities, revealing underlying imperial dynamics. The chapter ends with a view from the sky, looking at how technology propelled Fukuoka into a central role in imperial Japan's air networks and onto the global stage of aviation and world-spanning air routes.

With total mobilization and war, from Japan's invasion of China in 1937 to its defeat in August 1945, rhetoric about—and state power over—the region changed. In chapter 5 I view the urbanization occurring across the region from an empire-wide perspective via the proceedings from the first Korean Conference on Urban Problems, held in the colonial capital of Keijō in 1936. This source allows me to outline a new history, showing how Japanese National Land Planning emerged as a response to the growth of urban regions that spanned metropole and colony and was only later mobilized by the state in its pursuit of imperial expansion and war. Next, using debates in urban planning journals such as *Toshi Kōron* and *Toshi Mondai,* as well as radio broadcasts and speeches by Korean and Japanese elites, I show how the new scales of control and development required rhetorical shifts by planners, politicians, and locals in both Fukuoka and Pusan, and how this altered visions for the cities' roles in Greater East Asia.

In the last part of chapter 5 I look at the consequences of expansion and war for the inhabitants of Fukuoka and Pusan. I use a variety of personal accounts, oral histories, later interviews via the United States Strategic Bombing Survey, roundtable discussions featuring Korean and Japanese women, and the reports of institutions involved in labor mobilization to show how the wartime period was in some ways the crystallization of these cities' roles in the empire, as funnels of mobilized labor and extracted food supplies from the colonies, but how their increasing importance also made them more vulnerable to attacks from the air. The chapter ends with a study of the two cities' wartime experiences and looks ahead to the effects these would have on their postwar and postliberation development.

From August 1945, crossing the Tsushima Strait transformed colonial subjects into free citizens, and settlers into repatriates. Part 3 of this book, "A Sea Change," looks at what happened after an imperial border became a national one, how the cities and people of this region dismantled imperial structures and reoriented their urban plans, and how some patterns and networks of the imperial region were less easily removed.

In the immediate wake of Japan's defeat and Korea's liberation in 1945, the waterfronts of Pusan and Hakata became hubs of decolonization. Chapter 6 looks in depth at these formative and chaotic months using personal accounts from Japanese officials involved in the process as well as the pages of the *Minju Jungbo*, liberated Pusan's newly formed Korean-language newspaper. Via analysis of roundtable accounts from repatriation officials it shows how wartime structures evolved and influenced the dismantling of empire and redrawing of national boundaries across the Tsushima Strait. While most works to date have looked at either Japanese or Korean repatriation, this chapter looks at all those who passed through Pusan and Hakata, giving a snapshot of what "decolonization" really looked like on the ground for those struggling to make sense of it, via the local publications of Zainichi (literally, Japan-resident) Koreans in Fukuoka, and settler committees in Seoul and Pusan, as well as later publications for former settlers back in Japan. Formal repatriation between the port of Hakata and Pusan finished in 1947, although the movement of people did not stop there.

Military occupation in both Japan and South Korea and the outbreak of the Korean War in 1950 led to the extension of colonial structures beyond the collapse of the Japanese empire. The final chapter of this book first traces the new urban visions and lingering imperial structures in Pusan and Fukuoka via local and national newspapers, local Zainichi publication the *Seiki Shinbun,* and planning journals. It then turns to the effects of further military conflict on both cities by looking at how these cities at the end of empire were relinked as logistical bases at the front lines of the Korean War. Using Ministry of Foreign Affairs archives on the repatriation of Japanese-Korean families during wartime, I show how decolonization remained incomplete even after the two cities' trajectories diverged in the aftermath of occupation and the Korean War's ceasefire in 1953. The chapter concludes by discussing how traces of earlier networks would go on to shape later reconnections between the two cities in the 1960s and beyond.

There are of course many silences in the archives of colonial Korea and imperial Japan. The key imbalance in this book remains that between the voices of Japanese and some Korean elites, and those of non-elite Koreans, who are the object of many a colonial report but rarely get to speak with their own voices in the materials found in archives. I have tried to supplement these absences by using Korean-language newspapers, oral histories gathered by other historians, analysis of photographic images of urban scenes, the reading of sensationalist newspaper reports against the grain, and the occasional archival source in which non-elite Koreans speak in their own voices. However, there are urban spaces and lives that remain beyond the reach of this project, just as there are for any work of historical enquiry. Acknowledging and mapping these erasures and silences is itself a key part of history writing, and indeed was the inspiration for the project that became this book.

Alongside archival silences are their inverse: the submerged ideological grammar that structures nearly everything one reads and finds its way into one's own sentences.[72] While the echoes of colonial archives and their language stood out to me in the language of earlier scholarship on the lives of "rootless" or "model" Koreans in Fukuoka, it took me longer to spot a similar uncritical echoing in my own work, steeped as it was in the discourse of urban "development." Once it was pointed out to me, I noticed it everywhere. Writing a more complete history of this region did not mean to simply "write in" Asia or empire to a positive city biography, or echo boosters in reciting statistics showing Fukuoka or Pusan's preeminence. A more complete history is one that shows how such erasures and marginalization were structural—integral to the processes of urban and imperial expansion. Wrestling with this topic has forced me to think more deeply about how to decouple urban history writing tropes from these developmental discourses and the positive valences they still carry and project. What follows is my attempt to do so.

PART I

Watersheds

Fukuokans and the Making of an Imperial Region

ON APRIL 21, 1898, Hayashi Komao received a telegram to his inn in Fukuoka, informing him that his steamship, the *Kōchi Maru*, had arrived in the city's port of Hakata. Hayashi was one of countless Fukuokans who, from the final decades of the nineteenth century, contributed to the creation of a new imperial region spanning the waters of the Tsushima Straits. Their actions would enmesh northern Kyushu and southeastern Korea in a profoundly unequal but mutually transformative relationship. Hayashi was an assistant technician at the newly opened Fukuoka Prefecture Experimental Fisheries Station and had orders to travel on the *Kōchi Maru* across the Tsushima Strait to survey the waters off the eastern coast of Korea alongside two fishing boats crewed by the Chikuhō Fishing Union.[1] He boarded the ship after midnight. After a rough passage, the ship arrived that morning in the port of Izuhara on Tsushima, the island whose lords had for centuries acted as intermediaries between Japan and Korea. The *Kōchi Maru* then rounded the southern tip of the island, docking at the port of Sasuna on the island's northwestern coast before departing for Pusan at one in the morning of April 23.[2] Hayashi finally reached Pusan at six o'clock that same morning. Japanese made up over a quarter of the port's inhabitants in 1898, and Hayashi headed for the Japanese settlement, taking a room at the Ōike Inn, one of several businesses in the growing town that was run by Ōike Chūsuke, a Tsushima islander who had made Pusan his home since 1875.[3]

As he waited for the rest of his crew to cross the straits, Hayashi met with a number of figures involved in Pusan's fishing and canning industries, learning more about the port's importance as the sole fish market and trading center along the inhospitable coastline of southeastern Korea. Among them was a fellow Fukuokan, Ogata Toshitarō, from the city of Kurume, who had set up a canning factory in Pusan. Processing fishing catches was key to transporting them safely to markets in both Japan and Korea, but Ogata told Hayashi that the lack of transportation links on the Korea side was hampering expansion and supply lines—a common complaint among Japanese entrepreneurs in the port.[4]

In some ways, however, Pusan's location could work to the advantage of its Japanese residents: The town was the only place for Japanese fishermen in the region to stock up on daily goods, as well as sell their catches at a good price. Korean laborers hired in Pusan were also more likely to have some understanding of Japanese than those from small fishing villages along the coast.[5] Hayashi observed that, as a result, there were several hundred Japanese fishing boats anchored in Pusan's harbor during his visit.[6] With Pusan's growing Japanese settlement and maritime presence, it is not surprising that when Hayashi returned at the end of his expedition, he remarked that "it was like returning to the mainland [*naichi*], seeing the white Japanese houses dotted everywhere, and the Rising Sun flag flying on our legation."[7] By 1898 Pusan was more than just a key fishing port. It was a critical outpost for Japan's informal imperialism in Korea—a process in which growing numbers of Fukuokans were involved and invested.[8]

When the members of the fishing union that had accompanied Hayashi's expedition returned from Korea, it did not take long for them to consolidate their position as players in the Korean fisheries. Within months they had created a Korea fishing union for the prefecture.[9] In 1900, Fukuoka City was chosen as headquarters for the Korea Sea Fishing Union Federation, a new umbrella organization for Japan's growing Korea fishing fleets. Local newspaper reports on the federation's first meeting noted that the port city was a wise choice for the role. The *Fukuoka Nichi Nichi Shinbun* (*Fukunichi*) remarked on not only the convenience of Hakata Port as both an entrepôt for further redistribution of marine goods, but also its proximity to the growing populations of the Chikuhō coal mining area and newly industrializing regions in northern Fukuoka prefecture. Fishermen who caught Korean marine products in high demand in Chinese markets, such as shark, dried abalone, and sea cucumbers, could sell them to Qing merchants through Pusan or Nagasaki, but rather than dumping catches of fish in Korea, where they would have to be sold cheaply, Japanese fishermen would make more profit by meeting the growing demand for food in the expanding industrial, urban markets near Fukuoka City.[10]

The extraction of marine resources from Korean waters would be sure to help Fukuoka's growth too, the article continued. Supplying the federation's ten thousand–strong fleets and their crews with locally made goods would boost the prefecture's industry. What was more, the region's farmers would benefit from buying fish-derived fertilizer direct, without going through middlemen in Kanmon or Osaka as they had in the past. All this necessitated investment in both transportation links and the fishing ventures themselves, but, if their efforts were successful, this growth could propel Fukuoka's port into trade with markets yet further afield: Siberia and northern China. The newspaper ended by assuring its readers that this wasn't just a coldhearted business venture but was a divine calling for the people of Fukuoka: "Seeing as heaven has bestowed upon our fishermen the keys to this goldmine, it is our divinely ordained duty to develop these natural resources."[11] This rallying call appears to have been heard. By 1905 Fukuoka prefecture's Korean fishing fleet had grown from 18 boats employing 121 people in 1897 to 543 boats employing 1,785 people. Their catches brought in over thirty-three times the value of those in 1897.[12]

The expansion of Fukuokan interests into southern Korea in this period, exemplified by the growth of fishing, was facilitated by developments playing out on a larger scale.[13] It was Meiji Japan's use of gunboat diplomacy that led to the signing of the 1876 Treaty of Kanghwa, under which Pusan became Korea's first modern "treaty port," opened that year for trade and settlement by Japanese merchants. In 1889, ongoing pressure from the Meiji government also led to the signing of a new fishing treaty between the two countries.[14] Although the treaty spoke of "equality" between the two nations, this meant little considering the technological advantages of Japan's fishing industry. This, along with the support provided by newly established experimental fisheries stations, like the one Hayashi worked for in Fukuoka, ensured the rapid expansion of Japanese fishing boats into Korea's rich waters as Japan's own waters were becoming exhausted from overfishing.[15] From the late 1880s, Japan's growing urban populations were increasingly dependent on Korean fish, rice, and soybeans.[16]

The most important development of all was the Sino-Japanese War of 1894–95, fought over influence in Korea. For Fukuoka prefecture, Japan's victory over the Qing dynasty represented the first iteration of a pattern of military success, industrial growth, and labor migration that would be repeated multiple times over the following decades, each time increasing the links across the Tsushima Straits. Coming just three years after the conclusion of the Sino-Japanese War, and at a time when new national laws were creating even stronger incentives for Japanese fishermen to push into Korean waters and beyond, Hayashi's visit to Pusan took place at a pivotal moment for Japanese expansion across the Tsushima Strait.[17]

But this process of expansion cannot be understood completely from the national or international level. Japan's imperialism and the visions of development (*kaihatsu*) associated with it had local geographies, local factors, and local effects, which in turn drove broader change. In this regard, too, the case of Hayashi Komao is worth attention.

Hayashi's family history was entangled with Korea. Born Sugiyama Komao, he was adopted as the heir of his uncle, Hayashi Masayoshi in 1891, when he was around twenty. His older brother, Sugiyama Shigemaru, appears to have brokered this arrangement, with Komao as collateral in exchange for government bonds, worth some seven hundred yen, that his uncle, like all former samurai retainers, had received from the Meiji government as compensation for the abolition of hereditary samurai stipends in 1876. Sugiyama Shigemaru used these funds to bankroll a fishing venture in southern Korea, in which he was joined by two other former samurai from Fukuoka prefecture, Yūki Toragorō and Takeda Hanshi.[18]

Sugiyama, Yūki, and Takeda were all linked by their membership in the Gen'yōsha, the Pan-Asianist group often held up today as epitomizing the worst excesses of Japanese imperial expansionism. The group's local origins, and deep roots, in Fukuoka are less well remembered, even though E. H. Norman's pioneering 1944 essay on the group made the link explicit, describing the city as "the spiritual home of the most rabid brand of Japanese nationalism and imperialism" and the Gen'yōsha itself as "peculiar" for its "organization on a local basis with headquarters in a city of rich historical traditions where intense local patriotism or clannishness gave it an inner cohesiveness."[19]

Norman's seemingly oxymoronic phrase, "local patriotism," with its suggestion of deep commitment to both Fukuoka and Japan, captures the dynamics at play in many of the Gen'yōsha's actions. But the group's purported goal of unifying Asia against the forces of Western imperialism also led it to build relationships with like-minded allies abroad. This included the Korean radicals involved in the ill-fated Kapsin Coup of 1884, who sought to implement modernizing reforms of the kind launched in Japan after the Meiji Restoration. Many of the failed coup's leaders, including Kim Okkyun, were then exiled to Japan. Among them was a man named Yi Chuhoe, who, after three years in Japan, returned to Korea, where he was posted to the remote island of Kŭmodo near Yŏsu in Chŏlla province, possibly as a continuation of his punishment.

Yi was well known to members of the Gen'yōsha by this point, and it was for this reason that Sugiyama, Yūki, and Takeda chose Kŭmodo as the destination for their fishing venture. While the three former samurai provided the capital, fishermen from the Fukuokan fishing village of Shingū provided the expertise.[20] As it turned out, neither this connection to a local official nor the rich waters around Kŭmodo were enough to ensure the venture's success.[21] However, the relationship between Yi and Takeda, in particular, proved a consequential one. In 1894 Takeda and other Gen'yōsha members helped form a paramilitary group in Pusan, hoping to foment war with Qing China and gain control over Korea. The following year, Takeda and Yi were both involved in the assassination of Queen Min (posthumously renamed Empress Myŏngsŏng), who had long been seen as an obstacle to Japanese ambitions on the peninsula. The incident is still remembered today as representative of the brutality of Japan's push into Korea, and in its aftermath Yi was sentenced to death and executed. Takeda, meanwhile, was eventually released from custody and went on to play a significant role in agitating for Japan's formal "annexation" of Korea in 1910.[22]

The connections between high-profile incidents of political violence involving Gen'yōsha and self-styled *Chōsen rōnin* (masterless samurai in Korea) on the peninsula, and the expansion of Japanese fishing into Korean waters, may seem coincidental, but they were both important elements in early Japanese expansion in Korea. And, as the involvement and investment by Gen'yōsha members in fisheries and marine products, as well as the publication of numerous reports in their publications, attests, they were deeply intertwined.[23]

If a focus on Fukuoka allows us to reconnect these aspects of the dynamics behind Japanese expansion, it also offers us a way to better understand how they connected to urbanization as well. In general it has been noted that port cities in Japan flourished during the Meiji period (1868–1912).[24] By the period's end, two ports (Yokohama and Kobe) and one industrial city (Nagoya) had joined the three early modern megacities of Tokyo, Osaka, and Kyoto as the "Big Six" cities at the top of Japan's modern urban system.[25] That elites in Fukuoka were well aware of the key role that ports played in linking Japan's regions to overseas markets and settlements, natural resources, and battlegrounds helps explain why they were not content for their city to remain just an administrative outpost of the newly centralized Meiji government. They could see that the port of Hakata was key to the city's future and in particular to local visions for "development" (J: *kaihatsu*) of the Tsushima Strait. The same, of course, was true on the other side of the strait, where Pusan was to serve as a critical satellite port for Japan's, and Fukuoka's outward expansion.[26]

In spite of what local boosters in Fukuoka might say, however, there was nothing preordained or automatic about the growth of an imperial region that came to connect these two port cities. The remainder of this chapter will explore how, over several decades and two imperial wars, a shared vision for development began to take root in Fukuoka, helping to overcome earlier divisions; and how many other non-elite actors were also involved in connecting Fukuoka to Pusan via acts of regional imperialism, some mundane, some violent. By the time Korea was declared a colony of Japan in 1910, the modern urban growth of Pusan and Fukuoka, and of the wider Tsushima Strait region, were already enmeshed.

REORIENTING FUKUOKA

The borders of Fukuoka prefecture took their current form in the summer of 1876, the same year that the Meiji government signed unequal treaties with Chosŏn Korea and forced the opening of the port of Pusan. These two events, and the wider processes they were part of, were linked by more than synchronicity: The making of the modern nation-state of Japan entailed the involvement of its inhabitants in expansion beyond its national borders. Local former samurai (*shizoku*) elites, as well as commoner merchants and businessmen, laborers, fishermen, farmers, and their families, responded to and engaged in the socio-spatial shifts that accompanied domestic processes of unification, centralization, and peripheralization.

As people in Fukuoka experienced and engaged with the processes by which Japan became a capitalist, imperial nation-state—a process Kären Wigen describes as "the subordination of scores of overlapping but quasi-autonomous economic regions to a single national center"—their actions involved redefining their relationship to their immediate locality.[27] Their responses depended on their access to capital, but what linked many of their searches for opportunity is an outward gaze.

For those without capital or land, this redefinition often involved leaving their homes and selling their labor. Some became domestic migrants, moving from their rural communities to the growing conurbations of Meiji Japan's developing industrial economy. Some also moved beyond the archipelago. Those with the power and influence—local and national—afforded by capital and education responded to these changing circumstances, and their fears of peripheralization, by reimagining and reorienting their hometown.

Animating their actions was a vision of and desire for development on several scales and in various registers.[28] Development was seen as vital to succeed in the competition that Fukuokans found themselves in with other cities and prefectures in regard to both the region's relationship with Japan's new national center and with Japan's growing sphere of influence in East Asia. Fukuokan elites were keen to make use of their local past to imagine a new future for themselves. And, for many in Fukuoka, their eyes turned to the waters of the Tsushima Strait and the Asian continent over the horizon, especially Korea.

But this overseas reorientation required an internal remaking too. The modern-day city of Fukuoka is divided in two by the Naka River, which flows into Hakata Bay to the north. From the completion of Fukuoka Castle in 1607 until their merger as Fukuoka City in 1889, the river marked the division between the castle town of Fukuoka and the merchant town of Hakata. The Kuroda clan had been granted Fukuoka domain in 1600 and had a martial lineage that linked them to Korea. Kuroda Nagamasa had been one of the most ruthless military leaders in the Imjin War, the 1590s Japanese invasions of Korea. Later, in their regular visits to Edo, Kuroda lords gifted the shogun reminders of this connection in the unlikely form of pottery from the domain's Takatori kiln, made by generations of craftsmen descended from Koreans kidnapped during the invasion.[29]

After the Meiji Restoration, Fukuoka's former samurai felt slighted by the dominance of the nearby domains of Satsuma and Chōshū in the new regime and felt singled out when the domain was abolished early as punishment for its use of counterfeit currency—common across Japan in the aftermath of the expensive Boshin War.[30] Several senior members were executed, and former domain lord Kuroda Nagatomo was imprisoned in his home. Fukuoka domain had been the seventh largest and one of the richest domains in Tokugawa Japan, and the residual pride of its former samurai is evidenced by their actions in early Meiji. Fukuoka *shizoku* took part in a string of antigovernment uprisings across Kyushu, including the Saga Rebellion in 1874, led by Etō Shinpei, who had resigned from the Meiji government the year before for its failure to "punish" Korea for refusing to enter into new diplomatic or trade relations with the empire of Japan and its head of state, Emperor Meiji. In 1876 the Akizuki Rebellion was led by retainers from a Kuroda branch domain. What united all these rebellions was conservative anger and loss, as well as frustration over the denial of a chance for former samurai to regain their pride via military campaigns, especially in Korea.

In 1877 *shizoku* attacked their former domain seat of Fukuoka Castle. The target was the newly installed Imperial Army, which was using it as a base for troops to be deployed south to the Satsuma Rebellion, the largest of the samurai rebellions of the 1870s. Led by Saigō Takamori, and gaining support from those who opposed the reforms of the new government, the forces of several Kyushu domains had laid siege to the Imperial Army troops based in Kumamoto Castle since late February. Many Fukuoka *shizoku* participated in the Satsuma Rebellion on the anti-government side, and generations of Gen'yōsha members would continue to idolize Saigō after his death. The attack on Fukuoka Castle was an (ultimately unsuccessful) attempt by Fukuoka's former samurai to help the rebel cause, and it became mythologized as one of the Gen'yōsha's founding tales of Fukuokan exceptionalism.

Prior to housing the local regiment of the new Imperial Army, Fukuoka Castle had also housed the new prefectural headquarters. Replacing its role as domain seat, Fukuoka had become the center of the new prefectural government. In 1889, when the Meiji regime implemented top-down reforms creating a modern municipal system, the castle town of Fukuoka and merchant port of Hakata were merged to become a new city, which was eventually named Fukuoka after much disagreement between the two parties. But old divisions lived on well after the abolition of status groups in 1869, and after the merger in 1889. Perhaps most importantly, in a hangover from its division along mercantile and samurai lines, the new city now had two ports: the merchant port of Hakata and the domain port of Fukuoka.

Attempts to take advantage of Fukuoka's geographical position and natural harbor began early, but the city's halting progress was partly due to this continued rift, which created rivalries and stymied growth. The reimagining and reorientation of Fukuoka City toward Asia would require its local elites—*shizoku* and commoners—to engage in what David Harvey calls a "growth coalition," one that was capable of transcending local rivalries in order to engage in regional boosterism for the increasingly entangled interests of urban elites.[31]

The Gen'yōsha and Korea

Gen'yōsha members were among the most influential Fukuokan actors to undertake this reimagining. The group had formed out of a nucleus of disaffected *shizoku* active in the anti-government rebellions of the 1870s. Both its own members and historians have memorialized the group mostly as a far right, Pan-Asianist organization involved in violence and political intrigue within Japan and across Asia.[32] The usual subjects of these accounts are Tōyama Mitsuru (1855–1944), the de facto leader of the organization from its founding in 1881 until his death, and Uchida Ryōhei (1874–1937), the figure behind the affiliated ultranationalist and anti-Russia group the Kokuryūkai, or Amur River Society, founded in 1901.

However, the group had a much wider membership that at first glance is hard to square with the popular image of them. Members' lists and biographical data reveal roughly two key generations. The largest group for whom we have dates of birth—nearly a third of the total—were born in the 1850s, coming of age in the 1870s during the period of *shizoku* rebellion and debates over conquering Korea. Nearly one-fifth of those were involved in the *shizoku* rebellions. Many of those were taught at the Takaba *juku*, the private academy led by Takaba Osamu, between 1873 and Takaba's death in 1891.[33] This first generation contained many who would play a role in politics at the local and national level, as well as large numbers involved in journalism.

Members of the second key generation were born in the 1880s. After the closure of Takaba's *juku*, the later generations of Gen'yōsha members were mainly educated at the Shūyūkan, a prefectural school named after the old domain academy, which opened in 1885 with financial support from local notables, including the former domain lords. Younger Gen'yōsha members, born too late for involvement in *shizoku* rebellions and educated in the new Meiji system, must have had different reasons for joining the group—perhaps viewing it more as a useful regional network than a band of brothers. This later generation contained fewer national political figures and more businessmen, and it had a distinctly more local character than the older generation. As this chapter will show, the Janus-faced nature of the group's membership can be explained by the changed environment, local and international, between the first and second generations. "Local patriotism" took different forms in the late nineteenth century compared to the 1920s and '30s.

It is rare, especially in English-language scholarship, that the Gen'yōsha is analyzed in its local context, but the group's membership was overwhelmingly local. The group was often referred to as the Chikuzen Gen'yōsha, another name for the region. Of over six hundred identified Gen'yōsha members, only six were originally from outside Fukuoka prefecture.[34] Although founded in 1881, the group saw their roots stretching back far beyond that. The *Gen'yōsha Official History*, published in 1917, makes many references to the geography and history of Tsukushi no kuni, the ancient province roughly equivalent to Fukuoka prefecture today. Tsukushi no kuni and its component parts Chikuzen and Chikugo were used in the names of other local political groups in the Meiji period, such as the Chikuzen Kyōaikai, formed in 1879, which shared members with the later Gen'yōsha. This rhetorical hearkening back to the "transcendent symbol" of the *kuni* took on a partisan air in a region with little love lost between it and the new Meiji state.[35]

The group's *Official History* accounts for the Gen'yōsha name as a reference to the Genkainada, or Genkaiyō, the notoriously rough stretch of water comprising the coastal waters off Fukuoka, from Munakata in the northeast to Hirado in the southwest. The waters of the Genkainada surround the islands of Oki, Iki, and Tsushima; to their east lies the Hibikinada, and the Kanmon Straits between Kitakyūshū and Yamaguchi. In the *Official History* the waters are used as a convenient rhetorical and physical link between the Gen'yōsha, Fukuoka's history, and its renewed focus on the Asian continent. In one passage the author directs the reader's inner gaze outward from Fukuoka's Hakozaki Shrine: "Now, as an experiment, if you pass straight through the first and second *torii* from Hakozaki Shrine's 'enemy-defeating' gate and look out across the sea, your gaze passing first over Shikanoshima and in a straight line out to the open sea, you would eventually reach Pusan in Chōsen."[36] The shrine's "enemy-defeating" gate was so called because of its calligraphy sign—"defeat of the enemy nation" (*tekikoku kōfuku*)—a gift from Emperor Kameyama after the twelfth-century Mongol invasions were repelled from Hakata Bay. The teleology is clear: By 1917, when the *Official History* was published, Pusan was now a Japanese port in its closest colony, after the defeat of both Qing China and the Russian empire.

Such teleological mythmaking also led Gen'yōsha members—and some historians—to argue that the group was a local response to geopolitics. For them, Korea was a site of possible expansion but also a threat of invasion, and their connection to Asia was an ancestral and cultural inheritance—something in their blood but also passed down, almost as a folk memory.[37] However, the Gen'yōsha historians had to dig quite far back into Fukuoka's history to find relevant links between it and the Asian continent. For some eight hundred years Hakata had been a key gateway to Japan for visitors from overseas—wanted and unwanted.[38] However, from the 1630s onward Tokugawa Japan's maritime edicts meant that the previously active merchant port was reduced to something of a domestic backwater. Nevertheless, the area was still linked to Korea and China via smuggling, and by the role of the

Kuroda lords of Fukuoka in maritime defense of the shogunal port of Nagasaki, one of Japan's early modern gateways.[39]

Due to this hiatus, the push for renewed overseas connections in Meiji was envisaged as a return to pre-Tokugawa martial (and mercantile) prowess. This partly explains why a group like the Gen'yōsha emerged in Fukuoka as opposed to Nagasaki or Tsushima. Mythical and martial references to the Mongol invasions of the thirteenth century, and Kuroda Nagamasa's role in the Imjin War of 1592–98, worked much better for Gen'yōsha rhetoric than would have the Tokugawa-era links of Nagasaki and Tsushima with Qing China and Chosŏn Korea. During early Meiji, the inhabitants of those two former "gateways" were involved in more pragmatic attempts at making use of their human capital than were the self-mythologizing Gen'yōsha.[40]

Shizoku and the Construction of a Region

The Gen'yōsha were only one of many political groups formed by local notables that emerged in Fukuoka during the final three decades of the nineteenth century, all linked to the growing Freedom and Popular Rights (J: jiyū minken undō) movement, which aimed to widen participation in government and strengthen Japan's international standing by pushing a hawkish foreign policy and demands for a constitution to match the nations of the West. However, as other local factions welcomed a wider range of members, the Gen'yōsha remained far more *shizoku*-oriented in both membership and ideology. These local *shizoku* elites had a key role in the workings of local politics, business, and journalism, all intimately connected with expansionism and regional development in Meiji Fukuoka.[41]

Men from Fukuoka's former samurai families were deeply involved in the region's modern transformations. They had power and influence in its political, economic, and media institutions. As was the case in most prefectures in southwest Japan, the early membership of Fukuoka's prefectural assembly was dominated by *shizoku*. In 1883 *shizoku* held a nationwide average of one-fifth of prefectural assembly seats. However, in Kyushu they averaged nearly a third, with *shizoku* making up over half of Fukuoka's prefectural assembly members.[42]

The Gen'yōsha's "turn to Asia" is sometimes characterized as a result of the failure of, or disenchantment with, earlier *shizoku* political movements—as a shift from popular rights to national sovereignty. However, it was often their members' status as *shizoku* that enabled their "continental adventures," and, as seen in the case of Sugiyama's fishing venture, that gave them access to networks of capital, media, and ideas that would affect both their home-town and its links with East Asia, especially Korea and the port of Pusan.

The early involvement of *shizoku* in key financial institutions in Fukuoka was in large part due to the program of interest-paying government bonds (*kinroku kōsai*) replacing *shizoku* stipends in 1876, and the particular socioe-conomic structure of Fukuoka's former domains. Lower-level samurai did much better out of the bond system than those higher up, and both they and their bonds were "unequally distributed across prefectures."[43] The total worth of bonds held by Fukuoka's former samurai was the fifth largest in Japan, and sixth largest per capita. Despite the *shizoku* rebellions that erupted across Kyushu in the 1870s, partly in response to the new bond system, this sudden injection of capital provided financing for *shizoku* investment in business, banking, and education.[44] In Fukuoka this resulted in *shizoku* investing in the Seventeenth National Bank and in the region's most profitable enterprises, including mining and railroad construction.[45] These bonds were an impor-tant factor in the business successes of key Gen'yōsha members, such as Tōyama Mitsuru and Hiraoka Kōtarō, and their ability to fund the group's various causes. Along with Fukuoka's relatively early construction of railways, its *shizoku* bonds are thought to have boosted the economic development—via urbanization and industrialization—of the prefecture as a whole.[46]

The role of *shizoku* elites in founding and editing newspapers in the 1880s, connected to the Freedom and Popular Rights movement's aim of educating the people, has been well studied.[47] The Gen'yōsha, with members involved in the running of both of Fukuoka's oldest newspapers, was a key example of this. The *Fukuryō Shinpō*, begun as the mouthpiece of the Gen'yōsha in 1887, was financed by donations from its members, as well as former domain lords the Kuroda and prefectural governor Yasuba Yasukazu. Donations were also solicited throughout the Chikuzen area—a sign of the paper's local support and reach.[48] In 1898, the paper was renamed the *Kyūshū Nippō* (*Kyushu Daily*), suggesting new president Matono Hansuke's expanded ambitions.[49] Fukuoka's oldest newspaper, the *Fukuoka Nichi Nichi Shinbun*, was founded in 1877 as the *Chikushi Shinbun* before becoming the *Fukunichi* in 1880. Like the *Fukuryō Shinpō*, it had *shizoku* founders and ties to the Freedom and Popular Rights movement in Fukuoka, and its second president, along with several of its journalists, were members of the Gen'yōsha. These newspapers are an invaluable source for understanding the ways local elites promoted their views on the links between Fukuoka and East Asia, shaping and mobilizing the "spirit of a place-bound geographical community" in its readership.[50]

Beyond Fukuoka, Gen'yōsha members were involved in the writing and publishing of newspapers in key ports and cities across Kyushu and Japan's growing sphere of influence in East Asia. Newspapers in these port cities of empire played key roles in creating "communicative circuits" that fostered a shared understanding of Japan's imperial mission across its growing colonial possessions, but also a localized understanding of how these different regions could prosper alongside the empire's growth.[51] Gen'yōsha members financed and ran two newspapers in the Kyushu port town of Moji: the *Moji Shinpō*, which included key Fukuoka industrialists among its financiers, and the *Kanmon Shinpō*, started by *Kyūshū Nippō* founder Matono Hansuke, who was also involved as a consultant on Dairen's first Japanese newspaper, the *Ryōtō Shinpō*.[52] Gen'yōsha members were also involved in the *Pusan Nippō* and its predecessor, the *Chōsen Nippō*, Pyongyang's *Heinan Mainichi Shinbunsha*, Taipei's *Taiwan Nichi Nichi Shinbun*, and Nagasaki's *Kyūshū Hinode Shinbun* and *Tōyō Hinode Shinbun*.

These newspapers could act as mouthpieces for the expansionist ideals of their backers, but they also formed physical semicolonial outposts on the continent for their other activities. Another group of Kyushu *shizoku*, the Kumamoto Kokkentō (the National Rights Party), set up Korea's first Japanese-language newspapers during the Sino-Japanese War.[53] The group sprang from origins similar to those of the Gen'yōsha—they were both deeply influenced by Saigō Takamori—and was also heavily involved in activities connected to Japan's advance into Korea and the wider Asia-Pacific. The Kokkentō began sending students from Kumamoto to Seoul to learn Korean from 1896.[54]

As well as media expansion, both the Gen'yōsha and Kokkentō shared an interest in "cultivation" or "development" (*kaitaku/kaikon/kaihatsu*). The trope of *shizoku* reclaiming both land and lost status through engaging in *kaitaku* was common in Meiji and came to be seen as a tool of the Meiji state's expansionist policies—such as the deployment of *tondenhei* (military settler colonists) and *tochi kaitaku* (land development) programs in Hokkaido.[55] In the late 1890s Kokkentō members were involved in setting up emigration companies that profited from sending laborers to locations across the Pacific Rim. A predecessor to the Gen'yōsha, known as the Kaikonsha, was engaged in clearing and cultivating land on Uminonakamichi, the spit of land that curves round Hakata Bay.[56] When sympathetic Gen'yōsha members visited exiled Korean reformist Kim Okkyun in the Ogasawara Islands, they were also surveying the land for a possible site for *shizoku* cultivation.[57] In Meiji, the concepts of *kaitaku* and *kaihatsu* developed new and more abstract meanings, often connected to economic development and imperial expansion: dominion over both nature and territory.[58] The "development" of the waters linking Japan and Korea were, to the Gen'yōsha named after them, a natural extension of their earlier activities.

Shizoku status gave Gen'yōsha members political power, financial connections, a platform in a network of local newspapers that they owned and wrote for, and an early interest in development and "pioneering," which was transferred to the Korean peninsula and beyond. Involvement in such expansionist activities in Japan's colonies and semicolonies into the early 1900s provided the human and financial capital for many local development projects, producing the "preconditions" for future growth.[59] In turn, *shizoku* involvement in local development, which propelled the region's industrialization and urbanization, would also have rippling effects on the nature of links between Fukuoka and the empire, and the patterns of migration across the Tsushima Strait region.

Hakata Merchants and Hakata Port

Given what its boosters referred to as Fukuoka's "locational advantage" (J: *chi no ri*), the development of its port was recognized from even before the city's founding as the best catalyst for its urban growth, and, as seen in Hayashi's account above, this was deeply connected to the creation of new networks in and out of the port—of migration, trade, and the extraction of natural resources. In Meiji Japan, port development required connections with other open ports: Those of Korea, especially Pusan, were close by and had historical links that made them the obvious base for regional expansion by those from the Tsushima Strait region.[60] These plans were at the center of developmental visions for not only Fukuoka *shizoku* but also Hakata merchants and other business elites.

As discussed above, Hakata had soon emerged as the more important of the city's two ports, to the initial consternation of *shizoku* elites. After the opening of Korean treaty ports to Japan alone, and a period in which trade with Korea had been treated "just like domestic trade," new restrictions were brought in once Korea signed treaties with other countries.[61] In 1883 Hakata was one of three Japanese ports—all located in the Tsushima Strait region—

designated for trade with Korea.[62] Pusan was the closest open Korean port for all. In 1889, the same year that Hakata and Fukuoka were merged under the new Fukuoka City government, Hakata Port was designated a Special Import and Export Port, which allowed the trade of rice, wheat, flour, coal, and sulfur with Korea. The port was still a backwater, however, with most of its trade being done by Japanese sailing boats, not modern steamships. Despite its designation, there were few regular shipments between Hakata and Korean ports.

In this early period, initiating a trend that Hakata businessmen would find difficult to overcome, Hakata Port, and by extension Fukuoka City, were marginalized by the ports of Moji and Shimonoseki. Lying on either side of the Kanmon Strait, these were outposts of the central government and capital from Tokyo and Osaka, and they linked the inland sea and its shipping lanes to Osaka with the Japan Sea and the Asian continent. During the Sino-Japanese War, Moji became the hub for trade and military links to the peninsula from Kyushu, while Shimonoseki, on the Honshū side of the strait, had the superior transport links to Tokyo via railroad.[63]

From the late 1880s to the early 1890s, business groups and *shizoku* figures in Fukuoka saw their interests align through shared hopes for expanding trade links with China and Korea, entangled as these plans were with other motives for Japanese expansion on the continent. In December 1889, Pan-Asianist and China hand Arao Sei visited Fukuoka, scouting for potential research students to study at his new Institute for Sino-Japanese Commercial Research. Through this recruitment process and Arao's links with the Gen'yōsha, students from Fukuoka were well represented when the institute opened in Shanghai the following year. Several of those who became students would go on to positions of local influence in Fukuoka on their return.[64]

In October of 1892, vice president of the Hakata Chamber of Commerce, Isono Shichihei (who became mayor the following year) and city assemblyman and Gen'yōsha member Okabe Satoru undertook a research visit to Korea. Their mission was to look at possible markets for expansion. In their report on this business trip, printed in the *Fukuryō Shinpō* in March 1893, the two urged Hakata businessmen to harness the power of their forebears: "Our shrewd Hakata businessmen should not fall behind others but consider their Hakata Merchant ancestors ... who long ago set sail for ports in Chōsen, Shina, Annam, Siam, Burma, and beyond. ... The time is here for our city's businessmen to make known the talents bestowed upon them by their forefathers—home and abroad."[65] This joint visit by Okabe and Isono, and their references to both Hakata and Fukuoka's history in their research report, suggest an early attempt at reconciliation of the rival groups in order to imagine a shared local identity that could foster regional development. Their rhetoric was explicitly violent, linking the mercantile and martial. Isono and Okabe described Fukuoka's modern businessmen as participants in the "Meiji Imjin war"—a rather flippant reference to the fact that both 1892 and 1592 (the first invasion of Korea by Toyotomi Hideyoshi) were years of the Yang Water Dragon in the Chinese sexagenary cycle.[66] Presumably, the two were hoping for a different outcome this time. Although we could see this comment as reframing commerce as a battle itself, these two facets—the martial and mercantile—would be tightly linked in the city and region's future growth.

WAR, EXPANSION, AND OPPORTUNITY

Two regional wars punctuated the three decades between the opening of Pusan to trade in 1876 and Korea becoming a protectorate of Japan in 1905. Both military conflicts were fought over control of the Korean peninsula—first against Qing China in 1894–95 and then against the Russian empire in 1904–5. Members of the Gen'yōsha and the Kokuryūkai were deeply entangled with these events, often as a vanguard attempting to shift the course of national policy and deepen Japan's involvement in Korea. However, the actions of Fukuoka's Asianist elites, like Sugiyama and other Gen'yōsha members, as well as the reactions of local politicians and businessmen, often relied upon the prior networks, actions, and movements created by large numbers of non-elite actors, who had also been responding to these regional and national changes.

Fukuoka prefecture began accepting applications for *ryoken* (travel documents) in 1878.[67] In the 1890s, with labor migration programs to Hawaiʻi and the colonization of Taiwan, yearly overseas migration from Japan rose into the tens of thousands.[68] In Fukuoka at this time, the two most common destinations were Korea and Hawaiʻi. The nature of "migration" to these two places was very different. Most Fukuokans who left for Hawaiʻi were men and women from poor and isolated rural areas that suffered from high rates of tenant farming.[69] Mainly second sons and their wives, their remittances helped support family back home, and their journeys created "migrant grooves" that made Fukuokan village and Hawaiian plantation feel less "socially distant."[70]

Those who traveled to Korea at this time were a much more diverse group. They included groups of migrant laborers from fishing villages, *shizoku* from urban centers, and commercial migrants hoping to set up businesses in Pusan. Whether we would classify all those who applied for and received *ryoken* for travel to Korea as "emigrants" is debatable. Many were more mobile than the term suggests, both within Japan and overseas. Their movements brought together the uneven domestic processes of rural stagnation, urbanization, and industrialization, and the spread of Japanese trade networks across the Tsushima Strait and beyond. These networks were both local and transnational, and were formed by frequent movement between origin and destination. They helped to form a region whose networks, centres, and peripheries spanned an international border, and reveal an informal imperialism with a deeply regional character.

The outbreak of hostilities between Japan and Qing China saw a large increase in travel to the Korean peninsula. Applications for *ryoken* from Fukuoka in the period surrounding the start of the war reached five hundred in six months—the highest numbers since the *ryoken* system began. The port of Inch'ŏn was the early hub of Japanese military activity on the peninsula, and the port soon became the most popular destination for Fukuokan travelers over the much closer Pusan.

In October of 1894, Sano Katsubei, a forty-two-year-old resident of the old castle town of Kokura, applied for a *ryoken* for Korea, stating in his application that he would be working in military canteens. This is the only application for this peak period of travel that directly references the ongoing war on the peninsula. More representative of those traveling from Fukuoka at this time were Tokuda Ichitarō from Amagi village in Yasu county, who planned to sell vegetables in Pusan, and the Matsuki brothers, Kazuzō and Tatsuzō, from Kurogi village in Mizuma county, who applied to travel to Inch'ŏn to sell sundry goods (*zakka*).[71]

Looking at the *ryoken* application data reveals several different patterns of travel and types of travelers, uncovering a range of sub-prefectural economic structures at play, as well as new networks and geographies being formed. Over half of all Fukuoka prefecture's applicants applying for travel to Korea in the latter half of 1894 came from just three counties—Yasu, Kōzuma, and Mizuma—and the prefecture's two cities, Fukuoka and Kurume. In 1894, the combined population of these areas made up a fifth of the prefecture's population. Kōzuma and Mizuma were very populous counties, but Yasu remains the real outlier; between 1894 and 1895 it was the origin of 15 percent of the prefectures' migrants to Korea despite making up only 2.8 percent of its population. However, Yasu migrants had developed links to Pusan soon after it opened for trade: People had traveled from the county to Korea every year since 1884. For rural migrants, the safety in following in the footsteps of those who came before created networks of commerce between the prefecture's agricultural regions and Korea's growing urban regions.

Mizuma migrants to Korea were following new regional shifts in flows of money and goods that had resulted from larger political changes.[72] The county, at the mouth of the prefecture's Chikugo River (the longest in Kyushu), was home to the port of Wakatsu and the Fukagawa shipbuilding yards, and had been a domain port with shipping links to the Osaka rice market and across the Ariake Sea to Nagasaki.[73] However, as Japan's interests in continental East Asia advanced, the Ariake region was peripheralized—overtaken by the Tsushima Strait region. Mizuma's travelers to Korea were reorienting their trade networks across another sea.

Fukuokans' applications for *ryoken* reveal more about their motivations for travel than just their occupation and destination. For the initial postwar boom following Japan's victory over China in 1895, we can compare reasons given for travel with the current occupation of the applicant. For some applicants, Korea became an extension of an extant occupational network. For others, the advance of Japanese influence on the continent meant a chance to change their fortunes.

Nearly half of all applicants at this time were involved in commerce, and many of them were extending their occupational network into Korea. This entailed multiple journeys, facilitated by Fukuoka's proximity to the peninsula. For them, Korea was not a land of unbridled opportunity, but rather a constellation of urban centers and ports where previous skill, as well as experience and integration in regional networks, made expansion of their business prospects—in an increasingly Japanese-dominated market—an attractive option.

During wartime, the most highly represented among Fukuokan applicants for travel to Korea were people from agricultural regions with local industries or professions that transferred well to the Korean peninsula, such as tobacco growers, sake brewers, and itinerant merchants. These migrants, like Tokuda the vegetable seller, represented the incorporation of Fukuoka's agricultural regions as hinterlands not just for the prefecture's growing urban regions but also for Korea's cities and their Japanese communities. Such movement made particular financial sense during the Sino-Japanese War, when food prices on the peninsula skyrocketed.[74]

In this way, Fukuoka's own hinterlands became a labor frontier for its outposts in Korea, with the region's proximity allowing for a greater diversity of migrants.[75] In Korea, many of these migrants would enact a "relocation" of the peripheralizing processes Kären Wigen and others have traced in the domestic socioeconomic shifts of Meiji Japan's modern transformation.[76] In Japanese settlements and port cities like Pusan, this led to the exclusion or replacement of Korean labor by Japanese, discussed more in the following chapter.

Between 1894 and 1895 most migrants from Kōzuma, Mizuma, and Yasu counties were commoners, as were those from Fukuoka City. Most migrants from Kurume City, on the other hand, were former samurai. We know this because Fukuoka's authorities collected data on the class distinctions of its applicants, whether *shizoku* (former samurai) or *heimin* (commoner). This is unusual—other prefectures did not keep up this practice as judiciously, or for as long, as Fukuoka—yet it is another indication of the importance that status distinctions still carried in the region.[77]

Urban migrants had a wider variety of destinations than those from rural areas, which suggests a wider range of opportunities and knowledge informing their decisions. Furthermore, *shizoku* travelers from Kurume and Fukuoka cities were more likely to apply to visit Korea for professional or educational purposes, such as language learning or researching the peninsula's commercial prospects. In some cases the vague plans listed on their applications hid other intentions. One *shizoku* traveling to Korea after the Sino-Japanese War was Satō Keita, who received his papers for travel at the beginning of July 1895. Thirty-five years old and originally from a rural county of Kumamoto that bordered Fukuoka, Satō wrote that his plan for travel was "academic observation" in Seoul.[78] Only a few months later, on October 8, Satō joined other Kyushu *shizoku*, including Takeda Hanshi, in the attack and murder of Queen Min. While Fukuoka's commoner merchants saw Korea as a chance to expand their commercial networks, *shizoku* travelers to Korea saw the peninsula as a testing ground for regaining lost status—and shaping Japanese policy in East Asia. The base for many of their activities was the port city of Pusan.[79]

In May 1894, a group of fifteen *Chōsen rōnin*—four of whom, including Uchida Ryōhei and Takeda Hanshi, were Fukuokan, and nine of whom were Japanese residents of Pusan—decided to seek out and support the leadership of the Tonghaks, a peasant-led antiforeign and anticorruption movement that had emerged from a revival of the suppressed Tonghak (Eastern Learning) religion.

Hoping to support this rebellion, despite its anti-Japan sentiments, their aim was to bring about a wider conflict that could topple the current Korean government, lead to reforms, and increase Japanese control over Korea.[80] The group had been shocked by the assassination of Kim Okkyun in March that year—Kuzuu Yoshihisa and other Gen'yōsha members had been close to the reformer during his exile in Japan. This, along with the threat of Chinese military involvement, were two of the immediate reasons behind their plan.

The group, later self-styled as the Tenyūkyō (Knights of Providence), had set up a base in Pusan in the summer of 1893, which they named Ryōzanpaku after the stronghold of the rebel heroes in the classic Chinese novel *Water Margin*. Ryōzanpaku was otherwise known as the legal office of Ozaki Shōkichi, and its official purpose was to offer Japanese residents of Pusan legal advice connected to unpaid loans that they had made to Koreans.[81] While operating in opposition to the Japanese consulate, the group appeared to have the private support of its secretary, Yamaza Enjirō, and the Pusan Japanese settlement's chief of police, Utsumi Shigeo—both from Fukuoka.[82] The actions of this group were interwoven with local networks among Pusan's Japanese society.

The Tenyūkyō, according to their later accounts, met with Chŏn Pongjun, the leader of the Tonghak rebels in early July 1894.[83] The Chinese forces had already landed by the time they set out west from Pusan. This meeting, in which Tenyūkyō members proffered the rebels dynamite, was apparently one of mutual admiration. The Japanese also offered to act as scouts, gathering information for Chŏn's forces. However, this account is disputed by historians, and the swift outbreak of war between Chinese and Japanese forces at the end of July led to the group scattering, with some aiding the Japanese army and others returning to Pusan.[84] The narrative remains far more significant to the mythology of the Gen'yōsha and Kokuryūkai (many of whose founding members were in the Tenyūkyō) than it is to the history of the Tonghak Rebellion and Sino-Japanese War. For our purposes, it is significant for showing how these attempts at regaining lost samurai pride, along with increasing Japan's power on the Korean peninsula, were facilitated by local networks between Fukuoka and Pusan.

Creating a Postwar Merchant-Shizoku Alliance

Japan's victory against Qing China in 1895 was celebrated in Fukuoka much like elsewhere in the country. War prizes from the Sino-Japanese conflict were displayed at that year's Kyushu Okinawa Exposition, and celebratory parades—the first of their kind in the city—were held to commemorate Japanese victories at Lüshun (Port Arthur) and Weihaiwei and to celebrate the return of the Fukuoka 24th Regiment.[85] Members of the regiment were also sent to the new colony of Taiwan in the immediate aftermath of the Japanese victory.[86]

The victory had more lasting effects for the region too. The Sino-Japanese War produced regional changes—increases in transport and migration, both to and from the peninsula, and the promotion of industrialization—that were then intensified by the Russo-Japanese War in 1904–5. This connection between military expansion, trade, and urban growth was well recognized by officials and business groups in Fukuoka. In turn, these processes created new networks of movement and employment across the region. This period saw southern Korea became incorporated into Fukuoka's regional patterns of migration and trade as the result of local reactions to, and capitalization upon, war and expansion at the national level.

Japan's victory in war also focused the attentions of Fukuoka City's rival factions of local elites, *shizoku* and commoner businessmen. Old divisions remained, especially as electoral districts for the city's assembly were split into Hakata and Fukuoka wards. Hakata ward was often more politically divided than Fukuoka, and Gen'yōsha-backed candidates managed to gain the upper hand at the city level for much of the 1890s and into the early 1900s by exploiting these divisions.[87]

This influence extended to Fukuoka's national representatives too. *Shizoku* entrepreneur and first Gen'yōsha president Hiraoka Kōtarō was Fukuoka City's representative in the Diet's lower house from 1898 until his death in 1906.[88] Often running uncontested, with pressure exerted by his networks, Gen'yōsha and otherwise, Hiraoka barely needed to campaign beyond calling for local "unity" and emphasizing his credentials as a *kokushi* (selfless patriot). The Gen'yōsha were known for playing dirty in politics, and their heavy-handed control—suppressing opposition candidates by managing primary caucuses, for example—led to lowered participation in local elections.

While the *shizoku* who made up large numbers of the ranks of the Gen'yōsha often tied their visions for Fukuoka's future to its past military achievements in repelling attacks from the Asian continent, groups of businessmen, mostly commoners from more rural regions surrounding Fukuoka City and other members of the Hakata Chamber of Commerce, deployed the historical example of medieval Hakata merchants, with their networks of trade fanning outward to Pusan, Ningbo, and Naha, to promote their vision for Fukuoka's future as a hub of commerce and industry in Asia.[89] Eyeing Japanese victory in the Sino-Japanese War, local businessmen saw the opportunity to tie regional development to the expansionist mood. The year 1895 saw the founding of both the Overseas Business Association (Taigai Jitsugyō Kyōkai) and the Kyushu Business Association (Kyūshū Jitsugyō Kyōkai). In 1899 Fukuokans also set up the Japanese-Korean Business Group (Nikkan Jitsugyō Dan).[90]

The founding meeting of the Overseas Business Association, on January 16, 1895, featured a talk by founding member and *Fukuoka Nichi Nichi Shinbun* journalist Miyagi Kan'ichi entitled "The Founding of the Overseas Business Association: Its Most Urgent Tasks and 'Hakata Policy.'" Miyagi's plan for the future of the city relied not on the martial history of the castle town of Fukuoka but on the history of trade and commerce that defined the merchant city of Hakata.[91] Much of the early literature produced by this and the two other organizations was devoted to documenting the regional identity underpinning their prospects and the regional development that would be necessary for their success.[92] A desire to foster regional development and secure Fukuoka's future connections to Asia led to a new sense of shared histories and visions among the city's elites.

In the aftermath of victory, Fukuoka's local elites capitalized on Japan's military success and expanding interests in Korea. War reparations from China were invested in the state-owned Yawata Imperial Steelworks in the north of Fukuoka prefecture, which became the symbol of the region's industrialization from its opening in 1901. The Meiji government had been planning for the steelworks' construction since the 1890s, and a Gen'yōsha-backed campaign lobbied for the government to locate the steel plant in Yahata. Hiraoka Kōtaro and *shizoku* businessman Yasukawa Keiichiro both saw this as a chance to capitalize on the postwar mood for further military buildup and industrialization, and both were also heavily involved in the Chikuhō coal industry that would power the steelworks.[93] Their lobbying was a success: The site was formally chosen in October 1896 and recruitment for more than a thousand workers began in 1901.[94] From the early 1900s, Yawata relied on shipments of iron ore from the Daye (Tayeh) mines in central-eastern China in exchange for Chikuhō coal. By the Russo-Japanese War, it was said that "the bulk of armaments manufactured in Japan were produced from Tayeh ores."[95] With war and expansion on the Asian continent continuing apace, the interests at play in the development of this industrial region—*zaibatsu*, state, local, imperial—became more and more entangled.

The growth of Yahata and its connected ports and coal towns from the turn of the century onward initiated the formation of a new type of urban region linked directly to overseas expansion and industrial growth. Once created, these sites promoted the continuance of such overseas interests and flows. In the boom after the Sino-Japanese War, factory demand for coal reached record levels, and by the late 1890s the region's mines found themselves short of laborers: The internal migration of workers within Fukuoka prefecture was not enough to keep up with demand. This shortage led to the first small groups of Korean migrant workers arriving in Kyushu via Pusan and Moji to work in mines in Saga, Fukuoka, and Nagasaki. Figures in the Korean government were suspicious, fearing that the migrant workers might be trained as a secret military and join with political exiles in Japan to topple their regime. Although Yasukawa's large-scale plans to bring over as many as a thousand Korean workers to his mines in Chikuhō ended in failure, newspapers at the time recognized the impact this shift to foreign labor might have on the future of mining in the region.[96]

In Fukuoka City, attention turned back to the stalled project of the city's port development. The city founded the joint Port Development Survey Committee to move past Hakata-Fukuoka rivalries.[97] However, relations were not helped by only Hakata gaining the status of a special international trade port the following year, and separate city funds still being allocated to the two ports' development projects in 1898.[98] In 1899 renegotiations of Japan's unequal treaties finally allowed Hakata and forty other ports to gain full international status. To capitalize on this, plans were put forward for land redevelopment along the waterfront and rail lines to link the port directly to the coal-rich regions of Chikuhō. The Hakata Bay Railroad Company held its founding meeting in Tokyo on February 1, 1900.[99]

By the early twentieth century the rivalries between Fukuoka's aggrieved *shizoku* and Hakata businessmen had been replaced by new external threats: The growth of other cities in the region while Fukuoka lagged behind provoked local businessmen to put pressure on Diet representative Hiraoka, calling for plans for Fukuoka's economic and urban development. This involvement of the city's business elite in politics began to chip away at *shizoku* control in the region, but only slowly. In 1902 the first candidate to stand against Hiraoka, Ishimura Torakichi, a tobacco merchant and businessman from Hakata ward, pulled out of the race, but Fukuokans made their displeasure known, with 40 percent of votes returned as spoiled ballots.[100] Hiraoka even began to lose support among Gen'yōsha members, but only with his death in 1906, and the changed climate after the Russo-Japanese War, did Fukuoka's local political world escape *shizoku* hegemony, which had been based on divisions that were losing meaning in the changing national and international spheres.

Imperial Expansion, Imperial Urbanization

In the first few years of the new century, public opinion in Fukuoka regarding Japan's position in Asia and the world followed the trends of the times. After its victory in the Sino-Japanese War, Japan's remaining rival for influence in Korea was Russia. In 1902 a celebratory lantern parade in the city marked the Anglo-Japanese Alliance, which hoped to prevent Russian expansion. Fukuokans, especially expansionists like the Gen'yōsha, promoted the growing anti-Russian mood. When relations became heated over influence in Manchuria and Korea in late summer of 1903, the Anti-Russia Club (founded by Uchida Ryōhei) held a convention in Fukuoka at the Tokiwa-kan, an establishment close to the entertainment quarters to the east of the city that was popular with Gen'yōsha figures such as Tōyama Mitsuru and Hayashi Komao's brother Sugiyama Shigemaru.[101]

However, there were processes underway in Fukuoka that went beyond local inflections of national discourse. In July 1901 thirty-one-year-old *shizoku* Etō Kisei, originally from a mountainous part of neighboring Ōita prefecture and now living in the growing steel town of Yahata, was hired by the Seoul-Pusan Railway Company as an assistant engineer. That summer he moved to Pusan, the southern terminus of the railway, with his wife and three young children.[102] Work on the railway began in August 1901, with migrants from Fukuoka and further afield traveling to work on the project as laborers, engineers, and bureaucrats. Local elites in Pusan—Japanese and Korean—were similarly excited by what this meant for local development: The Pusan Civil Engineering Joint Stock Company, set up in 1901 "to provide labor and construction materials to build the section from Ch'oryang in Pusan," was a joint venture between Hyŏn Myŏngun, the magistrate of Tongnae county, and Fukuda Masubei, a Tsushima merchant who had lived in Pusan since 1875.[103]

Etō represents a new type of migrant whose numbers were increasing among those heading to Korea as Japanese involvement on the peninsula expanded. The first move of these migrants, who were originally from rural areas, often outside the prefecture, brought them to the growing industrial areas of northern Kyushu, and from there they moved to the Korean peninsula. At the time of their application, some 80 percent of those originally from outside the prefecture were based in the ports and industrial towns of northern Kyushu. These migrants were part of the region's imperial urbanization, a two-stage movement that linked domestic and international migration with urban growth and overseas expansion across the Tsushima Strait.

This expansion took many forms. Islands and bays linked by the waters of the Tsushima Strait, a key corridor for Russian and Japanese navies as well as fishing and whaling fleets, became flash points for tensions between the two expanding empires. These tensions were at once interimperial and local. Chinhae Bay to the southwest of Pusan, ringed by the island of Kōjedo and the port of Masan, was a key flash point. Between 1899 and 1900, in order to prevent Russia from building a naval base in Masan's now open port, Fukuokans from various walks of life attempted to buy up land. Fukuokan fishermen were part of an unsuccessful plan to gain concessions on the island of Kōjedo through a fishing union acting as a private intermediary.[104] In 1902 Kokuryūkai members Kuzuu Yoshihisa and Uchida Ryōhei were involved in the purchase of two small islands in Chinhae Bay.[105]

The autumn of 1903 also saw a larger-scale island-grab attempt: a movement to incorporate the islands of Iki and Tsushima into Fukuoka prefecture, pushing its borders closer to Korea. Although the islands had been part of Nagasaki prefecture since the 1870s, Fukuoka was the islands' key link with mainland Japan in terms of trade and communications. By the turn of the twentieth century, mail to Tsushima and Iki came via Fukuoka prefecture, and the Tsushima garrison (*keibitai*) was also under the jurisdiction of the 12th Division of the Imperial Army, based in Kokura.[106] In late September the Hakata Chamber of Commerce held meetings with representatives of the two islands visiting the city before the proposal was put to a vote at the City Council on October 19.[107] The city council of Fukuoka City voted to put forward the motion to the prefectural governor of Fukuoka, Kawashima Atsushi, and the chamber of commerce sent a proposal as a direct letter to Prime Minister Katsura Tarō.[108]

The proposal requested that the two islands be incorporated into Fukuoka prefecture as part of the Prefectural Restructuring Bill (Fuken haichi hōritsu an) planned to be brought before the Imperial Diet in early 1904. The 1903 draft legislation framed the restructuring as a response to the development of

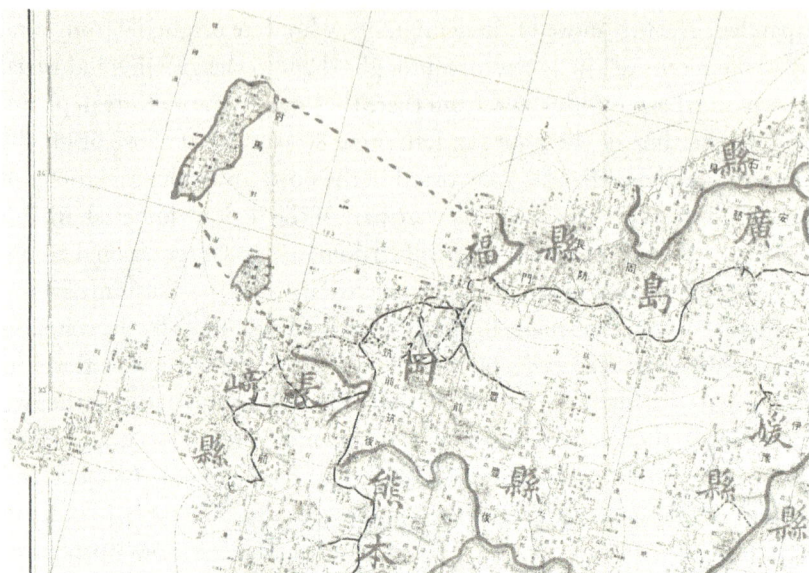

MAP 2. The envisaged new Fukuoka prefecture, including Iki and Tsushima. Credit: Detail from *Fuken haichi hōritsu an fuzu* 1903. Courtesy of National Archives of Japan.

transportation links with a slimmed down and economical administrative system, which included more effective management of the nation's ports.[109]

Looking at the draft of this legislation, the city council's request appears to have been heard: The draft shows that Fukuoka prefecture was to have been expanded to incorporate not only Iki and Tsushima Islands, but all of Ōita prefecture and even as far as the southernmost tip of Honshū (see map 2). With the outbreak of the Russo-Japanese War in February 1904, and the consequent breakup of parliament, the draft never made it to the Diet. If it had, Fukuoka prefecture not only would have become the fourth most populous prefecture in Japan, but also would also have cemented its position as the gateway to the Asian continent with control over the key port of Shimonoseki.[110]

The plan for incorporating Iki and Tsushima aligned with the new identity of Fukuoka as a city looking outward across the straits. The city council and chamber of commerce discussed Fukuoka's historical and geographic links to Tsushima and Iki in terms that regularly crop up in the discussion of the city's links with Asia. The city had a "locational advantage" that meant the port of Hakata had, since time immemorial, maintained strong links with Tsushima and Iki. The islands "held the key" to the Japan Sea (*inkō wo yakushi*), separated from Fukuoka "by only a reed's width of water" (*ichi itai sui*).[111]

As well as historical links, there were current time pressures, too: Business elites and city officials in Fukuoka wanted to take advantage of their location before the shifting geopolitical situation could be monopolized by Osaka- or Tokyo-based concerns. The minutes of the Hakata Chamber of Commerce meeting from September 19, 1903, reveal this strategy most clearly, stating that "we are hurrying to put forward this motion now, for once the Keijō–Pusan railroad opens Japan-Korea commerce will start to boom: We should strengthen our links to the islands before Tsushima and Iki become the center of these trade routes."[112] This plan would not only benefit businessmen in Fukuoka (two of the six businessmen responsible for the motion were members of a local shipping union). The same economic reasons also motivated those from the islands themselves: One of the two Tsushima representatives who visited Fukuoka was the head of the island's coastal steamship enterprise, Fujino Kisen, of which more in chapter 4.

The Russo-Japanese War

The growing rivalries between the Japanese and Russian empires over their interests in Korea and Manchuria led to all-out war in February 1904, with Japan's surprise attack on the Russian-leased port of Port Arthur. Due to its geography, the experience of the Russo-Japanese War in Fukuoka and the north Kyushu region was more immediate than elsewhere in Japan. The decisive naval battle of the war was so close as to be within earshot: Fukuoka residents reported being able to hear the blasts of guns on the battleships during the Battle of Tsushima in May 1905.[113] Of course, some elements of the experience were no different than in other cities and towns across the Japanese main islands. War bonds were sold and parades were held to celebrate military victories and commemorate the many war dead, especially those from the 24th Division, which saw some of the heaviest action in the conflict. This shared experience was part of an incipient nationalism built around imperial victories.[114]

However, even these commemorative events and their promotion of a sense of national pride had their own local significance. The celebration of the fall of Port Arthur took place on the grounds of the newly expanded Hakata Port. The end of the war saw the return of Japanese troops to Fukuoka, with victory parades taking place in the city's Higashi Park. It also saw the return of most of the soldiers from the Gen'yōsha-affiliated Manchurian Righteous Army. This was a paramilitary unit formed of members of Uchida Ryōhei's Kokuryūkai, which had been involved in intelligence gathering for the military in Siberia since 1903.[115] Over half of the Manchurian Righteous Army were Gen'yōsha members, and a monument to its war dead was constructed in Sōfukuji, a temple on the outskirts of Fukuoka City.[116] After the war, Uchida would continue to be involved in advancing Japan's position in Korea. Sugiyama Shigemaru recommended him to Resident General Itō Hirobumi as an advisor, and Uchida also worked with Takeda Hanshi to co-opt the populist pro-reform group the Ilchinhoe.[117]

During the war Japanese residents of Korea saw Fukuoka's proximity to the peninsula as a crucial lifeline. The head of the Keijō Japanese Residents' Association, Nakai Kitarō, wrote to the Hakata Chamber of Commerce less than a month after the outbreak of war informing them that supply lines had been interrupted and requesting that the city's businessmen load up a steamship with food, drink, and daily supplies, along with coal, and sail for Inch'ŏn as soon as possible. Nakai reassured them that the route was safe and that such actions would help not only the Japanese settlements but also their country's military, who were similarly suffering from supply chain issues.[118] Originally from Yamaguchi prefecture, Nakai was the president of the Kokkentō-affiliated newspaper the *Kanjō Shinpō*, as well as a member of an anti-Russian group with many supporters in Fukuoka. Such credentials can only have helped his request to the chamber of commerce. *Fukunichi* editor Miyagi Kan'ichi described this request as an "opportunity not to be missed," urging Hakata and Fukuoka's businessmen to capitalize on it in order to expand "Hakata trade in Korea."[119]

Indeed, for many in Fukuoka the war was seen as a catalyst to speed up local urban development, which had lagged behind that of other regions. "On paper, war might seem bad for business," Miyagi wrote in his op-ed, "but the reality is quite different. There are few chances like it to expand commercial supremacy. . . . As the prosperity of Fukuoka and Hakata depends on the use of Hakata Port, and that in turn depends on improving overseas trade, this is a once-in-a-thousand-year chance for the port's great development [*ichidai hatten*]." The war with Russia and the sacrifices of the Imperial Army would have been "meaningless" unless Hakata merchants managed to take advantage of it. Their "responsibility," Miyagi argued, was to follow the flag of the Imperial Army, expanding the region's trading links with Korea and China.[120]

In May 1905 the battleship *Mikasa* leading the Japanese Combined Fleet maneuvered out of Chinhae Bay and defeated the Russian Imperial Navy's Baltic Fleet in the Battle of Tsushima. In the room of the *Mikasa's* captain was enshrined an amulet from Fukuoka's Hakozaki Shrine bearing Emperor Kameyama's "defeat of the enemy nation" slogan.[121] Russia's naval defeat brought about negotiations for the end of the war and increased movement across the strait in both directions. A report from Pusan's Japanese Legation only weeks before the end of the war warned that ships leaving Japan for Korea were all full and the construction of Japanese houses in the area was continuing apace.[122]

The influx of Japanese migrants to the region was accompanied by an increased demand for transport between the peninsula and home islands for military and diplomatic staff. The rail link between Seoul and Pusan had already opened in January that year, and the first passenger ferry between Japan and Korea, the Shimonoseki–Pusan (Kampu) ferry, opened for business in the heady days of September 1905.[123] Its opening ceremony took place amid raucous protests throughout the country against the terms of the Portsmouth peace treaty, which did not meet the expectations set by the indemnity from Qing China upon its defeat in 1895. The anti-Portsmouth feeling was particularly strong in Fukuoka, where the Gen'yōsha and the *Kyūshū Nippō* took the lead in organizing and publicizing rallies in the city's Higashi Park that drew over a thousand people.[124]

Such patriotic anger was accompanied by, and perhaps in tension with, regional opportunism. Businessmen and boosters had begun to eye expanding links between the region and the continent even before the end of the war. They hoped their foresight would allow them to maintain their regional advantage over "big business" from Osaka and Tokyo: Such fears were part of a long discourse over the encroachment of central capital (*chūō shihon*) in Kyushu's economy. In the spring of 1905, while the war was still going on, the Hakata Chamber of Commerce sent petitions to Ishida Tokumaro, president of Hakata Steamship Company, stressing the need to expand Hakata's sea links to Asia. At that time Hakata was just one port of call for domestic and international shipping out of Osaka. For the sake of the city's growth, Hakata Steamship Company and the city's businessmen needed to act now, to take advantage of the "childlike" state of the Korean economy.[125]

Fukuoka City's first postwar transport link with Korea, a Pusan–Hakata shipping route, came in June 1906.[126] From September, the route was supported with funding from the city budget. The chamber of commerce sent a statement to Mayor Matsushita Naoyoshi on their hopes for the route's role in Fukuoka's growth; they envisioned the city as the departure point for a shipping link that crossed the straits to Pusan before fanning out along the coast of southern Korea and its newly opened ports. Due to southeastern Korea's mountainous geography and coastal towns, shipping along its coastline was a vital conduit of trade, and these routes were a target for many local businessmen hoping to expand into Korean markets.[127] Pusan acted as a hub for this second stage of regional imperialism. The port of Mokp'o had opened in 1897 and was linked to Pusan via coastal shipping routes, many managed by Pusan's Japanese residents. Soon Mokp'o's Japanese community was also full of migrants from the Tsushima Strait region, mirroring Pusan.[128] Through their expansion into regional networks within Korea, early settlers from the Tsushima Strait region consolidated and replicated their dominance along this second front.

After 1905 the waters of southern Korea were plied by increased numbers of fishing vessels as well as coastal shipping vessels. The Protectorate Treaty between Japan and Korea, signed in November 1905, removed Korea's diplomatic sovereignty and installed Japanese "advisors" in all sections of the government. An earlier agreement signed during the war included new rights for Japanese fishermen: Their activities were no longer restricted to fishing in Korea's waters and living in Japanese settlements in open ports but now included the construction of landings, warehouses, and migrant fishing villages along all of Korea's coastline, with fishermen's unions often clustered together by prefecture in villages built with prefectural funding.[129] Fukuokans had been quick to expand into Korean fishing waters, and the prefecture was also one of the earliest to be involved in funding these ventures. Ōta Tanejirō, the head of Fukuoka's Korean Fishing Union, was a key figure in one such location: "Irisa village" at Changsŭngpo on the island of Kŏjedo, twenty-three miles southwest of Pusan. To populate the village, Ōta recruited Fukuokan fishermen already based on the island of Yŏngdo in Pusan Bay.[130]

The island of Kŏjedo was also the first foothold in Korea for another Fukuokan: Kashii Gentarō (1867–1946). Born into the Oniki family in a rural part of Fukuoka prefecture, Kashii was adopted into a *shizoku* family with military connections when he was twenty-two and studied under Sugiyama Shigemaru's father at his private academy before moving to Korea. Kashii too was a member of the Gen'yōsha, and, like Sugiyama, he had both *shizoku* connections and commercial ambitions. Sugiyama had links via Tōyama Mitsuru to the Taiwanese Government General and to Japanese power in Korea via Itō Hirobumi.[131] Sugiyama and Kashii embody many of the characteristics of Fukuoka's local Pan-Asianist elites and reappear throughout this book. Both retained their local networks even as they built new ones that extended outward, often at the vanguard of Japan's expansion in Asia.

Kashii's career in Korea began when he opened a fish cannery operation on Kŏjedo during the Russo-Japanese War, supplying the Imperial Navy fleet based in Chinhae Bay. Canned food had been a part of the diet of the Japanese military since the 1880s, after which it slowly filtered into the eating habits of the general population.[132] After Japan's victory, thanks to the involvement of fellow Fukuokan Tsuruhara Sadakichi—the protectorate's general affairs secretary—and the new resident general, Itō Hirobumi himself, Kashii bought out fishing rights previously owned by Yi Kang, Emperor Kojong's fifth son. These rights spanned Chinhae Bay from the island of Kadŏkdo in the northeast to Kŏjedo in the southwest.[133]

His sudden rise to "king" of marine products in Korea soon drew Kashii away from the island to Pusan, where he would live for the next forty years, becoming one of the city's most prominent businessmen, brokering further links between the city and Fukuoka and at one point becoming the president and key stockholder of the *Pusan Nippō* newspaper.[134] However, his fishing rights and connections to the Fukuokan fishing villages that had sprouted up in Kŏjedo's coves meant that he was invested in the success of those still there: In 1910 his company, the Kashii-gumi, started trialing a daily steamship link between Pusan and Irisa, now the "base for Fukuoka migrant fisherman in Korea," in order to save the fishing cooperative money on expensive transportation by commercial companies.[135] On a memorial constructed at a shrine near his birthplace in Fukuoka, Kashii was described as a "developer of the sea" (*umi no kaihatsusha*).[136]

Kashii was just one businessman for whom Japan's war—and victory—against Russia meant new opportunities on the peninsula. Many Kyushu men who went on to become important figures in the metropole and colony had their first successes during wartime, supplying ships and logistical support to the Japanese military. This was a repetition and amplification of earlier patterns, like the provincial Fukuoka merchants who took their trade across to the peninsula during the Sino-Japanese War. Most of those Japanese who would become key "local" figures in Korea's cities had long since achieved these positions by the time Korea became a Japanese colony in 1910. In Pusan's settler community, the majority of this "local capital" was from the Tsushima Strait region, from people who had developed ties to the peninsula through shipping, fishing, and trade, as well as by buying up land, in the three decades leading up to Korea's colonization. Their regional imperialism shaped Japan's expansion, and their hometowns.[137]

In 1908, at the first general election after Hiraoka's death, Ōta Seizō, a businessman from a rich Hakata merchant family, won Fukuoka City's seat in the Lower House of the Imperial Diet. Ōta had been a city assemblyman and head of several business associations in the city. Hakata's business elites' pragmatic approach to Fukuoka's urban growth meant they valued closer ties to the government in order to gain central funds for local development. What they now shared with the Gen'yōsha and other *shizoku* elites, however, was the value they placed in developing Fukuoka's position in relation to Asia, and making use of the networks and "preconditions for growth" that, on the eve of Korea becoming a colony of Japan, had already been created through the decades of regional expansion across the Tsushima Strait region that had come before.[138]

CONCLUSIONS

On September 10, 1910, local figures from Fukuoka City, as well as those from surrounding villages on the verge of being absorbed into its growing urban area, gathered in front of the main pavilion of the 13th Kyushu Okinawa Exposition. Urban development in preparation for the exposition had required filling in the outer moats of the now obsolete domain seat, Fukuoka Castle. Fireworks marked the start of the event, and the guests filed into the pavilion, where, after the playing of the national anthem, Mayor Satō Heitarō read aloud the imperial edict on the Japan-Korea Annexation, promulgated on August 29. The event was to celebrate Japan's annexation of Korea, which, the imperial edict stated, "will serve as a fresh guarantee of enduring peace in the Orient.... All Koreans, being under our sway, will enjoy growing prosperity and welfare, and ... a marked expansion in industry and trade."[139] After the reading came speeches and three cheers for the long life of the emperor. Key Fukuoka constituencies were represented among the organizers of the event: the mayor and city government officials, members of the Hakata Chamber of Commerce, and the heads of the city's main newspapers, the *Kyushu Nippō* and *Fukuoka Nichi Nichi Shinbun*, as well as neighboring town and village heads.[140]

The imperial region that was brought into existence before the annexation of Korea in 1910 is something of an oxymoron. It was created through the development of regional networks, made possible by three decades of informal imperialism in Korea, and the catalysts of two wars that increased Japanese presence and power in the region. Many of the actions and decisions of those Fukuokans involved were made with one eye on reaping personal or local gain from Japanese military victories in Asia, but they were also in tension with central government control.

As the ceremony at Fukuoka's Exhibition Grounds attests, many in Fukuoka celebrated Korea's subjugation as a protectorate in 1905 and its colonization in 1910. However, when networks of regional imperialism were replaced by processes emanating from and subservient to the imperial center, Fukuokan locals had cause to be anxious. The development of Fukuoka's port of Hakata had eventually galvanized a coalition of rival factions of the city's *shizoku* and merchant elites. However, Korea's annexation was a mixed blessing for the port. Hakata's international trade, such as it was, was almost entirely with Korea. The removal of import tariffs took a huge chunk out of the port's income, even as colonization made other aspects of links across the straits easier and more profitable.[141] The shifting and uneven relationship that emerged between Fukuoka and Pusan, discussed in later chapters, began with this lopsided reliance on Korean trade by Hakata Port and its boosters.

In the wake of colonization, other Fukuoka groups protested the loss of their livelihoods, which had been built up over years of informal regional imperialism. In December 1910, business groups and fishing unions in Fukuoka protested over the loss of Fukuokans' rights to monkfish (J: *ankō*) fishing off the coast of Korea, which had been made over to the new Oriental Development Company, a "semipublic 'national policy company.'"[142] Fishermen from the Ariake Sea, where monkfish were also common, had long been involved in fishing off Korea and protested this intrusion: "Despite the long hardships we faced developing [*kaitaku*] fishing in this region, fishermen from Fukuoka [and other Kyushu prefectures] are now unable to fish these waters, despite their bountiful catches. We have no choice but to sell our ships and return home."[143] National imperial expansion centralized earlier regional forms of extraction.

Fukuoka's demographic and commercial links with Korea, created as preconditions for the city's capitalist development via its port, were especially strong with the port city of Pusan. These continued after Korea became a protectorate in 1905 and after annexation in 1910. With annexation, the demographics of the Japanese settler population in Korean cities changed, reflecting the countries' shift from a regional relationship to a colonial one. However, despite the influx of other settlers, Fukuoka was among the few Tsushima Strait prefectures that increased its representation within Pusan's settler community.[144] The city had become a key ferry and rail terminus linking Japan and Korea, but its Japanese population reflected the three decades of inroads made by Japanese from the Tsushima Strait region. As the following chapter discusses, Fukuokans' early involvement in informal imperialism and the urban growth of Pusan would continue to shape the direction of the city's development even after annexation.

Local Development and Regional Imperialism

IN 1902, FORTY-FOUR-YEAR-OLD Ueno Yasutarō, originally from Kumamoto prefecture, was working as an itinerant salesman, selling clothes and supplies to Japanese workmen employed in the construction of the southern stretch of the new Seoul–Pusan railroad. Perhaps it was on the job, among the comings and goings of Korean and Japanese laborers and technicians, that he heard about the new licensing rules for opening brothels in Korea. After all, with their mobility and daily grassroots interactions, merchants and other itinerant groups have been widely used, in Korea and elsewhere, as a network for gathering intelligence.[1] However it was that Ueno found out, he wasted no time applying for a permit to open the town's first "special restaurant" (J: *tokubetsu ryōriten*), to be located just outside the western limits of Pusan's Japanese residential zone, in what was still a "Korean area."

Even before receiving his permit, Ueno traveled to Hiroshima, a region many Japanese residents in Pusan had local connections to, and purchased eleven young women, probably from other brothel owners, and brought them back to Pusan to work in his as-yet-unbuilt brothel, to be named Anraku-tei.[2] "It feels like a dream to think about it now," Ueno recalled in a 1918 article looking back on his career, "hundreds or thousands of men, living in a strange land, starved of comfort, hankering after these girls like ants flocking to sugar. . . . The girls didn't even have time for proper meals—just a rice ball eaten in the corridors as they worked." Based on selling these young women to ten or twenty men a night, Ueno made fifty or sixty thousand yen in the first four months, which allowed him to finally replace his temporary structure with a grand three-story one. Others followed Ueno's lead, and the former farmland inhabited by Koreans to the west of the Japanese settlement soon became populated with more and more "special restaurants" employing young women from Western Japan.[3]

Only five years later, in 1907, the entertainment district that had grown up around Anraku-tei was being enveloped by the expansion of the port city. The Seoul–Pusan railroad had been completed, Japan had won a war against Russia, and Korea was now its protectorate. The city was growing rapidly. Petitioned by the local residents' association, the Pusan Japanese Legation ordered the relocation of the entertainment district to a new marginal location, further west and south along the bay, in between the shoreline and the foot of the slopes of Mount Ami (J: Gabi-san) (see map 3). The new entertainment district, Midori-machi, was ready to house its first inhabitants by 1911. In the 1912 *Guide to Pusan*, the relocation project was listed among those managed by the Residents' Association of Pusan, bearing witness to the involvement of local Japanese residents in the shaping of the now colonial port city. At seventy thousand yen, it was one of the most expensive of their schemes.[4]

The 1912 *Guide*, under a list of "Pusan's neighborhood names," reveals the extent to which Japanese residents of Pusan had already altered the contours of the port city by the time of Korea's colonization by Japan. In the *Guide*, Pusan's now-central neighborhoods were grouped into four categories: "former Japanese settlement," "new urban area," "North Harbor reclaimed land," and "new urban area on site of Mount Eisen."[5] Aside from the historic center of the city, built around the early modern Japan House (K: Waegwan; J: Wakan) and the hill of Yongdu-san (J: Ryūto san), the city's neighborhoods were built on "redeveloped" Korean districts that were flattened out of hillsides and reclaimed from the sea. The Residents' Association had been involved with all these projects. After annexation, Pusan's urban areas continued to grow. Midori-machi, the new brothel district, would only stay on the growing city's margins for so long. Soon the harbor views from the windows of its many "rooms for hire" (J: *kashizashiki*) would become more distant, as further land reclamation works inched outward into Pusan Bay.

When he died at the age of sixty-seven in 1925, Ueno was hailed as "an old-timer who dedicated himself to the prosperity of Pusan . . . who realized that the development of newly settled lands [J: *shinkaichi*] must start with the creation of entertainment districts."[6] Ueno had begun his career in Korea in the same wave of turn-of-the-century imperial urbanization as Etō Kisei, discussed in chapter 1. He brought his "troupe" of young girls across from Hiroshima, not on the Shimonoseki–Pusan ferry, but on a smaller vessel,

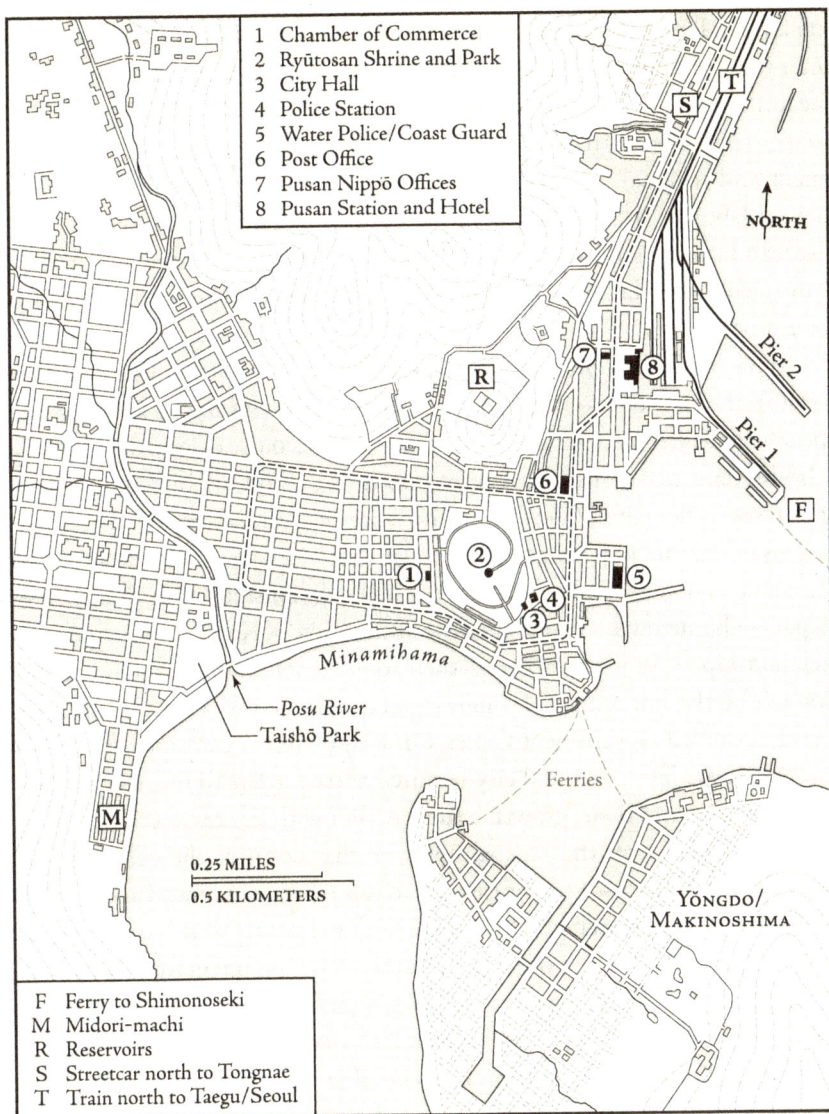

1	Chamber of Commerce
2	Ryūtosan Shrine and Park
3	City Hall
4	Police Station
5	Water Police/Coast Guard
6	Post Office
7	Pusan Nippō Offices
8	Pusan Station and Hotel

NORTH

Pier 2

Pier 1

F

R

Minamihama

Posu River
Taishō Park

Ferries

YŎNGDO/
MAKINOSHIMA

0.25 MILES
0.5 KILOMETERS

F	Ferry to Shimonoseki
M	Midori-machi
R	Reservoirs
S	Streetcar north to Tongnae
T	Train north to Taegu/Seoul

MAP 3. Downtown Pusan, ca. 1920. Credit: Kate Blackmer.

which stopped halfway on Tsushima, where he was questioned by police under suspicion of trafficking. Travel across the straits in 1902 was still relatively rare, unlike in 1918, when the article was written.

Like many other settler businessmen from Western Japan drawn to the peninsula in Meiji, Ueno first used the profits from his initial venture to buy up land in Pusan. In the 1920s he also invested money back across the straits in a tract of land in Kyushu's coal belt, whose mining operations had not begun before he died.[7] These circular exchanges of labor, capital, and land across this imperial region encapsulate the key dynamics of local development and regional imperialism that this chapter explores. And, while the sexual labor of the young girls from Hiroshima and the expropriation of Korean farming land are not dwelled upon in the 1918 article, both deserve our attention as they were part and parcel of these exclusionary and exploitative processes.

In the first half of this chapter I look at the Japanese settlers who sought to control the local development (J: *chihō kaihatsu*, K: *chibang kaebal)* of Pusan prior to and after its colonization, and how this discourse of local development also brought regional Korean elites into urban—and urbanizing—politics. For most settler elites, Pusan grew into a port city that exceeded their hometowns in size and importance but was still part of a colony to be exploited for Japanese ends. Not only did these settlers' relationships with their nearby Japanese hometowns change after the annexation of Korea in 1910, but their relationship to—and power over—their adopted hometown of Pusan was also altered by the imposition of a municipal government that answered to the newly installed Government General in Keijō. Pusan's transformation from an open port into a colonial city required these settlers to incorporate local Korean elites into their "growth coalition," but with limited success.[8]

Recent works on the Japanese empire that connect the colony to the metropole have focused on the ties and tensions between central and colonial government, and the cities where these nodes of power were based. In these works the "local" is more often than not used as a synonym for the colonial. In the case of Korea, the majority of works that focus on the "local" ramifications of colonial rule position settlers in Keijō (colonial Seoul) and the Keijō-based policies of the Government General as representative of the entire colony. "Local" as a blanket term to describe settlers in Korea implies a point of view based in the imperial capital of Tokyo, from where "local" means anyone present "on the spot" in the Korea colony.[9] However, "our man in Pusan" has, I would argue, a different meaning than "our man in Keijō."

Although Pusan was a key node in Japan's growing imperial network, its deeply entrenched settler elites often had visions for the city that were at odds with the Government General and they resisted externally imposed change. Theirs was a local imperialism, and they saw themselves as empire's locals—transplanted settlers embedded in the regional networks that had enabled expansion across the strait. Settlers from the Tsushima Strait region in Pusan triangulated their claims to locality in response to local Koreans, but also to central government power. In the Korean colony, settlers' limited political power was tied to local landownership, and thereby local political enfranchisement, something that has also been used to define Korean "local notables" (K: *yuchi*) of this period.[10]

Although Japanese settlers in Pusan co-opted local Korean elites, their presence and visions of "locality" relied upon exclusion and division. Their actions incorporated Pusan into an imperial region and tied its growth closely to that of the home islands—more so than other parts of Korea—with long-ranging effects. Locality for Japanese settlers in Korea was worn as a badge of pride: it was considered a reward for the common narratives of hard work and suffering for the sake of their adopted hometown, as shown by the article on Ueno above. Through this, claims to locality in the colony became predicated on one's industriousness and contribution to "development"—as an often urban, or urbanizing, process of imperialism. However, as Haunani-Kay Trask has noted in the case of Asians in Hawai'i, the language of locality is a rhetorical strategy that elides the violence inherent in settler colonialism, and the implication of self-styled "locals" in these violent processes of dispossession.[11]

The worldview of these settlers—or, as I refer to them elsewhere, these "local imperialists"—also highlights the ongoing effects of the regional imperialism of the nineteenth century on the settler communities on the peninsula, and the effect that the shift between Japan and Korea from a regional to imperial relationship had on them.[12] A focus on these groups and their claims is a call to disaggregate our view of the nature of Japanese imperialism in Korea, to place it in a longer historical setting, and to embed it more deeply in the geography of the region.

Studies of the local effects of Japan's overseas expansion have looked at the "grassroots imperialism" present in prefectures' attempts to connect local development to the expansion of empire in the 1930s, and at the creation of "transnational hometowns" via the effects of migration of large numbers of residents. They show the role of networks that linked the growth of regional towns and cities to the hopes of empire from a single, metropole-based point of view.[13] This chapter, and part 1 of the book as a whole, offers a case study of grassroots or regional imperialism that transcends the metropole/colony divide.[14]

Settler communities across Korea, especially those beyond Seoul, had significant diversity in population and in regional and socioeconomic backgrounds. This in turn affected interactions on the ground with colonized Koreans, both local elites as well as rural and urban working populations. In the growing cities where most Japanese clustered, this impacted the nature of urban growth. In this chapter's second half, I put local imperialism in Pusan in a regional context. I do this by focusing in on the community of Fukuokan settlers in Pusan through their own publications, first showing how Fukuokan elites continued to connect their two "hometowns" through local networks and visions, and then using members' lists of Fukuoka prefectural groups as a starting point to expand our view of Pusan's inhabitants in terms of gender, class, and ethnicity and to connect these demographics to a longer history of regional imperialism.

"THE MEN WHO MADE PUSAN"

The first pages of the *Guide to Pusan* of 1912 offer a visual overview of the changes wrought upon the port city by Japanese settlers between the turn of the century and the annexation of Korea. Panoramic photographs of the harbor and surrounding urban areas taken in 1897, 1904, and 1911 (figures 1 and 2) show the steady expansion of the livable area of land out into Pusan Bay. Most of these images were taken from the southern slopes of Pokpyŏng-san, directly north of Yongdu-san and Pusan's harbor. In the image from 1897 (top of figure 1), Pusan's urban area was clustered around the wooded hills of Yongdu-san and Yongmi-san—the "dragon's head" and "tail"—home to the Japan House and several Japanese shrines since the late seventeenth century. The port facilities consisted of a single pontoon that protruded out from the fishing harbor near Yongmi-san. By 1904 land reclamation on the northern harbor had extended out into Pusan Bay to the east of Yongdu-san, with a new harbor bristling with masts and the long pier for the soon-to-be-launched Shimonoseki–Pusan ferry clearly visible. Rows of warehouses lined the waterfront. The houses to the west of Yongdu-san now extended along the bay of the Southern Harbor. Developments clinging to the shoreline of the island of Yŏngdo (J: Makinoshima) can be made out in the distance. This decade's developments set the direction of the colonial city's future growth.

Seven years later, in 1911, Pusan was undergoing further dramatic expansion and changes to its urban environment (figure 2). In the top image, Pusan's railway station and hotel stand amid continued construction to the east of the new ferry pier, the freshly laid roads around it an empty grid. In

FIGURE 1. Pusan Harbor in 1897 (above) and 1904 (below). Credit: Pusan shōgyōkaigisho 1912, front matter.

FIGURE 2. Pusan Harbor (above) and the city viewed from Ami-san (below), 1911. Credit: Pusan shōgyōkaigisho 1912, front matter.

the far right of the photograph, between the base of the hill and the water's edge, lies the new entertainment district of Midori-machi. In the bottom image, a panoramic photograph taken from the hill of Ami-san, just northeast of Midori-machi, shows Pusan's expanding urban areas as viewed from the west.[15] The tightly packed houses in the distance, stopping at the bases of the wooded hillsides, become more generously spaced as they move further west. The plain between Yongdu-san and Ami-san, divided by the Posu River, would become a site for key developments and urban planning projects of the Pusan municipal government in the 1920s and '30s, and the basic grid layout of roads are visible in maps and images from 1912. However, long, low buildings and visible plots of open land suggest this area was still used for agricultural purposes around the time of annexation.

The three main administrative institutions during this transitional period were the Pusan City Hall, formerly the Japanese Legation, built in 1879; the Pusan Police Station, built in 1902; and the Japanese Residents' Association, built in 1901, all located on the southern slopes of Yongdu-san.[16] The urban center of Pusan, from the Kampu ferry pier and railway station in the east, following the main shopping street of Nagate-dōri south of the base of Yongdu-san, to the Posu River in the west, was, by the end of the Meiji era in 1912, replete with markers of the power of the Japanese settlers: the power to alter their built environment, but also the power represented by the institutions they chose to construct and control; the power to buy and sell; the power to heal the sick; the power to annihilate space and time; the power to enforce their own power.

Pusan's Residents' Association and Urban Space

Power over Pusan's urban spaces was often based on ownership of land, which, as Carter Eckert points out, "had always been the preeminent Korean investment" and remained profitable for Japanese, and a certain stratum of Koreans, even after annexation. The first wave of Japanese merchants and settlers, using the profits from their early commercial activities in the open port, had the best opportunities to buy up land in and around Pusan. These investments bolstered their financial clout and social position in the settler community and aided future ventures. Their investment in land gave settler "local capital" (J: *jiba shihon*) an interest in the city's local development.

Settlers from the Tsushima Strait region (Yamaguchi, Fukuoka, Saga, and Nagasaki prefectures), and Western Japan more broadly, made up a large number of those who first came to Pusan. The Tsushima Japanese were some of the earliest to arrive in the city. These included Fukuda Masubei (arrived 1871), Ōike Chūsuke (1875), Ōmiya Manjirō (1878), and Toyota Fukutarō (1880). Hoke Sadahachi, also from Tsushima, broke the *kaikin* (maritime edicts) to move to Pusan in 1863, five years before the Meiji Restoration, and three years before Japanese were officially allowed to leave the country.

Prior to Korea becoming a protectorate, the early Pusan residents wielded their power through various residents' groups. Japanese settlers in Pusan had formed a representative association in 1887, the oldest of such settler groups in Korea, renamed the Residents' Association (J: Kyoryūmindan) under the Residents' Association Law of 1906. In 1879 they also founded the oldest chamber of commerce in Korea, predated in Japan only by those in Tokyo, Osaka, and Kobe, all founded the previous year. Looking at the eleven local figures who were members of all the port city's early organizations, we find two Tsushima locals, Fukuda Masubei and Ōike Chūsuke; two Fukuokans, Kashii Gentarō and Ishikawa Shinpei; and a Yamaguchi native, Gotō Jinkichi.[17] The remaining six were from Wakayama (Hazama Fusatarō), from Kyoto (Ishihara Hanemon), and of unknown background. Even within the Residents' Association there were cliques based on geographic origin: The Ōchō Chikuhō Hiroshima rengō contained members from Yamaguchi, Hiroshima, and Fukuoka, while members of the Taihō jitsugyō dan all hailed from Tsushima.[18]

This influential group of settlers shaped the city in its early stages and were loath to relinquish their power over its growth. Members of this generation have been described as "products of the Meiji era" who formed the main constituents of Japan's "brokers of empire."[19] Age was indeed important, but so was the long residence of these brokers in Korea, their financial and property investments, and the networks that they forged with each other and back to their homes in the metropole. The men who became known as the "three magnates" (J: *san kyotō*) of Pusan—Kashii, Hazama, and Ōike—were remarkable for not only their business power, but also the length of their experience in the city. Ōike arrived in Pusan in 1875 and Hazama in 1880, followed by his brother Yasutarō four years later. Only Kashii was a relative latecomer, arriving, as discussed in chapter 1, at the end of the Russo-Japanese War in 1905. Kashii was born in 1867 and lived until 1946, his life covering the span of Japan's empire, and he was the only one of the three to see the end of Japanese colonial rule in Pusan.

In the 1870s Fukuda had shifted his business from coastal shipping and trade based out of Tsushima to shipping and trade between Pusan and

Japanese ports. He made his biggest profits from land bought in Pusan, as well as military contracts in the Sino-Japanese War.[20] Ōike, like Fukuda, had diverse business interests and investments that relied on Japanese expansion across the straits—shipping, supplying, hospitality—and his inn was where Hayashi Komao stayed during his 1898 fishing expedition. Others arrived in the 1880s: Ishikawa and Gotō in the rice trade, and Hazama as the head of a branch of an Osaka merchant house that was expanding into Korea after failures on the mainland. Kashii arrived much later, but the patterns of his business successes are similar to those of Ōike, Fukuda, and Hazama.

As scholars have discussed, the autonomy and extent of the powers of Japanese residents prior to Korea's annexation was often greater, and subject to less central oversight, than their equivalents back in Japan.[21] They involved themselves in construction of hospitals and schools, urban hygiene projects, sewage and water works, and the physical extension of the urban space of Pusan through land reclamation and earthworks projects that changed the face of the city. Although the days of the Residents' Association's authority were numbered due to the new municipal system that would be implemented in 1914, it was still listed as a self-governing institution in the 1912 *Guide to Pusan*. The list of works of the Residents' Association shows the extent of Japanese settlers' ability to shape and create the modern city of Pusan (table 1).

Pusan's geography further affected the colonial city's uneven development (see map 3). From the opening of its port in 1876, Japanese and other merchants settled in the narrow strip of land between the hills and the sea near the site of the early modern Japanese settlement. The port's topography was often compared to that of Kobe, and Pusan's ambitious settlers also saw its future role in the Korean colony's economy as similar to or even surpassing that of the Japanese port city. The expansion of the city, like that of Kobe, could only move in two directions—up the hillside or out into the harbor.

As the list of projects in table 1 indicates, expanding into the harbor was the first choice of the early businessmen and settlers, who were required to submit their petitions for urban development to the Korean government. The first wave of these ventures began at the turn of the century. By involving themselves with such projects, private companies run by Japanese were not only laying the groundwork for later Government General action, but also shaping the future city in the most fundamental way. They were creating new urban areas that expanded the city and, crucially, the proportion of the city monopolized by the Japanese. Of all the land reclamation works that took

TABLE I Works of the Pusan Japanese Residents' Association

Year	Projects Completed [1]
Meiji 38 (1905)	Construction of quarantine hospital Drainage construction on two mountainsides Construction of Pusan Common Elementary School Founding of firefighter brigade
Meiji 39 (1906)	Construction of Sōryo Jinjō Elementary School
Meiji 40 (1907)	Relocation of Residents' Association Offices Construction of new commercial school Relocation of graveyard Improvement of roads within Japanese settlement Reconstruction of Ryūbi-san (Yongmi san) Shrine Construction of branch of Pusan Common Elementary School on Makinoshima
Meiji 41 (1908)	Purchase of land for new military practice grounds Removal of Koreans from land [2] Relocation of prison Expansion of schools in Sōryo and Makinoshima Survey of roads in Sōryo, Kokan, and Pusan-chin districts Creation of park
Meiji 42 (1909)	First forest cultivation project at reservoir (1,980,000 trees) Construction of new health center New hospital buildings New buildings for girls' high school constructed Expansion of schools in Sōryo and Makinoshima
Meiji 43 (1910)	Relocation of pleasure quarters to Midori-machi Improvement of roads of urban area, to include Saka township Laying of waterworks to reach 55,000 people.

Year	Ongoing Projects
Meiji 41~ (1908~)	Urban reforms
Meiji 42~ (1909~)	Planting school forest on Makinoshima Planting Residents' Association forest on Makinoshima Earthworks and land reclamation project around British legation and Eizen-san Satsuma-bori land reclamation project
Meiji 43~ (1910~)	Second reforestation project Planting and managing bamboo plantation near reservoir on Kōenmi Makinoshima new urban district management Riparian works to Hōsui River (K: Posu ch'on)

(continued)

TABLE 1 *Continued*

Year	Ongoing Projects
	Survey for new urban district in Sōryo area
	Survey for new road at mouth of Nakdong River
Meiji 44~ (1911~)	Relocation of commercial school and construction of new buildings
Meiji 45 (1912)	Relocation of hospital for infectious diseases
	Expansion of health center
	Expansion of settler hospital

CREDIT: Data from Pusan shōgyōkaigisho 1912, 41–45.

[1] The projects listed here began after Korea became a protectorate in 1905. However, the association's previous incarnation was responsible for many other projects before this date.

[2] Pusan shōgyōkaigisho 1912, 43: "From hygienic necessity, Kanjin [Koreans] living in villages occupying hills to the north of Pusan's urban areas were paid a removal fee and evicted."

place in Pusan in the colonial period, not one was funded by a Korean company or businessman.[22]

The earthworks project undertaken from 1909 to 1913 highlights the Residents' Association's capacity to dramatically alter the urban space of Pusan. This project used the land gained by flattening two hills to extend Pusan's urban area out into Pusan Bay.[23] The Residents' Association raised 150,500 yen themselves before petitioning the Japanese resident general to allow the work to go ahead. Included in this project was the construction of harbor walls and some 40,490 *tsubo* (thirty-three acres) of new roads extending out into the freshly created land.[24]

Although it was smaller in scale than later imperial projects involving investment from metropolitan capitalists, the project is important for understanding the level of power that the Residents' Association wielded over Pusan's urban space, even before annexation. Perhaps most notable is the residents' ability to amass this significant sum of money. The capability of settlers to "inscribe their influence" on Pusan was due in no small part to their sheer financial power, which, often based in landownership, gave them a clear financial interest in funding this project.[25] Those members of the Residents' Association with the most financial clout were the old-timers discussed above, whose ability to leave their mark on the urban spaces of Pusan would last until Korea's liberation in 1945.

Japanese settlers also wielded power over the urban space of the city through discourses of hygiene and scientific knowledge.[26] While the Japanese built out into Pusan Bay, poor Koreans were forced onto Pusan's hillsides.[27]

The list of projects in table 1 makes its sole mention of Koreans in a description of a reforestation project, where, citing "hygiene" issues, the Residents' Association evicted Koreans living in a hamlet (J: *buraku*) on the hillsides to the north of the urban center in 1908.[28] The often-marginal presence of Koreans in the colonial archives mirrored local authorities' desire for control over their presence in urban spaces.

These reforestation projects were considered necessary for improving the city's water sources, and also, the association's 1912 report argued, because Koreans were ignorant or incapable of acting on the connections between forest growth and water supply.[29] Such rhetoric around colonial backwardness was common in Japanese forestry management in Korea.[30] In 1908 the removed Koreans were paid 3,271 yen—a not insignificant sum in total, but hard to parse further without knowing how many households it was divided between.[31] Whether they were truly "relocated" or left to find new accommodation on their own also remains unclear. As Pusan's population grew, and migrant Koreans built makeshift settlements on the hills surrounding the bay, Japanese landowners and city officials continued to deploy racist discourses of backwardness and hygiene to remove them.

By annexation in 1910, the sheer length of the Japanese presence in Pusan meant that the new local government inherited a city with significant Japanese-run institutions and facilities already in place. For example, the new Pusan City Hall, built in 1879, had originally housed the Japanese Legation. By 1928 it already needed replacing.[32] This was a built environment that reflected the vested economic interests—in land and business—of significant local settler elites.[33] After annexation, and especially after the Independence Movement of 1919 and the Government General's policies of "cultural rule" that emerged as a response, these elites had to adapt to a system of regional government that encouraged the involvement of colonized locals—Korean regional elites—as well as local imperialists.

Local Elites and Local Development

When Korea's colonial municipal system (J: *fusei*) came into effect on March 31, 1914, the administrative area of Pusan was made up of ten districts and neighborhoods centered on the former international settlements clustered around the port.[34] The boundaries of the city were defined along the lines of Japanese capital and interests. In contrast, while nearby Tongnae (J: Tōrai), the Chosŏn-era center of regional power, had been turned from a district (J:

gun) into a municipality (J: *fu*) under the resident general's reorganization of local administration, this decision was reversed in 1914. With this, Tongnae was demoted to a district but remained a center for local Korean elite politics, with far fewer Japanese residents than Pusan proper. The area was also incorporated into a colonial network of leisure and travel as Tongnae and Haeundae hot springs became popular as spa resorts for wealthy Japanese.[35]

In 1914, on the same day that the municipal system came into effect, former members of Pusan's Residents' Association and its school board formed the Pusan Kōinkai, named for the year it was founded in the sexagenary cycle. The Kōinkai members met monthly and petitioned for the return of the precolonial system of local rule that the 1914 municipal system had removed. Now that Korea was part of the Japanese empire, the Government General argued, there was no need for the settler groups to have the level of autonomy that they had considered necessary when living in a foreign country with "inferior" legal, educational, and judicial institutions. Through new elite groups such as the Kōinkai, as well as their ongoing presence in the city's new colonial institutions, long-term settlers continued to exert their influence in the city.[36]

Key figures of the former Residents' Association retained significant lobbying power over the local government through their roles in the city's chamber of commerce. Despite its merger in 1915 with its equivalent Korean organizations (originally set up to counter Japanese encroachment in the open port period), the chamber of commerce remained an overwhelmingly Japanese institution.[37] The chamber's members had ambitions and interests that went beyond the city and connected it to the rest of the colony and metropole. They often directed their petitions to the Governor General in Keijō, bypassing local government altogether. After their merger, with the bar for entry to even regional groups much higher for Koreans than for Japanese, the few Korean business figures that made it into the new chambers of commerce alongside Japanese members were usually those with Korea-wide, or at least province-wide, business interests.[38]

When protests calling for Korea's independence erupted across Korea in March 1919, Koreans in the areas surrounding the city of Pusan joined in. Protests were held by student organizers in Tongnae and Kupo. Although the activities of those calling for independence took place away from the colonial center of the region, their eventual punishment was meted out in Pusan, with many protesters incarcerated for months or years in Pusan Prison. One of the Japanese Government General's responses to the Independence Movement—

and to this divide between the city and its surrounding areas, between Japanese settlers and colonized Koreans—was a shift to so-called cultural rule (J: *bunka seiji*) after a decade of military rule (J: *budan seiji*).

With this came the reorganization of local government. This was an attempt by the Government General to create popular consensus about issues connected to regional development, which were entangled with the interests of local landowning elites—mainly Japanese, but some Koreans too.[39] However, for Japanese settlers this attempt to co-opt Korean voices—both a veneer of colonial equality and a safety valve for Korean frustrations cynically designed to prevent further unrest—was something they had feared from the moment they discovered that they would be losing their pre-annexation powers.[40]

From 1920 onward, local councils (J: *kyōgikai*) in municipal areas (J: *fu*; K: *pu*) and designated townships (J: *men*; K: *myŏn*) were made up of elected rather than nominated members. Koreans were better represented on provincial and township councils like Tongnae than on municipal ones like Pusan due to a franchise based on tax payment and the clustering of Japanese voters in cities.[41] These councils mobilized local elites to promote regional development projects in which their own interests—as both landowners and locals—aligned with those of the colonial state. Historian Hong Sun-kwŏn argues that even outside municipal areas, because the townships with elected councils were mainly county seats in industrializing regions with large numbers of landowners, the system created a feeling of connection between colonial modernization and urban development.[42] For historian Dong Sŏn-hui, the discourse of development and modernization resonated with many of the local Korean elites on provincial councils. In the 1920s there was still much overlap with the old local elites, who, prior to Korea's colonization, had ruled as county magistrates (K: *kunsu*) and had been involved in enlightenment groups focused on ideas of modernizing Korea's economy and military.[43]

Although local councils in the 1920s had no legislative power, they allowed space for discussion and, through elections and other residents' meetings, mobilized both Japanese and Koreans behind local projects, securing legitimacy for development in urban and industrializing areas. These residents' meetings (K: *myŏnmin taehoe/pumin taehoe*) were most often held to discuss urban development issues such as land readjustment or road and rail routes; although they were relatively common in the 1920s, they appear to have happened less frequently in the 1930s, perhaps due to the expanded powers of the new assembly system introduced in 1930.

From 1920, representatives were elected to the Pusan municipal council (J: Pusan fu kyōgikai). The Japanese members included familiar faces from the Residents' Association, some of whom were also members of the chamber of commerce. Those Koreans who were elected as members of Pusan's council were mainly those from commercial backgrounds—grain merchants and merchant brokers (K: *kaekchu*)—that reflected the local strata of Koreans that had benefited from Pusan's position as a treaty port, and the commercialization of agriculture that was taking place in its rural hinterland, and southern Korea more broadly.

Connections to Japanese settlers also helped. The three Koreans elected to the Pusan council in the 1923 election were Chu Nae-yoo, a grain and marine products *kaekchu*, Moon Sang-woo, a bank president with Kyŏngnam Bank, and Yi Cho-won, a lawyer. Both Moon and Yi had connections to Japanese settler elites that undoubtedly helped them get elected; Moon had studied in Tokyo, and his close links to Hazama Fusatarō had furthered his banking career.[44]

In the 1920s Koreans never held more than four out of a total of thirty council seats. To reflect the city's growth in population, in 1926 the number of seats on the council in Pusan increased from twenty to thirty. However, the number of Koreans on the council stayed the same. In 1929, the last election under the council system, only two out of thirty seats went to Koreans, and the percentage of Koreans among the electorate also slid from 10 percent in 1923 to 6.7 percent.[45] Across the colony the situation was somewhat better than that in Pusan, with an average of 30 percent of council seats going to Koreans. Despite incremental changes that brought Korean elites into local government, Pusan's established settler elite continued to exert control over local urban politics, and urban space.

The two were connected. The franchise for local elections was based on taxes, and Japanese elites in Pusan held more land than Korean elites. Settler elites had a tight grip on urban real estate, with a small number of Japanese landlords, including Hazama, controlling the rental market. This situation resulted in a housing shortage in the early 1920s, which led a group of Korean local notables to set up an organization to help those struggling to find housing, as well as to hold residents' meetings to protest for a change in the laws around renting. These rallies were an early sign of the city's growing urban issues. They drew the involvement of local elites who supported independence, such as An Hui-je, head of the Baeksan Trading Corp, but also others who would go on to play a role in the city's politics in the 1930s.[46]

Settler elites also used their personal wealth to shape the city. During the interwar years, when the municipal budget could not stretch to cover (or would not prioritize) the spending required to maintain the urban spaces constructed by the settlers themselves, these dignitaries dipped into their own pockets to come to the rescue of such institutions. The Pusan Theater was rebuilt and the Pusan Public Hall constructed with the help of the deep pockets of the settler elites.[47] Their munificence was never private: At the hall's opening in May 1928, Ōike, Kashii, and Hazama were honored in front of local and regional government officials with a lavish celebration featuring a film screening and geisha performances.[48]

These figures' power in the city was memorialized in more obvious ways, too. Pusan's Japanese residents saw themselves as part of a history of Japanese people exerting their authority on the Korean peninsula that went back centuries. Settlers from Tsushima drew historic parallels with figures from the Tsushima domain, who had acted as go-betweens for the Tokugawa government and the Chosŏn court. In 1928, in the same month as the opening of the Pusan Public Hall, an expansion of the park on the site of the old Japan House was announced. Tsushima-born Ōike Chūsuke had donated land for the project, for which he was rewarded with a statue of himself, placed next to a monument for Tsunoe Hyōgonosuke, a Tsushima samurai who had taken part in negotiations over the relocation of the Japan House in the early seventeenth century.[49] Settler control over Pusan's urban space went as far as using it to write a new, colonial version of "local" history, with Japanese settlers and their regional ancestors at its heart.

Political and Economic Stagnation

From the end of 1930 Pusan's council became a municipal assembly (J: *fu kai*) with legislative powers, although the municipal prefect (J: *fuin*) was still chosen by the Government General. The late 1920s saw a decline in the number of powerful Korean *kaekchu* business figures represented in local government. They were replaced by a more diverse group of Korean members who had made their money and connections under the colonial regime, notably professionals such as lawyers and doctors and those with interests in the booming brewing industry, such as Kim Chang-t'ae, first elected in 1929.[50]

As we saw in the previous section, Pusan's local government was mainly controlled by powerful settler elite figures who often remained in post for decades. The ratio of Korean to Japanese members was so low—one of the lowest colony-wide—that it required intervention from the colonial government. At its first election in May 1931, ethnic quotas were forcibly applied to those elected to Pusan's municipal assembly.[51] This had only limited effects, however. Throughout the 1930s Koreans never formed more than 35 percent of the total assembly membership in Pusan.

Furthermore, the increase in the number of Korean representatives compared to Japanese did not keep up with the demographic shifts in Pusan throughout the 1930s. As the city's growing industry pulled in Korean laborers, and the exodus from the countryside increased, Korean residents in Pusan went from 67 percent of the city's population in 1931 to 77 percent (170,699 people) in 1939.[52] Throughout this period Korean assembly members remained a minority, and many had loyalties to and interests that aligned with the assembly's more powerful Japanese members.[53]

By the early 1930s the power that these early settlers had become accustomed to wielding over Pusan's urban growth had caused tensions with the Government General and resentment among other, less well-off Japanese settlers, as well as with Koreans. Most Japanese, as well as most Koreans, were unable to vote in assembly elections.[54] This came to a head with a council rift over plans for a public takeover of the city's electricity. Fukuokan settler elite Kashii Gentarō was president of the Chōsen Gas and Electric Company. Unsurprisingly, he opposed the takeover, and Pusan's council was divided between Kashii's clique and those members, representing public opinion, who supported it. By 1929 the takeover bid was dead in the water.[55]

In 1931, in response to the affair, Pusan resident Inoue Kiyomaro published a tract entitled *The Men Who Made Pusan*. The Japanese title (*Pusan wo katsugu mono*) suggests the ambivalence felt toward these figures, the merchants and self-made men who shaped Pusan. The verb *katsugu*, as Inoue explains in his introduction, contains within it several meanings: "A kind reading is that these men created Pusan, expanded and developed it. . . . A less kind reading is that they poisoned it, swindled it: To put it bluntly, they've taken it for a ride."[56] Elsewhere Inoue used the simile of Pusan's oligarchs riding in a cart up a steep hill, pulled and pushed by the "masses" of Pusan's population.[57] The hard work of Pusan's inhabitants only resulted in an easy rise to the top for its settler oligarchs.

The power of the Pusan assembly to protect the property rights and interests of the city's settler elite, and, conversely, its lack of interest in incorporating the demands of Korean representatives, is apparent in an incident from 1934. In December 1933 thirteen-year-old Kim In-hwa, a Korean resident of the poor neighborhood of Taesin-dong, was collecting dead leaves in the woods around the Kōenmi reservoir, presumably for kindling. She was attacked by a German shepherd guard dog—employed by the city, along with its handler, to stop illegal felling of the woods around the reservoir, which acted as a water catchment forest (J: *suigenrin*; K: *suwŏllim*).[58]

The following spring, when Korean assembly members gave the assembly an ultimatum over the continued funding of the "inhumane" guard dog system, along with the lack of funding for the improvement of overcrowded Korean residential areas including the hill villages around Taesin-dong, the Pusan assembly refused to listen to the demands, and all nine Korean assembly members resigned in protest.[59] In his resignation speech, assembly member Kim Jun-sŏk, a rice merchant, criticized the Japanese assembly members and municipal prefect for ignoring the presence of Korean members, but even a drastic measure such as mass resignation did nothing to improve the situation, as the Korean members had no leverage over the prefect or the majority of the assembly's Japanese members. The budget was passed without them. After Municipal Prefect Ōshima called for the members to retract their resignations, seven of them did—without gaining a response to any of their demands in the process.[60]

In an urban political system like Pusan's, the interests of poor Koreans—indeed, the opinions of all "regular" Pusan residents whom the Korean assembly members said they were representing—had no way of being heard.[61] As in the days of the Residents' Association, discourses of hygiene and environmental protection were deployed by settler elites to legitimize discriminatory urban politics, despite the fact that, as the Korean assembly members argued, the improvement of conditions in the Korean hill villages would have benefitted Pusan's population at large. "Local development" in Pusan was a discourse for the few, not the many.

In the 1930s, with an entrenched settler elite unwilling to listen to the voices of its inhabitants or make room for the demands of a newly empowered number of Korean assembly members, Pusan's politics were stagnating. So was its economy: According to Inoue Kiyomaro, although the value of goods coming in and out of Pusan had quintupled between 1914 and 1931, the number of Japanese paying municipal tax had only doubled. This was a sign not only that Pusan's wealth was not trickling down to everyone, but that the municipal budget was also suffering. Pusan, for Inoue, was a plutocracy. The "big three" figures of Kashii, Ōike, and Hazama were "uncrowned kings" who, between them, were members of the city's four most important bodies and held positions on or investments in over two-thirds of the city's businesses.[62] Although this might have been acceptable in the open port era, Inoue argued, settler control was causing the autointoxication of Pusan's economy.

By the early 1930s this divided city, constructed for the benefit of a few, was in decline. Even after the colonial economy as a whole had recovered from the financial crises of the late 1920s, Pusan's urban economy was too structured around the interests of an entrenched settler elite to allow more than a chosen few Korean businessmen a chance at success. Following the founding of the client state of Manchukuo in 1932, even Japanese capital from the metropole, making inroads into Korea as part of the drive for the peninsula's industrialization, found it hard to break into the Pusan economy. It took until 1936 for Pusan's economy to recover to pre-1929 levels, despite national output being above 1930 levels by 1932. Only from 1937 onward, thanks to the boom upon the outbreak of Japan's invasion of and war with China, did Pusan's industrial economy show signs of real growth.[63]

The cause of Pusan's alternating stagnation and growth was the city's close links to mainland Japan and the resultant control of Pusan's economy and urban politics by long-present settler elites and a limited number of Korean elites whose interests mainly aligned with theirs. The modern economic and urban development of Pusan, just like that of the wider Tsushima Strait region, had become tied to cycles of Japanese expansion. During the first decades of the twentieth century Pusan was less and less a part of a "Korean" economy and increasingly enmeshed within an imperial region built on war and continental expansion.

We have seen above, then, how local imperialists in Pusan built on their long presence in the city to shape its local political economy in their interests. But their self-professed identity as "local" was twofold. Pusan's proximity to their hometowns back in Japan meant that for many settlers, their old as well as their adopted "hometowns" were incorporated into plans for local development. These effects weren't limited to those with political power or capital. Even the regional nature of migration by working-class settlers—those without connections or capital—affected the city's growth and pushed Koreans further to the city's margins. To undertake a closer study of the many layers and dynamics of the continued regional imperialism that shaped Pusan's urban space and political economy, as well as its position in the wider region, I turn to one regional group of settlers in particular: the Fukuokans of Pusan.

FUKUOKANS IN PUSAN: REGIONAL IMPERIALISM,
LOCAL GEOGRAPHIES

At nine o'clock in the morning on August 28, 1932, two Fukuokans left Fukuoka City's port of Hakata aboard the *Chōhaku Maru* ferry, the pride of the Kitakyūshū Shipping Company. As the ferry navigated its way out of Hakata Bay, passengers aboard could look back at the ongoing expansion works at the port of Hakata and witness, some for the first time, the growing city of Fukuoka as viewed from the sea.[64] The two passengers, Naitō Rikizō and Tsurusaki Shin, were editors of the magazine *Fukuoka Kenjin* (*The Fukuokan*), a monthly publication that connected Fukuokans living across Japan and its colonies.[65] Naitō and Tsurusaki had embarked on a continental tour to meet with, interview, and collect data on Fukuoka's overseas communities in colonial Korea and the new client state of Manchukuo. Their first stop was Pusan.

In 1932 the journey between Fukuoka and Pusan took ten hours. The *Chōhaku Maru* arrived at Pusan's pier at seven in the evening. This was Naitō's first trip across the straits, and his first steps on the Asian continent. Tsurusaki, however, had been to the city before; several years previously he had taken the Kampu (Pusan–Shimonoseki) ferry back to Japan after a trip to Manchuria. Compared to then, a new feeling surrounded the city: The old Pusan that Tsurusaki remembered was gone. At customs, the *Fukuokan* staff ran into a group of their compatriots: newspaper reporters from Fukuoka, also visiting the city. It was a small world, on either side of the straits.

Tsurusaki and Naitō were staying at the villa of Yoshioka Shigezane in the seaside resort of Matsushima (K: Songdo), southwest of the city center. From the villa they could see Pusan Bay before them and, beyond that, the Tsushima Strait, with the lights of fishing vessels blinking in the darkness. The house was built on top of a sturdy stone wall, a symbol not only of its owner's wealth and status but also of his pen name, Sekijō (stone castle), which was also a former name for Hakata itself. Yoshioka was a businessman with connections to Pusan's land reclamation operations, Nikkan Warehouses, Ōkura Construction Company, and Chōsen Industries, and had been involved in Matsushima's development as a beach resort. Like many figures in the empire at this time, Yoshioka had interests both in the business world and in local politics—he was a twice-elected member of the Pusan's council. Originally from Asakura district in Fukuoka, he had been making a name for himself on the peninsula for many years although he was still only forty-two years old. Over dinner, Yoshioka promised to arrange meetings for the journalists with prominent Fukuokans in the city.

These notable Fukuokans included Kashii Gentarō, who, as president of the Fukuoka Prefectural Association (*kenjinkai*) and the Pusan Chamber of Commerce, was seen as the head of the Japanese settler community in Pusan. Kashii's vice presidents at the association were Yoshioka himself and Sakada Bunkichi. Sakada was originally from the rural Yame district of Fukuoka prefecture and became head of his family trading company in 1905. Like Yoshioka and Kashii, Sakada was involved in politics as well as business. Fukuokans were at the head of Pusan's branches of the Bank of Chōsen and Chōsen Shipping and managing director of Kashii's marine products company. As well as being involved in business and politics, Fukuokans were well represented in education, as the principals of Pusan Middle School and Pusan Commercial School, and in journalism. Shinozaki Shōnosuke and Naganobu Seishirō, the vice president and sales manager of the city's Japanese-language newspaper, the *Pusan Nippō*, were both from Fukuoka.

Founded in 1907, the *Pusan Nippō* boasted Kashii as its largest shareholder.[66] It had other connections across the strait to Kyushu: Its predecessor, the *Chōsen Nippō*, had been founded by Kokuryūkai member Kuzuu Yoshihisa and had financial links to the Gen'yōsha, featuring columns by several members of the two organizations.[67] In 1930, ahead of the opening of the new Hakata–Pusan ferry link the following year, the *Pusan Nippō* opened a branch office in Fukuoka City. Reports hoped the "increase[d] traffic, communication, transportation, and economic connections" would lead to the two cities "becoming one" (J: *isshindōtai*). With its own expansion back across the strait, the *Pusan Nippō* hoped to strengthen Pusan and Fukuoka's geographic and economic connections and to serve as a "steadfast linchpin" between them.[68] In 1933 it moved into new offices shared with the *Fukuoka Jiji Shinpō*, with whom it also shared some staff.[69] This move followed an earlier plan for the Pusan municipal magazine, *The Fusan*, to expand its distribution across the straits to Fukuoka, although it is unclear whether this plan was realized.[70] It is worth noting here that the expansion of media networks that accompanied the growth of transport links between the two cities appears to be one-sided, consisting of Pusan publications expanding into Fukuoka and Kyushu—a mirror image of the activities of Fukuoka's local imperialists and their involvement in precolonial Pusan's newspaper and government worlds.

After a whistle-stop tour of the city and meetings with prominent Fukuokans brokered by Yoshioka, Tsurusaki and Naitō collected their thoughts on Pusan and its settlers as they headed north on the night train to Keijō. Their most lasting impression was of their fellow Fukuokans, who, "unlike in Japan," they noted, "were not constricted by petty emotions but viewed things from a confident, wide-ranging perspective. They were working hard, with purpose. This impressed us most considerably."[71] To the journalists, it appeared that moving to the colonies had a positive effect on these Fukuokans' ambitions and confidence, the language of constraint versus expansiveness adding a spatial dimension to the power and motivation these settlers appeared to gain by moving from the metropole into the empire.

Elite Visions: Regional Development and Regional Imperialism

The "wide-ranging" perspectives of Fukuokan settlers in Pusan did not mean they forgot their hometown. Rather, it was often through the lobbying of local settler elites like Kashii Gentarō and Shinozaki Shōnosuke that Fukuoka became connected to imperial schemes of Asian development. Although he was often the chosen representative of Fukuokans in Pusan, the magnate and electric company president Kashii Gentarō was, to some extent, an outlier in terms of his sheer success, power, and presence on both the colonial and metropolitan stage. However, while Kashii participated in lobbying the Diet as one of three chosen representatives of Japanese industry in Korea, he was also, as the head of the chamber of commerce, involved in brokering deals between his adopted colonial hometown of Pusan and his metropolitan hometown of Fukuoka, which is discussed further in chapter 4.[72]

Vice president of the *Pusan Nippō* at the time of Tsurusaki and Naitō's visit, Shinozaki Shōnosuke was also involved in forging links across the straits. His activities were on a decidedly more local scale than those of Kashii. Shinozaki was born in Fukuoka in 1896, three decades after Kashii, and graduated from the city's Shūyūkan High School in 1911. Shūyūkan alumni moved among Fukuoka's elite and its alumni network was intertwined with other regional networks: Like many of the school's graduates, Shinozaki also became a member of the Gen'yōsha. After studying at Keiō University, Shinozaki returned to Kyushu and worked for the *Kyūshū Nippō*. This paper and the *Pusan Nippō* have been described as almost "sister publications" in terms of their founding history and backers.[73] After the First World War, Shinozaki toured Europe and America before taking up his position in Pusan. Compared to Kashii's larger sphere of influence, Shinozaki's life and work centered on the straits region: He maintained strong connections to Fukuoka that appear to have been a key motivation in many of his activities and visions.

In the autumn of 1934 *The Fukuokan* sent Tsurusaki on a second trip to the continent. This trip was more ambitious than the first, spanning North and South Manchuria, Korea, the Kwantung peninsula, and parts of Mongolia. Upon arriving in Pusan at the very end of his two-month journey, Tsurusaki had been able to entreat Shinozaki to share his views on the past, present, and future of the city and the industrialization of the Korean peninsula in a series of opinion pieces entitled the "Construction of Great Pusan" ("Dai-Pusan kensetsu").[74] Published over three editions of the magazine and addressing Pusan's position in the flow of goods from the continent to the home islands, these articles linked the industrialization of Pusan to the economic development of the Fukuoka region. Shinozaki was thirty years Kashii's junior, and his technocratic plans show a generational shift away from the types of networks promoted by the older brokers of empire such as Kashii, whose rise to prominence through his business ventures in Pusan embodied the Meiji ideal of *risshin shusse*—making it in the world.

Geography was front and center in Shinozaki's plans for Pusan's future: The city's locational advantage (*chi no ri*) allowed it to act as a conduit for flows of goods and capital between the continent and Japan's home islands. From 1932 onward, Japan's exploitation of Manchuria's natural resources required recalibrating the various supply networks that spanned the Japanese empire and its economic sphere of interest. Shinozaki argued that instead of simply transporting raw materials from Manchuria via the northern Korean port of Rashin (K: Najin/Rajin) to Japan Sea ports such as Niigata and Tsuruga, investment in Pusan's industry could allow the processing of these goods on the spot before transportation to the home islands. This, for Shinozaki, was the key to the city's growth as both an industrial city and a port city.

Locational advantage also boosted Fukuoka's position on the border between empire and metropole. Shinosaki's argument for his new route for raw materials from the continent into Japan stressed the effects that "so called city-centrism" had wrought on land and labor prices in metropolitan cities like Tokyo and Osaka, which had been priced out of competition as possible sites for further industrialization.[75] The industrialization of Pusan, "only separated by a thin strip of water" from northern Kyushu, would affect Fukuoka too: "Setting up the required facilities for Pusan to become this industrial port is not just the most urgent business of Pusan, but . . . also a pressing problem for the heavy industries of North Kyushu."[76]

In his connection of urbanization, labor, and rising land prices in the cities of the home islands with flows of goods and urban growth in the Japanese empire, Shinozaki's plan was in some ways a harbinger of Japanese National Land Planning (J: *Kokudo keikaku*) and Great East Asian Land Planning (J: *Daitō-a kokudo keikaku*) in the 1940s, which offered solutions to problems spanning the Japanese empire and its economic bloc.[77] The plan was also, however, deeply inflected by a regional Pan-Asianism that was native to Fukuoka.

Fukuoka City, unlike those regions of northern Kyushu that had already industrialized by the early 1930s, faced a water supply problem, and its current plans to expand through industrialization were in danger of ending up hamstrung by this environmental scarcity. Shinozaki explicitly addressed his articles in *The Fukuokan* to Fukuoka's capitalists, informing them that "what Fukuoka lacks in terms of water supply can be found in Pusan, only seven or eight hours away."[78] These plans for Pusan involved diverting water supplies to newly reclaimed land along the waterfront areas northeast of the railway and main pier, which was ready to become prime industrial real estate. Investing and running industries in Pusan should be seen, Shinozaki argued, as simply extending the economic activity of the city across the Tsushima Strait.

By exhorting the capitalists of Fukuoka to make economic what had always been geographic—the "co-existence and co-prosperity" (*kyōson kyōei*) of the two cities—Shinozaki tapped into preexisting concepts of the connections between the Kyushu region and southern Korea and appealed for a regional form of colonialism that would secure the two cities' position in Japan's growing empire. In Shinozaki's vision Pusan would become an extension (J: *enchō*) of Fukuoka through the expansion of the city's capital and industry. Using what David Harvey calls the "tentacles of economic power," one city would enact a capitalist annexation of another by incorporating it within its own urban region.[79]

In his editorials Shinozaki, who referred to both "our Pusan" and "my hometown Fukuoka," advanced an idea that he considered mutually beneficial to both cities, but he left unsaid who the beneficiaries of this scheme would be: Japanese from the same circles as his own—investors in empire in all its forms. This group of elite men funded the newspapers that Shinozaki wrote in and profited from the coal mines that powered the ships plying the straits joining the two regions, whose ports and land reclamation projects were also being expanded thanks to money from these self-same Pan-Asianist businessmen.[80] Shinozaki's editorials helped to convey to the magazine's readership in the metropole just what Naitō and Tsurusaki meant by the "wide-ranging perspective" from which Fukuokan settlers in Pusan viewed their ventures and Pusan's place in the expanding empire. However, while the scale of these visions was broad, often couched in Pan-Asianist rhetoric of "developing Asia" (J: *Kō-A*), they had at their heart a rather narrow self-interest.[81]

Everyday Realities: Class and Gender in Colonial Urban Space

The stories told in the metropole about the "pioneers" who left their hometowns as an "advance guard" of Japanese imperialism often leave out descriptions of internal struggles, divisions, and hierarchies. When viewed from the metropole, or in the pages of *The Fukuokan*, the fractured picture of local, colonial, and imperial politics that existed in Pusan coalesced into a more triumphal portrait of local success stories on an imperial scale, allowing readers to connect the advance of Japanese imperialism to hometown pride.

Although Kashii, Shinozaki, and indeed all the figures that Naitō and Tsurusaki named in their 1932 report on Pusan were members of an elite settler class—the kind of figures that feature prominently in other works on Japanese settlers in Korea—they were but a fraction of the Fukuokans and Japanese who lived in the city. Those eligible to vote in municipal elections held from 1920 onward had to be male, over twenty-five, an "imperial Japanese subject" (J: *teikoku kōmin*), and pay five yen in tax. This amounted to only 2 or 3 percent of Pusan's Japanese population, and only half of 1 percent of the city's Korean population.[82]

The overwhelming majority of Japanese settlers in Korea's cities were not "brokers of empire." In Pusan they were blue-collar workers, housemaids, schoolchildren, fishermen, waitresses, hawkers, housewives, shop assistants, clerks, carpenters, and prostitutes. Many of them were migrants who had left rural Western Japan for Korea in the late nineteenth and early twentieth centuries, as discussed in chapter 1. And just as we saw in the case of Fukuoka, both urban elites and regional migrants (from both sides of the strait) played a key role in shaping Pusan's urban growth and incorporation within this urbanizing region. Not least, these working-class settlers' interactions with and impact on the livelihoods of colonized Koreans—Pusan's other urban majority—deserves more attention.

Contemporaneous sources produced by urban elites, like *The Fukuokan* or chamber of commerce publications, provide historians with historical information that if reproduced uncritically can produce a "Great Men" view of colonial history. Conversely, if we view the actors that appear in these texts as the main agents of colonial oppression, extraction, and violence, our conclusions change but the focus remains settled on the same actors. However, there are other figures within the pages of these settler publications that were also involved in shaping urban growth and excluding Koreans from the city. *The Fukuokan*, at the end of its report on the first leg of Naitō and Tsurusaki's trip in 1932, printed membership lists that included occupation, address in Korea, and hometown in Fukuoka for the Keijō and Pusan Fukuoka Prefectural Associations, as well as for the newly formed Pusan Chikugo Association.[83]

So many Fukuokans were present in Pusan that subgroups within the community had emerged: The large number of Fukuokans from the prefecture's southern, largely agricultural region, Chikugo, had inspired the formation of a separate Chikugo Association the previous year, in 1931.[84] The association had recently constructed a branch of the Kurume Suitengū (a guardian shrine of water transport located next to the Chikugo River) in Pusan's Taishō Park, itself bordered by the Posu (J: Hōsui) River, which flowed into Pusan Bay.[85] Taking the membership of these Fukuoka Prefectural Associations as a more representative, but still incomplete, reflection of the makeup of the Japanese community (compared to those settler elites discussed in Naito and Tsuruzaki's report) reveals a very different image of settler life.

What the membership lists reveal are, first, patterns of migration and settlement on a colony-wide level suggesting geographic and socioeconomic divisions that mirror the local origins and backgrounds of settlers. Many more Fukuokans from the urban areas in and around Fukuoka City are represented in the member lists for Keijō than for Pusan.[86] Second, we can see similar class divisions within Pusan's own settler community mapping onto the geographic origins of Fukuokan settlers.

This was a regional but also a rural-urban divide. The fifty-eight members of the Pusan Fukuoka Association were involved mostly in administrative white-collar work at companies or the municipal government. The Chikugo Association, however, had a more diverse range of occupations among its 188 members: restaurant owners, government clerks, merchants, postal workers, bakers, coopers, joiners, and even farmers. Comparing this with a

TABLE 2 Professions of Fukuoka Association members and other Japanese settlers in Pusan

Profession type	Fukuoka Association (1932)	Chikugo Association (1932)	Settler survey (1926)
Agriculture/Livestock	0 (0%)	4 (2%)	943 (2%)
Fishing/Salt production	1 (2%)	1 (0.5%)	2,463 (6%)
Industry	0 (0%)	14 (7%)	8,230 (20%)
Commerce/Transport	8 (14%)	56 (30%)	17,394 (43%)
Public/Professional	38 (66%)	45 (24%)	9,708 (24%)
Other	5 (9%)	16 (8.5%)	1,166 (3%)
No job/no answer	5 (9%)	52 (28%)	899 (2%)
Total	57 (100%)	188 (100%)	40803 (100%)

CREDIT: Data from "Pusan fu kyojūmin no shokugyō shurui betsu kokō no henkan," *The Fusan*, February 1927, 12–17, and *The Fukuokan*, October 1932, 36–40.

survey completed by the Pusan City Hall five years previously, it seems the Chikugo Association members were more representative of the wide range of occupations of most Japanese living in Pusan (see table 2). Over a quarter of the Chikugo Association's members chose not to give their profession, suggesting that many of them were involved in more hand-to-mouth or piecemeal work than those in the Fukuoka Association. The larger number of people involved in agriculture and food production (10 out of 188 members) could reflect the rural origins and skills of the Chikugo members compared to those in the Fukuoka Association. Based on these surveys, we can surmise that the settler majority in Pusan had moved from rural areas, and they had made journeys far more reminiscent of domestic migrants than colonial settlers of other empires.

This brief analysis sheds light on how Pusan's physical and social geographies shaped its development, and it reveals how the movements and networks not just of its settler elites but also of the many thousands of other regional migrants who worked and lived in the city had an impact on local and migrant Koreans. Analysis of census data from 1930, two years before Naitō and Tsurusaki's visit (the only Korean census that included detailed information on occupation and nationality) offers the most fine-grained portrait of Pusan's Japanese and Korean populations and their roles in the city's economy.[87] It also allows for comparison of Pusan with other cities in Korea—in terms of demographic makeup and the distribution of labor between colonial and settler communities—that fills in what is missing from the portrait painted in the pages of *The Fukuokan*.

Pusan in 1930 was Korea's second largest city, with a population of 146,000 people. Japanese in Pusan made up one-third of the city's population—the highest percentage of any large municipality in Korea. Slightly less than two thirds of Pusan's working population were Korean, mirroring the city's ethnic makeup. Most of these were men: Korean men made up just over half of the city's workforce, Japanese men just over a quarter, Korean women 13 percent, and Japanese women only 8 percent.

Hong Sun-kwŏn's analysis of the 1930 census has shown that, contrary to the outsized presence of the settler elite in histories of Pusan's settler population, 45 percent of Japanese employed in Pusan worked in some form of blue-collar occupation.[88] Among employed Japanese men, the ten most common occupations were general merchant, shop assistant, civil servant, carpenter, fisheries worker, general transportation worker, bookkeeper, public employee, general clerk, and "commercial assistant" (J: *shōgyō tedasuke*).[89] Among employed Japanese women, the most common jobs—nearly half of all employment—were commercial assistant, live-in domestic servant, maid or waitress in an inn, bar, or restaurant, and prostitute.[90]

Though rarely discussed in settler publications or included in the member lists of the Fukuoka prefectural associations, women made up nearly half of the Japanese settler population in Pusan. The only identifiably female member on the members' lists of the two Pusan Fukuoka associations in 1932 was Tsutsumi Hanako, the head nurse of Pusan Municipal Hospital, originally from Yame. This absence is not representative of the settler population of the city at this time.[91] Even in 1912, women made up 44 percent of the Japanese settler population. While men like Ueno Yasutarō, who set up pleasure districts such as Midori-machi, were hailed as pioneers of Pusan and Korea's development, the role of women's labor of all sorts—sexual, reproductive, manual—in the growth of the colonial city went largely undiscussed in settler publications at the time and remains understudied today.

Although this high ratio of women to men among Pusan's Japanese settlers has been used to suggest a "mature" population, the low birth rate among settlers also indicates a more precarious existence for many than simple statistics might imply.[92] Both of these are blunt metrics for attempting to understand what life was actually like for Japanese women in the city and how their presence affected its growth. The 1930 census offers us an overview, inevitably restricted, of women's work—Japanese and Korean—in the city.[93]

In 1930s Pusan there was more overlap in the occupations of Japanese and Korean women than there was among the more diverse occupations of

Japanese and Korean men. This could be because much smaller numbers of Japanese and Korean women worked outside the home compared to men, and they were confined to a narrower range of occupations.[94] Like Japanese women, many Korean women worked as domestic servants or in restaurants and bars. Unlike Japanese women, a large number of Korean women worked as peddlers or street hawkers or in thread and textile production in Pusan's booming spinning and weaving enterprises.[95] Of course, Japanese and Korean women who were classed by census categories as "dependent" would also have done significant unpaid domestic labor not mentioned in census data. In Pusan married women made up nearly a third of all those—Japanese and Korean—who were classified as dependents, with children under eleven making up half.[96]

Less overlap between the work of Japanese and Korean men suggests a more rigid ethnic hierarchy among traditionally male occupations. Of all Korean men employed in 1930, nearly a third worked as day laborers. This was a sector that Korean men in Japan were "institutionally channeled" into.[97] In this chapter we have seen this happening in the case of Pusan too. The other most common occupations for Korean men were fisheries worker, general merchant, hawker, odd-job man, and longshoreman.[98] Although Japanese settlers in Pusan were indeed working in more blue-collar roles than is common in other colonial settings, there was a division of labor at the unskilled level. Japanese settlers occupied roles in the commercial sector of the city, while Koreans, mainly from rural regions around Pusan, were funneled into work as day laborers and textile factory workers. These occupations contributed directly to Pusan's emergence as an industrial city in the 1930s.

Just as the occupations of working-class Japanese settlers overlapped and encroached on the lives and livelihoods of Koreans, so did their residential areas. Analysis of the member listings in *The Fukuokan* also allows insight into the social and colonial geographies of the city of Pusan through the members' addresses. Professional members of Pusan's settler community, including those who had been there since before annexation, mainly lived in the historic center of the colonial city, around the old Japanese settlement. Clusters of Fukuoka Association members and a few Chikugo Association members lived in the Sakai, Daichō, and Benten neighborhoods.[99]

Japanese who arrived in later waves of settlers were likely to settle in the newer areas of the city on what were described as previously "undeveloped" lands on the outskirts or hills overlooking the bay—land often owned by wealthy Japanese settlers like Hazama Fusatarō. Indeed, at this time some 80 percent of all Japanese in Pusan rented rather than owned their accommodation, usually from settler landlords.[100] Members of the rural Chikugo Association were more likely to be living in these newly developed areas of the city, especially on the island of Yŏngdo (J: Makinoshima) and in areas to the east and west of the city center, such as the Kusaba, Tomihira, and Sōryō neighborhoods.[101] Not only were these areas more recently developed, but they were also home to Korean residents as well as Japanese settlers.[102]

Precarity, even among the settler population, is a reminder of the particular geographies at play in Japan's imperial urbanization. Unlike longer-settled colonial elites, Pusan's settler precariat came from a wider range of often rural areas across the Tsushima Strait region. Their livelihoods indicate they had not found the path to certain success sold to them in literature about pioneers in the colonies but were instead doing work similar to that which they might have been doing if they had migrated instead to growing urban areas in the home islands. As discussed in the study of applications for travel documents in chapter 1, this was a function of the proximity of Japan's metropole to its colonies, which allowed the colonizers to easily replicate urban society back home without relying so heavily on colonized populations, unlike the situation in the more distant colonies of Japan or other imperial powers.

This phenomenon was especially noticeable in colonial Pusan, where, until its industrialization from the mid-1930s onward, Koreans were marginalized by precarious Japanese settlers, doing the labor of economically and socially reproducing empire. Poet Yu Chi-hwan, in an article from the magazine *Sindonga* (*New Orient*) in 1936, described Pusan as feeling "like a city initially created by Japanese in which a lot of Koreans live."[103] Yu's article was written after the economic shifts of the mid-1930s, when the industrializing economy of Pusan, as envisioned by figures like Shinozaki, could no longer survive without an influx of Korean labor. However—as will be discussed further in chapter 3—these regional Korean migrants did not always want to stay in Pusan, and their onward movement created further networks and links across the Tsushima Straits region.

CONCLUSIONS

Many of the Japanese who crossed the straits even before the annexation of Korea and who wielded significant power over the urbanization of the settler city of Pusan came from the prefectures bordering the Tsushima Strait. Their actions built on networks stretching back through Meiji into the early modern period. The city grew unevenly in the interactions between local elites and influxes of both Japanese settlers and Koreans, as well as the battles between settlers, the municipal government, and the Government General over Pusan's position as a city between metropole and empire.

The locality that these settlers relied upon and developed was a double one, encompassing both the local networks from their hometown, often expanded to incorporate a whole prefecture, as well as their adopted home in the colony. Pusan's spatial and socioeconomic development was built upon the gains of its earliest Japanese settlers, as well as a small number of Korean businessmen and local elites who did business or owned land in and around the growing city. This pattern of urban growth also relied on migrant labor from nearby Japan, and together these patterns resulted in the physical as well as socioeconomic exclusion of colonized Koreans from Pusan. In the following chapter I look more closely at the processes of exclusion and extraction upon which urban development was built in both Pusan and Fukuoka.

Fukuokan elites in Pusan used their connections in both cities to press for policies advantageous to both, whether related to transport links or economic investment. The monopolization of land by those self-proclaimed "local" settler elites who had been living in the city since the late nineteenth century was echoed by calls for the economic "extension" of Fukuoka's industrial zone across the Tsushima Strait—another form of colonization on a regional scale. The "wide-ranging" visions of these settler elites spanned metropole and colony, and their Pan-Asian visions were replicated in the pages of *The Fukuokan*. The Japanese empire, as seen through the eyes of the magazine's reporters, was a local one in which a mobile class of Japanese used their regional networks for social, political, and business ends.

While regional imperialism led to settler elites from the Tsushima Strait region, along with some local Korean elites, claiming local identity and shaping local development in order to dominate the management of urban life in colonial Korea, a long history of movement prior to annexation and the short distance across the straits also meant that Pusan had a large and diverse blue-collar settler population. Working-class Japanese settlers may have been unhappy with the settler elites' grip on the city, but their presence also acted as another form of imperial exclusion, to the detriment of Koreans' livelihoods.

Down and Out in Pusan and Fukuoka

KOREAN WRITER YI NAM-WON'S short story *Pusan*, from 1935, starts with the protagonist Kim Sang-bin, a migrant laborer, arriving in the port city. He doesn't have much of a plan: "First, I'm going to Shimonoseki and wherever after that." Kim lacks the requisite papers to cross to Japan and is tricked out of money by a range of characters. He is further disoriented by the mix of Japanese and Korean food and language he encounters. Finally, having spent all his money on a place on a broker's boat, he is captured by the harbor police. The authorities, anxious to move Kim and his fellow would-be migrants on, offer them train tickets to Manchuria, where the Japanese were building railroads and needed workers. Kim accepts: "As the train departed and sped further away from Pusan Station, I felt as if I had been to hell and back. Pusan was a den of robbers and a rotting human hell. . . . If I had the power, I would lift the streets of Pusan and sweep them into the sea."[1]

This chapter follows the authorized and unauthorized journeys of Koreans through Pusan and across to the industrial cities of northern Kyushu.[2] I attend to the complex and changing circumstances that informed the decisions of Koreans to cross the strait, and the effect that their movements had on the urbanization of the Tsushima Straits region. I argue that, as with the migration of Japanese discussed in chapter 1, this movement from Korea to Japan is better viewed as several disaggregated regional and social processes spanning an imperial border. Some Koreans were drawn to Pusan as an imperial gateway, while others simply found their way to this city at the edge of empire. Some succeeded in making a living there, while some, like Kim Sang-bin, were swindled and left destitute.

Pusan's local government was on the front line of Japan's imperial border policies and, along with migrants themselves, had to adapt to these often-changing regulations. Policies developed on the spot to deal with Koreans who "drifted" to Pusan spurred further uneven development of the city. Pusan's urbanization took place at the nexus of two processes: first, as seen in the previous chapter, the expansive development schemes of Japanese settlers, local Korean elites, and the colonial state, and second, the influx of provincial Japanese migrants and rural Koreans. Those Koreans who did make it across the straits to the shores of Kyushu contributed to the urbanization and industrialization of Fukuoka prefecture and beyond.

The travel of both Koreans and Japanese across the imperial border of the Tsushima Strait revealed contradictions and gaps in imperial Japan's labor policies. Such contradictions were especially apparent to those on the ground on either side of the maritime border of the Tsushima Strait. Japanese settlers and municipal planners both relied on "free" Korean labor for the development of urban infrastructure, but they also attempted to control and minimize its visible presence in the city. By the 1930s attempts were being made to force migration networks to conform to Japan's imperial borders and to a hierarchy of labor, with metropolitan Japanese at the top. Kim Sang-bin's rerouting by the authorities to Manchuria is one reflection of this.[3] At the local level, however, the logic behind such hierarchies and borders disappeared from view for both migrant laborers and their employers.

SOCIAL POLICY AT THE FRONT LINES OF EMPIRE

Changes in Korea's rural society and the commercialization of Korean agriculture, which especially affected its southern, rice-producing provinces, led to worsening conditions for both small owner-cultivators and the increasing numbers of tenant farmers by the mid-1920s. Japan's rice production promotion plan (begun in 1920 in the wake of rice riots in the Japanese home islands) had left the region especially exposed to global market forces and had left Korean farmers increasingly in debt. Agricultural prices in Japan began to fall in 1926, and this soon affected Korea too.[4] But the rise of a new class of agricultural wage earners had begun earlier: In the 1920s they could not all be absorbed by labor-intensive commercial agriculture, nor was there enough industry in Korea's cities. What had emerged was a group of what Soon-Won Park refers to as "floating" laborers, who moved between urban and rural work, and who "suffered from a vicious circle of extremely low wages, job insecurity, and long periods of unemployment," conditions that created, in the eyes of (mainly Japanese) employers, "an abundant, cheap, surplus pool of colonial labor."[5]

These people were part of a rural-to-urban shift that spanned the straits, a shift that for many was accompanied by a change from working as agricultural labor to working as industrializing labor. I use the term "industrializing" rather than "industrial" because, as Park and Ken Kawashima have pointed out, day labor (often in construction) rather than factory labor made up a large proportion of Korean workers' occupations in Korea and Japan.[6] Koreans worked as day laborers on both sides of the straits, constructing Pusan's port infrastructure and bridges and working in Fukuoka's coal mines, ports, quarries, and steel mills.

While imperial bureaucrats hoped the gaining of new colonies would help to solve the issues of overpopulation and rural poverty on the Japanese mainland, for them, the agglomeration of poor Koreans—and some Japanese— in port cities like Pusan was unanticipated and problematic. From both a public health perspective and a public image one, the colonial urban poor required an official response in order to maintain the assertion that Japan was a civilizing force on the peninsula. A city on the threshold of Japan's empire, Pusan experienced and reacted to "urban issues" that were also imperial ones, often ahead of both the colonial capital Keijō and the metropole itself.

So-called urban issues (J: *toshi mondai*) had first been identified in Japan's cities in the late 1910s and early '20s, when the sudden economic boom brought about by the First World War was followed by an equally sudden bust in April 1920. In Korea, certain mainland Japanese social policies were modified and implemented as part of Governor General Saitō's new Cultural Rule in the wake of the 1919 Independence Movement.[7] While the Great Kantō Earthquake of 1923, and the reconstruction of Tokyo that followed, intensified metropolitan debates on urban society in Japan and the growing gap between the city and countryside, the colony of Korea was seen as existing in rural opposition to urban Japan. Although social programs were no less needed in the cities of Japan's colonies, in the late 1920s Seoul-based colonial bureaucrats were focusing their efforts on tackling Korea's social problems at the source—in the countryside itself.[8] By this point, however, local efforts to deal with urban issues in Pusan had been long in place. Officials had made their own networks spanning the imperial border of the Tsushima Strait. For them, colonial Pusan's urbanization was a reality that could not be ignored.

Pusan's role as a gate between metropole and colony, at the edge of an imperial border, led to the converging of various flows of people within its urban areas. For authorities, this required cross-straits coordination at a regional level; indeed, it led to the conception of new regional networks by those attempting to control and co-opt the consequences of imperial urbanization.

Many so-called urban issues in Pusan were the result of the uneven mobility of Koreans and Japanese across the border of the Tsushima Strait. Poor Japanese, even those with little in the way of job prospects, could easily make it across the strait, while Koreans were subject to fluctuating border-crossing restrictions. This disparity led to Pusan becoming a "gathering place for surplus populations of the two nations."[9]

For Japanese from the provincial cities of northern Kyushu, Pusan must have seemed alluring in its proximity and familiarity, along with the advantages that their imperial privilege would have given them in traversing the strait. A description of the waiting room for the Kampu ferry from Shimonoseki to Pusan in Japanese poet Takahama Kyoshi's work "Chōsen" (Korea) gives us a sense of both the ease and lack of preparation with which, after annexation, Japanese people could cross the strait to Pusan:

> My wife looked to me with a troubled expression on her face. "Are all those people going to Pusan?" she asked, pointing at the people gathered there.
>
> "Of course. Everyone in this waiting room is a passenger on the Kampu ferry."
>
> "But those families with their packed lunches, and that woman carrying a baby on her own, why, they're dressed as though they're just headed out into the neighborhood."[10]

In this way Pusan became a "gathering place" for working-class migrants from Japan, especially the Tsushima Strait region, as well as for Koreans from surrounding areas, and municipal social work projects addressed both groups. The causes of Japanese settlers' precarity were similarly connected as well to Pusan's location—just a ferry ride away—but they show the difference that being Japanese could make to one's ability to traverse this threshold. Unlike the situation for Koreans, there were no restrictions on travel for Japanese crossing the Tsushima Strait.

The earliest municipal-level reaction to the increasing problem of urban housing and unemployment—among both Japanese and Koreans—was the creation, in 1923, of a municipal employment center only meters from the

Kampu ferry quay, along the main thoroughfare leading to Pusan Station. The center, and the hostel that opened the following year, was set up to deal with the ever-increasing numbers of unemployed members of the so-called proletariat class (*musan kaikyū*) after the end of the First World War. This was a practical step that outstripped the official central response by the Government General. While the governor general had set up a Korean social policy research group in Keijō in 1921, Pusan's municipal organization favored practical action over research.[11]

The center drew in both Japanese and Korean unemployed workers from a cross-straits hinterland. Although consistent yearly data is hard to come by for the 1920s, one report suggests the norm was around a 40 percent to 60 percent split between Japanese and Koreans. In 1926 the Pusan center registered over two thousand unemployed workers, with an almost even split between Japanese and Koreans. In 1926, while the overwhelming majority of Koreans registered at the center were from the immediate provinces around Pusan (over half from North and South Kyŏngsang provinces alone), the Japanese who sought employment at the center were from a wider range of prefectures—an indication, perhaps, of the inequality in mobility between the two groups. The most heavily represented areas were, however, the same three prefectures—Fukuoka, Yamaguchi, and Nagasaki—that made up the majority of Pusan's Japanese settler community. Most people, whether Japanese or Korean, who sought out work via the center were new to the city; in a survey of reasons for coming to the center, only 17 percent of the 2,267 who responded were previously living in Pusan. Forty-five percent had arrived in the city with no particular plans for employment.[12]

The center's data from the 1930s also suggests the impact of increased numbers of Korean tenant farmers forced to leave rural areas, as well as the demand for industrial labor in cities like Pusan. In the final extant set of data from the winter of 1934, the number of Koreans seeking work at the employment center was nearly double that of Japanese. In the 1930s the center also had a day labor exchange program that found work for over a thousand urban poor every month, but the data does not provide a breakdown by nationality for those offered employment in public works programs, which are discussed further below.[13]

The municipal hostel attached to the employment center was opened in 1924 in reaction to the large number of unemployed and unhoused workers who were driven to sleeping in the city's public spaces. From the perspective of sanitation and public health, the center's founders argued, it was impossible to ignore this situation. They created the facility with clean and cheap accommodation to "better the characters of these urban poor."[14] The workers who stayed in the hostel were of similar geographical makeup to those looking for employment: Most Koreans were from nearby South and North Kyŏngsang provinces, while the Japanese were from a wider range of prefectures, but with the highest numbers from the Tsushima Strait region. In 1927 there was a relatively even split overall between Japanese and Koreans.[15] Over the first four years of its opening, the center registered a total of six thousand Koreans and nine thousand Japanese.[16]

The programs organized by Pusan's municipal authorities and local groups in order to deal with the problems facing the city in the 1920s and '30s were developed not with other cities in Korea, but in coordination with those of cities on the other side of the strait, such as the key ports of Moji and Shimonoseki. These services were bankrolled by and benefited port bosses too. The Pusan Labor Mutual Aid Society (J: *Rōdō kyōsaikai*) was set up in 1923—three months before the municipal employment center. It offered similar programs and support and was funded by private donations as well as some financial aid from the Government General. The organization was run in coordination with the Moji Labor Mutual Aid Society. The president of Moji's society, Kimura Kiyoshi, also became president of Pusan's. Kimura, a cargo handling boss in Moji, had set up the mutual aid group to suppress the formation of a stevedore union.[17] Across the straits, the organizations provided a variety of services for "proletariat workers" (J: *musan kaikyū rōdōsha*), both Japanese and Korean, in the two linked port cities.[18]

Branches of central institutions were also set up that treated this cross-straits region as a single space and attempted to control the movement of labor across it. In 1926 the Western Employment and Advice Federation, "comprising the employment centers and advice bureaus in provinces south of Kyŏnggi and in Fukuoka and Yamaguchi prefectures," was set up to further coordinate labor supply and demand across the strait.[19] The center of gravity of this federation was on the metropolitan side, with its first meeting held in Shimonoseki's chamber of commerce, which was attended by police chiefs from Moji and Shimonoseki and social work bureaucrats from Pusan and Taegu city governments as well as South Kyŏngsang province. The aims of the federation included "improving the communication between employment centers across the Kanmon-Pusan region."[20]

Cross-strait social work connections included fact-finding missions. In 1926 Pusan dispatched municipal employee Kobayashi Umejirō to visit key cities in the Japanese metropole to report on their social facilities and programs, and his findings were published over four editions of the municipal magazine *The Fusan*.[21] Information on a sister organization in Shimonoseki was featured in the magazine's March 1930 edition. The center, known as the Shōwa-kan, was set up in 1928, five years after Pusan's employment center, and was run by a team of Korean and Japanese staff to help Koreans arriving in mainland Japan off the Kampu ferry who were looking for employment.[22] Like many social work programs, the Shōwa-kan was referred to as a Naisen Yūwa institution—supposedly working for the "reconciliation" of Koreans and Japanese. Those involved in its founding had visited schools and employment centers in Korea too.[23] In the creation of these organizations, we can see anxiety among regional bureaucrats and labor bosses, and their desire to control the movement of labor across the straits, resulting in the formation of regional networks that tracked and overlaid the hinterlands of labor migration.

Even after the opening of municipal and private hostels, Pusan's parks, waterfronts, temples, and shrines remained home to large numbers of unhoused people who had gathered in the city from other parts of the peninsula. In March 1927 *The Fusan* published an article on the subject entitled "Pusan Homeless Diary: An Excerpt." In contrast to other governmental reports on "social problems" in the city, which were reliant on statistics and conveyed little to their reader in the way of detail or context, this "diary" provides a close-up view of the lives of unhoused people in the urban spaces of colonial Pusan. The anonymous piece, thought to be the work of *The Fusan*'s editor Yoshida Masahiro, is a mixture of literary journalism and social documentary, and it stands out from the magazine's surrounding articles in both content and style.[24] Similar to George Orwell and his 1933 memoir *Down and Out in Paris and London*, Yoshida wrote the article after spending time observing such figures in the city.[25]

Yoshida's "Homeless Diary" exists as part of a journalistic tradition, which had emerged in the Meiji period, of documenting the effects of modern urban life on the lower classes. A new wave of such works became popular in metropolitan Japan after the Shōwa Financial Crisis of 1927 and the Great Depression.[26] This second wave of popular media and sociological research was characterized by its "grotesquerie"—"culture resulting from such deprivation as that endured by the homeless and by beggars."[27] The "Homeless Diary" came at the start of this second wave, out of a colonial city rather than the imperial capital, precipitated by the extremity of the urban unevenness found at this city at the edge of empire.[28]

The article traverses Pusan's margins to reveal an underside to the city's better documented modern spaces, focusing on unhoused people and rag-pickers (J: *monohiroi, borogirehiroi*) observed on the beach near the city's Taishō Park. It follows one of these groups in order to describe the day-to-day activities and economies of the ragpickers in detail. Yoshida contrasts their aimless presence in the park with the busy, modern lives of other city dwellers who use the space, combining the common tropes of modern urban life in the Japanese empire—the cinema, cafés, and strolling the streets—with Pusan-specific references. The difference between the unhoused people and other Pusan citizens, Yoshida argued, was instructive. He requested his readers—city dwellers themselves—not to "pass by so quickly as to forget what you've seen: Take a minute to observe the life of the homeless. There you will find many moral lessons."

At first the city appears to be a place where people eventually washed up after their meandering. As the diary unfolds, however, wider social and economic factors emerge. It becomes apparent that many of the unhoused people, "their faces pock-marked and swollen purple, their fingers, noses, and lips warped, their hair all fallen out," are suffering from leprosy.[29] Yoshida explains how "they came [to Pusan] hoping to enter Mackenzie Hospital, however, it being already full, they had no choice but to become vagrants, as no one was likely to give them employment either."[30] "Mackenzie Hospital" refers to the first leprosarium in Korea, opened in Pusan in 1909.[31]

In the same year that the "Homeless Diary" was published, the city announced new measures to deal with unhoused leprosy sufferers. Four hundred sufferers who were unable to find accommodation in Taegu and Pusan hospitals would be sent to the newly expanded Kogashima (Sorokdo) leper colony, on an island off the southwest coast of Korea. The following year, Mackenzie Hospital, unable to cope with the growing number of leprosy sufferers arriving, expelled those without severe symptoms from its care, no doubt increasing the number of unhoused people in Pusan.[32]

Pusan's urban margins were a gathering place for those with nowhere else to go and those attempting to reach the mainland. The city represented different things to those who ended up there: the hope of treatment, the hope of onward travel, and, for many, simply the last outpost of their wanderings, precipitated by the rural immiseration discussed above—a place where they could scrape together a living from the waste produced by a growing urban population. At the front lines of empire, in the city and the wider cross-straits region that these movements of people tied together, local policies often preempted colony-wide ones.

Social Policy and Urban Space

By the late 1920s there were many Japanese among the city's lower-middle and working classes, and many new would-be settlers, who, after coming to the city without money for lodgings or plans for employment, were forced to rely on the social services of the municipal authorities. However, the urban poor in Pusan who came under the gaze of local authorities (and therefore accounts of whom are preserved in the archives) were mainly Korean, especially those living in dwellings that the city authorities classed as illegal.

In 1928 the Pusan Social Work Research Group announced a plan for a new residential zone for the city's Korean poor, which would not "have a negative impact on the urban area" but still be "close enough to commute for work within the city."[33] There were also plans to set up bamboo-weaving and fan-making projects to give the poor an income. The suggested location for the residential zone was west and out of sight from the city center, over the brow of the hill from the Japanese cemetery. Each family was to be given a meager plot of land of around 10 *tsubo* (355 square feet) paid for by the city, upon which they would each build their own house. Although this project shows some improvement from the actions of the pre-annexation settler association, discussed in chapter 2, the municipality continued to use the language of urban development to justify the removal of Koreans from the center of Pusan.

The urban poor of Pusan came under the surveillance of the municipal authorities again at the end of 1928, when a survey was undertaken to assess their living conditions. The neighborhood divisions of the Pusan police department carried out the survey.[34] The results revealed that Pusan's urban poor were indeed overwhelmingly Korean. While there were no Japanese who could be defined by the term *saimin* (literally, deprived person or people) per se, there were some twenty Japanese households that had fallen into poverty as a result of changed circumstances. There were three neighborhoods in the Japanese colonial center of Pusan—Hon-machi, Ōkura-machi, and Fuhei-machi—that had no registered poor Korean households and only a handful of Japanese ones. We can surmise that the poor Japanese households in these generally prosperous settler neighborhoods had been reduced to their current circumstances due to a sudden death or illness of their family breadwinner rather than being in a precarious economic position to begin with.

Among Pusan's Korean population, there were 287 households—some 884 people—classified as being in poverty. These households were eligible to receive charitable donations (J: *jizenkin*) from the municipal government, and the Women's Association planned to donate money to them from their collection. The survey revealed a clustering of poor Koreans in certain areas, particularly newly expanded urban areas: on the island of Yŏngdo (Makinoshima), the Taesin (Daishin) neighborhood, and the hillside villages of the Yŏngju (Eishū) neighborhood. According to the survey this was also where those few Japanese households classified as living in poverty also called home: As discussed in chapter 2, they were popular areas for Japanese laborers and blue-collar workers. Looking at a map of the city from the time, the neatly arranged grid system of Daishin-machi's streets contrasts starkly with the piecemeal divisions of land within these blocks, suggesting a chaotic street-level reality of squalid and dense housing inhabited by the city's working poor—both Korean and Japanese.[35]

Both Korean and Japanese critics saw the city of Pusan as built on inequality. In a 1923 article in the Korean-language magazine *Kaebyŏk*, author Kim Ki-chŏn bemoaned how the city "is a den, a lair. It goes without saying that the Taesin neighborhood is a slum full of the poor, but the city is also a nest where the powerful Japanese cluster for the extraction of Korean wealth; a lair of the vain and idle, the ignorant rich; a cave where pathetic propertied Koreans lose their rights and money."[36] Kim continued, complaining how one of these "powerful Japanese," Hazama Fusatarō, "has more economic strength than all the 10031 Korean households in Pusan put together."[37] The socioeconomic range among Japanese settlers meant that there was resentment toward Pusan's major business figures, such as Hazama, from many Japanese as well as Koreans. Critiques by fellow Japanese also compared their taxes—with Hazama leading the pack—to illustrate their economic power. According to Inoue Kiyomaro's 1931 pamphlet, discussed in chapter 2, the taxes paid by Hazama alone were the equivalent of those paid by 2,995 Japanese individuals, or 699 Japanese households.[38]

Lower-class Japanese, however, who might have been frustrated or envious of the wealth and power of the city's settler elite, were still in a vastly superior socioeconomic position than the majority of Koreans in Pusan. And, in their complaints about the economic stranglehold that the settler elite held the city in, Japanese critiques make no mention of the poverty of the Korean inhabitants, which, as Kim pointed out as early as 1923, far outweighed the inequality between poorer Japanese and settler magnates. Although both Koreans and lower-class Japanese settlers had the same target in their sights, and despite the city's working poor living less segregated lives than we might have imagined, the subjectivity of their critiques and the relative extremity of their comparative positions were not the same.

Kim Ki-chŏn and Inoue Kiyomaro, both critics of Pusan's settler elites, argued that the same elites who had "made Pusan" into the supposedly enlightened modern city it had become were responsible for, and indeed profited from, the "dark" side of its development. This became more apparent in the 1930s, as increasing numbers of poor Korean inhabitants in Pusan lived in cramped conditions on the fringes of the city, often on land owned by Japanese landlords. But it was also visible in more high-profile urban development projects, such as the construction of the Makinoshima Bridge, which exemplified this intersection of settler elite interests, Korean labor, and urban development.

In 1930 plans finally crystallized for this long-called-for bridge that would link Pusan's southern harbor, near the new city hall, with the developing residential and industrial zone on the north coast of the island of Makinoshima (K: Yŏngdo). The bridge had been lobbied for by settler elites like Hazama and Ōike Chūsuke—both of whom owned land on Makinoshima that would dramatically increase in value with an improvement to the transportation infrastructure connecting the island to the city proper.[39]

After years of delay due to city budget limitations and disagreements over tenders, the construction of this new landmark bridge, "first in the Orient," was realized as part of the first Korea-wide public works plan.[40] The bridge was completed in 1934, and two years later the new city hall opened at its base. In the process of constructing both the bridge and the new city hall, Yongmi-san, the "dragon's tail" hill, was flattened. At the peak of the project, some five hundred of the city's unemployed Koreans were projected to be employed on it every day. The Pusan employment center even opened an office on-site to regulate the laborers involved.[41]

In the metropole, public works schemes employing out-of-work Korean laborers played a key role in building Japan's cities from the Great Depression onward.[42] Such plans were implemented in Korea too, with aims specific to colonial policies for the development of the colony and the circulation of Korean labor. The first round of poor relief public works projects (J: *kyūmin kyūsai doboku jigyō*) ran from 1931 to 1933, with a budget of some sixty-five million yen.[43] The project was framed as a way to distribute labor wages more "rationally" across the regions and help agricultural laborers recover from bad harvests and the economic depression.[44] This attempt combined earlier policies aimed at the countryside and rural populations with the colonial government's new focus: industrialization.

Facilitating Korea's industrialization was a secondary but large-scale aim of the Government General's public works project, mainly by improving transport routes. These projects were a boon for big business and cities like Pusan, far more so than offering real relief for the individuals employed by the works schemes.[45] In Pusan, unemployed laborers, some from the city and others from the surrounding countryside, were employed in infrastructure projects that would increase the port city's standing as a gateway of empire. Laborers on these projects were paid through a subcontractor, who often deducted fees for food and as "forced savings." In the case of Pusan, discontent with these working conditions reached a breaking point in June 1932, when workers went on strike to protest their meager wages—around thirty to forty *sen* a day after deductions by subcontractors.[46] These approaches to controlling Korean labor, taken by authorities on either side of the strait, would form the roots of patterns of exploitation and labor movement that were strengthened during the wartime years, and in some cases existed even into the postwar era.

The Makinoshima Bridge project shows how, by the early 1930s, the relationship between urban growth, poverty, and development in Pusan had grown close—almost to the point of symbiosis. In municipal and settler publications Koreans are rarely mentioned as anything but an impediment to the development of a sanitary and modern city, but evidence of their key role as mobilized labor can be found in the photographs of the city's bridges, dams, and landfill sites, manned and constructed by colonial subjects for the benefit of the local settler elite and the imperial expansion they envisioned.

The urban poor in Pusan were simultaneously wanted and unwanted. Kept close enough to remain a source of labor but removed from land within the urban center, they were treated with ambivalence by the authorities and settler elite and were dealt with in ways that required close ties with those cities across the straits facing similar problems, such as Moji and Shimonoseki. Since 1927 there had been local attempts to redirect those not allowed to cross to Japan to work on construction projects in the city.[47] One of the aims of the Government General's poor relief public works schemes was to reduce the number of unemployed Koreans crossing to Japan using methods such as "forced saving" to keep them tied to work in Korea.[48]

However, for many of the itinerant Koreans caught up in the labor schemes of Pusan's local government, the city was a waystation, with their ultimate destination being industrial Japan. By crossing the imperial border, they hoped to sell their labor for a higher price in the metropole. From the end of the 1920s into the 1930s, as the imperial state strengthened its restrictions on travel by Korean laborers to the home islands of Japan, many of those without permission to travel had to rely on the help of "brokers" (K: *ppurokŏ*) who promised to smuggle them over the strait in journeys that often resulted in arrest, deportation, and occasionally drowning and death. Following these Koreans across the maritime border, to the industrializing port cities and coalfields of Fukuoka, reveals their roles in constructing this imperial region.

ROUGH CROSSINGS: BROKERS, BORDERS, AND LABOR CONTROL

As seen through their early funding of a municipal hostel and employment center, the municipal government in Pusan keenly understood the link between imperial migration and the problem of urban homelessness. The ferry and rail links that connected Pusan to the metropole and to the rest of Korea and beyond had both pros and cons for the city's planners and settler elites. Many Koreans who came to Pusan or other port cities in the hope of work or transit to the Japanese mainland lacked the means or documentation necessary to gain passage and found their onward journey barred. For poor Koreans Pusan could be a site of purgatory, a liminal space where they were forced to remain if they lacked the ticket fee, language ability, or employment certification to travel to the Japanese metropole.

From 1919 to 1923 the Japanese government required would-be Korean migrants to carry a crossing permit (J: *tokō shōmeisho*) until they imposed a blanket ban on travel, active from September until June 1924, in the wake of the Great Kantō Earthquake of 1923. Then, from October 1925, new preventative measures were put in place for the "protection" (J: *hogo*) of Korean workers.[49] These new regulations, just like those before them, appear to have had little effect in stemming the increasing numbers of Koreans who made it across the strait to Japan. The inability of the Japanese government to affect the overall trends of population movement within its empire is apparent in the figures: No year between 1919 and 1927 saw a decrease in the net number of Koreans who traveled to the metropole.[50]

Not included in the official statistics were the increasing numbers of Koreans who resorted to traveling across the Tsushima Strait in boats run by gangs of people smugglers. As Tonomura Masaru points out, there was no law against Korean travel throughout the Japanese empire, so contemporary discussion of "illegal" immigration, while common, was inaccurate.[51] As early as 1923, the Fukuoka-based newspaper *Kyūshū Nippō* had discussed how "recently crossing to the *naichi* [mainland] has become so difficult that these brokers, promising Koreans an easy way to get across, have been extorting huge sums of money from them, then sending them across to Yamaguchi or Fukuoka prefectures in tiny boats."[52]

The shifting requirements of travel regulations between Japan and Korea—across a semiporous border that was easier for some imperial subjects to traverse than others—highlight the contingent nature of many imperial migration policies. These changing regulations have been studied as a barometer for attitudes toward Koreans within mainland Japan, as well as a reflection of the metropole's changing labor market.[53] For the Government General in Korea, Tonomura posits that it was not in their best interests to enforce these regulations too strictly, as it could have led to unrest on the peninsula, with anger directed toward the colonial rulers.[54] At the local level, Pusan's metropolitan government had to adapt its own institutions in order to both complement and supplement the responses of the Government General and central Japanese government.

After October 1925 new regulations meant that any Korean attempting to cross without confirmed employment, the ability to speak Japanese, and one hundred yen in savings would be prevented from traveling to the metropole. Such regulations might have prevented Koreans from making the journey once they reached the final barrier of checks between them and Japan, but it seemed to have no effect on those coming to Pusan to try their luck at crossing. This meant that the city's municipal authorities were forced to come up with their own policies in order to supposedly protect Korean laborers by preemptively stopping them from coming to Pusan. If that failed, they implemented policies that would send them back to their villages instead of them remaining in the city after their hopes of migration to the metropole were dashed. And, as seen in the previous section, in 1930s Pusan, if all these measures failed, Koreans who had left their villages and had nothing else to sell but their labor power were mobilized into laboring on public works projects.

In early September of 1925, local authorities first carried out a survey of Koreans leaving for Japan. Of the one thousand Koreans they surveyed, 544 of them had no confirmed employment in Japan, and 520 of them had only three yen of savings. As a matter of "protection," migrants who were leaving Korea as an "experiment" or in response to calls for labor were prevented from traveling, had their ticket fees returned, and were sent back to their hometowns. New rules and regulations, as well as fines, were put in place to deal with recruitment activities for jobs in the metropole.

Pusan was the last chance to stop the migration of Koreans with little money or job prospects, but local police stations in rural areas and towns along the train line were also engaged in preventative activities to stop would-be migrants before they swelled the ranks of unemployed Koreans in the peninsula's port cities. Urata Shōzo, editor of *The Fusan*, remarked acidly that "originally, after annexation, Koreans should have been able to travel freely to the metropole, and except for circumstances like after the Kantō Earthquake, stopping their travel lacks logic, and seems to be clearly a problem resulting from Japanese control of Korea."[55] From the perspective of the local authorities in Pusan, they were being forced to deal with problems created by the ambiguous nature of the imperial border—issues that, as noted above, neither the central nor colonial government seemed capable of addressing.

The role of local police in attempting to prevent laborers from traveling from rural areas was vital to this attempt to tackle migration at its roots, as was the involvement of the harbor police (J: *suijōsho*), who set up an office at the foot of the pier and expanded their staff to carry out checks on those leaving on the evening and morning ferries to the mainland. The new checks began to be carried out on October 7, 1925. Figures from 1925 to 1927 suggest that over three thousand Koreans were rejected from travel to the mainland every month—a third of the total number of crossings to the mainland in the same time span.[56]

Such figures reveal both the pressures to leave Korea for mainland Japan and the issues that this population increase—a hundred or so every day—would have posed to the city of Pusan if it went unaddressed by local authorities. Koreans from rural areas were often known to sell everything before trying to cross to Japan. Since they had nowhere to return, authorities feared they would remain in Pusan, attempting to make the crossing by any means possible.[57]

In 1927 the Pusan harbor police surveyed Koreans who were attempting to cross the Tsushima Strait to the Japanese metropole, as well as those coming back to Korea from Japan. The figures for travel between Japan and Korea by both Koreans and Japanese shed light on the social and economic situations of both places. Most Koreans traveling to the Japanese metropole were "free laborers." The report's authors argued that they might become comparable, in their effect on the labor front (J: *rōdō sensen*) and harm to Japanese laborers, to "those *shina* laborers in Korea."[58] Such comments, using the offensive term *shina* for Chinese, articulate a hierarchy of labor across Japan's sphere of influence that later policies would try to control and redistribute.[59]

In the survey from 1927, South Kyŏngsang province accounted for some 40 percent of all Koreans crossing the strait to Japan. Also heavily represented were migrants from Kyŏnggi province, as well as North Kyŏngsang and South Chŏlla, key rice-producing provinces along with South Kyŏngsang. The state of agriculture, geographic proximity, and regional transport links all played a key role in the likelihood of Koreans leaving home for the metropole. The coastal cities of South Chŏlla were connected by local shipping routes to Pusan, and Kyŏnggi (the province surrounding Seoul) was connected by the Seoul–Pusan railroad.[60]

Of those Koreans leaving from South Kyŏngsang province for Japan, as well as those arriving back to Pusan from the metropole, the statistics show that even within the province, those living closer to the port of Pusan were more likely to attempt to make the crossing. The province's largest city, Pusan, was both a site of employment for rural migrants themselves and a gateway for the movement of other rural migrants to the metropole. Merely viewing the migration that took place across the Tsushima Strait from the national level obscures these local mechanisms at play. Until the 1930s, when large numbers headed beyond the borders of Korea, or into its industrializing regions mainly clustered in the north, the movements of wage laborers have been characterized as mainly short distance and "intra-provincial."[61] However, we could interpret the statistics above as showing that, for Koreans in the regions around Pusan, short-distance movement for work might also include crossing the Tsushima Straits—or at least attempting to.

Brokers and Unofficial Crossings

Despite local preventative efforts in the late 1920s, the effect of Japan's economic depression on Korea's rural society in the 1930s meant that the numbers of migrants crossing from Pusan did not go down but in fact continued to increase by astonishing amounts.[62] Even a government publication like *The Fusan* admitted that "a side product of stricter policies was the so-called 'stowaway,' causing no small problem for those attempting to control the situation in their destination prefectures in the metropole: Yamaguchi, Fukuoka, and Nagasaki."[63] The underground system that existed to subvert the increasingly strict "proper crossing" system contained unlicensed recruiters for jobs in the metropole, underground guesthouses (J: *aku ryokan*), brokers, scalpers, and touts.

These networks, like the routes they were smuggling people across, spanned Japan and Korea. Fines and imprisonment for involvement in these activities in the two years of the new program appear limited: 169 cases of fines, amounting to a total of 8,096 yen (roughly 47 yen per case), and some 144 people detained.[64] When these brokers could be charging anything up to around twenty or thirty yen per person to smuggle Koreans to the mainland, it seems unlikely these fines would do much to put them off such a lucrative business.

By the early 1930s, for Japanese on the other side of the strait, accounts of such "illegal" crossings formed an important part of how Koreans were constructed in the imperial gaze. Newspaper reports on the topic highlighted the seemingly ever-increasing numbers of migrants reaching the coasts of Kyushu. These reports on Koreans smuggled across the Tsushima Strait also provide crucial details that fill in the space of the maritime border, which is often little more than a footnote in work on (authorized) travel between the metropole and colony. They emphasize the need to look holistically at travel to Japan by both authorized and unauthorized methods as constituent parts of the staggered process of imperial urbanization.

The waters of the Tsushima Strait were dangerous, notoriously rough in winter, even for ferry steamers. Unauthorized immigrants traversed the choppy seas in motorboats manned by brokers who extracted from them amounts of money often much more than the cost of the Pusan–Shimonoseki ferry, but with no questions asked. A report from the *Fukuoka Nichi Nichi Shinbun* (*Fukunichi*) on January 7, 1930, describes the discovery of a particularly large group of Korean immigrants on the coastline encircling Hakata's harbor:

> The Hakozaki police office has learned that the Koreans are all peasants and were taken advantage of by so-called "smuggling brokers." They set off from Pusan harbor in a motorboat around midnight on the fourth of January and came ashore at Saitozaki around eleven p.m. on the same day. They were swindled out of anything from three yen and fifty sen to twenty yen and are all now penniless, while the motorboat appears to have gone missing. After investigation the Koreans were sent back on the morning of the sixth, on Kitakyūshū Shipping Company's *Chōhaku Maru*.[65]

Days later another group of Korean immigrants came ashore in the port of Shimonoseki, having made a perilous journey across the strait in a tiny motorboat. Responsibility for smuggling these stowaways was apportioned to "dishonest sailors, preying on ignorant Koreans trying at all costs to reach the mainland."[66] The group of exhausted Koreans was promptly taken into custody on suspicion of being "illegal immigrants."

> On the night of the fifth, two or three sailors wearing padded kimono jackets arrived in Taesŏng village, Ch'ŏngdo county, on the border of North and South Kyŏngsang provinces and tricked locals into stowing away to reach Japan. One of these locals, barber O Pu-kŭn, twenty-four, told how around thirty people were tricked into paying ten yen each to get to Shimonoseki, a journey you can make for four yen.[67]

The reporter's inability to comprehend why these rural Koreans were compelled to make this journey for much more than the price they would pay to take the Kampu ferry shows the uneven experiences of Japanese and Koreans crossing the strait. With the incident ascribed to ignorance on the part of the "peasants" and the power of the smooth-talking sailors, these reports reinforced Japanese readers' common stereotypes about Koreans from their position of imperial privilege on the other side of the strait.

These journeys reached their peak in winter, when the waters were at their roughest. The agricultural offseason or spring famine (K: *ch'un'gunggi*) between January and April, when rice supplies from the previous harvest had run out, was the busiest time of year for both brokers and coast guards. Years with bad harvests also increased the rural-to-urban flow in the region.[68] One 1940 newspaper report described heartless touts "flooding into" rural villages during the spring famine trying to drum up business. The report was prompted by the deaths of over a hundred people in an overturned smuggling boat, with the drowned "countrymen" (K: *tong'po*) described as restless "water spirits" (K: *mulgwisin*).[69]

The maritime border of Tsushima Strait became crisscrossed by official and unofficial routes, as well as networks of imperial surveillance that monitored its waters. Travel into Japan across the straits and from Shanghai had been surveilled since the 1920s, not just for "illegal" Korean migration, but also for the movements of suspected anarchists, socialists, and communists, exiled independence activists, and smugglers and traffickers.[70] The increasing numbers of these unofficial migrants in the 1930s spurred further integration between Kyushu and South Kyŏngsang province in the form of cooperation between the coast guards on either side of the strait.[71] The cross-strait ferries, while also acting as vital conduits of labor between the Japanese mainland and Korean peninsula, were also responsible for deporting immigrants and former stowaways back to their homeland.

These unofficial border crossings remind us how tightly the processes of colonization and urbanization were linked in imperial Japan. They serve as physical evidence of the effects Japan and its colonies' proximity had on urbanizing the border region. Even the French Empire's *port des colonies*, Marseille, was around twenty-four hours by boat from Tunis or Algiers. The port cities of Pusan and Fukuoka were only eight hours apart.[72] The economic and social pressures that led to Koreans' decisions to stow away, and the changing options that were open to them, are crucial pieces of evidence for understanding the consequences of colonization on this region of empire. Tracing their routes and changing demographics allows us to map the human geographies of urbanization and migration that existed outside of official purview.

Labor Mobility and Labor Control

From 1932, Korean police departments and the Pusan harbor police were no longer able to use their discretion to decide how strictly to enforce the new rules on checks for those applying for a travel permit; they now had to double-check with authorities in the home islands to make sure offers of jobs were legitimate. This led to a significant drop in the number of migrants crossing via the Kampu ferry and an increased demand for the services of brokers. It also changed the demographics of those who resorted to such measures. As Tonomura Masaru argues, there was a significant increase in demand by those with money and some level of Japanese-language ability who had previously been able to meet government requirements to cross.[73]

Japan's central government immigration and border control policies were, as seen above, subject to alteration in response to real or perceived threats to the metropolitan labor market and to public order. They also were often out of step with the desires or policies of the Government General in Korea, and with local government in both Korea and the metropole. As one of the prefectures closest to the southern coast of Korea, Fukuoka bore the brunt of costs for repatriating those Koreans caught trying to enter Japan "illegally."

In March 1939 officials in Fukuoka held a roundtable meeting, presided over by the prosecutor's office of the Fukuoka regional court, to discuss issues connected to Koreans in Fukuoka prefecture, including the gap between local issues and central policy. The numbers of Koreans attempting to smuggle themselves into the Japanese metropole had increased during the 1930s, due in part to increasingly strict border policies. Fukuokan officials, however, faced with a shortage of labor following the outbreak of war with China in 1937, complained that sending Koreans back was not only expensive but also a "waste" of good labor (*mottainai*).[74]

The official policy of Fukuoka prefecture with regards to migration of Koreans could not differ from the central government policy, which was to create an empire-wide hierarchy of labor and to prevent, to the extent they could, Korean laborers from entering Japan without evidence of employment in the metropole. However, officials were aware of the policy's shortcomings, both with regards to the needs of regional industries and its failure to take a holistic approach to the movement of labor throughout the empire.

By 1939 the industrialization of the Korean peninsula, especially in the north, meant that there were labor shortages in the colony as well as in the industrial regions of Kyushu. First to speak at the roundtable meeting, Gotō Kichigorō, head of the Fukuoka prefecture special police, pointed out that it would be better for Koreans from the southern part of Korea, who made up the majority of those attempting to come to the metropole, to go north instead. The Korean Government General was attempting to deal with the lack of enthusiasm for migration to the northern provinces and with the often-dire consequences of Koreans attempting to reach the metropole.

According to Gotō, Korean stowaways who were caught by *naichi* authorities and sent back to the peninsula, numbering some two hundred every month by the end of the 1930s, were paying extortionate sums of money to brokers. To pay the brokers' fees (which had risen to some thirty or forty yen by 1939) and raise money to start a new life in Japan, poor rural Koreans would have to sell their houses, fields, or other lands. When these people were sent back to Korea by the metropolitan authorities, they were now destitute, with nowhere to go, which in turn added to the number of Koreans leaving rural areas for the growing slums on the margins of the peninsula's cities.[75] Gotō's comments about Koreans selling houses or land to afford the brokers' fees supports Tonomura's claim above about the changing demographics of those crossing the straits.

Industrialists and factory owners in Fukuoka prefecture whose businesses were booming in the wake of the outbreak of war with China in 1937 were short of labor, yet many also remarked on their inability to pick and choose between workers and to stop "good" workers from leaving for positions with better pay or conditions. Japanese employers, and their Korean laborers, were aware of the weakness of their position, which resulted in increased wages, especially among the longshoremen working in the ports of Wakamatsu and Moji, who were in high demand due to military supply contracts.

In an inversion of the situation in Pusan, where so-called "floating" or "surplus" labor was both wanted and unwanted by employers and authorities, and Koreans who sold their labor were left in a marginalized limbo, employers in Fukuoka discussed the need for "fixing" labor in one place and stopping demands for increased pay in terms of *naichi dōka* (assimilation). "Good" Korean workers were those who had "set down roots" (*dochaku senjin*), not those who would uproot their family to move from Kyushu to Hokkaido for better pay and working conditions. More harmony programs (*kyōwa jigyō*) were needed, employers suggested, in order to instill a Japanese work ethic into Korean laborers and increase their productivity.[76]

These complaints about worker mobility echoed grievances that had been made in earlier decades with regard to metropolitan labor in industrial Japan. High turnover rates had troubled managers in factories and shipyards since the late nineteenth century, and, as the longshoremen bosses learned in the late 1930s, the problem increased in times of war and uncertainty. What was different in the case of labor mobility in the home islands was the nature of the policies chosen to address it, such as promotions and bonuses based on seniority. These policies reveal that *Japanese* laborer mobility had been just as much a problem for managers only a decade or so earlier, but, in the intervening decade, these managers came to view loyalty to one's job as an innately Japanese characteristic.[77]

In the case of migrant Korean labor in the late 1930s, employers argued that what was really needed was "a national long-term system" that would allow only the "good" laborers to stay and would send the "bad" ones back.[78] The desire to tie Korean laborers to their jobs was a perennial one for Japanese employers, whether in the metropole or colony. As seen in the public works schemes in Pusan, Korean laborers were able to be employed by such schemes for the construction of imperial infrastructure due to their movement into Pusan but were then often coerced into "stable" employment through the withholding of wages.[79] This method mutated into the forced labor systems of the war period, when laborers brought to Japan from Korea would see their (nominal) wages be paid into "savings" accounts that they did not have access to.

Forced saving was not only a common method of "fixing" Korean labor used by both colonial and metropolitan employers, but it was also connected to the common racist stereotype of Koreans being "irresponsible" savers. In accounts of "model" Korean workers in Fukuoka prefecture, one key characteristic was their dedication to saving money.[80] These solutions to the mobility and "bad" traits of Korean laborers were significant precursors to the wartime solution to Japan's labor problems. In Fukuoka prefecture, many (nationalized) coal mining companies in Chikuhō used these methods, and worse, to control Korean labor between 1939 and 1945, when the Kampu ferries became vehicles for transporting forced laborers from the peninsula to Kyushu's factories and coal mines.[81] These structures continued to play a role in processes of decolonization too.

The forces that propelled the rural-urban movement of populations within and through the Japanese empire were subject to logics of capitalism and imperialism—which were often in tension with each other. Migrant labor had to be readily available but also dismissible. This was a different proposition in Fukuoka than in Pusan. Although both places were rungs on a hierarchical ladder of destinations for migrant labor, they could not be articulated as such. Special Police Chief Gotō summed up the problems with the metropolitan and local attitudes toward immigration and industrial labor thus:

> [The opinion] that it would be best to send back the bad Koreans has strong opposition from the authorities in Korea. Metropole or Korea, both are the same Japan, so "sending back" means sending them back to Japan. As a rule we should not be returning them. "Sending them back" only amounts to banishing them to another part of the same jurisdiction. For the police authorities this would be a dereliction of duty, and we should refrain from doing it.[82]

Gotō here reveals the contradictions in attempting to create an even supply of labor across an uneven imperial domain. Empire-wide policies dictated by the central government were often not only ideological rather than practical, but also ran counter to policies for Korean industrialization and demands for labor at the regional level.

The perceived mobility of Koreans was seen as a problem, then, not just for authorities like those in Pusan, who were attempting to control flows of labor across the empire, but also for authorities and employers—increasingly working together—in their attempts to monitor and assimilate communities of Korean laborers within the metropole. The Koreans of Fukuoka prefecture, who came predominantly from the rural regions around Pusan, migrated to the Kitakyūshū region in the north of the prefecture over several decades. A study of the formation of these communities reveals important links between urban Korean labor, its local organization, and the nature of Korean society in Fukuoka.

THE KOREAN MINORITY IN INDUSTRIAL FUKUOKA

Imperial migration fueled urban growth and industrialization across Japan's empire. Both the settler populations of Japanese in Korea and migrant Koreans in Japan were concentrated in urban areas that acted as hubs for imperial networks of transport and labor. While Japanese settlers—elites and blue-collar workers—had built and expanded urban areas in Korea's open ports and key cities from the 1870s, Koreans had been involved in Japan's industrialization from the early years of the twentieth century, mainly in Western Japan. Early migrants from Korea became inhabitants of urbanizing, industrial environments that would have been as unfamiliar to the large majority of Japanese people in the prewar period as they were to these rural Koreans. In Fukuoka, migrant labor—Korean and Japanese—played a key role in the growth of the prefecture's industrial areas and in its incorporation within a wider imperial region. Just as the presence of transitory migrants in Pusan points to the city's liminal position in this imperial region, the lives of Korean laborers who worked and lived in the coal towns of Chikuhō and worker cities (*rōdō toshi*) of Kitakyūshū—two key urban and industrial environments in Fukuoka—point to its long history as a destination for Korean migration as both a regional and imperial phenomenon.[83]

Sea routes across the straits—official and otherwise—connected Pusan and its rural hinterland to Shimonoseki and Fukuoka. Immigrant communities in any country have demographics that reflect the nature of the networks that brought them. A significant proportion of Osaka Koreans, for example, came from the island of Cheju, due in large part to a direct ferry, the *Kimigayo Maru*, that linked the Korean island and the Japanese city from 1922.[84] These geographies and networks are, once constructed, self-reinforcing. However, geographical factors alone cannot explain the colonial Korean presence in Fukuoka. Without demand for labor in the region, most migrants would have traveled on to other urban, industrial areas, such as Hyōgo, Osaka, and Tokyo.

The Kitakyūshū region needed workers for its mines, ports, and factories and drew its labor from surrounding regions, both colonial and domestic. Indeed, the migration patterns of Koreans to the region are similar to that of rural-urban migration patterns of Japanese from within Kyushu to its industrial areas.[85] For Koreans from the southernmost provinces of the peninsula, Kitakyūshū was not just the first port of call after disembarking from the Kampu ferry but a destination for laborers itself. Between 1920 and 1940 around three-quarters of all Koreans living in Fukuoka prefecture came from North and South Kyŏngsang provinces combined.[86]

In some ways, then, southern Korea can be understood as existing within a watershed of labor for the industrial regions of Kitakyūshū, but there are limitations to this vision. The ease of cross-straits travel that is suggested by descriptions of colonial as well as postwar Zainichi Koreans as living "cross-border lives" suggests an uncritical echoing of imperial sources.[87] Despite the difficulties faced by Korean laborers both entering and leaving Japan, their movement was often depicted in newspapers and reports as a "flood," and, ironically, their increasing numbers were described as akin to "colonization." Descriptions in Japanese reports on Korean migration that paint the Kitakyūshū region as a "virgin colony" for the Korean laborer highlight the paranoid and racist discourses that have long permeated the subject of migration.[88]

Crossings of the imperial border were policed, making travel across it the site of racial tensions and discrimination, on both the docks and the ferries themselves.[89] Policing also led to the loss of predominantly Korean lives, those who drowned in their attempts to circumvent imperial controls. Furthermore, mobility was connected to financial and educational capital. Most firsthand accounts available are by Korean students and intellectuals who memorialized their trips across the strait. For laborers, returning home on the Kampu ferry was often a last resort after suffering illness or injury, and many had to look to their fellow Koreans or to local aid groups for financial assistance in order to make the journey.[90]

After Japan's invasion of China in 1937, bosses of mines and other industries in the home islands had called for a relaxation of the strict border policy that had been in place since 1932. For the next five years increasingly violent and forceful measures were put in place to ensure a supply of labor to key industries in the metropole.[91] In the summer of 1939, the first plan for labor mobilization from Korea to Japan was implemented. From this date, under increasing levels of duress and violence, Koreans were brought to Fukuoka to work in its industries and mines as "group" labor.[92] The Korean population in Fukuoka prefecture nearly tripled from 1935 to 1940, from some 42,000 to 116,000 people.

Understandably, much scholarly work on Koreans in Kyushu to date focuses on their labor, especially in the mines of the Chikuhō region of Fukuoka, and especially during the period between 1939 and 1945.[93] However, it is important to understand this later, forced movement of labor from Korea to industrial Fukuoka within a longer history of migration and labor in the region, and to connect it, as I do in later chapters, to the postwar history of the Tsushima Strait region. In this chapter I focus on exploring the geographic, spatial, and social aspects of the large presence of Koreans in industrial Fukuoka prior to the beginning of labor mobilization in 1939, and what their presence tells us about processes of colonial migration and urbanization across the strait.[94]

Korean Communities and Kitakyūshū's Urban Development

Although Fukuoka, and Kyushu more widely, was historically the destination for the first Korean labor migration in Japan in the late nineteenth century, after annexation it began to be overtaken by other urban regions such as Osaka and Tokyo. However, the numbers of Korean immigrants arriving and living in the region continued to increase year after year. By 1918 Kyushu and Yamaguchi prefecture accounted for some 30 percent of the total Korean migrant population in Japan.[95]

From the onset of the economic depression that occurred after the end of the First World War, Japanese workers at the Yawata Imperial Steelworks were kept informed by their union newspaper of the rising number of Korean laborers arriving by ferry, similar to the accounts of the stowaways above, which became almost a daily bulletin in Fukuoka's local newspapers. According to a 1921 article in the paper of the in-house union at Yawata, "90 percent of Korean workers [senjin rōdōsha] arriving in Moji are headed for Yahata."[96] At that time Yahata was home to the largest population of Koreans in the Japanese home islands, and to Fukuoka prefecture's first social work institution, Maruyama Gakuin, a school and boarding house for Koreans set up in 1912.[97] Nearly half of the city's Korean population, some eight or nine hundred people, lived outside the city limits in what the Yawata newspaper called "a Korean slum."[98] As Ken Kawashima has shown, discrimination against Koreans in Japan's housing markets became commonplace in the

1920s, and these laboring communities were increasingly pushed to the margins of the metropole's expanding urban areas.[99] Over the next decade or so the situation in Yahata would be replicated across industrial Japan.

After the post-1919 restrictions on Koreans traveling to the metropole were briefly lifted in 1922, migration increased rapidly, even though, as the paper remarked, the postwar slump meant that "the metropole is suffering economically too." By 1923 the Kitakyūshū area, in the eyes of Japanese laborers, was overrun: "In Moji now it's hard to find any Japanese workers, so overwhelmed is it with Koreans."[100] The anxieties were clear: Koreans were coming to the region, disrupting the local labor market by taking Japanese workers' jobs, and altering the local urban environment. Although Japan's imperial growth relied on the cheap labor of its colonized populations, their presence in the metropole was thought to require government intervention to avoid "destabilizing" local labor markets and urban areas. Just like Pusan's authorities, Fukuoka's local governments were at the front lines of dealing with and implementing such policies.

The majority of Koreans living in Kyushu in the prewar period lived in Fukuoka prefecture, and of these nearly 80 percent lived in the Kitakyūshū five-cities area (Kitakyūshū goshi).[101] While Fukuoka city acted as the region's administrative, cultural, and educational center, the Kitakyūshū region was its industrial base. Its cities bled into each other in a winding industrial belt that spread from the waterfront and climbed up mountainsides, from the redbrick warehouses and factories of Moji at the northeastern tip of Kyushu to the coaling ports of Wakamatsu and Tobata on either side of Dōkai Bay. The steelworks at Yahata faced the water too: Coal that had been dug from the mines of Chikuhō was delivered to both the steelworks and the ports via rail (see map 4). Working along all stages of these processes were large numbers of Koreans.

Korean laborers not only worked across this urban region; they also helped to construct it. Koreans worked in construction in Fukuoka prefecture from as early as 1908, when twenty Koreans were employed on railroad construction near Yame, in the south of Fukuoka prefecture.[102] Unlike the castle towns of Kokura and Fukuoka, Moji and Yahata were newly urbanizing areas. From the mid-1930s until the evacuations and bombings of the war's end, Yahata was the second largest city in Fukuoka prefecture, and briefly Kyūshū, growing larger than Nagasaki.[103] Some Koreans even lived in houseboats in the ports they were building or in makeshift barracks on the landfill sites where they worked.[104] Their work was dangerous: Some of the only times

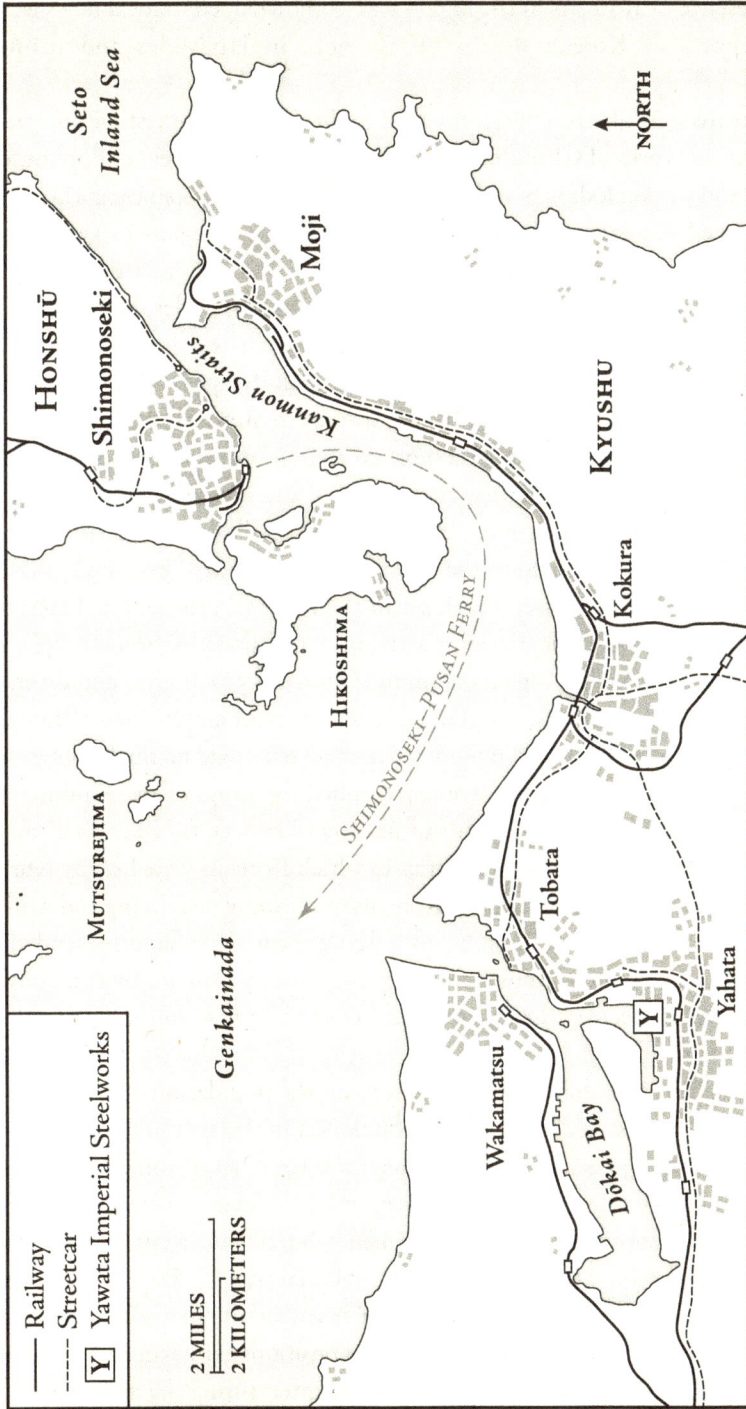

MAP 4. The Kitakyūshū five-cities industrial region, ca. 1933. Credit: Kate Blackmer.

the presence of Koreans in the region was acknowledged in local news were the reports of Korean deaths on the job, in landslides and tunnel collapses.[105]

Koreans were also heavily represented in the coalfields, limestone quarries, and cement works of Chikuhō and their self-contained system of flophouses (naya) and worker lodgings and canteens (hanba). While Japanese authorities categorized Koreans in Yahata and the Kitakyūshū region in general as "urban" and those working in mining towns and villages as "rural" (inaka) in order to distinguish between differences in their lifestyles, I would argue that the mining town was just as much a site of urban, imperial modernity as industrial Yahata. Although these "operational landscapes" might not be the modern environment that most readily springs to mind when one thinks of prewar Japanese urban life, they comprised an important portion of it, fueled others, and were representative of the type of uneven conditions of urban modernity experienced by most inhabitants of the Japanese empire. Urban modernity was not limited to the café waitress or modern boys and girls; it encompassed the unhoused ragpicker in the city park, the colonial factory worker in a flophouse, the stowaway arriving on the shores of the metropole.[106]

From the 1920s the Korean community in Kitakyūshū grew and diversified in terms of both its demographics and nature of employment. Though the majority of Koreans throughout this period remained manual laborers in the docks and factories, some workers climbed the rungs of these industries to become labor bosses and heads of mining camps, or they ran their own businesses connected to the industries in which Koreans were heavily represented. In the 1920s most migrant Koreans were young men living and working in mining camps or in cramped lodgings near their factories, and the ratio of Korean men to women was 16 men for every woman. By 1930, however, this ratio decreased to 2.5 to 1, and in 1940 it was around 1.5 men for every woman.[107]

While historians have used the increase of the population of women as a marker for how "stable" the Korean population in the area became over the two decades, the presence of these Korean women deserves our attention for more than just its statistical importance, and they deserve their own historical narratives beyond those of Korean men, whose histories, as Sonia Ryang argues, have become the sole legitimate "colonial past."[108] For these women life was no more "stable" than it was for many of the men. Indeed, some Korean women worked the same day-laborer positions as men in Kitakyūshū's ports.[109] Some earned money by serving and entertaining the male working populations of the region in lodging houses, restaurants, and bars, often with connections to the sex trade.[110]

These jobs could be dangerous too: Doubly objectified in sensational news reports of the time—as women and as Korean—those Korean women who worked in the service trade were also often the victims of sexual and other forms of violence at the hands of Japanese and Korean men. Newspaper reports from the time (which must be viewed with caution due to their propensity to focus on and sensationalize cases of Korean crime) discuss rape, abduction, and attacks on Korean women, both those working in Fukuoka and those trafficked across the strait against their will.

Colonial Korean communities in Japan were formed through the labor of Korean women, and Korean men—along with Japanese men—subjugated Korean women even as they were being subjugated themselves. Korean women were trafficked to work in so-called Korean restaurants (J: *Chōsen ryōriten*) that sprung up in mining towns across Japan with large numbers of Korean laborers.[111] From 1937, women in the northern Kyushu Korean communities were also some of the first targets for recruiters for military "comfort stations" on the continent.[112] Korean women were later recruited or purchased to work in similar "special comfort stations" located near, and sometimes run by, the mining companies of Chikuhō, which employed forced labor from Korea.[113] Understanding the earlier histories of these communities and geographies is important for understanding their mobilization during wartime.

Local Politics, Korean Representation, and the Assimilation Trap

By the 1930s Fukuoka prefecture was home to over thirty thousand Koreans. In 1935, twenty-five thousand Korean men and fourteen thousand Korean women lived in the prefecture. A second generation of Koreans was growing up in the region, attending its schools, learning to speak Japanese fluently, and considering it their home, if not their homeland.[114] After the advent of universal male suffrage in 1925, there was a significant Korean electorate in the industrial cities and coal-mining villages of the Kitakyūshū region. Just as the numbers of laborers arriving from Korea had been noted with apprehension in the local press, so too were the rising numbers of Koreans with the right to vote.

Anxiety surrounding the subject of Korean political representation was palpable. In January 1932 the *Fukunichi* printed the article "Sounding Out the Korean Vote: Will There Be a Korean Candidate from Kyushu or Not?" In the prefecture's second electoral district, more than three thousand Koreans had the right to vote that year.[115] Racist fears over elections and Koreans' lack of assimilation (J: *dōka*) converged on the use of Korean script on voting slips. This began as early as 1922 in reports on elections of union representatives, and it continued as Koreans gained suffrage in general elections in the Japanese home islands from 1928 onward. A report in the *Fukunichi* from 1930 announced that voting slips written in "Korean script" (J: *Chōsen moji*) would be included in the count, and the paper gauged the number of Koreans with voting rights in Japan at "over 100,000."[116]

The political activities of Fukuoka's Koreans are both quantitatively and qualitatively significant. While the political representation of Koreans in the Kyushu region has been addressed in terms of its statistical import, the nature of these political activities at the local level remains understudied.[117] Fukuoka prefecture had the highest number of Korean city council members in pre-1945 Japan, with four out of five of Kitakyūshū's cities including Korean representatives on their councils by 1938.[118] However, no candidates from Fukuoka ran for election to the lower house of the Imperial Diet; it seems their ambitions were closer to home—in local, mainly city government. It is at the regional level that the nature of this political representation comes into focus.

Fukuoka Koreans' political representation, especially in urban areas, was directly connected to community and labor networks. As the numbers of Koreans represented on local councils increased in the late 1930s and into the 1940s, the representatives were drawn increasingly from the upper spectrum of the Korean community, those with links to local Korean organizations and labor brokers. Even prior to wartime mobilization, Koreans elected in Fukuoka were moderates, with a platform of "Japan-Korea reconciliation" (J: *naisen yūwa*). This did not, however, stop their political activities from being seen as inimical to Japanese interests by the authorities, or from being the subject of much research and debate.

The discussion of the political leanings and activities of Koreans in Fukuoka was on the agenda at the meeting on the prefecture's Korean population held in March 1939. The minutes were published as the twenty-sixth edition of the Ministry of Justice's *Research into Social Conditions* series, begun the previous year.[119] The topic of politics was monopolized by the opinions of Special Police Inspector Nishiyori. The Special Higher Police (Tokkō or Tokubetsu Kōtō Keisatsu) were heavily involved in surveilling the

Korean communities in Japan. This amassed knowledge, gathered via continued surveillance of Koreans in Japan since the colonies' annexation in 1910, meant they were also involved in Naisen Yūwa campaigns. That a policy purporting to promote "reconciliation" was implemented by the special police gives us an indication of how these discursive campaigns and slogans were experienced by Koreans.

The Fukuoka report was the only publication in the Ministry of Justice's series that dealt with Koreans, or any migration-related issue.[120] As well as the special police, participants included figures from business and education considered to have knowledge and experience on the topic. These included representatives from Chikuhō's mining industries, Yawata Imperial Steelworks, schools in the Kitakyūshū region, and other industries in which Koreans were employed in large numbers. As far as can be deduced from names and the reported content of the meeting, no Koreans were present to give their opinions. However, there were significant differences of opinions about Korean residents in Fukuoka among the members, who often appear more openly racist and ignorant than their counterparts in colonial Korea, as suggested by the official language found in comparable sources.

This was probably a result of the stereotyping of Fukuoka's Korean populations. Inspector Nishiyori informed the roundtable members that "Koreans living in this prefecture are mainly laborers . . . mostly ignorant and illiterate, without the intellectual capacity to critically engage with political questions. Because of this we haven't seen many examples of political movements in the prefecture until recently."[121] Nishiyori went on to pinpoint this recent shift in political activity to the election in 1932 of Korean Pak Ch'un-kŭm to the lower house of the Imperial Diet. Pak, the first Korean to be elected as a representative, was originally from South Kyŏngsang province, as were many of the Koreans living in Fukuoka. After the franchise was extended in 1925 to all male imperial subjects living in Japan over the age of twenty-five, by moving from Korea to Japan, Korean men became able to vote in elections, and, as Nishiyori put it, they "saw this as an opportunity to improve their circumstances by their own hands."[122]

The extent of Pak's influence is open for debate. Whether the general trend toward Korean representation after the introduction of universal male suffrage would have led to political representatives from Fukuoka or not is worth further investigation, but the timing certainly supports Nishiyori's claim: The very next year, 1933, saw the first Korean candidates contesting local government elections in Fukuoka. All three of the candidates who stood for election in 1933 were mine laborers from Kaho and Kurate districts.

From 1933 onward every local election in Fukuoka saw Korean candidates fielded and a significant proportion of them elected to office. All three who stood in 1933 were elected. The first Korean elected to a city assembly in Fukuoka was Pyo Sŏng-cho, elected to the Wakamatsu city assembly in 1934. Like the three Koreans elected the previous year, Pyo, a restaurateur with ties to the construction trade, was from South Kyŏngsang province. Out of the thirty candidates who stood for local elections between 1933 and 1942, twenty-one of them were originally from the province surrounding Pusan. This is significant but not surprising considering that in 1935 over 40 percent of all Koreans in the prefecture hailed from South Kyŏngsang province, and 70 percent from North and South Kyŏngsang provinces combined.[123]

Although the political activity of Koreans was ascribed to their "incomplete" assimilation—an attempt to get "one of their own" elected, as Nishiyori put it—a significant proportion of those involved in politics had connections to Korean organizations like the Sōaikai, which were involved in "reconciliation" activities.[124] Although Nishiyori saw the chief motivation for Korean involvement in politics to be the improvement of their own living conditions rather than "cooperation with metropolitan politics," the Sōaikai, a national mutual aid society for Koreans in Japan, often cooperated with the Japanese government and employers to counter more extreme socialist Korean organizations. Indeed, Diet member Pak Ch'un-kŭm was a founding member of the organization.[125]

Koreans in Fukuoka, and elsewhere in Japan, were in a double bind: Involvement in politics gave some an opportunity to improve the conditions of their countrymen, yet it was seen at the time as a sign of incomplete assimilation. However, assimilation itself was a chimera: At the 1939 roundtable Special Police Chief Gotō admitted that complete assimilation—no longer being able to tell who was Korean—would make the job of the special police harder, despite being national policy.[126]

In May 1934 union chief and candidate for the Moji city council Kang Rae-u was interviewed by the Ōsaka Mainichi newspaper about his plans were he to be elected: "First I plan to fight for the citizens of Moji, and to deepen the understanding between Japanese and Koreans. We require more than 'harmony'—now is the time for action. On top of this, as Moji and Korea are geographically so connected, I believe it's my job to work for the historic development of both."[127] Kang's language here is reminiscent of the grander regional plans of Fukuokan settler elite figures like Shinozaki. His use of this local discourse of historical and geographic proximity shows its multivalence, able to be repurposed for many ends in 1930s Japan and Korea.

Despite gaining a respectable 209 votes, Kang failed to get elected in 1934. Four years later, in 1938, he was finally voted onto the Moji city council. Kang's position as an association head for the Moji Purchasing and Savings Association, an organization for Koreans in the city, was significant in gathering him votes. However, as the war worsened and opposition became politically dangerous, Kang's options for showing "support" for fellow Koreans narrowed. In 1944 he visited mobilized Korean laborers, bringing them chili peppers, an important ingredient in Korean cuisine.[128] It is hard to imagine this was the "deepened understanding" Kang had hoped to promote between his countrymen and the Japanese.

The demographics and networks of Koreans running for local political office reveal the changing dynamics of Korean communities in Fukuoka. In the first election in which Koreans gained positions on three village councils, all were in mining towns. At the 1939 roundtable a representative of Kaijima Mining admitted the company's involvement in getting one of them elected.[129] Over the next decade the nature of the vote machine mobilized to get Korean votes shifted.[130] Koreans standing for positions on city councils outweighed those standing for village office, although city council candidates were less likely to get elected—probably due to the increased competition and relatively smaller Korean vote outside of mining areas.

By the late 1930s most successful candidates were older Korean migrants in stable employment and social positions that allowed them to garner the necessary support of employees or mutual association members. Many were labor brokers or involved in "Japan-Korea reconciliation" organizations. Pyo Sŏng-cho, the Wakamatsu city assembly member, was head of the Wakamatsu Sōaikai branch. In 1937 labor broker Yu Kyong-sun used his first speech at the Kokura city council to call for more funding for the Kokura Dōwakai, a "reconciliation" organization, and more representation of Koreans as local district members (J: *hōmen iin*) responsible for social welfare and assistance for the poor.[131]

Fukuoka's position as the prefecture with the highest number of these Korean local political representatives has led some historians to see it as a "model" region of Korean minority and Japanese coexistence. Not only does this view overlook the important history of labor action and strikes in this region, but it fails to ask who benefited from this representation and ignores the reality of urban life for the majority of those Koreans working under the bosses and brokers that ended up representing them. A deeper analysis uncovers a more complex story. The involvement of Koreans in the supply of migrant labor to industrial Fukuoka's factories, ports, and coal mines created new social relationships that led to their advancement onto local city, town, and village councils, as well as their being made heads of Korean organizations that worked to promote "Japanese-Korean harmony"—what Kawashima refers to as the "divided margin."[132] Such representation can hardly have been for the benefit of the majority of Korean workers. The internal dynamics of Korean communities in northern Kyushu, like Japanese settler communities in Pusan, are a reflection of a regional history of imperial urbanization.

CONCLUSIONS

Korean workers who, in the 1920s and '30s, traveled from the rural villages of South Kyŏngsang province to Pusan, and across the Tsushima Strait to the industrial belt of Kitakyūshū, were reacting to forces that were both local and imperial. Their journeys were markedly different from those of Japanese traveling in the opposite direction. Both groups of migrants, however, would make their new homes in the empire's cities, as well as contribute to the construction of these spaces.

This movement of rural labor across the Tsushima Strait can be seen as an indication of the incorporation of southern Korea's rural areas into the "watershed" of the Kitakyūshū region's expanding market of labor, but it also shows the effects of incursions of Japanese capital into the peninsula. These networks that formed across the strait can be seen as part of a regional imperial urbanization that was informed by "local" Fukuokan interests attempting to counter the contradictory policies, and unintended consequences, of Japan's colonization of Korea. Studying the reactions of metropolitan and colonial authorities and businesses that attempted to control the flow of labor and took advantage of the large numbers of unemployed Koreans in both colonial and metropolitan cities reveals the *regional* context of many of these policies, and their role as predecessors to wartime policies of forced labor movement between Japan and Korea.

Finally, this chapter's study of the language and policies around the mobility of Koreans across the Tsushima Strait has shown how discourses around labor movement in the media and among authorities came to define Koreans in both archival and secondary works. In response, this chapter has tried to place their movement within a web of cross-border processes of urbanization, industrialization, and the expansion of transport links. The urbanizing environments in Kitakyūshū, co-constructed by Koreans working in the region's mines, ports, and factories, created opportunities for a growing class of Korean labor brokers and other businessmen to gain positions in local politics. However, Koreans in the region were caught between the "harmonizing" attempts of their bosses as community leaders and the desire of the Japanese authorities to keep them from assimilating totally.

The three chapters that make up part 1 of this book have looked at the co-creation of an urbanizing imperial region across a maritime border. By co-creation, I do not mean that different groups worked together in lockstep with a singular vision in mind; the opposite. Urbanization and human mobility—planned and unplanned—as well as the reactions by locals to wider-scale events all had an effect on the imperial region that emerged across and narrowed the maritime border of the Tsushima Straits. Part 2 of this book focuses on the intensifying development of the region's national and imperial connections and how inhabitants of Fukuoka and Pusan co-opted and reacted to these changes. The following chapter looks at the development, in the late 1920s and '30s, of several of the transport networks linking Fukuoka and Pusan to each other and to the expanding Japanese empire—via the construction of new harbors and airports, and their ferry links and flight routes. These increasing links between colony and metropole, and the expansion of Japan's sphere of influence on the Asian continent that drove them, led to a new era of booster politics and regionalism, with elites in both cities hitching their future to that of the empire.

PART II

High Tide

4

Imperial Gateways

FUKUOKA AND PUSAN WERE CITIES styled by their citizens as "gateways"—to the Asian continent or to Japan, depending on one's perspective.[1] Originally this was due to their roles as ports. Port cities, as some of the earliest forms of urban agglomeration, are a type of urban morphology that changes in form as the technology of shipping changes yet remains the same in function. However, the term "gateway," used in an age of empire, also suggests the presence of a porous border between differing political, cultural, and economic zones—a threshold that, as we have seen already, makes these locations attractive for investment, for selling one's labor power, and as a foothold for expansion.[2]

To write the history of a single port city is in some ways an act of amputation, cutting off the node from its network and from the impulses that animate its growth and shape its development. Instead, by tracing the modern history of Fukuoka's port of Hakata alongside that of Pusan, I argue for a more connective approach to the study of these gateways. This chapter tracks the shifting relationships formed by transport and technology between these two cities, which were repeatedly recalibrated due to war, the expansion of empire, and the advance of technology. While we might see the relationship between Fukuoka, a metropolitan city, and Pusan, a colonial one, as inherently uneven, in many cases power was balanced in favor of Pusan—a far more important city and port in the eyes of both the colonial and central government. How boosters and bureaucrats in both cities attempted to navigate this imbalance is the subject at the core of this chapter's examination of the development of the two cities' ports and their effect on urban growth.

As well as port development, this chapter also looks at imperial transport links between metropole and colony—via sea and air—to offer new perspectives on connectivity, expansion, and scales of imperial power. The interplay of local, colonial, and metropolitan forces shapes every stage in these histories, often in the form of regional elites attempting to take advantage of geopolitical shifts at the national or international level. The first of these links is the Hakata–Pusan ferry. In comparison with the history of the Kampu ferry—the first government-run sea link between Shimonoseki in Japan and Pusan in Korea—the story of the Hakata–Pusan link is much less well known. The Kampu ferry began in 1905, when Korea became a protectorate of Japan. Its forty-year existence has been written about as a metaphor for the changing relationship between Japan and its colony.[3] In contrast, the history of the Hakata–Pusan ferry link offers a different kind of narrative to the Kampu ferry's microcosm of national interactions, and it is with this history that the chapter begins.

This book begins in the age of coal, and coal-powered steamships, but it ends in the age of the fighter jet. The speed with which air transport and communication developed after Fukuoka's new airfield opened in 1936 soon created new power imbalances and geographies. While aviation can be said to strengthen "power at the center . . . at the expense of the periphery," it also had the power to create new peripheries out of old centers.[4] However, the outbreak of Japan's second war with China in 1937 and the closer attention paid by the central government to networks of sea and air marked, to some extent, a narrowing of horizons for the possible urban futures imagined by the citizens of both Pusan and Fukuoka. The development of air links across the Japanese empire altered the cities' relationship with each other, as well as their positions in the empire as a whole.

CROSSING THE GENKAI WHILE ONE DREAMS: THE
HAKATA–PUSAN ROUTE

The first regular sea link between Hakata and Pusan began as a "designated shipping route" (J: *meirei kōro*) financed by Fukuoka's city government in 1905 in the wake of the Russo-Japanese War.[5] It began service with hopes of increasing Fukuoka's trade with Korea. From 1908 the city contracted out the route to the Tsushima Transport Steamship Company (TTSC). Over the course of its forty-year service, this ferry link became a barometer for the relationship and power balance between Fukuoka, the strait's island communities, and Pusan.

TTSC had been founded in the late 1890s as the Tsushima Steamship Company, operating coastal routes around the mountainous and hard-to-traverse Tsushima Island and between the island and both Hakata and Nagasaki.[6] In the early 1900s the company appears to have been run by island notable Fujino Kojūrō, who had been active in the 1903 merger movement to make Tsushima and Iki part of Fukuoka prefecture, discussed in chapter 1.[7]

In its early years the line was mainly a trade link for Fukuoka with southern Korea. From 1908 onward the Hakata–Pusan route was operated by the *Tenyū Maru*, with six round trips per month.[8] The *Tenyū Maru* was only 472 tons, with room for a total of 139 passengers. Passenger rates were almost half the price of the Kampu ferry, while the shipping fees were between 10 and 30 percent cheaper.[9] In August 1920 the company was taken over by Nagasaki-based Kyushu Steamship Company and registered as a joint stock company under the name Tsushima Shipping Company, with its head office in Tsushima's Izuhara port and a branch in Fukuoka city.[10] At the time of Kyūshū Steamship Company's takeover, all seven of the company's ships were still of wooden construction.

Tsushima islanders remained central to the link for the first two decades of its existence. In 1925 islander representatives petitioned the government in Fukuoka and Tokyo, arguing that the current links across the straits were not sufficient, especially given the increasingly central position the straits held for Japanese continental ambitions, stressing that "with Korea's annexation and the return of Manchuria and Mongolia to within our sphere of dominance, today we should treat these islands at the center of the empire as stepping stones, as a vital national transport link."[11] At this time TTSC made only six sailings a month between Hakata and Pusan, via Tsushima. To the islanders, this seemed like a route that should no longer be handled by a private company but should be nationalized instead. As Fukuoka would benefit financially from a new daily line, its citizens were the main regional targets of the Tsushima delegates' attention. In Tokyo, the islanders presented petitions to both the communications and railway ministers, but they went unanswered. Only decades later, in 1943, would a Railway Ministry–run ferry briefly link Hakata and Pusan, and, unfortunately for islanders, it bypassed Tsushima and Iki in the name of speed.

From the mid-1920s the company's attentions shifted to Pusan. From 1925 to 1928 the president of TTSC was Sawayama Seihachirō, head of the Sawayama Shōkai, a Pusan-based shipping and merchant company that had operated as agents for TTSC in Pusan since the 1910s. In 1927, perhaps due to these strengthened connections in the city, TTSC set up its own offices on the passenger ferry pier. By this point the Hakata–Pusan route had ten round trips per month. The company's more visible presence in Pusan, as well as Fukuoka's developing tourism industry, made travel and interaction between the two cities more appealing.

In April 1927 the *Pusan Nippō* advertised two group excursions it was sponsoring to Fukuoka's East Asian Industrial Exposition, one via the Kampu ferry and one direct to Hakata on TTSC's *Tama Maru*. Pusan citizens would have had a particular interest in the exposition, as its Korea pavilion had been completed with the support and fundraising of Pusan notables, headed by Fukuokan Kashii Gentarō.[12] The *Tama Maru* group would leave Pusan on April 23, arriving the next morning, a Sunday. Members would have a chance to look around the exposition as well as time to explore Fukuoka before returning to Pusan the same evening. This "day trip" to Fukuoka was pitched at those who couldn't afford to take a day off work—bank clerks, office workers, and civil servants—yet wanted to make the most of their Sunday.[13]

Official visitors from Pusan to Fukuoka—including Mayor Izumisaki, delegations from the Pusan Chamber of Commerce, and journalists from the *Pusan Nippō*—attended both the expo and the fourth general meeting of the Japanese Port and Harbor Association (J: Nihon Kōwan Kyōkai, founded in 1922), held to coincide with the exposition. Celebrations were held on the roof of Fukuoka's city hall to inaugurate the Fukuoka branch of the Port Association. At the association meeting, Kashii Gentarō spoke on the need for increased funding for Pusan's third stage of port development, and Fukuoka mayor Tokizane called for Hakata to become a Port of Importance.[14]

As transporting passengers speedily between the two cities took priority, TTSC invested in upgrades to ships and new routes. In 1929 it changed its name again, this time to Kitakyūshū Shipping Company (KSC). KSC now had an all-steel shipping fleet and a separate company to operate its coastal shipping routes on Tsushima. Its first regular direct link between Hakata and Pusan began operation in the summer of 1929. This was the first time the two cities would be linked by such a regular, direct service.

Fukuoka magazine journalist Ariyoshi Kenshō wrote an account of his journey to Pusan via the *Tama Maru*'s new direct route in the summer of 1929. The speed of the journey and the evening sailing meant that one would fall asleep after leaving Hakata and wake up in Pusan—"crossing the Genkai while one dreams!" The twelve-hour overnight journey was a reminder of the closeness of the two cities and brought "Hakata folk to Pusan, and Pusan folk to Hakata." But Ariyoshi reminded readers that the ferry served a wider region than just Fukuoka; this new link meant that "southern Kyūshū … and the continent have been compelled to link hands."[15]

The new ferry did not yet seem popular with passengers—the middle deck of the ship was taken over by fifteen Japanese horses, accompanied on their journey by a Korean handler. The vessel usually carried more goods than human passengers to Korea: Its eclectic cargo included rubber boots, *tabi*, beer, enamelware, steam heaters, wheat, and coal. The return journey's cargo mainly consisted of soybeans and rice—a microcosm of the uneven trade relationship between Japan and its nearest colony.

Although the eighteen passengers were nearly outnumbered by the animals, according to a crew member, their number that day marked a record for the *Tama Maru*. Ariyoshi remarked that once a combined ticket with Korean Railways went on sale, passengers were sure to increase. However, he also struck a note of caution. The direct ferry was, he worried, late in coming and in danger of being overtaken by the speed of technological advancement: "One can already travel by plane from Tachiarai to Ulsan in less than two hours, after all."[16] Despite the fanfare of its early voyages, Fukuoka's long-awaited ferry link might soon be outshone by the region's new air connections that now linked Tachiarai in Fukuoka prefecture with Ulsan, north of Pusan, in Korea.

Cross-Strait Negotiations

This daily direct link had been brought into being after multiple calls for assistance from Fukuoka and lengthy negotiations between Fukuokans on both sides of the straits. In his position as head of the Pusan Chamber of Commerce, Kashii Gentarō was involved with the negotiations over the creation and funding of the link. In 1929 the Fukuoka mayor and head of the Hakata Chamber of Commerce had cosigned a letter to Kashii calling for his support, but Pusan's business world was less than confident in the city's ability to financially support a daily direct route.[17] In September 1930 a delegation from Fukuoka's city council and the Hakata Chamber of Commerce, again asking for financial assistance, arrived in Pusan. Kashii was in charge of hosting the delegates and organizing a meeting with Pusan's city government representatives to discuss the "shared problems of both regions."[18]

Mayor Kuse, chamber of commerce head Ōta, and KSC president Matsuo, in their interview with the *Pusan Nippō*, struck a tone that alternated

博釜連絡船 朝博丸 (重量噸数1650噸速力15浬)

FIGURE 3. The Hakata–Pusan ferry *Chōhaku Maru*, 1930. The caption reads "Hakata–Pusan ferry the *Chōhaku Maru*, 1650 tons, speed 15 knots." Courtesy of Kyūshū rekishi shiryōkan (*ehagaki mokuroku* no. 1077).

between humility and pride—Kuse hoping that the Pusan city government could manage to fund "even half" of the forty thousand yen they were asking for to support the route's yearly budget and reassuring readers that Fukuoka's future development would also benefit Pusan. Fukuoka's delegates seemed keen to cast their city, "Maritime Fukuoka," as the active player, with Pusan taking on the passive role of "gateway to the continent."[19] While Fukuoka's city and prefectural governments had in the past helped to finance the ferry, Fukuoka's delegates thought it fitting that the growing colonial city should now also contribute due to the mutual benefit the ferry would bring the two cities. However, that Fukuoka's city councilors had to petition Pusan for financial support suggests an uncomfortable (at least to Fukuoka) power imbalance between the two cities.

The ferry's financing shifted repeatedly from one side of the straits to the other. In 1930 the new "designated" Hakata–Pusan direct link was supported financially by Fukuoka prefecture.[20] The link was serviced by the *Tama Maru* and the larger *Chōhaku Maru*, some 1,280 tons, which the company had bought in 1929 (see figure 3).[21] However, from 1931 it was funded by the Korean Government General.[22] With the increasing use of motor vessels, coastal shipping routes were being consolidated, and the Government

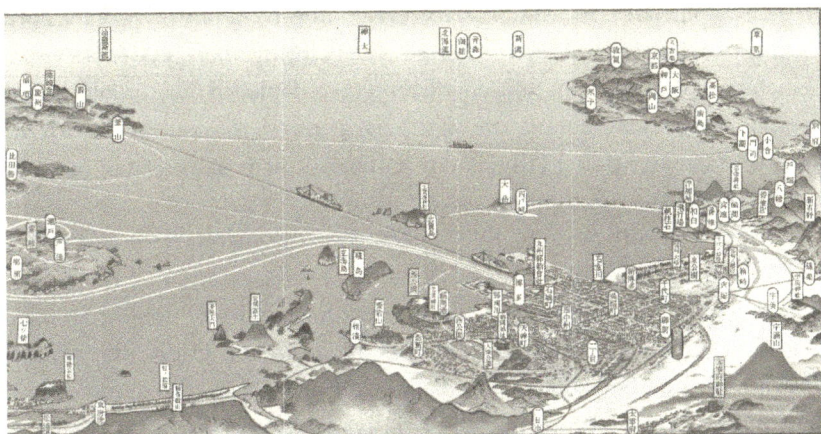

FIGURE 4. Detail from bird's-eye view of Kyūshū Yusen's routes, 1936. Credit: Yoshida Hatsusaburō 1936.

General was shifting its attention to funding links to the Japanese home islands and China, including the Hakata–Pusan route.[23] In 1933 the link was financed jointly by the Government General and Pusan city government.[24] In 1934, although the ferry link remained a Korean Government General designated line, joint funding responsibility moved back from Pusan to Fukuoka's city and prefectural governments.[25] The uneasy power balance between the two cities continued to fluctuate.

In 1935 KSC became Kyūshū Yūsen (Kyushu Mail Shipping Company) and moved its head office from Tsushima to Nagasaki City.[26] These were peak years for Kyūshū Yūsen's Hakata–Pusan route, perhaps best depicted by the bird's-eye view on Kyūshū Yūsen's 1936 route guide painted by Yoshida Hatsusaburo (figure 4).[27] Yoshida, known as the Taishō Hiroshige, was famous for bird's-eye views of cities and tourist sites. In the full image, the use of foreshortening allowed Yoshida to include the entire western coastline of Kyushu, from Moji and the Kanmon Straits south to Kagoshima. Front and center in the work are the islands of Hakata Bay, and beyond the bay lies the Japanese empire: from Dairen to the Korean peninsula to Karafuto. Tokyo is barely visible in the far eastern corner, behind Mount Fuji and a compressed Honshū.

While his paintings often viewed the subject city from the water, Yoshida's Kyūshū Yūsen panorama depicts the city of Fukuoka from inland, looking out over Hakata Bay and the Tsushima Strait. Fukuoka is depicted—and the viewer's gaze is directed—facing out toward empire, not back toward the

Japanese homeland. Kyūshū Yūsen's ferry routes head out of Hakata Port, linking ports and islands across the sea. The painting's perspective is a visual depiction of the common four-character phrase deployed by Fukuoka boosters and omnipresent in literature on the city's links to the continent, with the body of water separating Fukuoka from the continent narrowed to only the "width of a reed" (ichi itai sui).

In a publication from 1936, Kyūshū Yūsen's recent successes were described as a reward for the company and its director's tireless efforts to link Japan to its colonies.[28] Managing Director Matsuo Sadaichi was originally from Nagasaki but was seen as an adopted Fukuokan. In the mid-1930s he was also vice president of the Hakata Chamber of Commerce. In a roundtable discussion on Kyushu's economy that year, Matsuo described Nagasaki's economic development as slipping behind that of his adopted home region: "Nagasaki used to be booming, but the region is out of the way and lacks a hinterland [okuchi], therefore it is limited in its ability to develop.... If we compare Nagasaki to the Kitakyūshū region, they're in different leagues."[29] Matsuo's role in improving links across the straits was heralded by local boosters as expanding Fukuoka's hinterland further, increasing the city's importance, not only in Kyushu but in the empire. He was responsible for "compressing the temporal distance with Pusan, gateway to the Asian continent," for "this clasping of hands between Hakata and Chōsen,"[30]

From Local to Imperial Importance

As the Japanese empire repositioned itself as an autarchic economic bloc and, in 1937, invaded China, routes linking northern Kyushu and the Korean peninsula became even more important, even as some of Kyūshū Yūsen's local links were reduced or its ferries requisitioned. The Kyūshū Yūsen routes had a much smaller capacity than the Shimonoseki–Pusan (Kampu) ferry, and opening a secondary government-run route across the strait became a necessary pressure valve as the at-capacity Kampu route became a bottleneck. A Korean newspaper report from late 1939 describes the Railway Bureau's campaign to disperse Korean passengers traveling over the peak travel period of the New Year. Passengers were redirected from the Kampu ferry to routes between Shimonoseki and Yŏsu, and Hakata and Pusan.[31] While private companies like Kyūshū Yūsen struggled to keep lines running in wartime conditions, government transport policy, with its focus on improving efficiency and interimperial links, demanded a response.[32]

In 1940 the Ministry of Railways announced that it had chosen Hakata as the departure point for new links between the southern coast of the Korean peninsula and the home islands. The announcement was described as a godsend for both Fukuoka's citizens and city government, as the involvement of the Ministry of Railways would act as a catalyst for Hakata's still-incomplete port works and lead to the construction of new facilities, including a waiting room capable of accommodating some 250 passengers.[33] In these new facilities, cargo could be loaded from the newly constructed Hakata Port freight station straight onto the ferry, while buses transported passengers from Hakata station. The ferry was scheduled to connect to rail links out of Pusan at the other end.[34]

After many delays, in July 1943 the Ministry of Railways launched its ferry link between Hakata and Pusan. Celebrations were held in both Pusan and Fukuoka to commemorate the first sailings, and an exhibition entitled "Fukuoka's Leap Forward" was held in Keijō's Chōjiya department store to celebrate the opening of the route.[35] The steamships plying the new link, the *Tokuju Maru* and *Shōkei Maru*, were previously used on the Shimonoseki–Pusan route. Named after the Chosŏn-era palaces Tŏksugung and Ch'anggyŏnggung, they were bigger than any of Kyūshū Yūsen's shipping stock.[36]

Aboard the first voyage of the ferry to Pusan was a delegation of officials from Fukuoka: Mayor Hatayama and the heads of the city assembly and chamber of commerce. Upon their arrival the delegation emphasized the renewed importance of the two cities' relationship: "Pusan is Hakata's *tonarigumi*." Using the wartime term for a neighborhood association, they connected the two cities' shared interests to a familiar imperial movement.[37] When a delegation from Pusan made the return trip in August that year, their rhetoric shifted from a neighborly scale to an empire-wide one, with delegates emphasizing that "as bases of Greater East Asia, this link between Hakata and Pusan is not just for their benefit, but for a national purpose."[38]

When the Kampu ferry had begun in 1905, it symbolized the outward expansion of Japanese economic and military power into the Asian continent. In 1943, the ferry link from Pusan to Hakata was described as the "lifeline from the continent"—an "artery" that enabled the further extraction of foodstuffs and wartime laborers from the Korean peninsula and Manchukuo into the Japanese home islands.[39] The characterization highlighted a sea change in the nature of the relationship between the home islands and colonies that war had brought into stark relief.

The history of the prewar Hakata–Pusan link is little known in either Pusan or Fukuoka today. Since 1991 the cities have been joined by a jetfoil that speeds across the strait in under three hours.[40] This link is the descendant of the 1943 ferry, run by the descendant of the Ministry of Railways, JR Nishi Nihon. However, until 1943, when imperial considerations made intervention by the government necessary, it was local elites with networks spanning the Tsushima Strait, and the colonial government in Seoul, who backed the Hakata–Pusan route. The success of this link and other networks of trade and commerce relied on parallel developments in the harbors and port facilities of both cities. Such developments were also the result of negotiations between metropole, colony, and locality and shifted in priority and importance with the expansion of imperial power and regional networks.

A broader view of the importance of Hakata and Pusan as port cities in imperial and global shipping networks brings the disparities between the two ports into focus. At its peak in 1939, before war led to disruption of shipping, Hakata Port was a calling point for a total of nineteen regular ferry routes. Half were to islands in Kyushu, five were between Japan and Korea, two extended as far as Taiwan, and four went from Japan to China and Manchukuo.[41] In contrast, in 1939 Pusan was a calling point or terminus for some fifty-one regular shipping links. Nearly half of these were coastal routes around the Korean peninsula. Twenty-one connected the city to Japan, three to Taiwan and Manchuria, two to China, one to Vladivostok, and one to Surabaya, in the Dutch East Indies.[42] As negotiations over the funding of the line showed, for most of the history of this route, Hakata needed Pusan much more than Pusan needed Hakata. It is to the history of their two ports that we now turn.

PUSAN: GATEWAY OF ASIA

In numerous commemorative publications, 1926 was heralded as a year of celebration for the inhabitants of Pusan: The city was memorializing fifty years since it had opened for trade with Japan. Pusan's longtime Japanese residents, some of them present at the time of its opening in 1876, reminisced about the early days of Japanese settlement in the city and how far it had come since then. Back in the 1870s, the now-industrializing island of Makinoshima used to be so wild, old-timer Ōike Chūsuke recalled, that occasionally tigers or leopards would attack peoples' livestock.[43]

Such reminiscences often focused on the development of the harbor and its environs. Unlike Fukuoka, Pusan's growth centered almost entirely on its port area: The main train stations and thoroughfares in the city ran parallel to the waterfront. A commemorative booklet published in 1926 by the *Pusan Nippō* gives us an idea about the ambitions of Pusan's business elites for the city's future expansion, which was tied to the parallel growth of its port. Some 250,000 *tsubo* (about 204 acres, the equivalent of forty city blocks) of planned land reclamation, as well as municipal boundary expansion and new urban plans, all "form[ed] the basis for the founding of Great Pusan."[44]

The celebrations in the autumn of 1926 looked forward to further development of the city's harbor and its growing role as a gateway not just between the Japanese metropole and Korea but to the Asian continent and beyond. Pusan in 1926 was an urban center at the crossroads of expanding networks of rail and sea, "which this year will break through the twenty-five million yen mark in trade.... [The city] has a population nearing 110,000, both Japanese and Koreans. Such figures and growth are astonishing not only for Korea but also for the Japanese home islands."[45] The city's growth, as demonstrated via such statistics, led the authors of the 1926 booklet to envision Pusan's future not as a regional entrepôt but as a global one:

> Now, at a time when ports in our mother country are applying for free port status, the argument for Pusan becoming a free port too has reared its head. This is due to the fact that Pusan is at the eastern tip of the Asian continent, the gateway to East Asia, positioned at the crossroads between the Japan Sea and the East China Sea.... As a center for both trade and industry, Pusan has the qualifications and factors necessary to become the key free port in the Japanese empire, on a par with Hong Kong.[46]

The discourse on "free ports" had been recently reinvigorated in Japan following editorials in *Kōwan*, the new publication of the Port and Harbor Association, begun in 1923. Its proponents believed the future of Japanese ports was not as exporters of raw materials but as entrepôts like Hong Kong, where international trade could take place free of tariffs.[47]

While the vision of Pusan as the Hong Kong of the Japanese empire was still an abstract dream, in the fiftieth anniversary year of its opening to trade, plans for the construction of the new "Great Pusan" were already underway:

> In order to keep up with future expansion of trade ... the second stage of construction works for the development of the port, costing some eight million yen, is scheduled for completion in 1927. With this, Pusan's port

development will have had some fourteen million yen worth of investment. . . . Truly, the founding of Great Pusan, when it can live up to its name as the gateway of Asia, a way station on this global route [*sekai no kōdō*], is getting nearer every day.[48]

Pusan, viewed through the eyes of those Japanese and Korean citizens who relied on the development of the city for their own fortunes, had its best days yet to come. But several tempered their praise and visions with exhortations for Pusan's citizens to work hard on behalf of the city. Kashii Gentarō argued that "Pusan's biggest challenge still lies ahead," while municipal assembly member Yi Hyang-u reminded Pusan's inhabitants that "in this age that never stops for pause, we residents [J: *fumin*] of Pusan must keep working, to ensure that shining Pusan keeps on improving."[49]

On November 1, the governor general of Korea, Saitō Makoto, attended the ground-breaking ceremony for the second stage of Pusan's port works—a land reclamation project north of the train station in Pusanjin (J: Pusanchin) timed to coincide with the fiftieth-anniversary events. The event was described as "the first step in Great Pusan's founding."[50] But offstage, absent from commemorative speeches and publications, there had been many struggles that had led up to this ceremony. They are worth exploring, as both a corrective to the triumphalist narratives expounded by the city's boosters and to show the unintended consequences of such "development."

Imperial Ports, Land Reclamation, and Labor

Reclaiming land in both Pusan and Fukuoka was a vital part of the cities' urban expansion plans and the development of their harbors. However, the process of land reclamation (J: *umetate/maichiku*) was expensive and lengthy. In *A Short History of Pusan Harbor*, published by the Government General in 1937, the author lists the nine separate ventures that took place up to 1928.[51] Two were overseen directly by the Government General and seven by private companies. The protracted time frames of these ventures—especially those by private companies, which were still required to submit plans to the governor general—show the difficulty they faced in raising funds. This was not unique to land reclamation: The pages of newspapers and journals reporting on Pusan's urban works, many of which were never completed, are a testament to the collapse of companies, internal disagreements, clashes between municipal and central government plans, and budget cuts, which all took their toll on the lofty visions of the city's bureaucrats and boosters. As seen in chapter 2, plans that were unable to be supported by the municipal budget were often bailed out by the city's settler magnates. The settler triumvirate of Ōike, Kashii, and Hazama were constantly dipping into their own reserves in order to fund public halls, theaters, and other civic ventures. That they were also significant landowners in Pusan makes their investment in the city's economy and civic sphere less than completely altruistic.

Across the colony, tension existed between metropolitan Japanese and settler businesses. When tenders for regional construction projects were put out for bidding, competition ensued between "local" (J: *jimoto*) construction companies and larger ones, often with a metropolitan, conglomerate connection. Some regional organizations petitioned to keep metropolitan companies from receiving tenders.[52] In Pusan, such tensions during the land reclamation works in Pusanjin resulted in serious delays and multiple pauses in the construction of this crucial expansion to the city's urban area. Although the project was crucial for the city's expansion—both modern port facilities for coastal shipping and the creation of an industrial area for the city's growing number of factories—it could not be funded by the municipal budget alone, nor was the Government General keen to get involved, although eventually it was forced to intervene.

The area of Pusanjin lay to the north of the colonial city center and was first slated for development after the Nagoya-based Korea Development Company began land reclamation works along the waterfront in 1913. The company fell into difficulties around five years into the project, and although it had received a license for a two-stage reclamation works, it gave up its land-fill rights in 1918. The license was taken over by the Pusanjin Land Reclamation Company, but work on the second stage of the project did not begin for several years.[53]

One key metropolitan figure in the second stage was "cement king" Asano Sōichiro. Asano was a pioneer in the process of modern land reclamation, and in 1908 his Tsurumi reclamation company was the first to use modern pump dredgers on the Yokohama waterfront. Asano set up several industrial sites on the newly reclaimed land, starting the model for Japan's industrial port development, combining land reclamation with the creation of industrial zones.[54] Alongside Asano were two other major investors: the Kobe-based shipping tycoon Nakamura Junsaku and Pusan settler magnate Ōike Chūsuke.[55]

Asano's involvement in the Pusanjin project created tension with both Pusan-based Ōike and Nakamura, who did not live in Pusan but had an address there. In the months leading up to the founding of the company, Asano appears to have attempted to move the center of operations from Pusan back to the imperial capital of Tokyo. In January 1926 he sent his chief engineer, Tanba Sukihiko, who had also been involved in the Yokohama reclamation project, to begin on-site surveys. Tanba and his team of five engineers stayed for only a few days before returning to Tokyo. The sense that the project was being directed from the capital only increased with Asano's insistence that, despite the Pusan-based nature of the works, the company's office should be based in Tokyo, for "convenience."[56] Several months later, after more delays connected to changes in plans, Ōike was forced to make the journey to Tokyo in order to discuss the future of the company. Friction between the three camps slowed down their plans into the autumn.[57]

Asano's power plays eventually led to an intervention from Governor General Saitō himself to move the project forward. Nakamura became company president, Asano's position was reduced to an advisory role (from which he later withdrew completely), and the company's headquarters were to be located in Pusan.[58] In September, Ōike visited Keijō to give his thanks for the role the governor general played in resolving the company's problems.[59] Saitō's later presence at the ground-breaking ceremony in November was due to both his personal involvement in the project and its importance to the Korea colony as a whole.

Even after this high-level intervention, disagreements and local resentment remained. Fears were raised about the construction tender being given to companies that were not based in Pusan. An article in the municipal journal *The Fusan* aimed to allay fears among the city's inhabitants by reminding them, "It is of course the local residents, people of the port [*kōmin*], who will benefit the most. . . . You should all support the businessmen and help them to achieve their goals."[60]

By referring to the citizens (*fumin*) of Pusan as *kōmin*, the municipal journal linked their identity and responsibilities directly to the port and its development. However, the nature of the relationship between different groups of *kōmin*—whether Japanese or Korean, local elites or blue-collar workers—and their port city differed wildly. Although those funding the expansions were prominently featured in publications and represented on the city's various boards and institutions, those tasked with the port's construction were no less essential to its development but are far less visible in the historical archive.

They are discussed, however, in local debates over labor. In addition to concerns about the construction companies themselves, questions were raised about the workers that these companies would be employing. Fears were raised over the use of cheap Chinese labor in the architectural journal *Chōsen to Kenchiku* (*Korea and Architecture*) in April 1927. The article discussed how the "problem facing all of Korea, that of Chinese coolie labor undercutting Korean labor, while advantageous from the point of view of the company's budget, should be discussed with authorities."[61] Throughout the 1920s Chinese laborers had worked as *ninpu* (the lowest-skilled manual laborer position) on Pusan port works, but even at the height of their numbers, they made up less than a tenth of the *ninpu* workforce. In 1927 some three-quarters of the workers were Korean laborers, many newly arrived in the city.[62]

The port works of the late 1920s had many effects on Pusan's urban growth. While expanding the city into the harbor, they also attracted newcomers to the city—mainly Koreans from the surrounding countryside who came into Pusan to work as laborers. The newly arrived workers lived on the hillsides rising up from the northern harbor and outside the city limits to the north. This influx of Korean laborers into the city did not slow with the completion of these works in the north of the expanding city. The Asano model of development worked as predicted, and the development of newly reclaimed land in Pusanjin provided the city with more land upon which to construct new large-scale factories employing Korean and Japanese laborers. These included spinning factories with large numbers of female workers.

In 1929 this industrial development and the accompanying large and sudden increases in population led the city to announce an urgent need for research into the expansion of the city's administrative area. The areas to be incorporated into the city were mainly those adjoining these new industrial areas along the northern waterfront.[63] Piecemeal incorporation of land would not suffice, however. The city needed a new urban plan. In 1931, due to "Koreans residing in areas beyond what we imagined, and . . . an increase in the construction of Korean homes," city authorities not only called for a new urban plan but also planned "to apply to the Government General for an update to the architectural regulations."[64] Only two months after this report, at a meeting of the Pusan municipal assembly, questions were raised about damage caused by recent heavy rains. Assembly members noted that Korean laborers "built their homes on hillsides and along riverbanks that could be washed away with one heavy rain." The members stressed the need for the Government General to respond to these issues with new building regulations and to look to the advanced cities in the metropole that were responding to similar problems.[65] Planned development in Pusan, like port expansion and industrialization, brought with it unplanned urban growth that the city, and the colony, was unprepared to deal with. However, the growth often took shape in ways that echoed earlier waves of urbanization.

Geopolitics, Transport, and Technology

The founding of the new puppet state of Manchukuo in 1932 transformed Korea and Pusan's positions as links between the Japanese metropole and its expanding sphere of influence in continental Asia. As Louise Young has discussed in the case of the Japanese metropole, and scholars like Carter Eckert and Han Suk-Jung have noted in the case of Korea, these effects were wide-ranging and transformative.[66] In Pusan they were felt especially strongly. Pusan's railway connections to Manchuria and beyond became important not only for imperial tourists, but also for the transport of raw and processed goods, and later military transport after Japan's full-scale invasion of China in 1937.

Mainland Japanese, in the booming tourism market beginning in the mid-1920s and continuing into the '30s, were bombarded with appeals to visit Korea and the expanding Japanese territories to its north. Nearly all of them would have entered through Pusan. For many, their reaction was similar to Hayashi Komao's back in 1898: The city barely seemed Korean, but rather Japanese.[67] The transition was seamless in other ways too. By 1936 the facilities at Pusan connecting passengers from sea to land were designed to make the journey from ferry to express train as easy as possible: "When arriving into port in Pusan, the ferry moors alongside the wharf, and within a few steps from disembarking an express train connecting Korea and Manchuria awaits you."[68] From the mid-1930s there were attempts in Pusan to appeal to these imperial tourists and to develop the city, as well as the nearby hot spring resorts of Haeundae and Tongnae, into a tourist destination in its own right, not simply a stop on the way to Seoul, Manchukuo, or beyond.[69]

In addition to the transport facilities and rail infrastructure in the empire's gateways, the vessels that carried people between them also required upgrading. In turn, these upgrades necessitated improvement works in the ports themselves. In the 1930s the construction of new steamships for the Kampu ferry line meant that Pusan and Shimonoseki's port facilities needed expanding, with the new larger ferries beginning operation in the autumn of 1936.[70] The model for Pusan pier's redevelopment was another of Japan's key imperial ports: Dairen.[71] The new two-story waiting room and port building on the passenger ferry pier would have a top floor that housed amenities for passengers (including hairdressers and bathing facilities), to be connected by gangplanks to the moored ferries, while the ground floor contained facilities for storing and loading goods on board. However, the sophisticated passengers envisaged patronizing the hairdressers and bathing facilities of the new pier building were, in reality, overtaken in number by rather less well-heeled travelers. In 1934 the Government General's Railway Bureau announced plans to expand the third-class waiting room facilities at Pusan to cope with the increasing number of passengers at the bottom end of the market.[72] Although it is not discussed in the article, many of these passengers, who were buying the cheapest tickets available to Japan, were likely Korean.

While those Korean passengers were mainly heading to Japan's industrial zones, one of the most important results of the founding of Manchukuo for the Korean colony was the development of industrial facilities on the peninsula itself. These were for the processing of raw materials from Manchuria, Mongolia, and elsewhere in Korea. In the early to mid-1930s, these were mainly light industries such as spinning and canning; later, however, the north of the Korean peninsula and Manchukuo itself became sites of heavy industrial development.[73] Pusan, too, saw a shift from light to heavy industry over the 1930s and into the 1940s, discussed more in the following chapter. Plans by settler elites from this time argued for the necessary codevelopment of Pusan as a city of industry (sangyō toshi) as well as a port city (minato toshi).[74]

Pusan's port and its expansion were interlinked with the city's urban growth and with the expansion of Japanese imperial territory and its sphere of influence. In turn, the industrialization that took place in Pusan, especially in the newly expanded Pusanjin harbor area, expanded the city's trade horizons beyond simply Manchuria and the Japanese empire. In 1934 the Pusan Chamber of Commerce had a new region within its sights: Southeast Asia. The metropole-based shipping company Ōsaka Shōsen had announced the inclusion of Pusan as a stop on its goods shipping line to the Dutch East Indies via Taiwan. Members of Pusan's chamber of commerce traveled to the region and made reports on new markets for Pusan's marine products—especially canned goods.[75] According to the chamber of commerce director Ueda Kōichirō, the future looked bright for the sale of Pusan-canned sardines in Java.[76] This was an expansion of Pusan's markets that Hayashi

Komao could not have foreseen in 1898. Pusan's industrialization, a result of the creation of Manchukuo, aided the development of the city's role as an entrepôt between the Japanese sphere of influence in Northeast Asia and the markets of Southeast Asia.

The interaction of processes of industrialization, the expansion of Japanese shipping and rail links, and the work of local businessmen indicates that Pusan's development in the 1930s was not entirely in lockstep with imperial expansion. The ambitions of Pusan's elites were more expansive, referring as they often did to the city's position on the "global highway" (J: *sekai no kōdō*). Such visions were in contrast to the Government General's 1934 announcement of new plans for the three key ports connecting the southeast coast of Korea to Japan: Masan, Yŏsu, and Pusan. This was a three-year construction project from 1936 to 1938 that, in Pusan's case, was to build further outward into the bay in order to create new harbor facilities.[77] These new facilities were needed to deal with the increase in shipping that had returned to pre-Depression levels by 1933 and looked set to increase dramatically in the coming years.[78] While Pusan's boosters, Japanese and Korean, continued to imagine their port as a leading city in the Orient on the "global transport route" (K: *kukche kyot'ongno*), Government General plans for the city envisioned its future role as just one integrated part of a regional plan spanning metropole and colony.[79]

HAKATA: GATEWAY TO EMPIRE

Unlike Pusan's, Fukuoka City's modern growth was due to many reasons other than the development of its port; the city's position as a center of power in Kyushu and its ability to benefit from the industry of the surrounding areas were arguably far more important factors. However, this did not stop the development of both Hakata Port and an urban industrial base from becoming long-term goals for many of the city's businessmen and politicians.

Historically, both the castle town of Fukuoka and the merchant port of Hakata developed through land reclamation along their coastlines, the vestiges of which are present in local toponyms such as Kusagae (reedy estuary) and Nakasu (sandbank). Today the modern city of Fukuoka still experiences flooding and even sinkholes when construction crews attempt to tunnel too deep into its sandy foundations. This early history of Hakata Port and its

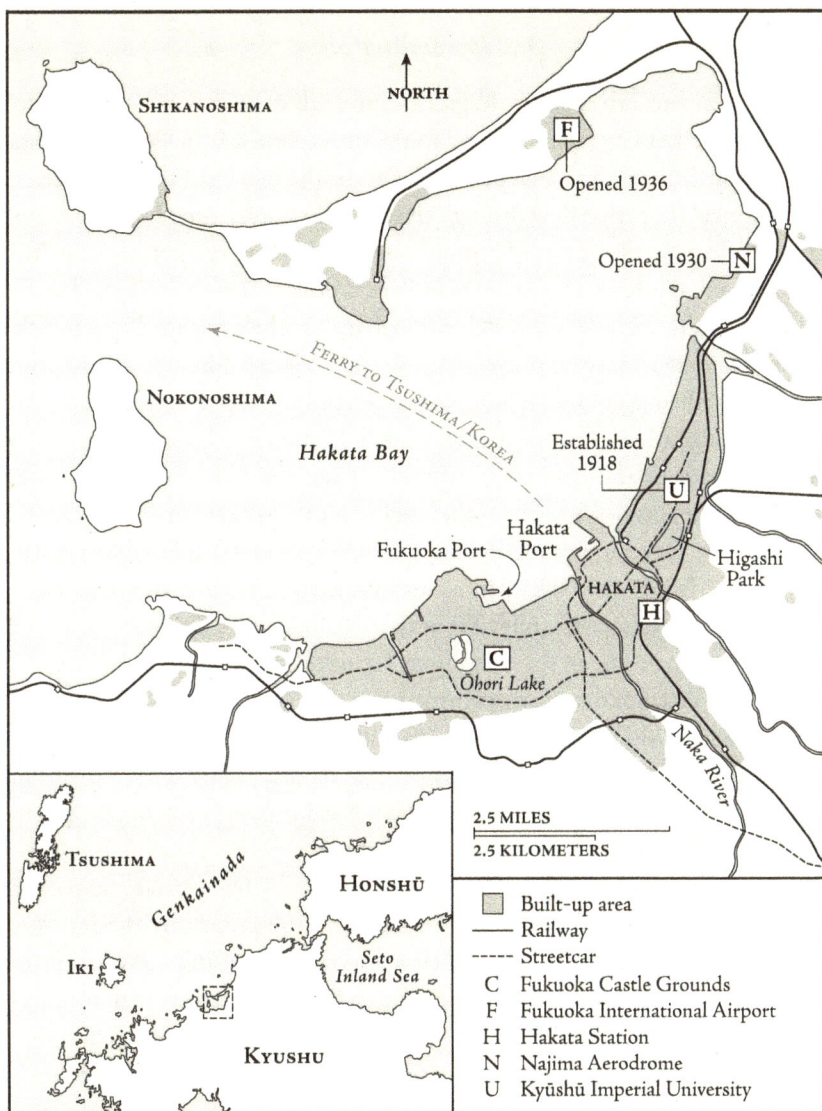

MAP 5. Fukuoka City and surrounding area, ca. 1940. Credit: Kate Blackmer.

Map labels:
SHIKANOSHIMA
NORTH
F — Opened 1936
Opened 1930 — N
FERRY TO TSUSHIMA/KOREA
NOKONOSHIMA
Hakata Bay
Established 1918
U
Fukuoka Port — Hakata Port
Higashi Park
HAKATA
H
C
Ohori Lake
Naka River

Inset:
TSUSHIMA
Genkainada
HONSHŪ
IKI
Seto Inland Sea
KYUSHU

2.5 MILES
2.5 KILOMETERS

☐ Built-up area
— Railway
----- Streetcar
C Fukuoka Castle Grounds
F Fukuoka International Airport
H Hakata Station
N Najima Aerodrome
U Kyūshū Imperial University

links to Asia were repeatedly raised as a model for future expansion. But it was only when the port's development became a national-level concern that local elites saw success for their somewhat parochial visions of *umi no Fukuoka* (maritime Fukuoka), and it would be national policies that again led to the port's rapid eclipse.[80]

In the late nineteenth century, despite its hundreds of years of history as "gateway to Japan" between the sixth and fourteenth centuries, the port of Hakata had become little more than a mooring place at the mouth of the Naka River, one of several rivers that flow through the city of Fukuoka into Hakata Bay (see map 5).[81] In 1883, along with Shimonoseki and Izuhara on Tsushima, it had been named as a Korea Special Trade Port, a designation that allowed trade with Korea only on Japanese vessels through otherwise "unopened" ports.[82] So began the modern history of the port's uneven relationship with the Korean peninsula. Silted up and with limited modern infrastructure or shipping, even after its designation as an open port in 1899, Hakata saw little of the growth brought about by the same designation for Moji and Shimonoseki. In 1898, with the open port designation in their sights, local businessmen had set up the Hakata Port Development Company (HPDC) and built a large new basin between the Ishidō and Naka Rivers, surrounded by some fifty thousand *tsubo* [forty acres] of reclaimed land.[83] From 1908 the Hakata–Pusan ferry was one of the first to make use of these new port facilities.

The next attempt by private companies to develop Hakata port came during the First World War, propelled in part by the annexation of Korea in 1910 and by Japan's increasing prominence in Asia, especially with European empires engaged elsewhere. This new plan was far more wide-ranging than that of HPDC and had the whole of Hakata Bay within its sights for development. The plans grew out of the vision of Gen'yōsha associate Sugiyama Shigemaru, who was called upon to assist with the project by three fellow Fukuoka businessmen around the time of the new basin's completion in 1908.[84] Sugiyama first submitted a petition to Fukuoka prefecture in 1912 and founded an association for local businessmen to support the port's development. His plans were rejected by the Imperial Diet in 1914: They argued such plans should be undertaken not by private companies but by local government or a public company. There were concerns, too, about the lack of clarity over the exact source of the money for this development and, if it was successfully completed, what the effects on the nearby port of Moji might be.[85] Moji's position as a state-sanctioned gateway and outpost of central power made it unlikely that the central government would want to create a rival port nearby without good reason.

Undeterred, Sugiyama put forward new plans to the local and national government based on the works being undertaken by a public company, with some 2.8 million yen in capital gathered from members of the association. In 1916 the Hakata Bay Port Development Company held its founding meeting in the Hakata Chamber of Commerce. From its founding, the company relied on both financial and human capital from imperial sources. The owner of the largest number of shares in the company was the shipping tycoon Nakamura Seishichirō. Born into a poor samurai retainer family from the Hirado domain near Nagasaki, Nakamura was based in Keijō, Korea, having made his fortune from shipping and military transport between Western Japan and the Korean peninsula during the Sino- and Russo-Japanese Wars. His company, the Nakamura-gumi, shipped iron ore from mines in northern Korea to the Yawata Imperial Steelworks and had numerous interests in Western Japan and Korea.[86] Other investors included Nakamura's two brothers, Sadazaburō (the company's first president) and Yūzaburō (a key figure in the marine and mining industries in Hokkaido) as well as Nakamura's close business associate in Korea, Kamihara Daikichi. The biggest Fukuoka-based investor was former mayor Satō Heitarō, followed by Kawauchi Uhee, also briefly mayor in 1938, and Shintō Kiheita, former Gen'yōsha head and father of postwar mayor of Fukuoka Shintō Kazuma.[87] The company's seventeen founders raised nearly half of the starting capital of three million yen themselves.[88]

As well as this investment by local and imperial business networks, Hakata Bay's development also relied on expertise gained through imperial expansion. Sugiyama was connected, through Itō Hirobumi, to Gotō Shinpei, head of civilian affairs for Taiwan, and had made regular visits to the island from its colonization in 1895.[89] The engineer that drew up Sugiyama's plans was Kawakami Kōjirō, a key figure behind the planning and construction of Keelung (Jilong) Port in colonial Taiwan.[90] Kawakami was also employed by Sugiyama to draft plans for another of his regional visions for Fukuoka: a tunnel linking the island of Kyushu with Honshū under the Kanmon Straits, discussed more in chapter 5.

The new port plans were much more ambitious than earlier ones, consisting of large-scale land reclamation projects that would create a vast new urban area between the Ishidō and Tatara Rivers to the northeast of the city center. Dredging of the bay, which was necessary to allow the docking of large ships, would provide sand and earth for the foundations of these new urban areas. These plans, just like Pusan's, appear influenced by the Asano model of urban port development, as Sugiyama's vision for Fukuoka extended beyond simply improving its port facilities to the industrialization of the city via the creation of new urban areas in the eastern area of Hakata Bay. His plan was to build, from scratch, an industrial zone complete with factories, transport and shipping facilities, and shipbuilding yards.[91]

This quixotic vision for an industrialized Fukuoka would take hold of many bureaucrats and private citizens in the prewar years. Paradigms about urban growth in this period favored the Osaka-Manchester model of industrial development, in which smokestacks were a measure of a city's success.[92] Fukuoka, however, lacked the access to water supplies on a scale that would allow its industrial development to compete with that of neighboring Yahata, Tobata, and Wakamatsu. As seen in the visions of Shinozaki Shōnosuke in chapter 2, one solution that was put forward in the 1930s was the incorporation of Pusan within Fukuoka City's economic zone. These visions of imperial urbanization occurred at the intersection of local imperialism and early twentieth-century models of industrial urbanization.

The inflation of goods, prices, and wages that accompanied the end of World War I saw the port works grind to a halt, with the completion of dredging works in 1923 their only real accomplishment. Attempts to negotiate with Fukuoka City to take on some of the financial burden of the inflated budget failed, and in 1924 Sugiyama looked to a Shanghai-based American company for foreign investment in order to realize his vision for the city.[93] The Asia Development Company (ADC), led by former US trade commissioner Paul Page Witham and his chief engineer, L. F. Patstone, had just completed reclamation works on the Yellow River in China for Shangdong province and had been investors in the port works at Takao (Kaohsiung), Taiwan.[94] Not content with simply raising funds for the port works, Sugiyama signed a contract with the ADC that included construction of a railway linking the harbor to the Chikuhō coalfields—a total investment of some seven million dollars.[95] The contract was announced in newspapers in Japan and further afield. The *Times of India* reported that "it is expected that with the completion of the harbor . . . Hakata will become one of the most active ports of Japan, taking away much of the coal traffic that now passes through Moji and Nagasaki."[96]

In October 1925 the Fukuoka city assembly put forward a plan for the city itself to take back control of these plans. They had expressed concern over taking on guarantorship of the massive ADC loan and had reacted strongly when Sugiyama and Gen'yōsha boss Tōyama Mitsuru, in an attempt to install someone more sympathetic to their plans to city government, used their influence to get former general Tachibana Koichirō elected mayor in

1924. Tachibana was forced to resign in August 1925, and this meeting, only months later, sounded the death knell for Sugiyama's attempts to mold the city as he pleased.

Local Dreams versus National Policy

These local shifts in power occurred at the same time that the central government was beginning to extend its interest and control over the empire's maritime gateways.[97] In early 1925 the Home Ministry's Port and Harbor Division chief Itō Takehiko headed a research tour of the ports of Western Japan. To raise public awareness of the national importance of port development he held public lectures and film screenings across Kyushu, accompanied by Port and Harbor Association director Fujimura Shigemichi and other association members.[98] The *Fukuoka Nichi Nichi Shinbun* reported how Fujimura had "come to the realization that . . . Hakata Port must be made a First Class Port of Importance, and put to use for our country."[99] Although the Home Ministry did not quite see the case in Fujimura's glowing terms, in 1927 it designated Hakata a Second Class Port of Importance, conferring on the port a rank that pointed to a larger role within the empire.

This designation came in the same year that Fukuoka City held its East Asian Industrial Exposition on the grounds of what would become the city's Ōhori Park and, in conjunction, hosted the Port and Harbor Association's fourth annual meeting, attended, as discussed above, by delegates from Pusan via the new ferry route. The 1927 exposition was the biggest such event held in Fukuoka to date and, as the 1910 exposition discussed in chapter 1 had, it relied on the filling in of part of Fukuoka castle's former moats to create new urban space. Solely relying on the development of the port for the expansion and development of Fukuoka's urban area was still too risky, and the city's authorities put greater stock in the development of transport infrastructure and tourism that such events precipitated. During the sixty days that the exposition was open to the public, it was attended by crowds numbering more than ten times the population of Fukuoka City at the time.[100]

Government-financed work on developing Hakata Port finally began in 1929, with some four hundred thousand yen invested by the central government and two hundred thousand yen by Fukuoka City.[101] The amount was far less than the city planners' projected costs, and local and central government did not see eye to eye on the length of time the works should take. Tokyo seemed far less concerned than local bureaucrats and businessmen with modernizing Fukuoka's port as quickly as possible. After all, nearby Shimonoseki and Moji were already much more advanced in terms of port facilities. The Home Ministry was more concerned with keeping the project under budget. In order to speed up what the central government projected would be a fifteen-year project, Fukuoka City planned to sell bonds, raising funds that would reduce the port works to a maximum of eight years.[102] The company contracted for the land reclamation and dredging works was Tobishima gumi, a construction company that had been involved with Pusan's port development.[103]

The city government, despite its reluctance to take on the responsibilities of overseeing the Port Development Project as a whole, entered into negotiations with Sugiyama and the Hakata Bay Port Development Company. In 1933 they came to an agreement, with the city taking over the land reclamation and dredging rights in exchange for compensation of some 180,000 yen and the pledge to return a portion of the reclaimed land to the company at a later date. The city government also began drawing up plans for the modernization and expansion of port facilities, which began construction in 1936. Sugiyama Shigemaru never got to witness the completion of his vision for Hakata: He died in 1935, at the age of seventy-two, two months before the groundbreaking ceremony for the Commemorative Exposition celebrating the completion of the first stage of the port works. His name lived on in Sugiyama-machi, a district in the newly reclaimed port area.[104]

The Hakata Port Exposition in 1936 signaled a city, and public, with increasing confidence in its past and future links to maritime and imperial expansion. The publicity for the exposition gives us a sense of this new vision. One poster design shows Hakata from the sea, with a gleaming white pavilion towering over the bay and seven steamships—funnels smoking, bows pointed outward toward Asia—as biplanes buzz overhead in a blood-red sky (see figure 5). In an interview with the *Fukunichi* newspaper, Ōta Kantarō, head of the Exposition Organizing Body and the Hakata Chamber of Commerce, remarked:

> The goal of the exposition is to announce, first to the rest of Japan and then the world, that Fukuoka is the best possible place for trade between Japan and overseas.... Fukuoka City is going to leap ahead, past its future as a commercial, university, and tourist city, and we need to make plans for its development that centers on the port. This truly is both Fukuoka City's destiny and the responsibility of all of its citizens [J: *shimin*].[105]

FIGURE 5. Postcard for Hakata Port Commemorative Exposition, 1936. Credit: Shūkōsha insatsu 1936.

Hakata's port development would have been limited in impact and significance had it not been connected to Fukuoka's hinterland, and with the other islands of the metropole, via local and national rail networks. In advance of the increase in traffic connected with the expo, and to facilitate better long-term transport links between the city's rail and sea terminals, the Fukuoka Urban Planning Board approved plans for widening the main road connecting the port with Hakata Station, and further plans for expansion were proposed in 1940.[106]

As the exposition was underway in 1936, the second stage of the port works at Hakata looked unlikely to receive serious financial backing from the central government. It was only with the outbreak of war with China the following year that the government and military acknowledged Hakata's logistical importance. From 1936 Fukuoka's Commerce and Industry Departments published multiple reports on Hakata Port and its links with regional ports in East Asia, totaling some fourteen publications in eight years.[107] These publications show the city responding to advances on the continent by including data on Hakata and target ports across what became the Greater East Asia Co-Prosperity Sphere. It is worth noting here the early focus of Hakata Port's boosters and bureaucrats on the Japanese-dominated "Greater East Asian" sphere for their future trade. While Pusan's urban elites had wider visions of their port's roles in global flows of trade and people, Fukuoka's seemed content with their city acting as a link between metropole and empire.

Hakata Port finally gained First Class Port of Importance status in 1939, but it was not long before war and subsequent shipping shortages reduced traffic to and from the port. The opening of the Ministry of Railways' Ferry in 1943 was a rare cause for celebration in wartime. Fukuoka City continued to publish reports until 1944, meticulously gathering and publishing information even as trade and commercial shipping were overtaken by military requisitions, and mining by US air campaigns began to make former routes impassable.

In 1941 the Hakata Chamber of Commerce published a fiftieth anniversary history that looked back over the city's modern development as well as forward to its future. The book's author, Nagashima Yoshirō, posited a shift underway from "traditional Hakata" to "modern Fukuoka."[108] Although by the early 1940s Hakata Port was finally living up to the historic reputation and international image that its boosters and bureaucrats had been attempting to realize since the late 1800s, Nagashima saw that Fukuoka's role—as a city hub in Kyushu and in the Japanese empire—was shifting, along with the bounds and networks of empire themselves, due to the expansion of another form of transport: aviation.

OUR CITY OF THE AIR: FUKUOKA AND THE EMPIRE'S NEW AERIAL GEOGRAPHIES

In June 1936 the inaugural flight took off from Fukuoka International Airfield at Gannosu—the "goose's nest"—out on the long spit of land that enclosed Hakata Bay. This was an event that would prove even more crucial for Fukuoka's geopolitical role in the Japanese empire than the expansion of its port. As Ariyoshi had foreseen in 1929, the age of the steamship was soon to be overtaken by the age of the airplane.

The opening of its international airfield placed Fukuoka at the heart of a reconfiguring of relationships within both the Japanese home islands and its overseas territories. The airfield was not the city's first, but its construction represented the quickening pace of change in technology and the ways in which Japanese advances on the Asian continent recalibrated imperial geographies. There had been a military airfield at Tachiarai, several miles inland from Fukuoka City, since 1919. The location was chosen because it was deemed safe from the danger of bombardment by enemy ships. By the time the Gannosu airfield opened, the age of battleship bombardment must have seemed over—or the desire to have the airfield within easy reach of the city center had won out over such concerns.

Air transportation in Japan was linked to the nation's imperial expansion from the founding of its first public-private civilian airline, the Japan Air Transport Company (Nihon Kōkū Yusō kabushikigaisha, or JAT) in 1928. Just like the Oriental Development Company before it, JAT was a national policy (J: *kokusaku*) company—set up as a private company but constrained by government policy.[109] The announcement of its inaugural routes made the news at home and overseas. The *Washington Post* announced in the spring of 1929 that Japan's "outposts of Empire" were to be "drawn closer to its centers of activity," with the trunk Tokyo–Dairen line cutting a journey of seventy-two hours by rail and sea to a "mere fourteen hours flying time." In this new network Fukuoka would be "the jump-off point in Japan proper for the 120-mile ocean crossing to Korea, and Seoul."[110]

In the early years of aviation, air had the advantage over ferries and trains only for "long, complex, or lightly-served routes"—often over sea or dangerous territory.[111] In his inaugural address to the Transport Research Association in 1929, JAT head Nishino Enosuke discussed the pressing need for connecting flights over long distances of water, especially flights over "our Korea Strait."[112] In Japan's case, the relatively short distances between its major cities in the home islands meant that, unlike the domestic market in North America, or the later market for domestic air travel between the urban centers of Manchukuo, the role of civil aviation in Japan was first and foremost to connect the home islands to the expanding empire.

Fukuoka in Japan's Civil Aviation History

Without its key geographical location at the imperial maritime border, a provincial city like Fukuoka would have been incorporated much more slowly into Japan's expanding air network. In the 1920s and 1930s, domestic routes took a back seat to those connecting the metropole to its colonies.[113] Flights to Tōhoku, Shikoku, and the Japan Sea coast only began operation in 1936 and were some of the first to be cancelled after the outbreak of war with China, when planes from these routes were commandeered by the military for use on the increasingly important routes to the continent.[114]

In early 1929 JAT constructed a branch office and hangar at the military airfield in Tachiarai. Its first flight was a mail link between Fukuoka and Osaka, but the number of routes expanded rapidly in the following months to include regular links between Tokyo and Japan's colonies. As well as mail and passenger flights, short pleasure flights were available to locals who wanted to view the nearby city of Kurume and the Minō mountain range from the air.[115] From July 1929 flights from Fukuoka went to Ulsan, on the southeast coast of Korea, and by September they flew to Dairen.

The first airfield in Fukuoka City proper opened in 1930—a seaplane aerodrome at Najima, northeast of the city center (see map 5). The Najima aerodrome was constructed on reclaimed land near Hakata Port. Originally there were plans for further construction to add a landing field, but this appears to have been replaced by the plan for a whole new airfield across the bay at Gannosu.[116] With little spare land for long runways, aerodromes like Najima made sense in Japan. In the early days of civil aviation, seaplanes, especially flying boats, were an answer to the country's topographical unsuitability for aviation infrastructure. Until the opening of the new airport at Gannosu in 1936, JAT used both the Najima and Tachiarai locations for its expanding network of air links to Korea and Taiwan.

In 1931, the year after its opening, Najima's aerodrome gained a place in aviation history as the final Japanese stop for Charles and Anne Lindbergh on their cross-Pacific flight from the East Coast of the United States to China, connecting the city, and Japan, to the international flying craze that had propelled Lindbergh to celebrity in the late 1920s.[117] Press in Japan and abroad followed the Lindberghs' journey across the archipelago in detail, with daily reports on their activities. Minutes before their departure from Osaka to Fukuoka, a boy of eighteen was found hiding in the aircraft: According to one report, he had been reading about Manchuria and hoped to make it as far as Nanjing aboard their Lockheed Sirius in order to learn Chinese.[118]

This particular security breach notwithstanding, Japan's civil aviation was highly regulated due to fears over espionage and military security. As Pusan's inhabitants would soon discover, security concerns played a large part in decisions about airfield locations. JAT English conversation manuals coached staff to remind passengers that they were forbidden from taking photographs from planes, and that their cameras would be confiscated for the duration of the flight.[119] Charles and Anne Lindbergh were accompanied on their route from Osaka to Fukuoka by a JAT plane, as they were traveling over the Inland Sea area, a route not usually open to foreign aviators.[120] On September 19 they departed Fukuoka for the Chinese capital of Nanjing, where they planned to survey the flooded Yangtze River from the air.

The *New York Times* saw the Lindberghs' visit in 1931 as recognition of Japan's emergence in the world of international civil aviation and believed its success or failure would help to "answer the question of whether Japan is to be a terminal or a link in the world's air services."[121] In 1931 the future for Japan's air service did not look bright; two years after JAT's inaugural flights, Japan's air network was still "a minute almost self-contained island system, stretching out one thin tentacle to Korea and getting ready to extend others to Shanghai and Formosa."[122]

On September 19, in the same hastily printed extras handed out by Fukuoka's newspaper sellers that announced the Lindberghs' safe departure, there were reports about an incident in Manchuria. Japan's Kwantung Army, using the pretext of an attack on a stretch of railway near Mukden, attacked and eventually subdued regional Chinese forces before advancing to control all of Manchuria. The following year, using the Wilsonian language of "self-determination," the nominally independent puppet state of Manchukuo was founded, under Japanese control. Over the next decade the utopian vision of a global network of "world air services" gave way to a struggle of autarkic blocs that extended into the skies.[123]

This shift in East Asian geopolitics would act as a catalyst on the Japanese air industry and strengthen Fukuoka's position as a link between the home islands and the continent.[124] The "tentacles" linking the home islands of Japan to its colonies, and to the Asian continent, did indeed grow in number in the following years. Test flights from Najima to Taipei took place weeks after the Lindberghs' departure in preparation for a regular link.[125] From 1934, the Tokyo–Dairen route connected to domestic flights run by Manchurian Airways via a Sinŭiju–Mukden link (see figure 6). From 1936, there were regular flights from Fukuoka via Naha to Taiwan.[126] Not only were the routes expanding but they were speeding up too. The journey from Tokyo to Manchukuo's capital city, Shinkyō (Hsinking), took fifty-two hours in 1932. By 1935, it took only fifteen and a half hours. By 1938—the tenth anniversary of JAT's founding—one could travel from Tokyo to the capital of Manchukuo in just nine hours.[127]

In 1936 work began on a new international airfield across Hakata Bay at Gannosu (see map 5).[128] The construction was under the direct control of the prefecture. Under the banner of "volunteer work" (J: *hōshi sagyō*), local youth and patriotic women's groups along with local veterans were all mobilized to help construct the airfield. On June 6, 1936, the completion ceremony for Fukuoka International Airfield was broadcast live across the empire via radio, combining two technologies of communication—one mass, one elite—to reproduce the "public spectacle of aviation," with "the fuzzy crackle of mass communication amplify[ing] the national drama."[129]

Whereas the Korea Strait could be crossed by fishing vessels, stowaways, ferries, and traffickers, the air link, in Japan as elsewhere, was the realm of the imperial class: well-heeled businessmen and government officials.[130] The largest plane could hold only around twenty passengers, and the prices were more than a Korean manual laborer's monthly wages.[131] However, just like the radio, these air routes were important in connecting many people in different ways. Mail, not cargo or passengers, was the real growth market. For JAT's first seven years, mail increased at an exponential rate that far outpaced passengers or cargo. After 1937 cargo began to see a similar growth rate, though it never caught up with mail.[132] The air link strengthened and sped up transimperial networks of communication, commerce, and colonial control far beyond the movements of its elite passengers.

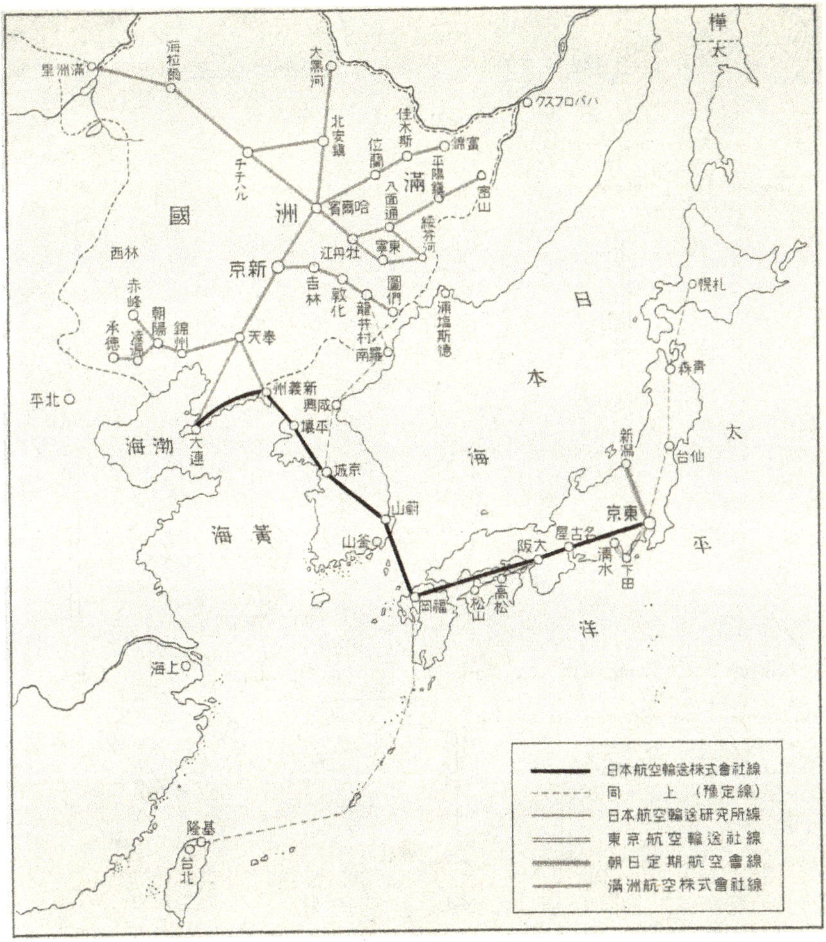
日本航空輸送株式會社線
同 上（豫定線）
日本航空輸送研究所線
東京航空輸送社線
朝日定期航空會線
滿洲航空株式會社線

FIGURE 6. Regular routes of Japan Air Transport (black) and Manchurian Airways (gray), 1935. Credit: Nihon kōkū yusō kabushikigaisha 1935.

In his speech at the opening ceremony, Ōta Kantarō, city council leader and head of the Hakata Chamber of Commerce, described the new airport as "a weapon in times of war and peace" for both strengthening the city's commerce and industry and protecting the country. Ōta continued by stressing the increasingly important role of air travel in the expanding web of Japan's imperial transport networks and the strengthened position of "our city of the air" (*sora no Fukuoka*) within this network. He closed his speech with a florid effusion of thanks to the "holy trinity of central, prefectural,

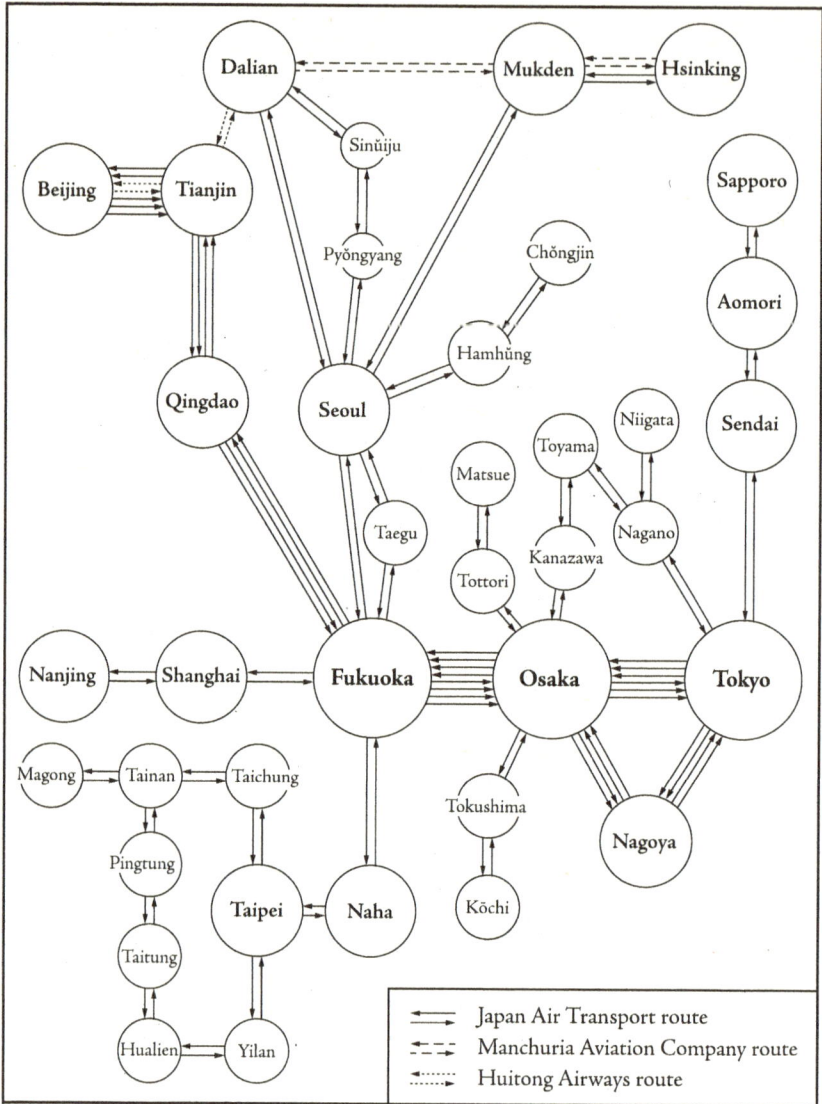

FIGURE 7. Japan Air Transport regular air routes, October 1938–April 1939. Credit: Kate Blackmer, based on Senkōkai 1986, 1037.

and city authorities for their role in advancing the position of our Fukuoka," which "now holds the key to Japan, controlling access to both the continent and the ocean: Let us celebrate this new dawn for Japan's airborne age, and for our city of the air, Fukuoka."[133] The term "holds the key" refers to control over a tactical position, suggesting that despite nods to national defense,

Ōta's outlook remained Fukuoka-centric, as he viewed the completion of the airport in terms of its benefits to the city.

Looking at JAT route maps from the 1930s, one can see why Ōta and his fellow bureaucrats and boosters felt this way. Fukuoka's new airport linked the Japanese metropole to all of its colonies (see figure 7). In order to travel to the Asian continent or to the colony of Taiwan, one had to pass through the city. Fukuoka's position, and the crucial role its airfield would play, only increased in the following years.

Flyover Country: Pusan and Korean Air Networks

In the first years of JAT's expansion, Fukuoka's counterpart on the other side of the Korea Strait was Ulsan, twenty-five miles northeast of Pusan. Ulsan's airport was the result of a compromise: Although Pusan was the obvious choice for an airfield in southern Korea, the location of military facilities at the nearby Chinkai (K: Chinhae) naval base precluded it from being the site for a civil airfield for security reasons.[134] Following the founding of JAT in 1928, the Korean Government General constructed several new airfields at speed in order to facilitate new routes between Japan and its expanding sphere of influence. The Ulsan airfield was one of these, alongside others in Sinŭiju and Keijō (on Yŏŭido Island).[135] Ulsan airfield opened in December 1928, and from 1929 it was the first Korean stop along the new route from Tokyo to Dairen.[136] However, increased traffic after the founding of Manchukuo in 1932, and Japan's invasion of China in 1937, as well as problems with the airfield's location, meant that Ulsan became almost obsolete within the decade: In 1937 a new, larger airport at Taegu became the main airport for southern Korea, while Ulsan languished. By 1938 it was used only for emergency landings and as a radio tower site.[137]

Pusan's boosters were not silent during this. There were attempts made to counter the bypassing of their city by the new geographies of air travel and their power to upend "conventional geopolitical assumptions."[138] Reports in the *Pusan Nippō* from 1934 contained enthusiastic responses to the governor general's preference for a cross-strait air link from Shimonoseki, with its Korean terminus in Taegu or Pusan rather than Ulsan.[139] This aerial replication of the Kampu ferry route appealed to citizens of Pusan. Plans for a large aerodrome complete with seaplane-landing facilities and runways, to be built on an island (Taejo-do) at the mouth of the Naktong River, had been put forward by General Shiōden, chairman of the Imperial Aviation Association, on what would be the eventual site, postliberation, of Pusan's Kimhae airport. *Pusan Nippō* reporters remarked that the proposed site was only twenty minutes by car from the Pusan city center, unlike the inconveniently located Ulsan airfield.[140]

In 1934 the Communications Bureau put forward plans to expand the air network within Korea itself—especially along the neglected east coast. Pusan was again nominated as the key regional hub for new air routes to link Eastern Korea with Japanese cities across the Sea of Japan.[141] However, it was not to be: Taegu was announced as the front-runner for the improved metropole–peninsula link in 1935, with Fukuoka retaining its position on the other side of the strait. As Taegu's position strengthened, the citizens of Ulsan, protesting the move of the airfield, called for Pusan's support, hoping citizens of Pusan would rather keep the airport within South Kyŏngsang province than lose it to a different province altogether.[142]

War in the Age of Air

In the months after the opening of the airport at Gannosu in 1936, there were indications that the age of air—which city council leader Ōta had seen as a new period of dominance for Fukuoka—was also an age of new insecurities and new "maps of vulnerability."[143] The industrial zones of the Tsushima Strait region were in danger of becoming targets from the sky. October 1936 saw a large-scale air defense drill held simultaneously across the Kitakyūshū and southern Korea regions. Although this was viewed from Fukuoka as very much a joint exercise—with commemorative stamps describing the event as the "Southern Korea and Kitakyūshū Region Air Defense Drill" and reports from Pusan featured in the local newspapers—both Korean- and Japanese-language newspapers on the Korean peninsula referred to the event as the "Southern Korea Air Defense Drill."[144]

The commander in charge of the joint practice was field marshal Prince Nashimoto Morimasa, who traveled between Kitakyūshū and Pusan on the Kampu ferry and toured the islands of Iki and Tsushima via Kyūshū Yūsen's ship the *Tama Maru*.[145] The "enemy planes" that filled the skies on the two nights of air raid drills flew loops across Kitakyūshū's industrial zones and the Chikuhō coal mining area before crossing the strait to Pusan and southern Korea.[146] These simulations, centered on the Tsushima Straits region, indicated simultaneously the strategic importance and vulnerability of the shipping links joining Japan to its colonies. On the first day of maneuvers, one headline referred to air defense as the "lifeline" protecting the skies. Arguably it was the skies themselves that, in this new age of air, were the

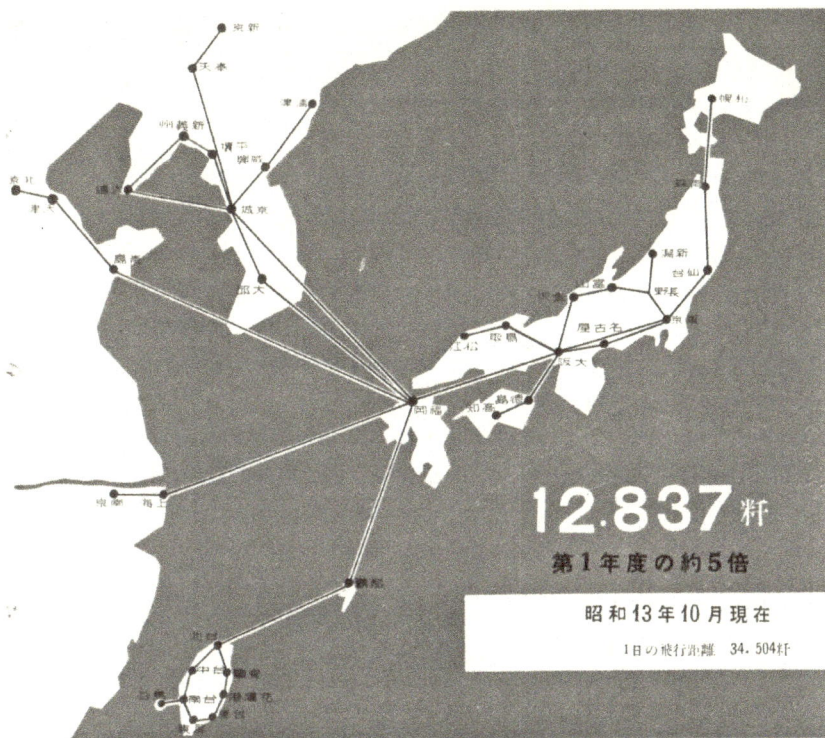

FIGURE 8. Japan Air Transport routes expand into China, late 1938. Credit: Nihon kōku yusō kabushikigaisha 1938b, 32.

lifeline that would protect, or render vulnerable, the Tsushima Strait and the urban regions on either coast.[147]

The following year Japanese forces began a full-scale invasion of China. With the advance of Japanese military power on the continent came the advance of long-awaited air routes into China proper. There had been proposals for an air link between Fukuoka and Shanghai since the founding of JAT in 1928, with several test flights between the cities in 1930. But JAT executives had long complained about the "recalcitrance" of the Chinese government, along with the advance of Western airlines into Chinese aviation, as reasons for the company's slow progress.[148] After the outbreak of hostilities in July 1937, the speed with which air links between Japan proper and newly fallen Chinese cities began shows the intimate connection between imperial military expansion and air power. Air route charts from 1938 show new JAT routes to Shanghai and Nanjing, Qingdao, Tianjin, and Beijing, all departing from Fukuoka (see figure 8).[149] These flight maps show no borders, only cities on a blank, abstracted continent "render[ing] invisible ... political, social and economic realities."[150] Such aerial visualizations had begun with dreams of a borderless "golden age" but now acted as "blueprints for geopolitical dominion."[151]

The year 1938 marked a shift in Japan's civil aviation industry and a further strengthening of Fukuoka's role within it. In December 1938, as Japan gained control over eastern Chinese cities and lines of communication, Japan Air Transport became Imperial Japanese Airways (Dai Nippon Kōkū), consolidating government control over all air transport. The day after the founding of this new company, plans were announced for a three-year expansion works for Gannosu, to begin in the spring of 1939, to transform it into the "ideal international airport."[152] The increasing importance of air transport and communications for Japan's war in China, and for links with its colonies and the new geographies that these technologies created, meant that it was no longer just local boosters and bureaucrats who saw Fukuoka as a gateway of empire.

CONCLUSIONS

The histories of these air and sea links, and the two ports of Hakata and Pusan, reveal the different scales and timelines at which their development occurred during the expansion of the Japanese empire. These histories also show how local, colonial, national, and international events interacted during these processes. The connected yet very different histories of the expansion of the two ports, and their role in the growth of their respective cities, invert many of the assumptions associated with the relationship between the colony and metropole. Fukuoka's peripheralization by the nearby ports of Moji and Shimonoseki put it in a far less important position in the eyes of central government than the colonial port of Pusan. These two cities were linked by networks of migration and capital, but with competing interests at stake. Whereas those with Fukuokan links were attempting to tip the scales in their favor, Pusan's other settlers, and their few Korean partners, were content to provincialize Fukuoka in favor of more wide-ranging and profitable partnerships. Such dynamics force us to pay more attention to the ways in which boundaries between empire and colony were constructed and manipulated at different scales, and along different chronologies.

Fukuoka's link with Pusan via ferry was established in the aftermath of Japanese victory in the Russo-Japanese War. Its history began at a time when naval power was the measure by which nations compared themselves against others, when steamships were the key link between metropole and empire. Its development shows how local networks reacted to, and were brought into the service of, regional and national plans for expansion. The ferry route had evolved out of shipping links of Tsushima's Transport Steamship Company, spreading out from this island at the center of the strait with a history of mediation between Korea and Japan. However, it eventually developed into a route that bypassed the islands entirely.

Although local boosters attempted to claim the emergence of Fukuoka as a hub of empire as a further sign of the city's importance, the Fukuoka-centric rhetoric of the mid-1930s would soon have to be replaced by more patriotic utterances. In January 1939 the newly elected mayor of Fukuoka, Hatayama Shiomi, gave an address to the city government in which he attempted this balancing act, reminding his audience first that "historically, Fukuoka has been at the front line of national defense and diplomacy. . . . The current situation is the perfect opportunity to recreate the Hakata of the Tang era." Looking forward as well as back into history, he concluded the speech by stating that "being involved in the self-governance of this city of great national standing is a great honor for me, and I am determined that we should aim for a huge renewal [J: *dai kakushin*] of Great Fukuoka."[153]

Hatayama's speech shows a new vocabulary of urban pride compatible with the New Order in East Asia announced in the final months of 1938. Fukuoka's geographical position was no longer to be used for the benefit or development of the city itself but for the greater good of the empire and for facilitating the expansion of the Japanese sphere of influence into Greater East Asia. The reference to the Tang hearkened back to Fukuoka's position as the starting point for diplomatic missions (J: *kentōshi*) between the Japanese court and Tang China, showing that some historical allusions to the glorious past of the city were still possible. However, as Japan's empire expanded, and war in Asia intensified, the "animating horizons" of what urban development was imaginable for these imperial bases began to narrow.[154]

Cities in Japan's Greater East Asia

FROM MONDAY THE 27TH TO WEDNESDAY the 29th of April 1936, the newly built Keijō Citizens' Hall hosted the first Korean Conference on Urban Problems.[1] Dignitaries, local officials, and journalists from across Korea, as well as planners from Tokyo and Osaka and mayors from the home islands' six biggest cities, arrived at the International Style building on Taihei Boulevard (see figure 9). Although there had been four iterations of conferences on urban problems held in the Japanese metropole since 1927, this was the first in, and on, Korea. The Keijō Urban Planning Research Group was responsible for the event's organization, along with officials from Keijō's municipal council and the city's chamber of commerce. Around a third of the twenty-six planning committee members were Korean, and the rest were Japanese.[2]

In his welcome address, Date Yotsuo, governor of Keijō, discussed the particular circumstances in Korea that made the event necessary. The recent upsurge in the population of Korean cities, not just of Keijō, was unlike anything seen before, he began. The outskirts of the cities were being urbanized faster than they were being incorporated within administrative boundaries, often causing chaotic and unhygienic conditions, which in turn created real problems for future planning. By gathering experts and officials from all urban administrations across Korea under the same roof, Date argued, they could discuss these mutual problems and find solutions together. He concluded by stating his belief that "this will be the start of a new age" for Korean cities.[3]

These issues were familiar to Ishikawa Hideaki, a top planner at the Tokyo Institute of Municipal Research. Ishikawa was the keynote speaker for

（館民府城京）場　　　　　會

FIGURE 9. The Korean Conference on Urban Problems, Keijō Citizens' Hall, 1936. Credit: Keijō toshi keikaku kenkyūkai 1936 (image via National Library, Korea).

Tuesday's afternoon session with his lecture "Recent Trends in Urban Planning."[4] The lecture focused on the issue of overpopulation across the empire's cities, with Ishikawa arguing that none of the problems discussed at the conference could be solved without addressing this key issue first. Ishikawa argued that by expanding the scale and scope of planning from a single city to an urban region, the new trend of regional planning could be a solution to these problems. He pointed out that in Korea, as well as back in Japan, there were already cities that showed signs of connecting to each other in ways that unknowingly mirrored these new planning theories.[5] Illustrating this statement with an anecdote, Ishikawa described how

> The other day I was talking to your governor, and we were discussing the possibility of factories being built in Suigen [K: Suwon, less than twenty miles south of Seoul]. "That's no good! Keijō will be in trouble!" one fellow remarked. Another chap disagreed, arguing, "This is a good thing, make no mistake." The fellow who thought this was bad for Keijō is a good friend of mine, but he's clearly an urban planner who believes in big cities. The chap who thought it was a good thing is a regional planner.

Ishikawa continued, arguing that

> It may seem like the best strategy is for Keijō alone to rake in whatever it can, but eventually autointoxication will occur. Instead, making the other areas around Keijō work, while it becomes the center of consumption at their heart, is a much better strategy. The best example of this is Fukuoka in northern Kyushu. Fukuoka isn't an industrial area, it hardly produces anything itself, but the cities around it have factories, and their wealth flows into Fukuoka.... Mutual coexistence isn't such a bad thing.[6]

For Ishikawa, the future was not in individual cities competing over industrial concentration, size, and population but in urban regions, with a division of labor like he described in his anecdote. This must have been an appealing vision, especially compared to the reality of what urban growth beyond the city currently looked like, as Date's speech attested to. Ishikawa made what he knew might be a controversial proposal to his audience:

> We have begun to doubt whether just making small-scale urban plans, rather than thinking about the country as a whole, is really the right course of action. Therefore, at the upcoming Toyama urban planning conference, my colleagues and I plan to put the case forward for no longer using the term "urban planning." Instead, we propose the term "national land planning."[7]

The old single-city scale of planning, Ishikawa argued, no longer matched the reality of urban growth across Japan's empire. Imperial expansion, migration, industrialization, and urbanization—all the processes that had impelled the growth of the imperial region spanning the Tsushima Strait—were forcing planners to come up with new paradigms to contend with their results. In cities like Fukuoka, Pusan, Seoul, and elsewhere, imperial urbanization had caused changes beyond the visions of boosters pitting their hometown against others. New scales of planning were required to match the new scale of change—in the built environment, transport networks, and human mobility across the empire.

BEYOND THE CITY: THE RISE OF REGIONAL PLANNING

Why did Ishikawa bring up Fukuoka and northern Kyushu as his example of an emerging urban region? It was not the only site of urban growth and change in Japan at this time: The cities of Japan and its empire had grown rapidly in the interwar period. By the 1930s, the location of this urban growth had shifted from earlier patterns. During the early 1920s, internal migration from rural to urban areas was centered on the "Big Six" cities on the Japanese mainland: the big three cities of the Edo period (Tokyo, Kyoto, and Osaka) that had been joined in Meiji by two key ports (Yokohama and Kobe) and the industrial city of Nagoya. However, from the mid-1920s onward, urban areas in Hokkaido, Fukuoka, Yamaguchi, and Hiroshima all joined those cities in drawing significant numbers of migrants from rural regions. This growth was mirrored on regional scales too: In Fukuoka prefecture between 1930 and 1940, the eight largest cities grew by nearly 50 percent, growing from a total population of 891,000 in 1930 to some 1.3 million in 1940.[8] In Korea, from the early 1920s onward, policies promoting industrialization were among the factors that also increased urban populations.[9] A decade later, the creation of a client state in Manchuria led to further industrial and urban growth in the peninsula's north, but also in its port cities, especially those on the Japan Sea coast.[10]

As well as location, the nature of this urban growth also changed. Urban centers grow both in size, via mergers, and in population. "Satellite cities" (J: *eisei toshi*) surrounding major conurbations grew in population more than the central cities themselves. Industrializing regions like Kitakyūshū, where five cities had grown rapidly in a short time, were another new feature of the urban landscape. Hokkaido also saw a rapid population increase in the 1930s, connected to internal migration and expansion of mining and other industries. The urban growth that changed and overflowed beyond these imperial cities in the 1930s was predicated on the connected processes of industrialization and colonial expansion. It created new problems, required new forms of governance, and generated new debates.

Tracing the early versions of the concepts of regional and national land planning and their gestation over various conference and lectures from 1935 onward, we find a different understanding of national land planning than that offered by recent scholarship, which sees it as emerging in the wartime imperial core, based on colonial precedents.[11] Japanese historians of planning have cited the 1936 Toyama conference mentioned by Ishikawa, held a month after the conference in Keijō, as the first public discussion of national land planning.[12] This attribution can be partially ascribed to the fact that Ishikawa himself fails to mention his Keijō talk in his 1941 work on the topic, and he even incorrectly dates his own first use of the term to 1937.[13]

Ishikawa's Keijō speech, which predates the national land planning announcement at the Toyama conference and expands our understanding of the term's origins, has not been discussed by historians until now. The speech's details offer a new insight into the background for national land planning as a response to urban growth *beyond the city* and *across the empire*. From the mid-1930s onward, new ideas like regional planning (J: *chihō ·keikaku*) and national land planning (J: *kokudo keikaku*) were a response to this change in the nature of urbanization in Japan and its colonies. Their promoters saw these new paradigms as offering regionally scaled solutions to urban issues that spanned empire and metropole.

A year before the Keijō conference, Fukuoka City hosted the second national urban planning conference. This was likely the source for Ishikawa's knowledge about the city, and the inspiration for his speech.[14] Attendees at the conference, and publications that came out of it, discussed the growing need for a new scale of planning, referencing the case of Fukuoka and the Kitakyūshū urban region.[15] Two proposals had been put forward, including one by the Fukuoka Regional City Planning Committee, for a new planning paradigm. Both argued that the current regime was no longer appropriate for "modern cities" and a regional planning system was needed to replace it—one that had "the entire nation" (*zen kokudo*) as its target.[16]

Even before this attention from urban planners, the cities of Kitakyūshū had long since begun to function as a single city for people from the region. The relationship between the five Kitakyūshū cities, Fukuoka City, and Western Japan had been the topic of a series of articles in *The Fukuokan* in 1932.[17] According to *The Fukuokan*, the regional urbanization of northern Kyushu was connected to both overseas expansion and industrial growth: The five cities "hold the wealth of the Chikuhō coal fields, and through their ports have a grip on overseas markets. As an industrial region they act as Japan's heart and are developing day by day into modern cities. In reality they already are displaying the appearance of a single urban belt [*renkei toshi*], but this is not yet mirrored in their administration."[18] We can see here language very similar to that of Ishikawa's speech—describing the emergence of an urban region in character but not in name.

The article in *The Fukuokan* then summarized the two decades of urban growth in Kitakyūshū that had led to the need for new urban planning paradigms:

After the Great European War, the area grew and grew, and by 1921 it had already developed into a single urban belt. In July of 1926 the Home Ministry designated Moji, Kokura, Yahata, Tobata, Wakamatsu, and the three neighboring towns of Kiku, Orio, and Kōjaku as the target of a single urban plan.... The prefectural urban planning division is currently undertaking detailed research based on a projected one million strong population by 1965.[19]

The first regional plan for the restructuring of this urban area involved rezoning across the five cities. The coastal regions and plains of Kokura City were to be the region's main industrial zone, with residential areas relocated to the hillsides and current urban centers devoted to commerce.[20] The term used in the article—*renkei toshi*—was not common in urban discourse at the time, but it had been used two years previously to refer to the Hanshin (Osaka-Kobe) urban region.[21] My translation of it here as "urban belt" is a nod forward to the industrial "Pacific belt," which in the postwar period would stretch from Tokyo to Kitakyūshū, and whose origins are found here, in the urban and industrial development of the 1930s.[22]

In the eyes of *The Fukuokan*'s editors in 1932, the future for a united, industrial Kitakyūshū looked bright. They believed a regional plan would further facilitate the area's imperial urbanization, looking ahead to how, "after resolving the contradictions of the five separate cities, Kitakyūshū will be free to pursue its own development, and with the Manchuria-Japan economic alliance, and its advantageous situation, it will no doubt show great development."[23]

The topic continued to animate local planners over the next few years.[24] Expansion beyond the single city was imagined at several scales, sometimes spanning the straits. This wider discourse offers context for Shinozaki Shōnosuke's 1935 plan to include Pusan within Fukuoka's economic zone discussed in chapter 2. In this light, Shinozaki's suggestion appears a natural extension of the emerging discourse around urban growth, imperial expansion, and regional planning taking place in northern Kyushu during the 1930s, which, by the time of Ishikawa's speech in Keijō in 1936, brought it attention from across the empire.[25]

These regional inspirations for new urban planning paradigms would soon be overtaken by more pressing, top-down concerns. In 1936 there were signs of administrative movement toward a future Kitakyūshū merger. Newspapers hailed new region-wide zoning plans as a "first step forward for Great Dōkai city."[26] However, after Japan's invasion of China in the summer of 1937, the local merger movement faded from the pages of local newspapers and magazines. What remained from the plan were those elements of it that were now considered vital to national policy, especially those connected to defense and transportation.[27] Priorities shifted from the merger of the five Kitakyūshū cities to the need for an overarching port administration and better transport links. Such comprehensive planning to link the region outward via its ports, new tunnels, and roads represents the subordination of regional planning to national policy and imperial visions, with a focus on increased rationalization and efficiency across the empire.

By the mid-1930s urban development had Japan's planners on the back foot across the colonies and the homeland. Regional planning was increasingly seen as the only way to control the pace of change and guide the interdependence emerging between formerly separate cities and their urbanizing hinterlands. At the same time, with the likelihood of conflict with China and the United States rising, and the empire's increasing international isolation, there was also a growing focus on improving transportation links and air defense, as discussed in chapter 4. In Keijō in 1936, the final lecture on the first day of the Korean Conference on Urban Problems was on air defense, given by Lieutenant Colonel Kawai Kiyoshi.[28]

After the outbreak of the Second Sino-Japanese War in 1937, and more definitively from 1940 onward, the needs of the empire began to take precedence over the needs of the residents of Japan's growing urban areas. Focus shifted from individual cities to the "nation-empire" and national policy. Regional planning goals made way for top-down plans to put the Japanese empire and its subjects on a wartime footing. I turn now to how this affected the imperial region spanning the Tsushima Strait.

CITIES FOR EMPIRE

From 1932, with the founding of Manchukuo, the movement of goods and people across the Tsushima Strait increased, and with this came an increased sense of the sea link's vulnerability. From the mid-1930s the Kanmon Strait between Shimonoseki and Moji and its coastal industrial zones became a focus for defense-minded planning on a regional scale, and, as discussed in chapter 4, in 1936 the local governments of northern Kyushu and southern Korea undertook coordinated air raid drills.[29] In a pamphlet published by the Fukuoka National Defense Association the same year, Army Major Fukuyama Kanpō discussed both the Kanmon Strait and Kitakyūshū five cities from the point of view of national security and military strategy.[30] For Fukuyama, the region was the "starting line" of an empire that must expand into the world—as logistically critical as the Suez or Panama Canal. It was vulnerable not only from the air but from the sea too. There was a need, he argued, for far stricter customs and coast guard policies to control the flow of vessels, goods, and people though this key imperial waterway.[31]

Upon the outbreak of the Second Sino-Japanese War in July 1937, the region's authorities increased the number of air raid drills. On February 24, 1938, Fukuoka City's air raid siren was sounded in earnest for the first time, following information that suspected enemy planes were headed for the city from Hangzhou. Aircraft had bombed targets in Taipei the previous day in the first raid by the Republic of China on Japanese imperial territory.[32] Although the information proved inaccurate, three months later there was a "successful" air raid originating from Ningbo, when planes dropped propaganda leaflets across Kyushu. Although they dropped leaflets, not bombs, this was the first ever raid on Japanese soil by enemy planes, proving that air attacks on Japan were indeed possible. As in the joint air raid drills of 1936, both the threat of attacks and the warning system against them spanned the Tsushima Strait region: The alert for the May 1938 leafleting and subsequent scouting missions by Chinese planes went out to both Western Japan and southern Korea.[33]

Defense planning was joined, of course, by military buildup and training. Japanese planes had attacked Chinese cities from the air for the first time in 1932. From 1937 the Air Services of the army and navy were involved in air strikes against several Chinese cities as the Japanese military pushed the Chinese nationalist forces west. The most destructive of these were the incendiary strikes on the temporary capital of Chongqing in 1939. Despite Japanese fears of an attack from the air, they had been the first to commit such an epoch-defining attack, against civilian populations with little to no ability to retaliate.[34]

Early sites of aviation in Fukuoka prefecture became key wartime hubs. After Japan Air Transport left for the new international airfield at Gannosu in 1936, the military airfield at Tachiarai developed into a linchpin of the Imperial Japanese Army's (IJA's) Air Service, connecting the home islands with Asia and the South Seas. From 1937 the site grew to include an arsenal, as well as training schools for technicians, radio operators, and pilots. In 1939 the IJA's Fifth Air Training Unit was formed at Tachiarai, followed in 1940 by an army flight school. As the war progressed, eleven branch schools of Tachiarai's flight school were opened across Kyushu, and four branch schools opened in Korea. They trained a total of ten thousand pilots of the Imperial Army Air Regiments.[35]

Despite the threats that their new significance brought, many figures saw their cities' connections to military victory and imperial expansion as a source of pride. In the case of Korea in particular, the peninsula's role as a key route to Manchukuo and China was a way to increase the colony's visibility in national land planning discourse, and the role of Pusan, as a gateway between Japan and Asia within the empire, was often characterized as a microcosm of Korea's.

In November 1938 Japanese-speaking residents of Pusan with access to a radio would have been able to hear how a Pusan local—businessman and vice president of the Pusan Chamber of Commerce, Kim Chang-t'ae—viewed the outbreak of war and the speedy progress of transport links across Japan's expanding sphere of influence.[36] Kim began his radio speech by directly linking the modern development of his city to Japanese expansion on the Asian continent. "Pusan is where Japan's continental expansion was born," he argued. "The past and present of Pusan is interchangeable with the past and present of Japanese expansion in Asia."[37]

Unlike the expanding urban zones of northern Kyushu, Pusan was linked to other urban centers in Korea by coastal shipping, or via railroad to the capital region around Keijō. The topography of Pusan meant that its own urban development was geographically restricted, but its marine industries developed vast maritime hinterlands, as did its manufacturing industries. Kim painted a portrait of this expansion for his listeners:

> Standing on the Pusan bridge, I could witness all these changes that have created our city: There is now a bridge linking [Yŏngdo] to Pusan, the city is full of trams and cars, islets have become industrial zones bristling with chimneys. Our imports and exports now count for some five hundred million yen. Pusan-made ironstone china and enamelware, lightbulbs, marine products, canned goods, rope, cotton fabric, rubber products, graphite, and many more are exported—not only to Manchuria and China, but also to British India, Britain, Germany, America, the Philippines, Siam, Argentina, Australia, and countries in Africa.[38]

Kim closed his radio broadcast with a final reminder of the key role that Pusan had played in the expansion of the Japanese empire and its increasing significance in wartime:

> It makes me uncontrollably happy to think that peace in the Orient—the aim of this holy war—is within sight. The fact that Japan's first step on its way to controlling all of the Orient was taken from Pusan means I feel incredibly strong emotion every time I talk about the city's past and present.[39]

Kim's speech trod a fine line between local boosterism and wartime jingoism. Prior to the outbreak of war with China, imperial expansion was seen as a boon for urban regions. But war shifted focus from the constituent regions and cities of Japan's imperium to the expansion of empire itself, which was now indivisible from the mission to bring peace to Asia through "holy war."

While expressing a desire for recognition of one's "home" as a key link in Japan's expanding imperial network, Kim also outlined the ways Japanese imperialism had made his city almost unrecognizable from the place he grew up. He expressed emotion for a lost Pusan, recalling how "when I was a boy, I remember hanging our school bags on the giant pine tree outside the Chinese consulate and swimming under its branches." The seashore of his childhood was now replaced by a city "built out upon layers of reclaimed land."

Kim's conflicted views about Japan's role in the simultaneous processes of Pusan's colonization and urbanization are further highlighted in an erratum notice published in the broadcast transcript: "Throughout this document, *Japanese* should be replaced by *mainlander* [J: *naichi-jin*]." "Mainlander" was a euphemistic term to blur territory and identity. After its annexation, references to the colony as "Korea" were often replaced with the term "peninsula" (*hantō*) and the term "Japan" replaced with "mainland" (*naichi*). The pride apparent in Kim's description of his hometown's growing importance for empire is tempered by his linguistic rejection of a flattened imperial space. Kim's listeners—Japanese and Japanese-speaking Koreans—would have heard his uncensored version, where the distinctions between nations remained.

Such complex enthusiasm is representative of many among the Korean bourgeoisie at the time, who saw opportunity in the post-1937 policies of Japan and Korea as One (J: Naisen ittai, K: Naesŏn ilch'e) and wartime economic development of the peninsula and Manchukuo, but who also pushed back against the erasure of their nation.[40] In Kim's case the growth of the city of Pusan was a source of pride, but it was not without its costs, and required a subtle rejection of the subsuming of Korea into Japanese imperial territory.

New Expansionist Visions

The locational significance of the Tsushima Strait region, and the desire of state-level planners to increase the efficiency and capacity of its ports and transport infrastructure, brought its cities new prominence in wartime

Japan. By the late 1930s the visions of state-led institutions, along with technological advancement, had caught up with the dreams of Fukuoka's local imperialists. In 1936 Sugiyama Shigemaru's long-held vision of a rail link connecting Honshū and Kyushu—the Kanmon Tunnel—finally begun construction, a year after his death. It was to be the first undersea tunnel in Japan, although not the first in East Asia. That had been constructed in Korea four years earlier in 1932: a tunnel reconnecting the Tong'yŏng peninsula and the island of Mirŭkdo, located west along the coast from Pusan. They had been newly separated by a canal to allow coastal shipping a shorter route between the key ports of Pusan and Yŏsu. The tunnel was a poor relief public works project, which paid its workers only thirty sen a day, another example of the symbiosis between imperial expansion and the exploitation of Korean day laborers.[41]

The Kanmon Tunnel inspired further visions, both metropolitan and imperial. In his 1936 pamphlet on defense, Major Fukuyama called for the construction of a road link alongside the rail tunnel to ease the transport bottleneck, which would only worsen, he argued, as the importance of Fukuoka City increased along with the westward expansion of the Japanese empire onto the Asian continent.[42] In 1939 his call was answered: The Home Ministry announced plans for a new highway between Tokyo and Fukuoka, including a road tunnel linking Honshū with Kyushu. That year the digging of test tunnels began.

These domestic links brought new attention to the region. In an article in the new engineering journal *Kōgyō Kokusaku* (*National Industrial Policy*), Home Ministry engineer Wada Shigetatsu outlined the importance of this new highway, not only for linking the imperial capital, Tokyo, with the imperial gateway of northern Kyushu, but also for promoting national industries such as the newly emerging motor industry.[43] Taking its inspiration from the German autobahn, the Japanese government's plan for this new highway also had domestic precedents: "Historically . . . this stretch has been the central artery of our country's transport. . . . [Now] it leads to the urban areas of Kanmon, the gateway to Korea, Taiwan, Manchuria, and China, and acts as a conduit to the industrial zone of Kitakyūshū."[44]

The Kanmon Tunnel was also used as a blueprint for a plan far bigger in scale and ambition: a rail tunnel linking Japan and Korea. Extant plans for this tunnel list various candidates for entrance points on either side. In Japan these included Fukuoka, Karatsu, and Shimonoseki, and on the Korea side, Pusan and Masan.[45] The tunnel would connect two planned rail projects. The first, in Japan, was a high-speed "bullet train" (J: *dangan ressha*) between Tokyo and Shimonoseki, under consideration by the railway ministry since 1938.[46] Like the new highway, the bullet train was planned to relieve pressure on the Tōkaidō rail line, now running at capacity. Secondly, on the continent the line would connect to a trans-Asian railway network, in development by the Railway Ministry and later the Cabinet Planning Board (J: Kikaku-in). One line was proposed to link Beijing in the north with Singapore in the south.[47] Another proposed east–west line, characterized as an "anti-communist" railway, would contain the spread of the Soviet Union and remove reliance on the Trans-Siberian Railway by linking extant German- and Japan-controlled rail networks between Tokyo and Berlin.[48]

Such grandiose, world-conquering schemes were not limited to Japan. Globally, the utopianism of late 1920s air travel had been overtaken by "high modernist" visions of aerial domination.[49] As tensions in Europe rose, nations were competing to plan their own routes spanning the globe. In 1938 the British Embassy in Tokyo became aware of German and Italian interest in opening up air routes to the Far East. In order for Britain to "remain a power in the Far East," officials considered offering the Japanese landing rights in Hong Kong or even Singapore in return for getting Britain's Imperial Airways landing rights in Fukuoka, which they recognized as "the 'hub' of the Japanese continental lines."[50] The following year Deutsche Luft Hansa planes twice landed at Fukuoka Airport, their first Japanese stop on test flights for a new link between Berlin and East Asia.[51]

Japan's expansionist visions would prove to be self-destructive. The eventual cancellation of the trans-Asian railway and Japan–Korea tunnel is often explained simply by citing "the intensification of the war," but this ignores the ideological role these visions played during wartime: The railways and tunnel were *symptoms*, not just victims of Japan's expansionary war in the name of Greater East Asia.[52] Imperialist ideology used the language of peace in order to wage war: Just as Kim Chang-t'ae described war with China as bringing peace to Asia, so these plans for an anti-communist railway were seen as a "kingly way to peace."[53] Ultimately, the bullet train was the only plan from this period to later be realized—mainly due to the fact it was the only one contained within the postwar borders of the home islands.[54]

In July 1940 Konoe Fumimaro—against the backdrop of the fall of France and the Netherlands to Nazi Germany and eyeing their newly vulnerable colonial empires in Asia—returned to power as prime minister for a second time. His August 1940 announcement of an expanded New Order in Greater

East Asia, and the articulation of a system of national land planning that was explicitly linked to imperial expansion, placed new demands on planners in metropole and colony alike. In September 1940 the new paradigm's basic goals and principles were laid out in the Cabinet Planning Board's "Outline for the Establishment of National Land Planning."

With the outline's publication the work of planners became subordinated within an overarching vision of the Greater East Asia Co-Prosperity Sphere, which now included not only Japan, Manchuria, and China but also new targets of Japanese expansion in Southeast Asia, Oceania, and beyond.[55] National land planning now took place at the newly founded Total War Research Institute.[56] These new visions for a Japanese-dominated Asia required the mobilization not only of the empire's peoples, but also its cities, ports, and industrial and agricultural regions. Japan's expansionist vision was epitomized by the phrase *hakkō ichiu*—"the eight corners of the world under one roof"—once a rhetorical term but now seen as the final goal of Japan's holy war.

Mobilizing National Land Planning

Japan's new imperium, as envisaged in both Konoe's 1938 and 1940 declarations, was a double-edged sword for figures involved in regional planning. It both tied their work to imperial expansion and made it harder to achieve their local goals. Top-down plans rarely addressed the reality of current conditions, and they also subsumed urban areas within a whole new scale of planning rationality. In 1940 Akaiwa Katsumi, member of the Fukuoka Regional City Planning Committee, outlined the importance of the Kitakyūshū urban region for the empire, but he also voiced his concerns for the region's future:

> For the time being it is a definite fact that Kitakyūshū, by its very nature, will continue to function as the powerhouse of New East Asia. Because of this, Kitakyūshū as the base for continental [expansion] is in desperate need of various infrastructure projects to be completed, reflecting the nature of these times. However, will its future be able to continue for long? . . . When the time comes, we will see an unprecedented shift in Japan's industrial regions . . . that is, the continent will become the biggest rival for Kitakyūshū's industrial zone.[57]

Akaiwa was concerned about the possibility of being peripheralized by the same expansionist impulses that had brought this region its new centrality. Although

Kitakyūshū and the Kanmon Straits region would only increase in geographical significance as a gateway to Greater East Asia, the newly comprehensive scale of national and imperial planning meant that if it was in the best interests of the empire (or, more pragmatically, the war effort), the region could end up losing out to industrial zones on the continent that were able to offer more competitive labor and land costs. Such fears had also been vocalized by *The Fukuokan* journalists Tsurusaki and Naitō on their visit to the coal fields of Fushun in 1932: After realizing that Chikuhō's mines paled in comparison to those of Manchuria, they announced the only way to move forward was by "seeing the bigger picture and connecting [Fukuoka] and Manchuria together."[58]

Akaiwa's concerns were prescient. The initial "Outline for the Establishment of National Land Planning," released in September 1940, was followed in early 1941 by the "East Asia National Land Plan Overview," which expanded on the brief discussion of Japan's colonies within the original outline: The key topics were plans for labor migration—the "increase and strengthening of the distribution of good-quality populations"—and the discussion of an autarkic industrial plan for the whole co-prosperity sphere.[59]

The official adoption of national land planning by the government was a catalyst for its wider dissemination, but not necessarily for its wider understanding. From 1940 onward articles on the topic were published one after another.[60] The journal *Toshi Mondai* produced a special edition on national land planning in January of 1941, which brought together colonial experts to discuss how the new paradigm would affect Korea, Taiwan, and Manchuria. The combination of national land planning's empire-wide scope and its ability to be interpreted in endless ways caused confusion and—ironically—promoted competition within the empire. The published essays showed planners, academics, and bureaucrats all attempting to leverage national land planning's new importance for the benefit of their chosen agendas.[61]

Realizing a planning regime to encompass Japan's ever-expanding "National Land" was a task that would only increase in difficulty as the war continued. Japan's expansion into Asia had become synonymous with both war and peace, and the visions for its future empire reflected the contradictions inherent in this duality. Ideological calls for spiritual mobilization were present in many aspects of imagining and planning for a Greater East Asia, as rhetoric and slogans attempted to mask the impossibility of the task at hand. This was the case for national land planning too.[62]

Growing gaps between vision and reality left Fukuoka planner Akaiwa despairing. In a 1943 article he lamented that centrally directed national land planning still did not exist. Stopgap measures brought in ahead of a national plan only had a regional scope, and in the case of Fukuoka, the problems of the "Kitakyūshū regional plan" were still those of a single "overgrown city."[63] Without an overarching national plan or government funds, the issues faced by this urban area—air defense, population growth, and food and labor shortages—could not be solved at the local level. The original aims of national land planning—addressing urbanization beyond a single city—had been overtaken by wartime planning that ignored and even exacerbated urban problems. Too often these plans went no further than the galvanizing rhetoric of their announcement.

In January 1943 Hatayama Shiomi, mayor of Fukuoka City, published a far more optimistic vision for the region's future as "an advance base for the Greater East Asia Co-Prosperity Sphere."[64] His article, published in *Toshi Kōron* almost six months after the Battle of Midway and just before the Japanese retreat from Guadalcanal, demonstrates the mobilizing rhetoric of urban visions of empire and their continued deployment even in the midst of war:

> From 1929 a great amount of money has been put into renovating the port, and by 1941, just as the work was completed and all our efforts put into showing its use, the Greater East Asian War happened to break out. Due to this, and to the glorious victories of the peerless Imperial Army expanding the area of Japanese activities, the port's importance increased again, exponentially. Thanks to state funding after its designation as a "National Policy Port" in 1941, the port has begun to be redeveloped further.[65]

Hakata Port's expansion and development was, Hatayama argued, the contribution his city could make to the "holy work" of the construction of the Greater East Asia Co-Prosperity Sphere. The "locational advantage that Fukuoka had held since time immemorial" (J: *senko chi no ri*) was finally paying dividends. Fukuoka and its port of Hakata would become the great gateway for Japan that their history up until this point had only hinted at.

What set Fukuoka above other cities with marine links to the Asian continent and the growing co-prosperity sphere, Hatayama argued, was the city's second role: as a hub in an imperial aviation network across Asia and the Pacific. The future possibilities for new air and sea links between Fukuoka and Japan's sphere of influence in Asia seemed endless: "Expansion of air links to Dairen, Tianjin, and Taiwan, and … ferry links to Tsingdao, Lianyungang, and Shanghai are currently being looked into from every angle." Hatayama described Fukuoka's busy airport as a "great symbol of

Japan's advance," marking a shift away from the Fukuoka-centric rhetoric of the airport's opening ceremony eight years earlier.[66]

Mayor Hatayama also pushed for Fukuoka's development as an industrial city, a long-held dream of many Fukuoka boosters but hampered for many years by a lack of water supply. In 1943 the city's urban space was still expanding, with newly reclaimed land along the city's waterfront slated for port facilities and industrial development. Hatayama used these developments to press his case "that the Hakata port area will become the obvious choice for sectors key to national policy, such as heavy, chemical, and precision industries."[67] This suggests that as long as boosterism was couched in the rhetoric of national policy, there was still some space for cities to push for their own advantage.

Mayor Hatayama concluded his 1943 article by offering a bird's-eye view of Fukuoka, describing it as the center of a region of industry and economic growth, with Hakata Port as the central gateway of empire. The north Kyushu urban region now ranked alongside Keihin (Tokyo-Yokohama) in the east and Hanshin (Osaka-Kobe) in central Japan as the key site for industry and economy in the west of Japan. As the "front line of the Greater East Asia Co-Prosperity Sphere," Hatayama declared, "Fukuoka's citizens [J: *shimin*] are painfully aware of their responsibility."[68]

By 1943 Fukuoka was at the convergence of land, sea, and air links, as well as being Kyushu's center for key governmental, educational, and communications institutions and home to a growing population. All were trends intensified by imperial expansion on the continent and by an increasing military presence in the region: The Western Command Headquarters had moved to Fukuoka from Kokura in 1940. Hatayama's view of the city, like most urban visions in this chapter thus far, was a bird's-eye one, at the abstract level of statistics, maps, and transport routes. However, his final invocation of the "painful" responsibility felt by Fukuoka's citizens hinted at the toll that this urban, industrial, and imperial expansion would soon take on the people of the region. The following section offers a street-level view of how the wartime actions of both the Japanese regime and Allied military forces affected the spaces of these cities and the lives of the imperial subjects of the Tsushima Strait region.

CITIES AT WAR

From 1937 to 1945 urban space became militarized space. With Japan's invasion of China, urban areas across Japan's empire became sites of military display and participation that aided the diffusion of military and wartime propaganda to their populations. Many inhabitants of Fukuoka and Pusan, like those across the empire, took part in the celebration of Japanese military successes and Japan's connections to the Axis powers. Such uses of city space were not new: Citizens of Fukuoka had taken part in lantern parades in the wake of victories in the Russo-Japanese War, and the rising militarism of Japanese society from the 1930s onward was displayed in the city in the form of mass rallies, expositions, and parades.

The outbreak of the Second Sino-Japanese War began with nationwide displays of confidence meant to unite Japanese imperial subjects. On July 21, 1937, Fukuokans took part in an "emergency citizens' rally" in the city's Higashi Park. According to reports from that evening's papers, around fifty thousand Fukuokans attended the event, including the city's schoolchildren, various youth and women's groups, veterans, and regular citizens. The rows of attendees waved banners emblazoned with slogans such as "Draw your swords!" and "Destroy tyrannical China!"[69] The rally was held below the statue of Emperor Kameyama, who was said to have prayed for divine intervention to stop the second Mongol invasion when it threatened the shores of Hakata Bay in 1281.

As the war spread, first on the continent and then, from late 1941, across Southeast Asia and the Pacific, supplying military demands required new state control over urban spaces, infrastructure, and industrial labor. Only the faintest traces of national land planning remained in these attempts to control the cities and inhabitants of the Tsushima Strait area and sustain flows of material and labor. These flows became targets. From 1944 onward the Tsushima Straits region—its cities, industrial regions, and shipping routes—was bombed and mined by Allied planes. By July 1945 Higashi Park had become an open-air refugee camp for Fukuokans whose homes had burned down in Allied air raids.

Militarizing Urban Space

In the months after July 1937, public space and time in Fukuoka and Pusan were synchronized with the progress of Japan's troops on the Asian continent: Both cities held parades to celebrate the fall of Shanghai on October 30, and Nanjing on December 12. In Pusan the fall of Nanjing was marked with the erection of an illuminated tower in front of Pusan station, around which people gathered with lanterns.[70] In Fukuoka prayers were held at the city's shrines for the safety of local regiments. In December, the strengthening of the National Spiritual Mobilization Movement was marked with a series of speeches held in the city's martial arts hall. Fukuoka's colonial minority was also incorporated within patriotic and military activities: Defense organizations for Korean residents of Fukuoka were set up in the months after the outbreak of war.[71]

In January 1938 came the first memorial ceremonies for Fukuoka's war dead. On January 18 a "silent triumphal return" (J: *mugon no gaisen*) ceremony was held for eighty-five members of the prefecture's Twenty-Fourth Infantry Regiment. A week later, a funeral was held at Fukuoka's Memorial Hall for another twenty-three soldiers killed in China. Similar events were held in Pusan, but in smaller numbers. The remains of Japanese soldiers being transported back home from the front often passed through Pusan, and such processions were noted in the local newspapers alongside notices about Pusan-born Japanese victims as well.[72] Later in the war, as the numbers of dead increased, such elaborate ceremonies were no longer held.

City streets were sites for parades by Japan's allies too. In the spring of 1938, as part of a campaign to celebrate Italy's joining of Nazi Germany and imperial Japan's Anti-Comintern Pact in November 1937, a delegation of Italian Fascists, headed by Ambassador Giacomo Paulucci di Calboli, was dispatched to tour Japan and its colonies. Daniel Hedinger argues the Italians' visit to Japan and its colonies "helped place the nation's regional war with China in the broader context of worldwide conflicts."[73] The visit's itinerary also brought symbols of worldwide conflicts and alliances to inhabitants of the empire's regional and colonial cities. In April, Fukuoka City was the delegation's last stop in the metropole. Paulucci addressed a mass rally in Higashi Park, and city authorities went to extreme lengths to impress their guests, including reenacting Fukuoka's most famous festival, the Hakata Gion Yamakasa, usually held in July.

Paulucci was an avid cinematographer and the president of the propaganda organ Istituto Luce. He documented the Fascists' visit on film, showing the scale of their welcome events and the reaction by Fukuoka's citizens to their arrival. Ranks of schoolchildren and youth groups, all waving Japanese and Italian flags, fill the foreground of the footage of the rally as the crowds raise their arms in salute to the ambassador. According to news reports, the rally was attended by some twenty thousand people.[74]

The planning and mobilization of ordinary citizens that went into the entertainment and receptions for the Italians' visit was documented by the

Hakata Chamber of Commerce. They noted how, by mobilizing all their members, "we were able to offer the Italian delegation the sincerest hospitality." Footage from the Yamakasa event shows Paulucci and the other Fascist delegates surrounded by the festival participants, the Italians lifted onto their shoulders, with some again breaking into an impromptu salute.[75] The organizers also mobilized schoolchildren to attend the rally, and over 150 geisha from Fukuoka's entertainment districts to entertain the delegation.[76]

The spaces of Japan's cities, and those of its colonies, had long been sites for public expositions and their imperial visions. After Japan's invasion of China in 1937, these events promoted Japan's war as the liberation of Asia from white imperialism. In 1939 Fukuoka held the Holy War Expo, sponsored by the *Kyūshū Nippō*, in Ōhori Park, and in 1942 the Construction of Greater East Asia Expo was held by the sea front in Momochi, historic site of the Mongol invasions. In 1943, work began on the prefecture's new Shinto shrine for the "defense of the country" on land close to Ōhori Park. Only three months after the ground-breaking ceremony, construction began on another military site nearby: the new headquarters of the Western Military Command on the site of Fukuoka's former castle.

Fukuoka, more so than Pusan, was the stage for parades, expositions, and military rallies that involved citizens in Japan's imperial and military successes. Unlike in Fukuoka, Pusan's population could not be relied upon to respond enthusiastically to such propaganda. Although there were attempts to hold parades in Pusan's streets, they had uneven results. On September 24, 1942, the *Fukkai Maru*, carrying hundreds of British prisoners of war from Singapore, which had fallen to Japan in February that year, docked in Pusan. The POWs were brought ashore, strip-searched in front of crowds, and then paraded through the streets of the city. The parade, its route, and timings were announced in the morning's newspaper, but while attendance was high due to it being an imperial holiday, the Korean population watched in "cowed" silence while some Japanese men and boys jeered and spat at the soldiers.[77]

More pragmatic aspects of militarization also shaped the two cities. The threat of war altered urban planning in Japan and Korea, and the rising military presence in cities across the empire reshaped their urban spaces. In the Japanese home islands, the Air Defense Law was passed in 1937, and, three years later, the 1940 revision of the City Planning Law also included air defense as an urban planning goal. During wartime, planning in Fukuoka City focused on widening main roads and creating new city parks to serve several purposes: They could be used for evacuation, or to house antiaircraft bases or fighter interceptor bases.[78] The construction of new parks in 1941 was directly linked to Fukuoka's increasing importance as a hub for continental expansion, and its likely targeting by air attacks. However, only one was completed by 1945. (The incomplete plans would be taken up again as part of the city's postwar reconstruction.)[79]

Aside from creating parks, Fukuoka's urban planners were involved in land readjustment projects, many of which were forced upon residents in a way not seen in prewar implementations. Such expropriation was now legal due to the 1940 City Planning Law.[80] Forcible land readjustment allowed planners to push ahead with the readjustment of three zones in Fukuoka in the name of improving air defense and traffic and expanding munitions factories.[81] As the war intensified, military demand for land in Fukuoka even led to requisitioning the city's schools to be used for offices and dormitories, reducing the city's educational capacity even before teachers were drafted into the military and students conscripted into the war effort.[82] When the threat of air raids became real, firebreaks were created through further forced evacuation and demolition.

Many urban planning measures that were only possible in the home islands after new wartime legislation had long been in use in Korea. Land readjustment in Pusan took place at the hands of the government, not private bodies. From 1937, expansion works began on the city's road network to link the port with the growing industrial areas around Pusanjin (J: Pusanchin) and Pŏmil (J: Bon-ichi), as well as with military warehouses in Uam-ri (J: Akasaki). From 1940, air defense legislation allowed cities in Japan and its colonies to use similar strategies to clear land and pull down houses.[83] In the case of Pusan, this legislation provided new language to justify heavy-handed solutions to what authorities saw as the perennial issue of shanty housing built on the hills above the city.

Pusan and its port were altered significantly by wartime processes of intensified industrial growth and a new focus on military supplies and logistics (see map 6). In Pusan Harbor the Government General developed three new piers and new reclaimed areas, although not all were in use by the end of the war. By 1944 military warehouses covered the new waterfront between Pusan and Pusanjin, and the second pier, next to the Kampu ferry jetty, was used for both military use and some private cargo shipping. Shipbuilding and repair yards on the island of Yŏngdo (J: Makinoshima) were increasingly used for naval purposes.

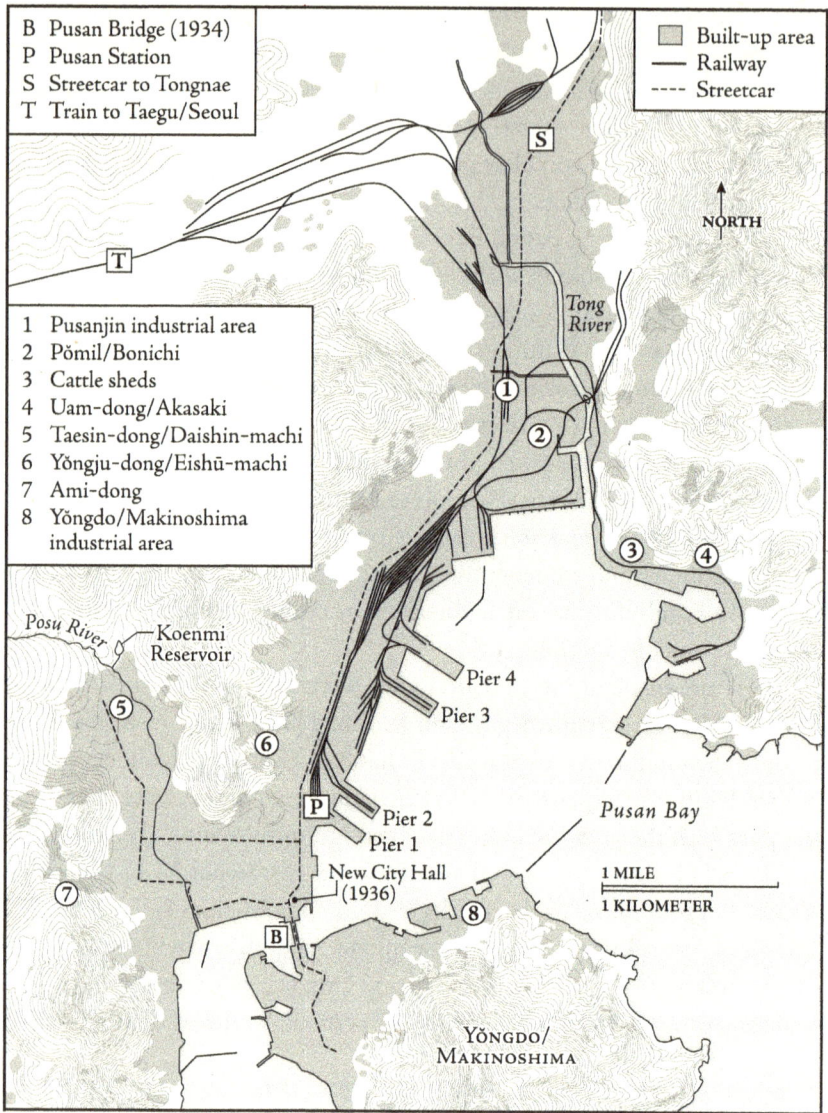

MAP 6. Pusan's expanded urban area, ca. 1945. Credit: Kate Blackmer.

As the Tsushima Strait became a focus for enemy attacks on shipping and port infrastructure, Pusan's importance increased. It was the center of a military zone encompassing the city and a nearby naval base at Chinhae. In 1940, the Japanese army built an airfield in nearby Haeundae, on the floodplains of the Suyŏng River, which required requisitioning land and mobilizing labor to construct it. In 1941, an air defense corps was posted in the city for the first time.[84] This new military presence only added to Pusan's housing shortage. By 1945 there were some ten thousand personnel living in the city's garrison near Daishin-machi, with many others commandeering Japanese settlers' homes.

The outbreak of the Sino-Japanese War in 1937 had catalyzed Pusan's heavy industrialization. In the 1940s, the spread of industry in Pusan was divided between heavy industries, such as shipbuilding and oil companies, based on Yŏngdo; and light industries, including spinning, rubber, and canning factories, in the northeastern neighborhoods of Pusanjin and Pŏmil. This industrial growth caused further population growth.[85] Between 1935 and 1940 the population increased from around 200,000 to 240,000, and then to 330,000 in 1942.[86] It is likely that not all those who lived in Pusan were included in these statistics, especially those in shantytowns on the city's outskirts and hills. By 1942 municipal authorities believed there to be some 4,600 households—around 23,000 Koreans—who were living in informal settlements spread across the hills above the city. Their report states that these workers had moved to the city to work in its growing number of factories.[87]

From the early 1940s plans were developed to construct new housing for some of this growing population—specifically "lower-class" workers in Pusan's industries. In a petition for funds from the Government General in 1942, Pusan governor Yamashita Shinichi described the new scale of the situation and the "danger" it posed the municipality. People living in shantytown conditions were not only seen as a threat in terms of hygiene (an outbreak of infectious disease would have escalated rapidly) and fire safety (there were no clear roads in the shanty areas and no checks on the use of fire) but, Yamashita argued, they also threatened the Japanese war effort.[88]

This was a new rhetorical shift in attempts to control Pusan's shantytown inhabitants. Governor Yamashita argued that the settlements were obstructing efforts to protect against air raids and that their presence was casting "a dark shadow over city life."[89] The petition stated that city authorities wanted to construct new, hygienic accommodation for their inhabitants. However, the project's plans reveal the municipal government's underlying attitudes toward the shantytown dwellers: In one blueprint they are referred to as *furyō rōmusha* (delinquent workers) before the term was replaced by *kakyū rōmusha* (lower-class workers).

The new accommodations would, Yamashita argued, strengthen the city's workforce in order to keep up production for the war effort.[90] The terminology for these accommodations was, again, revealing: Two "camps" (J: *shūyōchi*) were planned for Pŏmil and Taeyŏn, near Uam-ri, close to munitions and spinning factories (see map 6). The third was in distant Koejŏng—a decision reminiscent of earlier policies, established when the city's poor were seen by authorities not as part of an industrial working class necessary for the war effort but as a problem best kept out of sight.

Housing in the camps was cramped and the settlements were dense.[91] The Pŏmil and Taeyŏn camps are visible on a US Army map of the city, based on aerial photographs from this time.[92] In their confidential reports on the port, naval intelligence remarked on the new zones, describing them as "barracks, apparently laborers' quarters, some of which were still under construction in November 1944." Noting their dense construction, the report wondered whether the buildings could really be meant for human habitation.[93]

Controlling Urban Labor

During wartime, Japan's relationship with Korea became increasingly extractive: The route that connected Japan's home islands to its expanding empire was also a funnel through which the peninsula's rice and workers could be brought to feed the metropole and to replace labor lost to military conscription. As prime minister, Konoe Fumimaro passed the National Mobilization Law (J: Kokka sōdōin hō) in April 1938, allowing the state increased powers to mobilize and control labor within Japan and its colonies, which it implemented from August that year. Pusan played a double role in this process. As seen above, the city's road networks and port were improved for military purposes, but Pusan also acted as a hub for mobilized Korean labor.

Wartime policies regarding labor mobilization both within and through Pusan evolved from earlier iterations, using new wartime agendas for old aims. The conscription, from 1944, of Korean laborers to work in Japan— often referred to as *kyōsei renkō* (forcible movement)—marked the breaking point of a system of labor control, movement, and mobilization across the empire. Workers—especially the large numbers who traveled from southern Korea to northern Kyushu—traveled along a route with a long history.[94] Control over labor both for public works within Pusan and through Pusan's employment office had been a feature of city government from the 1930s onward, when unemployed Korean laborers had been paid a pittance to work on city construction projects. The desire for greater control over the quality

and movement of labor had also been a topic of discussion for Kyushu industrialists at their 1939 roundtable, discussed in chapter 3.[95]

Six months after the Fukuoka roundtable, in September 1939, government-
sanctioned large-scale recruitment of laborers from southern Korea to Japan
began. The target regions for this labor supply were to be the "densely populated" regions of southern Korea.[96] Later reports rephrased this reasoning,
describing the policy as another "poor relief" project aimed at regions
stricken by drought. Commentators also worried about how such large-scale
movement of laborers to the home islands would affect planned group migrations of Koreans to Manchukuo, as well as the supply of agricultural labor in
Korea.[97] It seemed that the metropole's wartime needs for labor were in danger of upsetting other empire-wide flows of migrants and workers. Putting
the forced and coerced movement of Korean labor in a regional context highlights how this mobilization relied on already extant institutions and routes
created through processes of imperial urbanization.

The Pusan employment office (J: Pusan shokugyō shōkaijo) had been
nationalized in January 1940 and had produced a report on "the delivery of
Korean laborers to the home islands" in August of that year.[98] The report
offers an insight into the logistics of how this so-called delivery (J: *kyōshutsu*)
of Korean labor was undertaken and organized, and into the cooperation
required at national, colonial, and local levels, especially as Pusan was a staging ground for the transportation of laborers to mining and war industry
sites in the home islands. The report's conclusions also show that the vision
for a far more comprehensive movement of Korean labor—and an awareness
of its dangers—was present in the minds of colonial bureaucrats several years
before it was implemented.

The report offered its own summary of recent changes in labor migration
policy, recounting how, after the outbreak of war with China, in order to aid
industries in the home islands, three national ministries (home, health and
welfare, and colonial affairs) along with the Government General of Korea
were forced to find "a solution that both sides could agree on."[99] This led to
the 1939 policy that allowed large-scale labor recruitment across the strait,
especially from southern Korea, through the mediation (J: *assen*) of municipal and county authorities and the colonial police.[100] In 1940 the Korean
Employment Ordinance further institutionalized the recruitment system,
nationalizing six employment centers across Korea. Pusan's office, which had
opened in 1923, found itself incorporated in a newly widened web of labor
control. Whereas it previously interacted with other regional centers such as

those in Shimonoseki and Moji, as discussed in chapter 3, Pusan's employ-ment office was now part of an empire-wide system that aimed to "plan for the best distribution of labor"—a concept echoed the following year in the Cabinet Planning Board's "East Asia National Land Plan Overview."[101]

Pusan's labor policy at this time bridged the gap between earlier labor recruitment methods and later, more violent methods. The 1940 report out-lines the process of recruiting, selecting, and supplying Korean laborers from Pusan's catchment area for three mining and construction companies from Hokkaido, Karafuto, and Okayama during the spring of 1940. Once they received permission to recruit, each company had an application period of around two weeks, during which time the employment center's various sec-tions would get to work—first by putting out announcements via radio, newspaper, and billboards. They also made sure that employees at regional offices knew to reassure applicants, nervous about the bad things they had heard about labor conditions in Hokkaido, that "conditions now are much better than in the old days." Notices were put out in both Japanese and Korean advising applicants to register at their nearest regional office (see figure 10).

Once registered, successful applicants underwent initial screening at their local police office. Their names and numbers were then added to a final reg-ister, and they were asked to report for further screening and health checks before receiving permission to cross to Japan (see figure 11). This process aimed to weed out those who were "simply interested in life in Japan, but without the physical strength for manual labor, for example hairdressers, insurance salesmen, or traveling performers."[102] Interviewers were also told to look out for those wearing extravagant clothes, or "someone . . . straight from the sticks, with no chance of passing the police screening."[103]

After a health check by a local Korean doctor, those deemed free from internal and infectious diseases and without developmental issues (J: *hat-suiku fuzen*) were sent to a local photography studio, where they had two identity photographs taken, to be added to their contracts. All successful applicants were then lectured on how to behave upon arrival in Japan proper by a member of the police. The report notes how "recently, due to the involve-ment of the Japan-Korea Association [Naisen Kyōkai], this training has become very professional."[104] This provincial-level association had been set up earlier in 1940. It held seminars to discuss the movement of Korean laborers to the *naichi*, and even stationed staff on Pusan's ferry pier to assist laborers with their paperwork.[105]

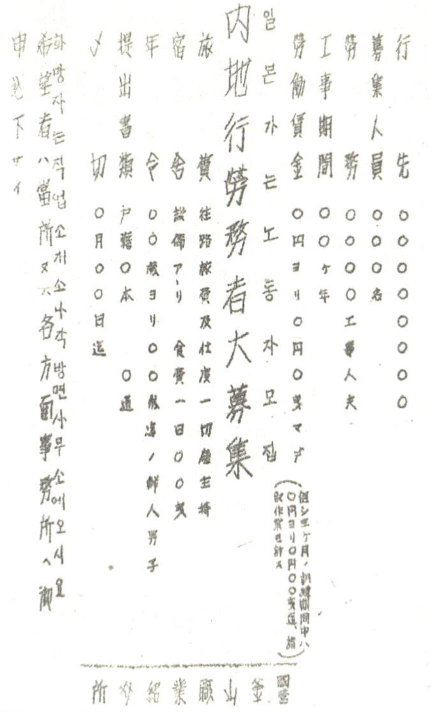
内地行勞務者大募集
일본가는 노동자 모집
行先 〇〇〇〇〇〇〇〇
募集人員 〇〇〇名
勞務 〇〇〇〇工事人夫
工事期間 〇〇ヶ年
勞働賃金 〇円ヨリ〇円〇銭マデ
（但シ三ヶ月ノ訓練期間中ハ〇円ヨリ〇円〇〇銭迄、請負作業モ許ス）
旅費 往路旅費及仕度一切雇主持
宿舍 設備アリ 食費一日〇〇銭
年令 〇〇歳ヨリ〇〇歳迄ノ鮮人男子
提出書類 戸籍〇本 〇通
〆切 〇月〇〇日迄
希望者ハ當所又ハ各方面事務所ヘ御申込下サイ
희망자는 직업소개소나 각 방면 사무소에 오시오
國營 釜山職業紹介所

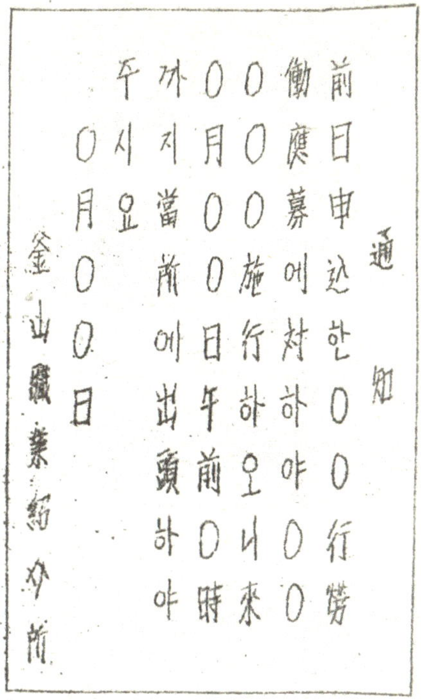
通知
前日申込한〇〇行勞
働應募에対하야〇〇
〇〇〇施行하오니來
〇月〇〇日午前〇時
까지當所에出頭하야
주시요
〇月〇〇日
釜山職業紹介所

FIGURE 10. A sample recruitment notice for Korean workers. Credit: Pusan shokugyō shōkaijo 1940b, 12. Courtesy of the Hitotsubashi University Institute of Economic Research.

FIGURE 11. A sample notice calling successful applicants for further screening. Credit: Pusan shokugyō shōkaijo 1940b, 14. Courtesy of the Hitotsubashi University Institute of Economic Research.

Only after this lengthy and expensive process to weed out "bad workers" would applicants receive notice of the date of their departure for Japan. In spring 1940, out of a thousand applicants for work at all three companies, only 499 actually left for Japan—a hundred fewer than the companies asked for.[106] The workers were sent off to Japan in groups from Pusan pier.

The report described how, on their day of departure on the Kampu ferry, these new "shining warriors on industry's front line ... dedicating their strength to the home islands' heavy industries" would gather at the designated meeting place in civilian uniform.[107] A leader, usually a school graduate who spoke some Japanese, was chosen for every group of ten. Group leaders would be responsible for distributing food and keeping their workmates in check on the long journey to their destination. Often the group would visit

Ryūdozan Shrine before reporting at the port police station and finally boarding the ferry to Japan.

"Modern war," the author of the 1940 report concluded, "is not won merely by military strength, but through the battle for production, which takes place behind the front lines, through the combined strength of all subjects. Therefore, from now on, we believe it our duty to do everything we can to facilitate the movement of Koreans as required for vital industries."[108] In order to do this more effectively, there were several points that needed attention, the report argued. The process should be sped up and streamlined and employment centers should be expanded, with proper training regimes for applicants in order to improve their "character." The author ended his report with the following prescient warning: "From now on the supply of workers is going to cause a giant movement in labor on the peninsula. The failure or success of this project has the potential to result in a dramatic shift in relations between Japan and Korea."[109] From 1941, with the start of the Pacific War, further labor control mechanisms and mobilization ordinances were implemented in order to facilitate the movement of workers to the home islands, and to find new sources of skilled Korean workers to maintain the peninsula's industries.[110]

Mobilizing Women and Students

In the final years of the war, both Pusan and Fukuoka were part of a complex network of labor replacement that was responding to military conscription and other shortages of labor and materials affecting Japan's industry. In wartime, Pusan was a funnel for mobilized and later forced labor, as well as a regional center of industry itself. Its industries increasingly relied on mobilized labor, including women and students, to replace male Korean workers sent to the Japanese home islands. Many of the city's industries suffered from shortages of materials as well as labor: From late 1943, in response to Government General orders, formerly booming shipbuilding yards such as those of Chōsen Heavy Industry on Yŏngdo increasingly shifted to the production of wooden ships in response to iron and steel shortages.[111]

Student labor mobilization had existed in both the home islands and colonies since the outbreak of war with China in 1937, with the amount of time students had to devote to this "dedication" increasing every year.[112] In addition to coordinating the movement of laborers from Korea to the metropole, the Pusan employment office was responsible for facilitating student labor service, in which both Japanese and Korean students would work in offices and factories for several weeks during their summer holidays.[113] After the office's nationalization in 1940 they also began placing graduates of the city's elementary schools (aged around fourteen) as "young industrial warriors" (J: *sangyō shōnen senshi*) in the city's shops and factories. Wartime mobilization was assimilatory: Students noticed the similarities between daily routines at school and the factory such as bowing toward the imperial palace and doing daily radio exercises.[114]

Hoping to increase the number of working women in the city, the employment office held a roundtable on the subject featuring Japanese and Korean women in September 1941. Women in Pusan worked on the front lines of labor mobilization: Some were involved in the Japan-Korea Association, offering advice to Koreans heading to the home islands, while others worked as supervisors over teams of Korean women in the city's spinning factories. Their work extended to the unpaid wartime labor of organizing family finances, finding substitute foods, sewing new economical outfits, and raising "the next generation of subjects [J: *kokumin*]."[115]

The port of Pusan was also a hub for the trafficking of "comfort women" from the Korean peninsula to Japan's expanding theater of war in Southeast Asia. In July 1942 some two hundred women and girls were trafficked out of Pusan to Burma via Taiwan and Singapore as part of a convoy of military vessels.[116] The port was the site of its own "comfort stations" too due to the increasing numbers of the Japanese army and navy members stationed in the city.[117]

From 1944 the Student Labor Ordinance (J: Gakuto kinrō rei) allowed for the conscription of Korean students, some of whom were sent in groups as "volunteers" (J: *teishintai*) to work in factories in the metropole, as well as in industrial areas on the peninsula.[118] In Fukuoka, too, university students and schoolchildren were caught up in this process, which drew on historic hinterlands of labor, reinscribing Fukuoka as a center of gravity within Kyushu. Students were brought to work in Fukuoka from surrounding rural regions such as Oita and Kagoshima, while Kyushu Imperial University students were mobilized to work in munitions and other war industries in Kitakyūshū, including the Kokura Arsenal.[119] In early 1945—the peak of student mobilization in Fukuoka's industries—there were around twenty-five thousand female and fourteen thousand male students working in the city's factories, making up around a third of the city's industrial labor.[120]

From July 1944, even the students of Fukuoka's elite school Shūyūkan, alma mater of many Gen'yōsha members, were called up for war work. The school's principal, Ōuchi Kakunosuke, recounted the experience in an interview with occupation forces in November 1945: "My school has a long tradition and is regarded as the best middle school in Fukuoka; thus, in a sense, if my boys failed others would fail: They had to be models."[121] By the end of the war, 850 of the school's 1,200 students were engaged in war work. Some of Ōuchi's students were even employed as drivers on the city's streetcars. The principal had worried most about these students during the air raids: "These boys I encouraged, saying, you must be the last to drive the cars. The bombing had grown worst [*sic*] and professional motormen had been called to the front. It was a terrible situation. Many a time at night in my sleep I have pictured my boys dead with their hands on the brake after having made their passengers go to shelter."[122]

Suffering and Collapse

Both Japanese and Allied military strategists saw the Tsushima Straits region as an indispensable lifeline for the home islands of Japan. After US forces gained control over the Marianas in the summer of 1944, air attacks on the Japanese home islands began in earnest from the autumn, focusing first on industrial sites and then, from March 1945, on the firebombing of Japan's urban centers. However, Kyushu, Manchuria, and Taiwan had been considered targets for US bombers from bases in China since late 1943. In June 1944 the region's cities, industries, and ports were the first parts of the home islands that Allied air attacks could reach. B-29s, flying from advance bases in Chengdu, had bombed industrial sites in Kyushu and Manchuria, including Yawata and Anshan Steelworks, and targeted shipping in the Shimonoseki Straits. The bombing of Yahata in June 1944 marked the first raid on the home islands since the Doolittle bombings of Tokyo in 1942.[123]

The Tsushima and Kanmon Straits were targets not just of air raids but also of the US mine-laying campaign, which cut off the home islands from continental resources and sank and destroyed more ships "than any other agent."[124] Submarines and B-29s had mined ports throughout the Japanese empire from 1942 onward. From April 1944 the Government General funded a twice-daily air link between Taegu and Fukuoka to make up for reduced maritime traffic.[125] The intensive mine-laying campaign in the "Inner Zone" of Japan's empire in the final five months of the war "resulted in a virtual blockade of shipping through the Shimonoseki Straits."[126] Between March 1945 and the end of the war, more than twelve thousand mines were "laid in every significant channel and harbor in Japan and Korea," cutting "the Japanese lifeline to the Asiatic continent."[127]

The fear of air attacks had animated planners in both Japan's home islands and its colonies since the 1930s. From 1941 the Pusan municipal authorities oversaw construction of the city's air raid shelters. The Air Raid Shelter Exhibition held in Pusan's Minakai department store in April of that year attracted large numbers of attendees.[128] The *Pusan Nippō* even boasted that one of Pusan's air raid shelters in Sakai-machi, constructed with the help of one of the city's many local notables, was "the best in all of Korea."[129] Tall buildings in the center of Pusan were used as sites for antiaircraft lights and guns, including the roof of the municipal offices themselves.[130] In the final two years of the Pacific War, Pusan and its harbor and industries became possible targets for air raids by US bombers. From June 1944, Pusan's antiaircraft post, headed by Captain Nagaki Junkichi, was given warnings of enemy aircraft approaching from bases in China, first via Japanese command in occupied China and then by a lookout post on an island close to the south-western port of Mokp'o.[131]

The first enemy planes to reach Pusan were spotted in the early hours of June 16, 1944. They flew over the city three times, caught briefly by the antiaircraft searchlight. Nagaki and his unit were at a loss about what to do. Although Pusan was not hit that night, bombs were dropped near the industrial towns of P'ohang and Kosŏng. Nagaki found out later that the bombers were part of the same B-29 mission from Chengdu that struck Yahata and other targets in Kyushu for the first time.[132] It is not usually noted that targets in Korea were also hit in this mission.

After this, US planes dropped significant numbers of mines into Pusan's harbor, while bombers also targeted the harbor walls. One mine sunk a ship, which was left half-submerged in the harbor until the end of the war. Mines dropped by the Americans needed to be defused, stopping all traffic and disrupting the vital shipping link between Pusan and the metropole.[133] After American forces took Okinawa in June 1945, the mining operation was increased, and submarines began to patrol the waters of the Tsushima Strait. Nagaki reported the hopelessness his unit felt at watching Japanese ships being targeted by US submarines "within sight of Pusan harbor."[134]

Although its harbor was considered a key target for mines, attacks on Pusan itself were limited and opportunistic rather than the main focus of missions, at least until the final weeks of the war. Nagaki kept a diary of his time as the captain of the Pusan antiaircraft unit, but at the end of the war he burned all his entries from June 30, 1944, onward. He later recalled several raids by US planes on the city between then and the end of the war, including one instance in which residents of Pusan were killed.[135]

As the site of several large plants connected to war industry, as well as the headquarters of the Western Military Command and "numerous regional administrative and governmental facilities," Fukuoka was a more important target than Pusan for US bombs.[136] The city was targeted in June 1945, at a juncture between the firebombing of Japan's six largest urban areas and the "night burn jobs" that focused on smaller cities with fewer significant targets.[137] In the report on its "target" city, US Bomber Command described Fukuoka as follows:

> The city had a population of 323,000 in 1940 and has probably grown since then due to the increase in shipping from Korea and the development of new industries.
>
> The city is a funnel for all types of transportation. Kyushu's main highway runs through the city, the harbor receives a large part of the shipping from Korea, and a major branch of the Kyushu RR runs through town with the Hakata Yard (Target 1270) serving it.[138]

Fukuoka had increased in population through the 1940s, to around 324,000 people by 1945. In 1940 it was the eighth most populous city in the Japanese home islands and the tenth biggest in the empire—around the same size as Taipei and Hiroshima.[139] There was a large gap between the empire's seven biggest metropolises, most with a population of a million or more, and the next group of cities, which included Fukuoka. This was a cluster of industrial and colonial cities with populations between 250,000 and 400,000, which also included Pyongyang, Pusan, Yahata, and Kawasaki.

By the final year of the war, however, Fukuoka's industry was collapsing. The boom had peaked at the end of 1944: Despite the increasing mobilization of students and workers from nonessential industries, it was impossible to overcome shortages of materials and rising absenteeism. Labor productivity had slumped along with morale.[140] After the firebombing of Tokyo and Japan's other big six cities, many in Fukuoka no longer held out much hope for a Japanese victory. By June the city's residents had been subject to air raid warnings so frequent and inaccurate that they were no longer taken seriously.[141]

The targets for attack in the June raid included the Watanabe Ironworks, listed in the target report as an "important producer of naval ordnance." By

1943 the company, renamed Kyushu Munitions, had several factories in the city and surrounding areas. While Watanabe Ironworks had produced plane parts and munitions before the war, production at their plants increased through 1943 and 1944. Indeed, some 80 percent of Fukuoka's prewar industries shifted to military production, and of this, the majority were engaged in aircraft-related construction. At their height in early 1945, aircraft plants in Fukuoka employed 30 percent of the city's population.[142]

The other targets for the bombing raid were Hakata's harbor, railway station, and three factories on the outskirts of the city.[143] This was not a precision raid, however, and the Bomber Command report stated as such: "Besides the destruction of a good deal of industry, an incendiary attack on Fukuoka should destroy or disrupt important regional administrative and governmental facilities. It should also post [sic] another problem for the already over-burdened Kyushu transportation system, and create a serious housing problem for government and industrial workers in the area."[144] The raid on the night of June 19, which continued into the early hours of the following morning, was the only intensive attack Fukuoka suffered, but it was enough to destroy around a third of the city's industrial structures and leave nearly a fifth of its citizens without homes. The majority of those who died had lived in the city's central residential areas.[145] The number of deaths, despite the intensity of the attack and population of the city, was considered surprisingly low, due in part to the dispersed nature of people's air raid shelters.[146] Fukuoka's public air raid shelters could only hold some 10 percent of the city's population, so most people had to construct their own in fields or on plots of land near their homes.[147]

Three days later, on June 23, an attack on the imperial army's Mushiroda air base east of the city—its runway only just completed at the hands of conscripted students—was the last significant raid on the city. In the wake of the destruction, plans were made by the city government and by the Jūtaku Eidan (Housing Corporation) to build around two thousand houses for those who lost their homes in the bombings, although five months later the US occupation forces noted no signs of these being built.[148] Indeed, after the end of the war Fukuoka's attempts to rehouse its population would be compounded by new and increased population flows that accompanied the collapse of Japan's empire.

At midday on August 8, 1945, 221 B-29s from bases on Saipan and Tinian bombed the Imperial Steelworks at Yahata for the third and final time. The long-scheduled raid, coming only two days after the atomic bombing of

Hiroshima, was now strategically obsolete. For the crew involved, however, there was a feeling of symmetry: Yahata had been the B-29 bombing mission's first target in June 1944, and, with what was to be this final raid, the city would become "part of its prologue and epilogue."[149] Yahata's steelworks had been a "single industrial area" target for the Twentieth Air Force's "500 plane attacks," but that campaign had been completed six weeks earlier. Yahata alone, "the Empire's largest steel center . . . the Pittsburgh of Japan," had had its attack postponed multiple times due to bad weather. The mission, referred to as a piece of "leftover business" by the American crew, killed nearly three thousand people and injured some fifty-two thousand more, including mobilized students and other conscripted workers, some of whom died in the air raid shelters of the city's war industries.[150] It is likely some of the city's large Korean population died during these raids, although no official statistics exist. One Korean resident, Kang Kŭm-sun, worked at the steelworks along with her husband. She recalled the "sea of fire" on August 8.[151]

The raid destroyed around a fifth of Yahata's urban area. The following day, lingering smoke from the fires is one reason why Nagasaki, rather than Yahata's neighboring city of Kokura, was chosen as the second target for atomic bombing. Kokura's military arsenal had been the mission's first choice, and the city had been left untargeted for that reason, but poor visibility on August 9, including smoke from the smoldering ruins of the raid on Yahata the night before, ruled it out.[152] On August 14, in a final all-out attack by the Far East Air Force, Pusan's harbor facilities and railway yards were bombed, along with sites in Taiwan, Shanghai, Hong Kong, and the home islands.[153] Before the last B-29 made it back to base in the Marianas, the news came that Japan had surrendered.[154]

CONCLUSIONS

At the close of the Second World War, Fukuoka City, the industrial belt of Kitakyūshū, the ports of Pusan and Hakata, and the Kanmon Straits had been bombed, mined, and blockaded. Crossing the Tsushima Strait meant risking an encounter with US submarines and the possibility of striking mines. A map made by the United States Strategic Bombing Survey showing "the situation on 14 August 1945" shows those areas "under intense Allied air attack" (see figure 12). They included the home islands of Honshū, Shikoku, and Kyushu and the islands north of the now-occupied main island of

FIGURE 12. Chart showing the "intense Allied air attack" across the Tsushima Strait region. Credit: United States Strategic Bombing Survey 1975, Summary Report: Pacific War 1 (1975). Detail from "Chart No. 2, The War Against Japan," insert after p. 32.

Okinawa. They also included the southern coast of Korea, parts of Taiwan, and the urban area around Shanghai. These areas are rarely thought about or discussed when the history of the Allied bombing of Japan is mentioned. Even in the immediate aftermath of surrender, the United States Strategic Bombing Survey spent little time surveying, and even less analyzing, the effects of Allied bombing outside the Japanese home islands.[155] This map is a reminder, however, of the strategic importance of these imperial regions to the Japanese war effort, and also a corrective to the presumption that the Allied attacks avoided targeting colonized populations due to the "professionalism and care" of the bombers, when the pragmatic answer seems to be that in most cases, large colonial population centers and military targets had not overlapped.[156] In the case of the Tsushima Strait region, however, the imperial importance of this maritime boundary, which by the summer of 1945 was "ringed with ports polluted with aerial mines," had brought populations in its urban centers, and those crossing its waters, under repeated attack.[157]

The importance of the Tsushima Strait region within the Japanese Empire had animated the visions of its inhabitants, planners, and politicians for decades. In the second half of the 1930s, Kitakyūshū had emerged as a new example of regional urbanization and Pusan had reprised its role as a microcosm of Korea's role in the empire—this time as an advance base for Japanese military expansion, in its holy war for "peace in Asia." Both visions left the cities and their inhabitants vulnerable. Their working populations, especially Koreans, were vulnerable to empire-wide policies of labor mobilization and control. Additionally, the drive for increased industrial production ignored the reality of the empire's crowded urban spaces, worsening living conditions for many and reversing Ishikawa's original aims for national planning that he had outlined in Keijō in 1936.

Finally, as a key industrial zone and transport corridor, the cities of the Tsushima Strait region and the shipping routes between them became vulnerable to attacks from air and sea. In the final days of the war, "in a desperate measure to get supplies to the mainland," shipping between Japan and Korea continued, despite the impossibility of clearing the sea-lanes of danger. The route linking empire and metropole had become so vital that authorities appeared to prefer to "take abnormally high losses rather than stop [using it] completely."[158]

PART III

A Sea Change

6

Decolonization across the Straits

AT THE END OF THE PACIFIC WAR there were around a million Japanese people in Korea—some 700,000 civilians and 300,000 military personnel.[1] Over two million Koreans, many of them from the peninsula's southeastern provinces, were living in the home islands of Japan. Of these, some 1.6 million were "regular residents," 300,000 were forced laborers, and 100,000 were members of the military.[2] The process of their repatriation was part of the worldwide movement of people in the wake of the Second World War, the East Asian history of which remains less studied than its European counterpart.[3] In the case of Korea and Japan, decolonization intersected with the concurrent processes of military occupation, which both catalyzed and complicated the nature of repatriation. This chapter follows the processes of decolonization that led to the majority of the two groups above—Koreans in Japan and Japanese in southern Korea—being repatriated across the Tsushima Strait. It is grounded in the experience of people, both residents and those who passed through, in the key ports for this process: Pusan and Hakata. These two port cities witnessed the repatriation and homecoming of over three million people in under two years.[4]

Official repatriation on both sides of the straits was overseen by the occupying forces of the US military. In mid-August 1945, "Japanese Korea" was divided between Soviet and US forces along the thirty-eighth parallel, with Soviet troops arriving in the north even before the announcement of Japan's surrender on August 15. US military forces, led by Lieutenant General John R. Hodge, landed in Korea on September 8 and set up a military government (the United States Army Military Government in Korea, hereafter USAMGIK), which replaced the short-lived provisional government of the People's Republic of Korea. US troops arrived in Pusan on September 16.

Occupied Japan was directly controlled by the Supreme Commander for the Allied Powers (SCAP), the head of which was General Douglas MacArthur, who arrived in Japan on August 30 from the Philippines. US army troops did not arrive in Fukuoka City until September 30.

The two groups focused on in this chapter—Japanese based in southern Korea and Koreans based in Japan—have often been discounted or overlooked by the historical focus on "official" or "proper" repatriation. First, Japanese repatriates from southern Korea often discounted their own histories by comparing them to the violence or misery experienced by fellow Japanese from Manchuria and North Korea.[5] In the literature on repatriation produced in the postwar period, both primary materials and memoirs written after the event, there are lines drawn between what did and did not count as "real" repatriation. Elsewhere, Lori Watt has shown how the image of Manchurian returnee women became the representative image of repatriates in postwar Japan.[6]

Second, this chapter includes the treatment and experiences of Korean repatriates, who have remained underrepresented in the historiography until recently.[7] The total number of "foreign nationals" who traveled through Hakata accounted for a quarter of all those who departed or arrived at the port, and yet in Japanese- and English-language works the history of their experience has often remained a footnote to the histories and testaments of Japanese repatriates. In a recent publication on the history of repatriation through Hakata Port, the departure of foreign nationals is addressed in a single two-page spread, with the rest of the book devoted to the experience of Japanese repatriates.

By presenting a history of decolonization that focuses on the activities of the people on the ground (officials, Japanese settlers, Korean aid groups, and occupation forces), I argue for the importance of attending to the regional and temporal links—both across the strait and with earlier wartime structures—that shaped how these events played out on the waterfronts of both these port cities.

LEAVING PUSAN

August 10, 1945: Firebombing. Several bombs hit the area around the railway staff dormitories in Suishō-machi, with a significant number of deaths and injuries. After this, until the end of the war, the Pusan urban area was hit several more times by enemy attacks. Houses were blown away, and many people were killed or injured. Every night we were kept on guard by air raid warnings and couldn't get a wink of sleep. These continuous raids left me tired and my body drained of energy.

August 15: Today there was another air raid warning at half past twelve at night. After about an hour the all clear was given and I managed finally to doze off. My secretary Nishida informed me that the 6 a.m. news had mentioned an important news announcement would be broadcast at midday. I wondered what it could be: "Prepare for the final homeland battle of a hundred million deaths," perhaps, or an announcement of surrender. Those were the two that came to mind. . . . At noon the head staff all gathered in my office and listened to the important news announcement. No one seemed that shocked. In my heart of hearts I too thought "thank goodness" and heaved a sigh of relief. I telephoned the central bureau to ask about the policy from now on, and at 3 p.m. gathered all the staff in the assembly yard and told them the nature of the radio announcement, and that we were waiting for our next orders.

August 16: While wondering what the first postwar orders we would receive from the central bureau would be, I was left speechless by a request I got, asking whether there were any boats available to set sail for the home islands. This was for the wife of Governor General Abe and her retinue, who wanted to evacuate as soon as possible.

Of course, with the surrender it is not surprising that in these circumstances rumors were flying round. For example, that the Soviet army had entered Keijō, or that a US warship had entered Jinsen [Inch'ŏn] port, and the Supreme Command had set up headquarters in a hotel: All these things sounded so plausible, but on checking with the central bureau we were told they were all rumors. However, apparently there were already groups of [Korean] demonstrators in front of Keijō Station, and the situation in the city was unsettling.

August 17: From this evening, the blackout in Pusan was lifted. For the first time in four years, since the outbreak of war, I looked out at the night view as lights across the hills and downtown of Pusan shone out, and a deep sadness came over me, that I was not witnessing this beauty as a result of our victory in war.[8]

Tanabe Tamon, the author of this account, was promoted to head of the Pusan Regional Transport Bureau when the Government General of Korea restructured its transportation and shipping departments at the end of 1943. The newly restructured Korean Transport Bureau (J: Kōtsū kyoku) was the most streamlined and powerful transportation authority in the Japanese Empire, and a point of pride for Tanabe, even with its untimely dissolution after Japan's defeat. Railways, shipping, air transport, and customs were all under its control. As Pusan bureau chief, Tanabe's most important job in 1944 and 1945 had been to improve the efficiency of Pusan port's land-to-sea links. At this point in the war, "efficiency" relied on increasing manpower: At its peak, the port employed twelve thousand laborers to load and unload cargo in the port.[9]

Tanabe's account, based on his diary, offers his perspective on the final days of the war and the situation in Pusan immediately after Japan's surrender and Korea's liberation. Wartime attacks on Japanese shipping meant that the Japanese home islands were increasingly reliant on goods from the Asian continent, transported via train to Pusan, where they took the shortest sea route possible to the Japanese islands. By 1945, however, shipping across the Tsushima Strait was also under attack. Cargo piled up in the port. Pusan's two ferry links with Shimonoseki and Hakata ran smoothly until March, from which point US mining of Japanese and Korean harbors resulted in constant rerouting and canceled sailings. In May, after the *Kongō Maru* ferry struck a mine in Hakata Bay, the link was rerouted to Senzaki, a small port on the East Sea coast of Yamaguchi prefecture. By July 1945 shipping across the Tsushima Strait was making use of any ports available—Masan, Ulsan, Senzaki, P'ohang—in order to keep the lifeline between the metropole and its continental colonies running.[10]

In the final months of the war, Pusan and southern Korea continued to be subject to intermittent mining and air raids by US planes, and reportedly even bombardment by US warships. In his diary Tanabe noted an attack on Tsuruhashi (Hakkyo) Railway Station, in South Chŏlla province, during a visit from Governor General Abe in late June.[11] In July, the Taejŏn region was targeted in an air raid that damaged railway stations and bridges. By the end of July, enemy planes over Pusan were frequent, and residents were kept awake by constant air raid warnings. What was to be the final wartime crossing between southern Korea and the Japanese home islands took place on July 23, when the *Tenzan Maru* ferry left Masan port for Kyushu. After this date the only link between Japan and the Asian continent was via ports in northern Korea, such as Rajin and Wonsan, with Japanese ports on the northern coast of Honshū.

Decolonizing Pusan

This chapter begins by reconnecting events in the final months and weeks of the war with those immediately after Japan's surrender. The conditions of shipping, transport, housing, and local and national government at the end of the war had an enormous impact on how repatriation took place. So did the attitudes of the different groups of people involved in its various processes and local iterations—as demonstrated in Tanabe's account of the war's end in Pusan. The postdefeat attitudes of Japanese residents in Korea toward US occupation forces were influenced by awareness of their newly changed circumstances, and fear of repercussions for their wartime and colonial policies toward the now newly liberated Koreans.

Pusan's wartime experience had been difficult for its inhabitants, both Japanese and Korean. Across Korea food shortages caused by both imperial policies and, later, shipping shortages had disproportionately affected Koreans and those without the economic ability to keep up with inflated prices. Korea's urban populations, unlike in Japan, had a relatively better food supply situation than those in rural Korea, indicative of the different attitudes toward colony and metropole, and the uneven experiences of war across the empire.

Unlike residents of Keijō and other less industrial regions of Korea, however, inhabitants of Pusan had been subject to frequent, sometimes deadly attacks by enemy planes in the final months of the war. Although the attacks on the Korean peninsula were far fewer and less intense than those on the Japanese home islands, they took their toll on residents, who, as seen in Tanabe's diary, had been subject to blackouts ever since the outbreak of the Pacific War in 1941.[12]

By the end of the war, the city's water supply was barely running. Supplies of food were low: The home islands took priority over Japan's colonies, and Pusan acted as a funnel for supplies to Japan from the rice paddies and soybean fields of Korea and Manchuria. Shipping into Pusan, which had slowed from a trickle to a full stop in the final weeks of the war, did not start up again immediately with the announcement of Japan's surrender, and the cargo that had built up on the docks in Pusan hampered initial repatriation efforts.

When the US forces arrived in Pusan, they found a city still very much under the control of the Japanese. Richard Johnston, a *New York Times* journalist, was with the occupation forces on their arrival:

> The reception in Fusan was a silent one, for huge numbers of armed Japanese have completely intimidated the people ... the citizens turned out in large numbers and gazed silently at the Americans. The narrow-necked port ... is filled with small boats and junks aboard which many Japanese was [*sic*] loading themselves and their goods today for the trip to Japan. The sizable harbor

shows no signs of bomb damage, but the city is pocked here and there by hits from United States planes.[13]

Captain Nagaki Junkichi of the Pusan Air Defense Unit also described the continued role of the Japanese forces in what he described as "keeping the peace," but he noted that after the arrival of the Americans, Koreans "took advantage" of the Japanese military's loss of power by driving trucks through the streets of Pusan and pasting posters with the name of Kim Ku, president of the Korean Provisional Government in exile, at every intersection.[14] The Japanese troops of the Pusan Garrison were ordered out of the city by the US forces and relocated to a fishing village some miles away.[15]

For those on the ground—both Japanese and Korean—the process of Korea's liberation and Japan's retreat was experienced in increments. Tanabe's experience, however, spanned the whole process of removing Japanese settlers from Korea, which drew to a close by the end of 1945. The US forces kept Tanabe in Pusan for much longer than most Japanese officials due to the importance of his position as transport bureau head in what was now the staging ground for repatriation between southern Korea and the Japanese islands. His diary for the first months after surrender documents the step-by-step removal of all symbols and apparatuses of Japanese control. When an announcement was made on September 8 that, from the following day, flying the Japanese flag would be banned, Tanabe noted discussions at the transport bureau over whether or not they should hold a final flag-lowering ceremony: "In the end, the feeling from most of us was that it would look too much like a once great nation that had lost all its spirit, and we decided regretfully not to go ahead."[16]

From 1941, the Korean Government General had forced the merger of newspapers in each province, with the *Pusan Nippō* becoming the only newspaper for South Kyŏngsang province until the end of the war. During the war years, many of the Japanese staff working on the newspaper had been conscripted into the army or other war work, with Koreans gradually becoming the majority of the paper's staff. With the arrival of US troops a committee of former Korean staff members, which had been publishing a Korean-language version of the newspaper since September 1, changed the newspaper's title to reflect the new era and its aspirations. The *Minju Jungbo* (*Democratic Popular Press*) published its first edition under this name on September 17, 1945.[17]

In the following weeks all the radio stations began broadcasting in Korean, and many Japanese-run companies were taken over by their Korean workers. Companies held meetings for their Korean staff, and *Minju Jungbo* editorials discussed policies about Japanese-run businesses, which "many Korean businessmen are hoping to take over the running of."[18] From late 1945, announcements of businesses renaming and reopening, signed by newly formed management committees made up of Korean staff, were a constant feature in the newspaper. Many mentioned their desire to contribute to national reconstruction, and some offered services to help repatriated brethren and war victims. The Western Japan Shipping Company, taken over by its Korean staff, offered repatriates priority on its coastal routes now that control of the route was "back in our hands."[19] The reclaiming of control over shipping routes and the sea was a constant theme in the port of Pusan. An article from October 11 announced that "for the past decades the fishing rights to our rich Korean seas have been almost entirely taken away from our people . . . but Kashii Gentarō, known for his huge fortune, has had his fishing rights and fishing equipment taken away by the US forces, as part of their 'economic liberation' policy, and returned into the hands of Koreans via consigned management [K: *uit'ak kyŏngyŏng*]."[20] The phrase "with our own hands" (K: *uri sonŭro*) was a constant refrain in these reports.

Other reopened companies under Korean management included heavy industries, metal workshops, rubber factories, soy sauce breweries, and restaurants.[21] One Lee Chu Sŏn, proprietor of Pusan Sushi, promised that "our former Japanese-style menu has been done away with entirely, replaced by pure Korean-style [sushi]—homestyle, cheap, fresh, hospitable, and delicious."[22] Companies also put out calls for new staff and advertisements for stocks. As was the case with the *Pusan Nippō / Minju Jungbo* newspaper, wartime conscription and mobilization of Japanese staff had led to a swift increase in Koreans working at companies throughout Pusan, enabling them to enact these takeovers in the first few months after liberation.

Repatriation from southern Korea to Japan relied on two key transport routes: the Seoul (Keijō)–Pusan railway and the Pusan–Japan sea routes. The US occupation required the continued and smooth operation of both in order to meet their targets for the swift repatriation of the Japanese military and other "undesirables" before beginning the repatriation of civilians.[23] Before his departure on December 26, Tanabe witnessed the repatriation of most Japanese staff from both Korean Railways and the transport bureau. By the end of October 1945, Korean Railways, as a colonial Japanese entity, was no more. However, after negotiations between the Hiroshima Railway Bureau chief, the provisional Korean authorities, and USAMGIK, it was decided that the Pusan branch would remain in operation due to its current importance.[24]

Both rail and sea routes suffered from issues stemming from wartime and long-term colonial policies. On Korea's railways, Tanabe and the other transport bureau staff were faced with the issue of trying to find skilled Koreans to replace Japanese train drivers, many of whom had left their jobs on Japan's surrender. Although they had been heavily represented in manual labor positions along Korea's railways, Koreans had rarely been allowed to train as engine drivers under Japanese rule.

Until enough Korean train drivers could be recruited and trained, the US Occupation forces offered the assistance of their railway unit, for without the smooth running of the line, the repatriation process would have been almost impossible. Tanabe also noted that many railway operatives had left for Japan wearing their uniforms, and that the new Korean staff were left without enough to go around. In the midst of the chaos of decolonization, the Pusan Transport Bureau began chasing down repatriated Japanese staff and ordering them to return their uniforms to Korea.[25]

Several accidents and deaths on the railways occurred in the aftermath of liberation. Indeed, the worst incident in Korean Railways' history occurred at the end of September 1945, when a Korean train driver missed a signal arriving into Taegu, colliding with the Pusan–Keijō train waiting in the station. The train was carrying Korean repatriates from Japan. Some seventy people, mainly Korean repatriates, died in the incident, and another eighty were injured.

The reaction of the transport bureau staff to this incident illustrates the shifting balance of power in newly liberated Korea. The Taegu Youth Association, acting on behalf of the deceased repatriates, called for the bureau to make an official expression of condolence.[26] Tanabe and the youth association worked together to organize a memorial service in the station square in Taegu, and in his diary Tanabe expressed relief at having avoided a serious incident between the mourning Koreans and Japanese transport officials. However, he recalled the "feeling of being surrounded by youthful Koreans, having to read out the only Japanese-language speech on behalf of the bureau."[27] Tanabe was out of place, not just as a representative of a culpable railway bureau whose employment practices had led to these deaths, but also as a remnant of Japan's colonial regime.

The Japanese relied upon the US presence to act as a buffer between them and the newly liberated Koreans. After a visit to a railway yard along the east coast rail line to Keijō, where nearly all Japanese had already left and there was a "dangerous air" among the Korean staff, Tanabe admitted that the Japanese were reliant on the "borrowed authority" of US officials to ensure their orders were listened to.[28] In exchange, the Japanese offered their local knowledge and cooperation. In his diary notes Tanabe described almost every US official he met as "kind" or "a true gentleman"—and, although he may have genuinely felt this way, there was also pragmatism in Tanabe's willingness to ingratiate himself with these new figures.

Upon their arrival in the city, US forces took over Pusan's spaces and structures of colonial rule and relied heavily on Japanese authorities to help coordinate the repatriation of their own military and civilians. The occupied city and its structures and spaces of military rule were adopted with little alteration from the colonial period. Reporter Mark Gayn, who visited Pusan during the autumn of 1946, described the "machinegun nest over the arched driveway" of the US Military Provincial Government headquarters, which was housed in the former regional offices of the colonial government.[29] The image captures the complexities of an occupation where the "liberators" came to treat Koreans with more suspicion than the colonial authorities they had freed them from, and, as the machine gun suggests, often with more naked threats of power.

Pusan, as a key site of repatriation that had a significant Japanese population and US military presence from early on in the process, was felt to be a far less risky environment for Japanese settlers and authorities than those rural areas where Japanese were now a minority who had lost the backing of their colonial authority. However, Korean workers in Pusan made their feelings known in ways that reflected the changed dynamic and the importance of the port: Dockworkers went on strike several times in the months after liberation, and also appear to have engaged in "go-slow" protests, hampering the process of loading and unloading cargo. As transportation companies were no longer under the control of the Japanese authorities and were now being run by Koreans, there was only so much that could be done by the transport bureau—although the US Occupation forces seemed to rely on them to act as a go-between, repeatedly ordering Tanabe to improve efficiency in the port's operation.[30]

As the port workers were aware, Pusan's port and its sea links to Japan were just as vital to repatriation as the Seoul–Pusan rail link. In the chaos of the aftermath of Japan's surrender, there was little coordination of or knowledge about shipping, even from the Japanese Navy, including what ships were where, which were seaworthy, or how safely harbors could be navigated after the US mining raids. It had been hoped, both by authorities and by the large numbers of Koreans who flocked to the port in the weeks after Japan's surrender, that Shimonoseki would play a large role in repatriation between Japan and Korea. However, the Kanmon Straits remained unnavigable for many months due to the intensity of the US mining blockade in the final weeks of the war.

On the first of September 1945, the *Tokuju Maru*, one of the former Hakata–Pusan ferries, which had been taking shelter in Susa, another small Yamaguchi port, departed for Pusan to begin the repatriation of Japanese from Korea.[31] The ship arrived in Hakata on the third of September, navigating the safest path it could through the mined waters. The following day it returned to Pusan as the first official vessel to carry Korean repatriates, mainly demobilized Koreans from the Imperial Japanese Army, back to their newly liberated homeland. Some 2,560 Koreans traveled to Pusan on that first crossing, and the *Tokuju Maru* continued as a regular planned repatriation vessel on this route for the rest of 1945.[32] By September 8 the Japanese government had compiled a list of possible ships to bring Japanese living in southern Korea back to the home islands; their route would be from Pusan to Hakata.[33]

Settler Networks and "Yamibune"

Initially, when it was still unclear that the end of the war would also require the end of Japanese settlers' residence in Korea, Pusan Air Defense captain Nagaki noted a city-country split in Japanese settler opinion over repatriation. Those living in Pusan who had land or significant capital hoped to stay on, while those from the countryside, most of whom were involved in agriculture, were among the first to leave in large numbers.[34] In September 1945 there were around 70,000 Japanese based in Pusan, some 60,000 of them settlers who had lived there for decades, as well as military forces.[35] By the end of 1945, however, there were only around 1,500 Japanese left living in the city.[36]

Official repatriation from Korea did not start in earnest until late September, when the repatriation of Japanese troops began. Japanese settlers wishing to leave sooner than official ships would be made available, especially those in Pusan and other areas along the southeast coast of Korea, took matters into their own hands. They crossed the straits by unofficial *yamibune* (black boats). The term used the same character as in *yamiichi*—black market—both booming businesses in the immediate postwar period.

Such unofficial repatriation was, in the early months, aided by new settler organizations. The Pusan Nihonjin Sewakai (Pusan Japanese Aid Association, hereafter PNS) was formed in the first weeks after Japan's surrender and acted as a broker in organizing unofficial repatriation of the region's Japanese residents back to the metropole. Enterprising figures in the settler community sourced various boats, charging people 150 yen for passage to Hakata, Karatsu, Shimonoseki, or Senzaki. Two hundred yen could get one as far as Osaka. These amounts, recalled later by PNS official Maruyama Hyōichi, referred to the prices implemented after the organization began price controls in October; "in September, before these controls, people were charging around a hundred yen more per person."[37]

The cost of these unofficial crossings may have been high, but they would have been appealing to settlers with significant capital. Repatriates traveling on official routes were only allowed to take a thousand yen back with them. Korean suspicion toward the Japanese settlers was further fueled by reports that "powerful Japanese" were flouting other restrictions on withdrawing money from savings accounts by using "cash brokers."[38] Several articles in the *Minju Jungbo* called for strict enforcement of all the rules relating to Japanese settlers leaving their former colony, as well as reporting on continued infractions by Japanese settlers who were still acting as though they were in control. At Pusan Port it was reported that "Japanese brokers were behind the scenes," trying to force out union workers who had long "been under the thumb of Japanese imperialism" and replace them with seemingly "free labor"—probably as a response to the strikes discussed above.[39]

When the PNS was set up by settlers at the start of September 1945, it was an iteration of the same kind of residents' associations that the city's settler population had been involved in since the late nineteenth century. Its initial organizational structure and representatives reflected this: For the first month of its operation, the president of the PNS was Kashii Gentarō; its vice president was the chairman of the Pusan Chamber of Commerce, Ueda Kōichirō; and its office chief was Ikeda Suketada, who had been president of the Pusan Port Development Company. Akutagawa Hiroshi, former president of the *Pusan Nippō*, also held various positions in the association. To give a further indication of the lingering colonial mindsets of its members, for the first month of its existence it was referred to as the Pusan Naichijin Sewakai (Pusan Mainlanders' Aid Association).

In the other direction, too, unauthorized crossings of the Tsushima Strait were common in these early months. Koreans, also frustrated by the slow pace of repatriation and the controls on money they could take out of Japan, paid brokers to carry them across the straits. Korean associations in Pusan, set up to help their repatriated countrymen and -women, reported Koreans arriving via *yamibune* at a rate of over six hundred people a day even at the end of November. Statistics suggest that this represented a slowing in pace from September and October, when between nine hundred to a thousand arrived every day.[40]

Attempting repatriation via these methods involved a calculated risk. Currency and luggage restrictions on the official repatriation ships made the *yamibune* an appealing option, but Koreans were at the mercy—again—of brokers and captains who could easily extort them when out at sea. Reports had reached USAMGIK of such incidents on both sides of the straits: "Captains of small ships would put to sea with a load of Koreans or Japanese, rob them, throw them into the sea, and return for another load of victims."[41]

Koreans returning in this way were also seen as a threat to both public health and order, with US military sources echoing the prejudices of their Japanese assistants. Captain William Gane, in his report for USAMGIK on the early months of repatriation, remarked that "the Koreans were bringing with them large sums of Japanese currency, which could only be exchanged on the black market, since Korean banks are unauthorized to exchange Japanese yen. Koreans not apprehended and traveling in this manner receive no medical health processing and become a serious health menace."[42]

The decolonization of Pusan relied, somewhat ironically, on the temporary continuance of many colonial structures, as well as the dismantling of others. It was also shaped by the recent experience of the city and its inhabitants during wartime, and the arrival into this tense situation of a new force: the military government of the United States. After the lull in shipping during wartime, Pusan soon regained prominence, this time as the main embarkation and debarkation point for people leaving from and arriving at the peninsula. Many of those leaving Pusan ended their journeys across the Tsushima Strait, in Fukuoka City's port of Hakata.

REPATRIATION ON THE WATERFRONT

From late August, boats from the southeastern coast of Korea began coming ashore along the northern coastline of Fukuoka prefecture, from Munakata

FIGURE 13. View of Hakata Bay from the top of Fukuoka's Iwataya Department Store, October 1945. Courtesy of the National Archives, photo no. 127-N-140415.

in the northeast to Itoshima in the southwest. Within Hakata Bay, "huge numbers streamed in along the stretch of coast from Hakata Port down to West Park."[43] The numbers of Japanese arriving via these *yamibune* outnumbered planned repatriation vessels for September and October. Large vessels as well as small *yamibune* made their way into Hakata Bay. Between August 18 and 24, around twenty-seven vessels, all cargo ships that had been based in Korea at war's end, arrived laden with passengers and goods. Some were so large they ran aground in the bay. When these first ships arrived in the harbor, there were no representatives from the prefectural or city authorities waiting to receive them: Staff from the port had to go directly to the prefectural offices and tell them that ships had arrived from Korea (see figure 13).[44]

Local Responses to the End of Empire

The 2,500 Japanese people who arrived on cargo ships from Korea in the last weeks of August prompted the prefectural authorities, who had received no orders from above, to come up with a solution to the situation on their own.

Their most pressing concern was paperwork. Repatriates who arrived at Hakata port needed proof of their situation in order to allow them passage to their final destination. The prefectural government improvised a "proof of repatriation" certificate, based on ones they had handed out to victims of Fukuoka's firebombing only two months earlier. This was later taken up as a model for certificates given out to all repatriates nationwide.[45] An account by a prefectural office employee vividly depicts the improvised nature of these first weeks after surrender:

> During August we had no communication with those boats coming into the harbor. We would keep a lookout from the roof of the prefectural offices, and when we saw a ship arriving we would grab *katapan* [hard tack], the repatriation certificates, and some food vouchers and run down to the wharf. There we would give out a single bag of hard tack, a certificate, and ten meals' worth of vouchers to each arrival. That was all we could manage.... There weren't any passenger lists of who was on board either. We just gave certificates to those who came ashore. If you didn't get one then, we didn't give them out later. There were also scuffles over the food vouchers if we doubled up by mistake.[46]

Former settlers arriving on small *yamibune* outside the port area caused problems for the prefectural authorities, who struggled to monitor repatriates and to ensure that they had the correct paperwork necessary for their onward journeys, and that they had received the various food and clothing they were entitled to. Prefectural employees were sent out to landing spots within Hakata Bay to give out repatriation certificates to those arriving by *yamibune*. In the prefecture's outlying coastal areas, where prefectural employees could not be expected to wait on the shore to distribute paperwork, certificates and food vouchers were sent to local officials to give out to any repatriates who might come ashore in their district.[47]

Ever since the war's end, demobilized Korean soldiers, as well as large numbers of demobilized laborers, both Koreans and some Chinese, who had been working in the region's industries and mines, had begun to arrive at ports in northern Kyushu. Shimonoseki and Hakata, as the departure points for the two ferry links to Korea, were the obvious goal for many of those hoping to leave for home. However, there was no planned repatriation of Koreans or other formerly colonized peoples from Hakata for the final weeks of August, and those arriving in the city had nowhere to sleep. Similarly, Shimonoseki was unable to be used as a repatriation port due to the large number of mines making the Kanmon Straits impassable. From late August into September, Koreans hoping to repatriate were stranded in both ports.

Although the Hakata Repatriation Office kept painstaking details of the repatriation and sending off of Japanese and Koreans from its opening in December 1945, the first overwhelmingly busy months of the repatriation processes on the Japanese side were far less well documented. A few weeks before the closure of the Hakata office in April 1947, its former employees gathered to discuss their activities in those first months. Some who were involved in the early months of repatriation continued their work at the Hakata office after "official" repatriation began in 1946. The roundtable held in 1947 brought together officials from both city and prefectural government with those still working at the office, as well as members of other organizations who had been present in Hakata Port and experienced the first chaotic months of Japan's de-imperialization.[48]

The initial response by the prefectural government to the Koreans arriving in the port area was to defer to existing institutions and organizations: namely, those that had dealt with the large number of Koreans, especially forced laborers, in the prefecture. The provision of food and shelter, as well as the eventual organization of repatriation of Koreans, was delegated to the prefecture's Minseika (Welfare Division) and Kōseikai branch.[49] The Kōseikai was the new name for the Kyōwakai, an "imperialization" organ of the state that had been centralized in 1939 and renamed in 1944. In wartime it had been involved in the control and assimilation of forced laborers as well as regular resident Koreans.[50] By fall of 1944, however, it was joined in this task by the prefectural level Welfare Division, which had branches in the four prefectures with the largest number of Korean (forced) laborers: Hokkaido, Osaka, Yamaguchi, and Fukuoka.[51]

During wartime, most of the Koreans working in Fukuoka's construction and mining industries had been brought there against their will. Utsunomiya Ichū, a former employee of the outgoing repatriation (J: sōshutsu) division who was present at the 1947 roundtable, admitted that even before conscription labor began in 1944, it had been conscription in all but name.[52] Koreans in Fukuoka, he continued, had been asked to contribute manually, but also spiritually, to Japan's war effort. In this they had been guided by the Kōseikai. But as the situation worsened and the Japanese war effort increasingly relied on the labor of Koreans, they were no longer willing to cooperate. It was at this point, in September of 1944, that the Welfare Division was set up.

However, "before [the Welfare Division] could solve the Korean problem, which had reached a breaking point, the war ended."[53]

Utsunomiya explained how the "nature of the relationship between Japanese and Koreans" during the war determined the nature of the authorities' postwar response and their repatriation to Korea. Despite Utsunomiya's acknowledgment of the amount of work and power that Korean laborers had given to the Japanese war effort—especially in the case of Fukuoka, where over 70 percent of all miners in the Chikuhō coalfields were Korean—his comments reveal the continuance of imperial attitudes and structures of control after Japan's surrender. Similarly, a report on Koreans in Fukuoka prefecture after the end of the war argued that the "few with any intelligence" would want to stay in Japan, while those without would be "cheering for independence" and want to return home as soon as possible.[54]

Fukuoka prefecture's Welfare Division and "imperialization" organizations like the Kōseikai had failed to solve the "problem" of Koreans while they were colonial subjects, and the authorities' immediate postwar attitude toward them showed little in the way of remorse. Other former colonized peoples were also treated with contempt mingled with fear. Chinese residents of Japan who arrived at Hakata were deemed the responsibility of the Keibika, or Guard Division.[55] Chinese workers in the Chikuhō mines—made up of forced laborers and prisoners from occupied China—had been more active than Koreans in labor protests in the wake of the Japanese surrender, and this postwar division of responsibility reflects both wartime administrative divisions as well as common attitudes toward the two different groups.[56]

Utsunomiya described large numbers of Koreans arriving in Hakata from Fukuoka's construction and mining industries, which, he reported, had been ordered to stop work at the end of the war. Other reports suggest that this was not always the case: Some Japanese mining officials had attempted to hide the news of Japan's defeat from their Korean workers, and some had even begged them to stay and keep working, promising them land if they agreed.[57] There is no doubt, however, that if even a fraction of Fukuoka prefecture's population of some two hundred thousand Koreans (by 1945, the largest after Osaka) had arrived in the city in those first few weeks, it would have been enough to overwhelm the authorities.[58]

The first response of the Welfare Division to this influx of Koreans in Fukuoka was to find accommodation for them—not an easy task considering the destruction of much of the city in firebombing raids only months earlier.

At the beginning of September they bought buildings from the Japanese Equine Association, an organization that, prior to the war's end, had been involved in breeding and supplying horses to the Japanese military. For most of September the Koreans waiting to return home were housed in what were "essentially just stables."[59] They were open to the elements, with only hay on the ground to sleep upon. In order to improve their living conditions, Koreans were encouraged by the Japanese authorities to engage in "volunteer labor" (*kinrō hōshi*—a euphemistic term used during the war for conscription labor) to search the city for wood from wartime building demolitions to use for fuel, and as building materials to board up the structure against the elements.[60]

Officials in Hakata categorized returning Koreans as either "planned" or "regular" repatriations—the latter being Koreans who arrived at Hakata Port on their own. Planned repatriation of "former countrymen" (as some official reports referred to them) included Korean members of the military and laborers brought over to Japan in the final months of the war.[61] There were estimated to be around 300,000 forced laborers present in Japan at the end of the war, counted separately from the 1.6 million "regular" Koreans. The planned repatriations of Koreans were, in some ways, mirror images of their outward journeys, reliant on the same mechanisms and institutions that had brought mobilized, conscripted, and forced labor to Fukuoka in the final years of the war. By the end of December 1945, the "planned" repatriation of these mobilized Koreans—former soldiers, "imported group laborers" (*i'nyū shūdan rōmusha*), and "conscript laborers" (*ōchōshi*)—was mostly complete.[62]

A photograph of Hakata Port taken by a US soldier in October 1945 shows one such group (figure 14). Around 180 young women are gathered next to a banner reading "Zenra hokudo joshi kinrō teishintai" (North Chŏlla Province Women's Volunteer Corps). All still dressed in their wartime national uniforms, with headbands and name badges, some of them are smiling for the camera as they wait at the docks to be transported back to Korea.[63] One of the women featured in figure 14, Ch'oe Hŭi Sun, who was fourteen at the time, later recounted her memories of the experience. Ch'oe, who had been conscripted to work in a munitions factory in Toyama City in March 1945, remembered the factory workers who had accompanied the group to Hakata and waved goodbye to them from the pier. When she arrived at the train station of her hometown in Korea, Ch'oe found her mother, "who had waited there until the last train every day since the end of the war."[64]

FIGURE 14. North Chŏlla Province Women's Volunteer Corps at Hakata Port before repatriation, October 1945. Courtesy of the National Archives, photo no. 111-SC-290861.

Unlike those sent back in groups as part of planned repatriation, "regular" Koreans, whose arrival and transport was unplanned, had to wait in the city for a place on a departing boat, and their numbers outgrew the prefecture's meager facilities. When Captain Nagaki Junkichi, head of the Pusan Antiaircraft Division, was repatriated through Hakata, arriving on the morning of September 30, he recalled groups of Koreans sleeping outside at the port waiting for a boat to take them home.[65]

Repatriation and Its Regional Effects

In Pusan, too, during the early weeks of their repatriation, "very little attention was paid to incoming Koreans."[66] Just like in Fukuoka, the city and port became easily congested without a system to swiftly move repatriates not only out of the port area but also out of Pusan altogether. The US authorities became worried about the possibilities of "refugees . . . unable to obtain tickets for trains and others [who] would remain in the area living off relief agencies. Such a condition would generally lead to severe overcrowding, create serious health hazards, and hinder repatriation."[67] Indeed, photographs from a US Army report from the autumn of 1945 show Koreans sleeping in Pusan Station, waiting for trains.[68]

In addition to raising the problems of overcrowding and the lack of places to sleep, USAMGIK expressed concern about Koreans arriving illegally with large amounts of Japanese yen, and those who avoided immunization. Plans were therefore put forward for a "reception compound" for Korean repatriates, including those whom the authorities caught arriving at Pusan harbor via *yamibune*. Incoming Koreans were processed through these compounds on the pier, "dusted with DDT," and had their currency exchanged. The process was overseen by the US military as well as "members of the local Korean welfare society." Such groups emerged among repatriates on either side of the straits.[69]

Pusan was not the only port being used for the official repatriation of Koreans from Japan, but it was the largest, and the port that saw the biggest influx. Mokp'o, Kunsan, and Inch'ŏn—three cities ranged along the western coast of Korea—all saw Koreans processed through their ports. However, early data collected by USAMGIK's Displaced Persons Office revealed that a significant percentage of those arriving in these three ports required onward travel to the southeastern provinces.[70] This is not surprising when we remember that Koreans from the southeast made up a large number of all Koreans living and working in Japan during the colonial and wartime period. In an attempt to limit the need for further long journeys upon arrival in Korea and reduce pressure on Korean Railways, by early 1946 US forces developed a system of "destination loading." This meant that Korean repatriates would be sent to and from certain ports in Japan and Korea depending on their final destinations. Although this new policy was meant to take the strain off the Korean railway system, it added to the numbers of Koreans traveling through Hakata and Senzaki and arriving in Pusan—the designated ports for those heading to southeastern Korea.

These policies, decided on by Japanese and Occupation authorities, would have both short and long-term effects on the cities involved in repatriation. Gane estimated in his report that two-thirds of all officially repatriated Koreans disembarked at Pusan, and the port was also the sole departure point for all Japanese on the peninsula during this period.[71] On the other side of the Tsushima Strait, a total of 340,000 Koreans passed through Senzaki and 494,819 through Hakata—around 33 and 48 percent, respectively, of all Koreans reported as "deported" by 1950.[72]

The differences between repatriation facilities at Senzaki and Hakata were notable. Gane's report for USAMGIK described Senzaki port and its connected reception centers in Shimonoseki and Ozuki as functioning "quickly and efficiently" and "in an excellent manner."[73] On the other hand, Hakata's Korean repatriation facilities, such as they were, appear to have been far from a model operation. Although Hakata was the largest such repatriation port for Koreans, there is no mention of the facilities in Gane's report, only a map in its appendix.[74]

One reason for the issues in Pusan and Hakata was that, unlike the smaller ports of Kunsan and Senzaki, with their well-controlled and well-maintained facilities, Pusan and Fukuoka were large cities. Pusan had long been a site where displaced and marginal populations had gathered in the colonial period, and where Korean housing was pushed to the city's margins. Furthermore, Fukuoka's unhoused population had dramatically increased after the firebombing of June 1945. As we shall see in the following chapter, the sudden influx of Korean and Japanese repatriates was to have long-term effects on the cities' populations and urban spaces, often compounding extant urban issues.

Repatriation through these two ports had wider regional effects too. Three years after the end of the war the number of repatriates in Fukuoka prefecture remained one of the highest in Japan, with other Kyushu prefectures also seeing large numbers of returnees. Maps from a report on repatriation produced in 1948 show the distribution of repatriates across Japan's prefectures, as well as their relative concentrations as a percentage of the population. Map 7 shows that only Fukuoka, Kumamoto, Tokyo, and Hokkaido had repatriate populations above three hundred thousand. Repatriates made up more than 15 percent of the population in the Kyushu prefectures of Kumamoto, Nagasaki, and Saga, as well as neighboring Yamaguchi prefecture (map 8). Although repatriates made up a larger percentage of these less-populated rural prefectures' populations, this does not mean that they were easily absorbed into more urbanized prefectures, especially considering the shortages of food and housing that these urban areas continued to experience for years after the end of the war.

Across the straits, repatriates were also overrepresented in Korea's southeast, around the repatriation port of Pusan, and in the provinces that originally had sent many workers to the metropole. South Kyŏngsang province had the highest rate of population change of any province in Korea between 1944 and 1946, especially in its smaller cities and rural counties.[75] This

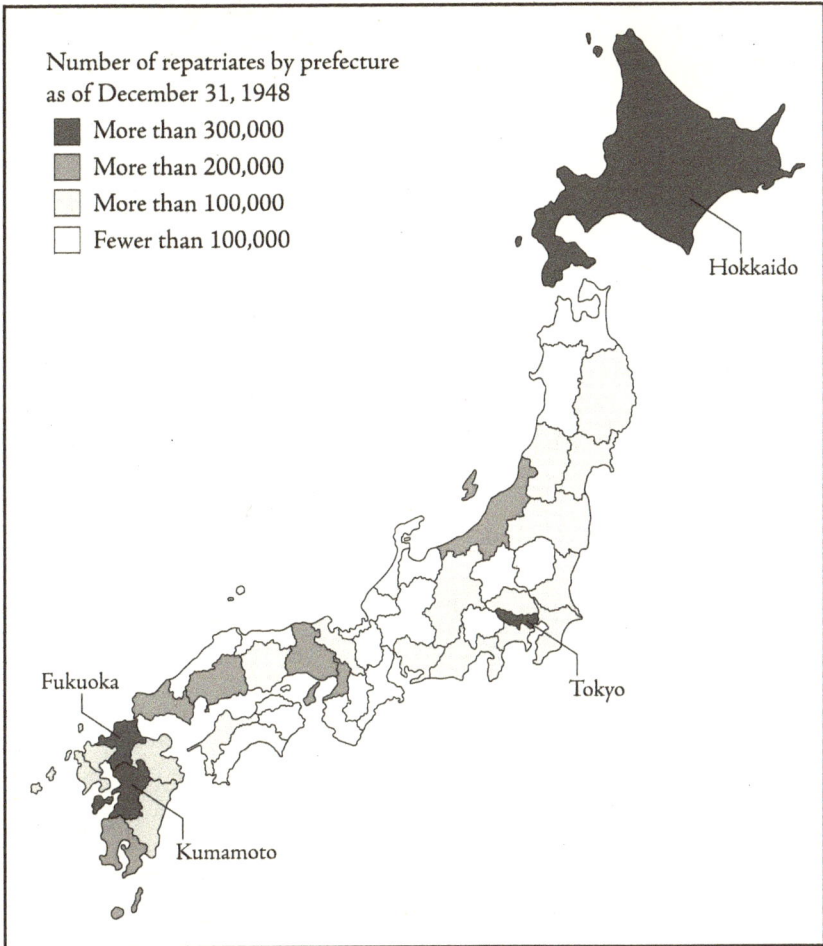

MAP 7. Number of repatriates in each prefecture as of December 31, 1948. Credit: Kate Blackmer; data from Hikiage engo chō 1950, front matter.

population movement, which Bruce Cumings refers to as a "continuing influx of profoundly discouraged and resentful people," alongside other regional socio-geographic factors, led to the province's political mobilization following the liberation of Korea.[76] In South Kyŏngsang province, those counties with high population change had some of the strongest local political organizations, which would play a role in the Autumn Harvest Uprisings of 1946. In Japan, how the presence of repatriates affected the sociopolitical character of Kyushu's rural prefectures in the postwar period deserves further investigation.[77]

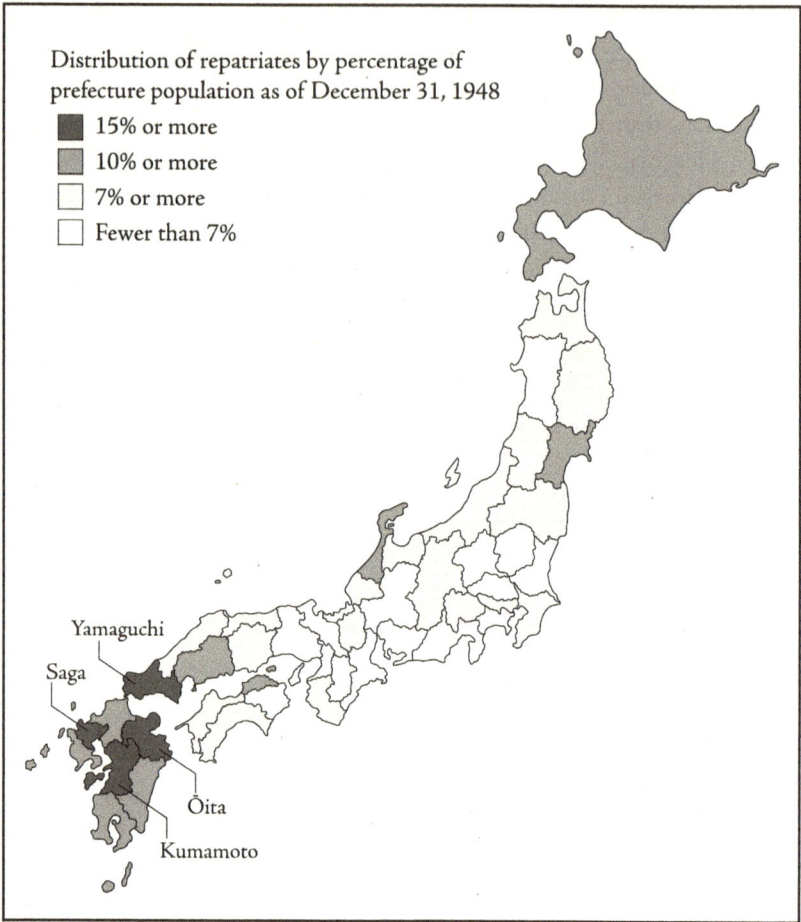

Distribution of repatriates by percentage of
prefecture population as of December 31, 1948

- 15% or more
- 10% or more
- 7% or more
- Fewer than 7%

Yamaguchi

Saga

Ōita

Kumamoto

MAP 8. Repatriates as a percentage of prefectural population as of December 31, 1948.
Credit: Kate Blackmer; data from Hikiage engo chō 1950, front matter.

Postcolonial Tensions and Occupation Forces

Upon their arrival in Hakata at the end of September 1945, occupation
authorities clashed with Japanese officials over the treatment of Koreans
waiting to leave the port. As mentioned above, poor conditions in Hakata
were exacerbated by the racist colonial attitudes of Japanese officials toward
Korean repatriates. The officials present at the 1947 roundtable remained
adamant that the stables in which the Koreans were living were the only
suitable accommodation that could be found in Fukuoka, despite clashes

with the occupation forces, who argued the stables were unfit for human habitation. In October they ordered Fukuoka officials to open empty buildings on the docks for accommodation, and although they could not ignore these orders, officials expressed regret that they could not "protect" the port from being used for such purposes.[78]

When the occupation officials ordered the Japanese to gather together all the Koreans waiting to be repatriated in order to move them into their new accommodation, their numbers surpassed their estimates: "I had thought there were maybe three thousand, five thousand tops, but there were over fifteen thousand Koreans gathered there."[79] By this point, some two months after Japan's surrender, Koreans in Fukuoka had formed their own local Aid Group for Returning Countrymen. The head of the group, Nam Jŏng Woo, appealed to the occupation forces to improve their situation and refused to recognize the authority of the Japanese police over Koreans.[80]

Photographs taken by the US Signal Corps after the move from the stables to the docks, however, show that the port buildings were also insufficient to house the numbers of Koreans arriving in Fukuoka (figure 15). Families crowded around improvised hearths, shielding themselves from the elements with umbrellas or straw screens, some wearing wartime civilian uniforms and others in Korean clothing. On the burnt expanses of land surrounding Hakata Port, hundreds of families with bundles and bags of their possessions waited for boats to take them across the straits. The local Korean community, including the Korean Christian Church in Fukuoka located near the port, formed aid societies (J: *kyūgokai*) to help repatriates.[81] At the end of 1945 there were still some fifteen thousand Koreans waiting for repatriation from Hakata.[82] One member of the Christian community in Fukuoka was Nam Chu Ya, a young Korean woman who had lived in wartime Fukuoka since she was fifteen. Her husband and brother had helped set up the port's aid societies. She later recalled how "we wanted to return home too, and got our belongings together. In February of 1946 my husband went across to Pusan to see how it was. A month later, when he returned, he told me . . . 'There's no way we can make a living back home right now,' so in the end we didn't go back."[83] Other Koreans who had decided not to repatriate after hearing rumors of chaos and poverty made money selling food to those waiting to return home.

Japanese officials linked the move of Koreans to the docks with the sudden appearance of black-market stalls along the port's main road; the goods being sold appeared to have been "liberated" from dock warehouses. As news

FIGURE 15. Koreans waiting for repatriation at Hakata Port, October 1945. Courtesy of the National Archives, photo no. 111-SC-290862.

of this traveled, women from downtown Fukuoka arrived "with shopping bags over their arms." Eventually the authorities cleared the black-market stalls, but only as far as Ōhama, one of the portside neighborhoods, where the black market—Fukuoka's first—was still in operation in 1947 and had become known as the "Korean market" (J: *Chōsen ichiba*).[84]

Only with the intervention of the Allied occupation forces were Japanese officials made to reflect on the disparities between their treatment of Korean repatriates and returning Japanese. Even then, and at the roundtable that took place nearly two years after the event, there is little sense that these officials saw their response as discriminatory; rather, they took pains to argue otherwise. On being accused by the US forces of providing more goods for returning Japanese than for Koreans, Yoshitake, a prefectural employee in the social affairs division, disagreed: "What I was doing was fair. That is, some of the people being repatriated from Korea had had all their money stolen from them. They were coming back empty-handed, with just the shirts on their backs. But those Koreans in Japan didn't have their clothing stolen from them, or suffer any kind of hardship. Of course we gave those people clothes who didn't have them. But the Americans would bring up the issue of food, [saying], 'The Japanese get all the best food, while the Koreans are treated coldly.'"[85]

Some officials were more open about their treatment of Koreans, utilizing their ambiguous position as "third-country nationals"—falling between the defeated Japanese and the occupying forces—to evade responsibility for their welfare.[86] Prefectural official Kawafuji, who was responsible for the distribution of clothing and bedding from military stocks, described redirecting complaints from the Koreans who came to his offices demanding goods: "We couldn't focus on our work, so when Koreans arrived we told them 'that's the responsibility of the Social Affairs Division' or 'that's a job for the Welfare Division, we don't know anything about that,' in order to get rid of them."[87] When these tactics didn't work and the officials were openly confronted by Koreans, Kawafuji "told them [that] according to the Potsdam declaration, the distribution of former military supplies is only to provide the minimum level of living conditions for Japanese people. We got these from the occupation forces, and we aren't required to share any of it with you lot."[88] Whether there were any orders from the Allied occupation about these goods being meant only for Japanese people remains unclear, but it is obvious that the reign of confusion in these early months allowed officials to use their own judgment, backed up with both old prejudice and the new jargon of the postwar settlement, to decide policy on the spot.

Kawafuji's statement vividly illustrates how the decisions of those on the ground were informed not only by long-standing colonial prejudice against Koreans, but also by the ambiguity created when Japan's empire—along with any imperial responsibilities—and its war ended simultaneously. It seems many metropolitan Japanese officials in the immediate postwar era treated Koreans not only with disdain—as former colonized subjects—but also, due to the bureaucratic black hole they had fallen into, as a group of people they no longer felt any responsibility for.

Japan's wartime treatment of and reliance upon Korean workers did have some repercussions in the immediate postwar period. One such case arose on the docks at Hakata, where all ships arriving and leaving required refueling with coal. However, the company responsible for this had a workforce composed almost entirely of Koreans who had left their posts at the end of the war. Port officials were reduced to searching for volunteers from within the crowds of Koreans waiting on the docks, promising them priority repatriation if they would offer their services shoveling coal for the ships in port.[89]

These examples of tense negotiations between the formerly colonized and their colonizers, forced to reenact their previous roles, are a reminder of the everyday realities and untidy demarcations between war and postwar, empire and aftermath.

By late 1945 these aid groups had coalesced into a single national body, the League of Resident Koreans (Zainihon Chōsenjin Renmei, or Chōren). The Fukuoka branch was founded in December 1945 with Nam Jŏng Woo as its first chair. In Kyushu, Chōren was involved in procuring *yamibune* for Koreans (similar to the PNS in Pusan), and from April 1946 the Fukuoka branch supported the publishing of a Japanese-language newspaper, *Seiki Shinbun* (*Century News*).[90] Chōren's Fukuoka branch offered office space to the newspaper editorial team, and many founding members of the two organizations overlapped.

In its early days *Seiki Shinbun* functioned similarly to an advanced version of the Japanese Sewakai newsletters. Articles focused on repatriation, as well as looked to the future of Korea. In its first issue the paper announced the opening of a branch office in Sasebo—another key repatriation port. The majority of the early issues of the newspaper were filled with reports on conditions back in Korea and cautionary tales for Koreans in Japan:

> [In Pusan] we saw those without money who were left with no choice but to beg on the streets to keep alive. Others were brought to the brink of starvation with no way to afford somewhere to live, or the bare daily necessities needed, because of the limited amount of money they were allowed to bring back. It's not a rumor that those without housing are being forced to live in air raid shelters—it's the truth. Recently there have been deaths from malnutrition, and an eighty-year-old woman threw herself off Yŏngdo Bridge because of her difficulty making ends meet.[91]

The conditions in both repatriation ports were topics of concern for all involved. Both occupation forces and Japanese colonial officials still present in Korea were aware of the possible repercussions on the peninsula from the poor treatment of Koreans in Japan. In late September USAMGIK had released a statement on the conditions of Koreans waiting in Shimonoseki in an attempt to combat rumors of disease and deaths from overcrowding, and to let it be known that the Allied occupation in Japan was working hard to facilitate the repatriation of Koreans based in Japan.[92] In response to news about the ill-treatment of Koreans at Hakata, the provincial governor of North Kyŏngsang province had sent a telegram to prefectural authorities in

Hakata warning of the effects this might have in Korea—presumably on the treatment of Japanese still present on the peninsula.[93]

On both sides of the straits, the Korean editors of local newspapers—Pusan's *Minju Jungbo* and Fukuoka's *Seiki Shinbun*—ran many stories about repatriating Koreans. They both had local readerships who were aware of activities in the two repatriation ports of Hakata and Pusan and had access to information networks spanning the straits. Following the immediate aftermath of the war, both newspapers also displayed an interest in promoting local development, although the *Seiki Shinbun* appeared far more interested in building a strong relationship between Japan and Korea—including Koreans in Japan as more than just go-betweens for a reborn trade partnership.[94] On the first of November 1946, a group of Korean businessmen came together to form the Korea Commerce & Industry League (J: Chōsen shōkō renmei). The *Seiki Shinbun* described how "our pioneering countrymen working in trade and industry and based in Fukuoka have joined forces to promote trade and friendship between Japan and Korea, to help the poor and needy, and promote the reconstruction of Japanese industry. There will be many obstacles ahead, but if they can be overcome, the future will lead us to a new history of prosperity and development."[95] In contrast, the editors of the *Minju Jungbo* focused on the swift and safe return of all Koreans in Japan in order for them to assist in the rebuilding of their country—although development in Pusan would again include the employment of jobless workers on projects in the city "to stabilize our countrymen's livelihoods and help the unemployed"—with the old employment bureau now part of city hall's Health Department.[96]

The closure of USAMGIK's Hakata Liaison Office in April 1947 also provoked a strong reaction in Korean newspapers, as well as a petition among Koreans resident in Japan (J: Zainichi Chōsenjin). The office's staff had penned op-eds in the *Seiki Shinbun* and had taken part in its roundtables, as well as acted as an advocate for resident Koreans with the occupation forces.[97] Korean newspapers saw its closure as the success of Japanese "counterpropaganda" against Koreans, although its timing also coincided with the closure of the Hakata Repatriation Office.[98]

The networks that continued to cross the straits during these processes of decolonization, whether networks of information, like newspapers and newsletters aimed at repatriates, or the higher-level communiqués between occupation officials, remind us that these processes were, especially at the beginning, ad hoc, and they were informed by officials on the ground responding to local circumstances. As in Pusan, the scenes on the waterfront in Hakata Port reveal these persistent mindsets and long histories of regional migration and imperial expansion, confronted with the uncertainties of a postimperial future.

AFTERLIVES OF EXPANSION IN OCCUPIED FUKUOKA

Fukuoka City's emergence as the center of Kyushu and Western Japan's transport, educational, military, and administrative networks was a key reason for its choice as a hub for occupation forces. Its port of Hakata was central in incoming and outgoing repatriation processes. Along with the movement out from Hakata Port by Chinese and Korean former colonial subjects, this postwar moment also revealed Fukuoka as a center for numerous centripetal forces—a regathering of the many networks of mobility that had unfurled from the region since the late nineteenth century. This included the arrival of groups linked to overseas migration to North America, Hawai'i, and the Asian continent. The presence of these different groups in the city made Fukuoka a crossroads in the process of decolonization and reinforced its position as the de facto "first city" of postwar Kyushu.

One such group were the first- or second-generation (J: *issei/nisei*) Japanese Americans who traveled to Japan to work for the United States occupation forces. Their histories also illustrate the fates of different migrant communities in the postwar period: Those from Japan's Asian colonies were returned as repatriates, while those whose families had moved to the United States returned as occupiers. Sergeant Yasuo Baron Goto was born in Japan but moved to Hawai'i as a child. His parents both came from Fukuoka prefecture.[99] During his posting in Fukuoka, Goto met with his relatives throughout the region and reported on their morale and feelings toward America as part of his work for the United States Strategic Bombing Survey (hereafter USSBS).[100] On a visit to one of his cousins, Goto noted that "it seems that they are all happy that we are in the army and that many families are waiting for their relations to come as United States soldiers."[101] Seichi Takeda, another nisei working for the USSBS, described how "when I suddenly was given the opportunity to be at Fukuoka City the first thing I thought of doing was to call on the parents of a couple living with us in the United States."[102]

American newspapers reported on some of these cases as "good news" stories in the aftermath of the horror of war; one story, for example, described a Japanese American soldier, "Seiyu Higachi [*sic*] of Los Angeles, interpreter for the Twenty-fourth Division," who found his father on Okinawa after the US occupied the island in July 1945—"their first meeting after eight years."[103] No doubt many such reunions took place in areas that, like Fukuoka and Okinawa, had long histories of migration to the United States.

As part of his work for the occupation forces in Fukuoka, in late fall of 1945, Japanese American translator Sergeant Goto filed a report on displaced Okinawans in the city.[104] Goto recorded an interview with a man from Okinawa who had been repatriated from Davao, in the Philippines, in October. The Okinawan, unnamed in Goto's notes, describes being evacuated first into the hills above Davao, where he waited until news reached him of the war's end. Upon coming back down in September, he was captured and sent back to Japan on an American freighter. When they arrived in Hiroshima on October 25, however, the Okinawans on board were "not accept[ed]" and were sent to Fukuoka because it had an Okinawa Office. According to the Okinawan informant:

> The Okinawa office requested Fukuoka Prefecture to assist in aiding the Okinawans but Fukuoka stated that Okinawa itself should do it and turned it down.... In this war, the greatest sacrifice was made by Okinawans. In the south, even prior to the war, Okinawans were made to work for various units; at Saipan women and non-combatants were made to die fighting; at Davao, many were killed by Japanese soldiers and food taken away. These are truths.... It makes us sad to think that we are discriminated because we are Okinawan even here in Japan. We are all thinking that it would be fortunate if Okinawa becomes a part of the US.[105]

The history of the "Okinawa Office" in Fukuoka speaks to the waves of Okinawan refugees and repatriates arriving in Kyushu, which began with the Battle of Okinawa in April 1945 and continued after Japan's surrender. Over sixty thousand Okinawans had arrived as refugees in Kyushu from the Ryūkyū archipelago before the Battle of Okinawa in the spring of 1945. Others were repatriated former settlers who had ended up in Kyushu after being brought back from the Philippines and Micronesia, some in the final months of the war and others after Japan's surrender.

Fukuoka's Okinawa Office staff consisted of Okinawa prefectural employees, including former mayor of Naha, Tomiyama Tokujun, and a skeleton staff of other Okinawans. After the Battle of Okinawa, Tomiyama had been ordered to stay in Fukuoka by the Home Ministry. In the early days—both before and directly after surrender—there were fewer than ten employees in the office, which, along with the Repatriation Office, operated out of the Iwataya Department Store in Tenjin, one of the few large buildings still standing.[106] Other Okinawan organizations were set up in cities with large groups of evacuees, such as Kumamoto and Kagoshima, but the Fukuoka office was the central coordinating link with the authorities and had its own branches in several other prefectures across Kyushu, as well as in Osaka and Tokyo.[107]

In September 1945 the Okinawa Office came under the control of the Kyushu Regional Government (J: Kyūshū Chihō Sōkanfu), one of seven regional bodies set up in the final months of the war, which was to oversee preparations for the "final battle" that was planned to take place upon Japan's invasion by the Allied forces. Kita Eizō, deputy councilor of the Kyushu Regional Government, took up a joint post as head of the office.[108] After Japan's surrender, the regional governments took on organizational roles before being ordered by SCAP to disband in November 1945.

The office's day-to-day activities focused on helping islanders living in Kyushu. It also became a hub for a new paper, the *Okinawa Shin Minpō* (*New Okinawa Popular Post*). In January 1946 Oyadomari Seihaku, former editor of the *Okinawa Shinpō* newspaper, was invited to Fukuoka by Kita and began publishing this new paper for the tens of thousands of evacuated Okinawans living in Kyushu, who were without any contact with their home islands or fellow islanders. With the repatriation of most Kyushu-based Okinawans to the Ryūkyū Islands by the end of 1946, the Okinawa Office wound down operations, and it finally closed its Fukuoka and Tokyo offices at the end of September 1948.[109] The *Okinawa Shin Minpō* continued publication out of Fukuoka until 1953.

Goto's account of the confusion over responsibility for Okinawan repatriates also speaks to the islanders' ambiguous status in this period. Like Koreans, these Okinawans were also viewed as a group that now fell between clear categories. This allowed Japanese officials to absolve themselves of responsibility for another group of displaced people. Repatriation Office official Kawafuji explained how

> unlike Taiwanese or Koreans, we had long had friendly relations with [Okinawans] as Japanese people. Also, as Japanese, they had worked tremendously during the war. But upon defeat they stopped being Japanese and were treated as "Okinawans" [*Okinawa-jin*].... However, the fact of the matter is that our orders from the central authority [*chūō no shirei*] were just to distribute goods to Japanese: We had no orders about distributing things to foreigners.[110]

Eventually the Okinawans repatriated to Fukuoka were housed in two schools on the outskirts of the city center, where they were visited by a Japanese employee of the occupation forces in November 1945:

> I visited the sleeping quarters. I found a pitiful sight of these people sleeping on the floor with a thin blanket underneath and a comforter on them, row in row. Due to weariness from a long voyage, lack of nutrition, cold (sickness) and recurrence of malaria, the entire group [some 850 "refugees"] lacked pep and were thin and weak, their eyes deep in their sockets. They were merely breathing—that was all.
>
> As I greeted them, some raised their heads and others looked at their children and wept. Some women, with their palms in praying position, asked: "is it not possible to return to Okinawa on American freighter?" ... They are in tropical clothing and bare-footed. Daily two die due to lack of nourishment.[111]

As suggested by this report, the US policy toward Okinawans was to call for their repatriation to the newly renamed Ryūkyū Islands as part of a process that "serve[d] as a justification for maintaining the separation of the Ryūkyūs from Japan, and for perpetuating the direct US military rule there."[112] The new borders of postwar Japan were being redrawn among refugee populations in repatriation ports and makeshift camps, across an empire in the process of being dismantled.

Pioneers Again: Former Settlers and Their New Networks

The largest of the groups that "returned" to Fukuoka were Japanese repatriates. In contrast to the language of contempt and even disgust that they had used to discuss their involvement with the repatriation of Koreans, and the bureaucratic handwashing that appeared to characterize their treatment of Okinawans, officials at the 1947 roundtable talked about their "devotion" (kenshin) to helping their fellow Japanese who arrived in the months following Japan's surrender.[113] This gap in treatment reveals the true feelings hidden behind hollow wartime rhetoric, and the pragmatic beginnings of a reconceptualization of the "boundaries of the Japanese."[114]

Provisions for those Japanese arriving from former colonies of Japan were initially the responsibility of the Health and Welfare section of the Fukuoka prefectural government, and after the first few weeks of chaos described above, an office was set up at a school near the port to organize the supply of food and accommodation and to help arrange the repatriates' onward travel.

In November 1945 the Health and Welfare Ministry set up their own head-quarters in the Iwataya Department Store, with a branch office by the port. From December 20, 1945, this became the Hakata Repatriation Office. In the final months of 1945 there were some thirty employees working for the office; by its peak in the autumn of 1946, there were nearly 1,500.[115]

Across the straits in Pusan, the Pusan Nihonjin Sewakai (PNS) shifted its role from procuring *yamibune* to assisting—as a junior partner of the US authorities—with the process of planned repatriation of Japanese settlers, which began on October 25.[116] Although the US Army's 160th Infantry Division was charged with running repatriation facilities at the port, they later delegated some parts of the process to the PNS, especially those involving care for repatriates waiting for ferries. At both ends of the Seoul–Pusan railway Japanese aid societies played important roles in spreading information, organizing groups of repatriates, and coordinating departures in an attempt to ensure there was no backlog or overcrowding on the docks in Pusan.

As well as coordinating with the US authorities, these groups formed information networks for anxious settlers, especially after newspapers and radio reports switched from Japanese to Korean. The newsletter distributed by the Keijō Nihonjin Sewakai (KNS) in the early months after surrender contained reports on conditions in both Pusan and Hakata. While some of these were letters from people who had been repatriated, others hint at the initial freedom of movement of officials and semiofficials who crossed back and forth across the straits. The first of these types of reports, from September 25, was by "Mr. Adachi, who arrived back [to Seoul] after observing conditions in Pusan and Hakata on the 24th." He reported how

> there were around twenty thousand pieces of cargo waiting to be shipped from Pusan, but with the *Unzen Maru* going into action this has now dropped to around ten thousand. . . . There are also several thousand passengers waiting who will also be repatriated in the next few days.
>
> The food situation is not good. The US occupation troops are being strict. The martial law [*chianrei*] has not yet been lifted, but there are no body checks. The *Pusan Nippō* has become a *hangul* paper, called the *Minshū Shinbun* [*sic*].[117]
>
> Upon arrival in Hakata, everyone receives a boxed lunch voucher and ten meal vouchers. People being repatriated should bring as much food as they can. People over there are having to make use of seawater instead of salt. There are no rental accommodations. . . . It is hoped that those who are sick or pregnant would hold off from repatriating at present.[118]

Later reports offered information on the prices of rooms in Hakata's inns, how best to use one's food vouchers, and the availability of hot baths and haircuts. Food in Fukuoka was cheaper than in Keijō, one report from December noted, but it was in short supply.[119] Despite the reports' gloomy content, settlers still based in Korea must have gained some solace from these information networks, with their reassuring depictions of ties across the Tsushima Strait and of the involvement of Japanese in the processes of repatriation at both ends. They also illustrate how Japanese settlers, involved in their own decolonization, fell back on the same organizational principles—settler groups and their publications—that had played an important role in their colonization of Korea. Such continuity, however, could not last forever. By January 1946 the nature of the Japanese presence in Korea, and the attitudes of the occupation forces toward it, had undergone a sea change.

Beginning in November 1945, announcements appeared in Korean- and Japanese-language newspapers about the increasing restrictions on Japanese traveling between Korea and Japan. The KNS newsletter on November 14 announced a directive from SCAP, which stated that travel by Japanese to southern Korea was in principle no longer allowed, but, if truly necessary, required the permission of the military government. The *Tong-a Ilbo* also reported a similar story a month later, citing a SCAP ordinance from December 22 that announced, "From now on, Japanese not allowed into Korea."[120] Despite these warnings it appears that Japanese continued to travel across the straits in large enough numbers to warrant a further announcement by USAMGIK, in early January, that personal trips by Japanese across the straits were now forbidden.[121]

One of the cases that may have necessitated the January reminder involved members of the repatriation aid organizations in both Hakata and Pusan. PNS official Yoshimura Yōzō traveled from Pusan to Hakata on December 4, 1945. He was in the market for a Christmas present—something "elegant and Japanese"—for USAMGIK governor general John Reed Hodge. Yoshimura and the PNS were not alone in this sentiment: The KNS newsletter also put out a call for "high-quality Japanese goods" to be given as a Christmas gift to the occupation forces in Korea to thank them for their kindness over the past months.[122] With the help of the Hakata Repatriation Office, Yoshimura managed to get his hands on a high-quality Hakata doll and returned to Pusan several days later. However, the new restrictions on Japanese entering Korea meant that he was kept "starving and shivering" on the docks of Pusan, unable to enter until he received an official letter from the US authorities to prove his business in Korea; letters from the PNS did nothing. Yoshimura later related his story to Foreign Ministry officials from Shimonoseki as a warning for future travelers.[123] By early 1946 even Japanese officials, who had previously been able to move between Japan and its colonies as they pleased, were given a taste of the restrictions and suspicion previously reserved for Koreans traveling across the straits.

Upon arrival in the Japanese home islands, Japanese who had been settlers in Korea faced a reversal of the ways in which they defined themselves in relation to each other, and to Japan. Where once they had identified with their home prefectures in Japan, now they identified with their former homes in Korea and their jobs in the colonial administration. But the ways in which they adapted to repatriation also reflected how they had created their settler networks. Before their repatriation settlers had been given the advice to "banish any naïve thoughts" and treat postwar Japan just as they had the Korean peninsula: "Return with the heart of a pioneer."[124]

One repatriate from Korea, artist Yamada Shinichi, began a magazine for his fellow returnees. Yamada (1899–1991) was a successful artist in postwar Japan. Born in Taiwan, he attended art school in Tokyo and worked as a teacher in Keijō's No. 2 High School. Yamada exhibited his works in the Imperial Art Institute Exhibition and Korean Art Exhibition multiple times, and in 1943 he was involved in the founding of the Tankōkai, a group of Japanese and Korean artists who produced work promoting Government General policies, such as the conscription of Koreans into the Imperial Army. After the war he was also commissioned by the Allied Occupation to return to Korea and retrieve works of war art.[125]

Renrakusen (*Ferryboat*), which Yamada not only edited but also illustrated, was first published in Kyoto in March 1947 as a "news magazine for repatriates from Korea."[126] The character and contents of the magazine, published monthly until the end of 1948, had a lot in common with that of colonial-era expat magazines like *The Fukuokan*, which had ended publication in 1943. Strangers in a strange land, new repatriates felt a connection with their fellow former colonists—a geographic bond and shared experience that now seemed to outweigh their previous association with their hometowns in Japan.

The repatriate experience shaped Yamada's designs for the magazine. *Renrakusen*'s different columns corresponded to the different parts of a cross-strait ferry, for example "Antenna," "Observation Deck," "Saloon," and "Meeting Room." The "Antenna" column, featuring a masthead with

Yamada's illustration of the Government General building, reported on developments in Seoul such as the new government's land policies. The preface of the first edition, entitled the "Fore(deck)word," set the scene:[127] "Inside, the harbor is splashed by waves of defeat, but tomorrow's weather will be fine, the Pacific is calm. When Makinoshima is lit by the dawn, it will be perfect weather for a stroll on deck. Until then, please be patient in the cramped cabins."[128] In their letters to the magazine, repatriates identified themselves via colonial-era job titles and former addresses in Korea before announcing their new addresses and positions. Similar to *The Fukuokan*, which included dispatches on Fukuokan settlers, *Renrakusen* ran articles describing Yamada's visits to now former settlers and their new lives. In one account of his visits to repatriates in Kyushu, Yamada let readers know that the former Pusan mayor, Tomiyama Osamu, was now running a "magnificent" restaurant in Nakasu, Fukuoka's entertainment district.[129] Akutagawa Hiroshi, former editor of the *Pusan Nippō* and head of the Pusan Nihonjin Sewakai, wrote in to tell readers that, after successfully founding another newspaper in Moji, the *New Kyushu Evening Post*, he had now retired to Tokyo.[130]

The magazine's writers and readers kept up the ferry analogy. In one article a writer remarked that it wasn't just Japanese "on board the ferryboat, but Koreans too."[131] In other articles the ferry's journey seems to stand in for the rebuilding of Japan itself. The magazine is just one example of how the redeployment of settler ambitions back within the confines of Japan's home islands relied, in style and in substance, on their former experiences and communities.

CONCLUSIONS

By the end of 1945, some 240,000 Japanese civilians, 66,000 army troops, and 16,000 naval troops had been repatriated through Hakata. In the other direction, some 283,000 Koreans and 9,700 Chinese departed from Hakata for their homelands between the end of the war and the end of 1945.[132] Koreans who left Hakata in the chaotic four months after Japan's surrender made up over half of all Koreans who would eventually leave through the port, and a quarter of the total estimate for postwar Korean repatriates from Japan.[133]

On the other side of the straits, in US-occupied Korea, the repatriation of Japanese troops from below the thirty-eighth parallel was complete by mid-November 1945. USAMGIK figures suggest that in December 1945 there were only 23,435 Japanese left in southern Korea, 5 percent of their estimate of 435,000 at the end of September.[134] Some 800,000 people, Japanese and Korean, had passed through the docks of Pusan in under four months. As the following chapter discusses, the impact of these huge flows of people on the cities of Pusan and Fukuoka would be felt for much longer than the length of the repatriation process itself.

The speed of this process and the crucial role these two cities played in the first few months of repatriation was a result of both geography and very recent history. Continuities with both wartime and colonial structures and mindsets did not end with the arrival of occupation forces either. In these initial months the new borders of postimperial Japan were still in the process of being redrawn—in people's minds, between the Japanese and their "former countrymen," and through the waters of the Tsushima Strait. In Korea, new postcolonial borders were being decided even as the straits continued to be crossed daily by Japanese and Koreans in ferryboats and *yamibune*—flows of people put in motion by empire and its collapse. Over the following years the links between these regions had to be unlearned. The animating role of empire in the personal histories of the region's inhabitants, and in its cities' imagined futures, would have to be redeployed, redirected, or replaced.

Cities after Empire

AFTER NEAR STASIS BY THE END of the war, flows between the two cities of Fukuoka and Pusan were reconnected in the initial postwar period by vessels involved in repatriation crossing the Tsushima Strait. However, as Japan's disentanglement from its former empire officially ended in the late 1940s, with the final repatriation ship entering Hakata Port in April 1947, the two cities found themselves on diverging paths. From 1945 onward both cities saw higher growth rates than at any time during the prewar period. By 1955 Pusan's population was just over a million people, while Fukuoka's was almost exactly half that. In figure 16 we can see that Fukuoka's population showed a temporary increase in its speed of growth between around 1925 and 1935 before a plateau followed by a rapid decline toward the end of the war, at which point Pusan's population overtook Fukuoka's for the first time. But these numbers, while useful, can only gesture at the changes seen in these two cities in the decade following 1945.

This final chapter examines how decolonization and the outbreak of another war affected patterns and processes of urbanization in both Pusan and Fukuoka and across what had become an imperial region. The chapter spans the eight years from Japan's defeat and Korea's liberation, through the military occupation of both South Korea and Japan, to the end of the Korean War in 1953. In the first half, I focus on the years between defeat and the outbreak of the Korean War and how the attempts to control movement—of people and things—across the maritime border down the middle of the Korea Strait affected both sides. I look at those who evacuated or repatriated into the cities of Pusan and Fukuoka, and the resultant urban spaces they repurposed and the conflicts this created in these temporal and geographic "ends of empire." I also look at what still crossed the straits in the aftermath

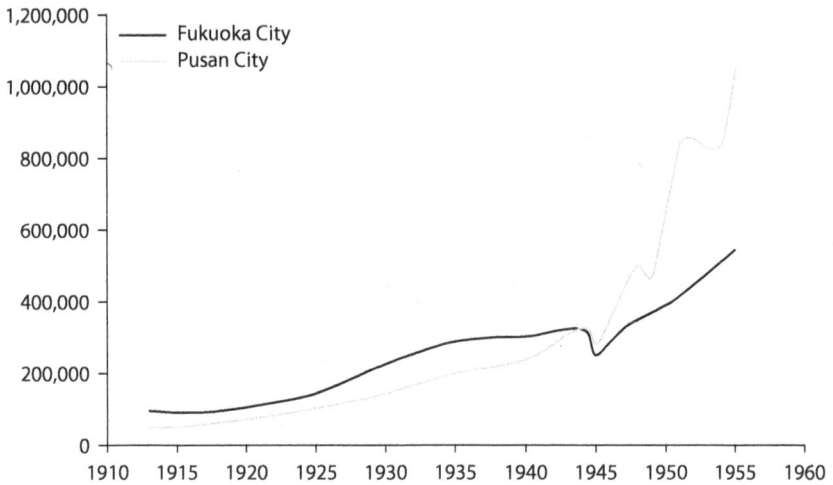

FIGURE 16. Populations of Fukuoka and Pusan, 1913–1955. Credit: Figures from Japanese census data, Pusan chikhalsi sa p'yŏnch'anwiwŏnhoe 1989, 2: 1127, and Lee 2017, 105–22.

of a rapid and incomplete decolonization, how those in each city envisioned their port cities reopening to the world again, and what these licit and illicit flows can tell us about processes of decolonization and remilitarization between Japan and Korea.

This book has argued that war had driven growth for the northern Kyushu region since the nineteenth century, and it tied Pusan's economy to that of Japan's during the colonial period. In the second half of this final chapter, I look at the different effects and aftereffects of the Korean War on the cities and their respective positions in their new nations. The outbreak of the Korean War in 1950 reconnected Fukuoka and Pusan once again through their use as frontline bases for United Nations and US forces, and through the movement of war refugees from Korea to Japan. But the redrawing and recrossing of this new national border happened again and again. It was redrawn down the middle of mixed Japanese-Korean families, reconnected by smugglers transporting daily necessities across it, and recrossed by new movements of troops and military aircraft. Next, I look at how war and military occupation affected housing and reconstruction on either side of the straits and trace the shift toward a new postwar discourse on "urban problems" and development, and the continued marginalization of certain groups within the cities. Finally, I briefly discuss how traces of earlier networks would go on to shape later reconnections between the two cities in the 1960s and beyond.

ENDS OF EMPIRE: PUSAN AND FUKUOKA IN
LIBERATION AND DEFEAT

Immediately after the Japanese surrender in 1945, plans for the future of Kyushu's cities filled the pages of the region's main newspaper, the *Nishi Nippon Shinbun (NNS)*.[1] Only two days after defeat, on August 17, what was to be the first of many such articles announced a "speedy return to civilian supply: New activity for Kitakyūshū's industrial cities."[2] The article argued that production in Fukuoka's factories needed to shift to civilian goods for Japan's reconstruction, but the discussion retained familiar wartime terminology, referring to "industrial warriors" *(sangyō senshi)*. In the following weeks reports on urban reconstruction discussed plans to turn militarized cities into centers of health, education, and peacetime industry.[3] Many of these plans repurposed air defense measures from the final years of the war to new ends.[4] An article on the Kitakyūshū five cities called for their "reconstruction from a city of air defense into a city of health," and for the redevelopment of urban areas destroyed in air raids. The new city plan would incorporate cleared and bombed areas, turning them into newly widened roads or public green spaces such as parks and market gardens.[5] Throughout August newspaper articles offered various outlines for the region's future. As long as there was a vision to work toward, it seemed, there was no need to draw breath and reflect on what had just happened.

A number of regional reports focused on the cities of Kyushu that had been hardest hit in the air raids of the last years of the war. The *NNS* series "Born Again: Western Japan's War-Torn Cities" ran over several weeks in late 1945 and included plans showing readers what these cities would look like after their reconstruction.[6] Many of these indicated a return to plans that had existed before the outbreak of war and that, with a certain amount of recalibrating, were still viable in the new postwar world. Reporters appeared unable to break free of imperial-era booster rhetoric, boasting, about the repatriation efforts currently underway, that "most of Japan's shipping has been coming and going through Hakata, so one could even call it the number one port in Japan."[7]

In the first few years after liberation, a certain amount of repurposing of old rhetoric to create new visions for the future went on in South Korea as well. In newspaper coverage of the city from 1947, the new Catholic newspaper *Kyŏnghyang Sinmun* contrasted the role of Pusan in the Japanese imperial days with its importance for "New Korea":

In the colonial period the port of Pusan was the advance base for imperialist invasionary policy, but after liberation it has made its glorious debut as the advance base for New Korea's overseas development. Before long, when our government begins its advance into overseas [markets] in earnest, Pusan's name will be known around the world, and boats from every nation, flying their flags, will come and go from this harbor.[8]

This panoramic view out from Pusan to the world has much in common with the wartime speeches of figures like Kim Chang-t'ae, discussed in chapter 5. And, similarly to Fukuoka, Pusan's future growth and success in both its new nation and the new postimperial world was still tied to the role of its port.

The Reality of Reconstruction

These visions of a new urban future for the two port cities existed alongside other unavoidable realities. Fukuoka City was reduced to ashes by US bombing in June 1945; as a designated repatriation port from October 1945, it was inundated with over a million returning Japanese repatriates and troops, as well as departing former colonial subjects, mainly Koreans. Even as the Allied occupation's General Headquarters (GHQ), via the Japanese government, put emergency measures in place to limit growing urban populations across Japan, Fukuoka's population was increased by inflows of Japanese from the surrounding regions—some returning after evacuation, and others seeking new opportunities in the city.[9]

In Pusan, although its housing stock had been left far more unscathed than in most cities in the Japanese metropole, many Koreans were already living in substandard housing on hillsides and riverbeds at the close of the war. As discussed in chapter 5, Pusan's housing shortages were also made worse in the final years of the war by military encroachment into former residential areas and the removal of "slum" or shanty housing under the guise of "greening" and "air defense" policies imposed by Japanese authorities. The city was unprepared to deal with the large numbers of repatriates who entered through the port in the months after liberation. As seen in drawings by a US soldier with the Fortieth Division, the streets of Pusan were soon full of homeless repatriates, whom the soldier depicted "huddled around improvised brick ovens and charcoal burners" (figure 17).[10] Many of them were forced to camp in spaces cleared during wartime or, as discussed more below, in areas long used by those on the margins of Pusan's society: the waterfront, parks, and fringes of the city.

FIGURE 17. Sketch by US soldier of Korean repatriates in Pusan. Credit: From "Evacuation," United States Army 40th Division and Barach, ca. 1945. Courtesy of Princeton University Library.

In the aftermath of war and liberation, poverty, homelessness, crime, and profiteering were rampant in urban areas on either side of the straits. In the case of Pusan, these issues became fuel for violent protests against the US Military Government and the Korean officials aiding its rule. As discussed in chapter 6, the population influxes caused by repatriation into South Kyŏngsang and the political mobilization of these regions are shown to have been contributing factors in the Autumn Harvest Uprisings, which occurred across Korea in the fall of 1946.[11] These uprisings, by Koreans calling for labor rights and political representation, spread across Korea after a strike begun by railway workers in Pusan in late September. They revealed the rifts present in a population reacting to their nation's unfinished decolonization process, as well as the tinderbox nature of cities like Pusan, which were crowded with repatriates and restive labor.

In 1945 and 1946 the United States Military Government in Korea (USAMGIK) attempted to quell popular opposition to its rule, promoting right-leaning local politicians, often with connections to the colonial administration, over those supporting policies such as land reform and unions.[12] USAMGIK was also wary of the role of Korean repatriate organizations, which it attempted to paint as political organizations that should be shut down. Almost as soon as they were formed in the autumn of 1945, such groups were treated with suspicion by the US authorities, who saw their aims as less than charitable. USAMGIK reports suggested that many only came into existence after hearing about the budget allotted for repatriate aid, and that it was impossible to work out which groups were "sincere" and "nonpartisan" in their mission. The head of the aid group's umbrella organization, Chŏng T'ae Hŭi, was asked to step down by US authorities in November 1945, charged with being "politically ambitious" and "welding the many welfare societies into one united society for the purpose of building a political party."[13]

After the initial repatriation of Koreans from Japan and its other colonies in the autumn of 1945, local groups run by repatriates themselves began to emerge. These groups soon turned their attention to employment and housing aid for repatriates in their area. Repatriates and repatriate aid groups called on the government for the release and redistribution of the former homes of Japanese settlers (K: *chŏksan'gaok*, or enemy properties) who had returned to Japan.[14] Despite touting their independence, these groups are thought to have cooperated with local authorities and USAMGIK due to the scale of their projects.[15] In the winter of 1946, local newspapers in Pusan and elsewhere ran campaigns to raise money for homeless repatriates.[16]

In housing policy, as in so many other areas, there were significant continuities between colonial plans and those of the Korean authorities under US occupation. Pusan's authorities responded slowly to the influx of displaced peoples and calls by repatriate organizations to house their "returned compatriots." Until the founding of the First Republic in 1948 and the creation of a housing bureau within the new government's department of social affairs, local authorities were often reliant on their own initiative, or on the examples and urban spaces left by Japanese colonial planning.[17] In November 1947 an announcement was made by the Pusan Welfare Council—a group that included municipal and provincial officials—that some two hundred homes for "indigents" (K: *kŭkpinja*) would be built in both Pŏmil-dong and

Uam-ri.[18] The location and number of these planned houses was almost identical to those in the municipal plans for homes for "lower-class workers" announced in 1942. Even after liberation, marginalized groups continued to be removed to the same peripheral spaces of the city.

Pusan's "Japanese Vestiges"

Pusan's supposed moral degeneracy and general seediness had been the subject of commentary in Korean-language media during the colonial period, and it continued to be seen as a lawless liminal zone after liberation as well. In 1947 *Kyŏnghyang Sinmun* reporter Lee Ju-yŏng considered the city suspect because of its stubborn "Japanese vestiges" (K: *waesaek*) that persisted even years after liberation.

Lee's reports from Pusan gave the impression of a city not fully decolonized and not fully Korean. Restaurants in Pusan continued to serve Japanese food, the noticeboards in the streets were hangovers from Japan's military rule, and Lee was shocked by the "brazen nonchalance" of young intellectuals using Japanese without any shame. He admitted that the city's proximity to Japan made the task of completely eradicating its "Japanese vestiges" impossible.[19]

In postwar Japan, repatriate orphans (J: *hikiage koji*) became a symbol of the innocent victims of the violence of war. In liberated Pusan the presence of repatriated Korean orphans was a complex reminder of both Korea's colonized past and its chaotic present.[20] In Lee's reports the children appear as an unassimilated, almost alien presence. Many of them spoke only Japanese and congregated around Pusan's train station: "There is no more tragic sight," Lee wrote, "than these children at the side of the road, or in streetcars, singing plaintive *naniwabushi* and begging for money."[21]

Postliberation Pusan was a city of contrasts and contradictions. While rice riots and railway workers' strikes broke out in Pusan in 1946, the city was also a hotbed for profiteers, who were subject to the same critiques of opportunism as the city's colonial-era businessmen had been. In Lee's reports the postliberation city had two faces: On one hand, it was a "tinderbox" of overpopulation, restive labor, and food shortages; on the other, it was a "gold mine" where profiteers could make money hand over fist, coming and going between the city and Seoul so frequently that they were "wearing out the seats on the Liberator Express."[22]

Such contradictions were also present in the cities of Fukuoka prefecture. Its geography and history meant that the region faced a perfect storm of incoming populations combined with housing shortages; bombing and forced clearances (*sokai*) meant that the prefecture had lost nearly 15 percent of its housing stock at the end of the war.[23] In the aftermath of surrender—indeed, since the air raids of summer 1945—the entire urban belt of northern Kyushu was suffering from an overwhelming and immediate need for housing. The prefecture's six largest cities had lost some fifty thousand homes.[24] The problem was only exacerbated when Fukuokans whose houses had been destroyed or damaged in air raids were joined by repatriates and returning troops. The severe deprivation and poverty experienced by the citizens of Fukuoka in the aftermath of the war is visible in the number of deaths registered in the city: 1946 saw a higher number of deaths than 1945, despite the firebombing of the city in June 1945, which claimed nearly a thousand lives.[25]

The unevenness of postwar reconstruction was a problem both within and between the prefecture's cities. Shibata Masafumi, an engineer with the Fukuoka prefectural construction department, offered an overview of the prefecture's reconstruction in November 1948.[26] Of those urban areas that had suffered severe bombing, reconstruction of Fukuoka and Wakamatsu led the way, with around a quarter of their war-damaged areas rebuilt, whereas in Moji and Yahata only a tenth of reconstruction or less was complete. As we saw in chapter 5, war had set back earlier plans for the integrated administration of the five cities of Kitakyūshū, meaning that in the immediate postwar period, redevelopment of the five cities occurred at vastly different paces.

National policy dictated some of the priorities. Three years after the end of the war the Yawata Steelworks were still silent, while the centrality of coal as "the driving force behind Japan's reconstruction" meant construction of miners' housing and the redevelopment of mining towns like Ōmuta outflanked that of Yahata. Nearly two-thirds of all "emergency housing" units constructed in Fukuoka between surrender and the end of 1949 were miners' housing.[27]

Between 1945 and 1947 Fukuoka City saw its population increase by 30 percent. Indeed, statistics in the first city handbook (*shisei yōran*) of the postwar era show that unlike Japan's six largest cities, five of which had suffered severe bombing followed by migration restrictions, Fukuoka's population

TABLE 3 Pre- and post-1945 populations of Japan's bombed "Big Six" cities and Fukuoka

City/Population	February 1944	November 1945	April 1946	October 1947
		(as % of 1944 population)		
Tokyo	6,569,819	2,777,610 (42.3%)	3,442,106 (52.4%)	4,177,548 (63.6%)
Osaka	2,842,083	1,102,959 (38.8%)	1,293,501 (45.5%)	1,559,310 (54.9%)
Nagoya	1,348,061	597,941 (44.3 %)	719,382 (53.4%)	853,085 (63.3%)
Yokohama	1,033,474	624,994 (60.4%)	706,557 (68.4%)	814,268 (78.8%)
Kōbe	918,101	379,166 (41.3%)	443,344 (48.3%)	607,202 (66.1%)
Fukuoka	315,890	250,601 (79.3%)	287,322 (91.0%)	**325,554 (103%)**

CREDIT: Statistics from Fukuoka shi 1948, 22. Baseline statistics for Kyoto in 1944 were missing in the original report, and the city was not subject to bombing, so figures for Kyoto are not included here.

quickly recovered, surpassing prewar levels by the final months of 1947 (see table 3). Repatriates were not subject to the 1946 urban migration regulations, and we can assume this accounts for Fukuoka City's position as an outlier compared to these other cities.

Just like Pusan, occupied Fukuoka was an uneven patchwork of misery and moneymaking, where "war orphans, now a familiar sight," camped in air raid shelters and bombed-out houses, steps away from the newly booming entertainment district of Nakasu. Furthermore, a thriving black market in construction materials and labor meant official construction schemes often lost out to private ones.[28] A year after it had been firebombed by US planes, Fukuoka City's reconstruction had begun, but with uneven effects: "If one looks at the results," argued a piece in the *NNS*, "what do you find but cabarets, movie theaters, restaurants . . . beer halls, and shopping arcades." A few blocks away from the bright lights of Nakasu lay empty plots "where all that has changed from a year ago is the height of the weeds."[29]

The earliest phase of reconstruction work in Fukuoka operated out of the prefectural offices, but the city government had also been monitoring the situation, creating a Reconstruction Committee in early September, and, after taking over the reconstruction work from the prefecture at the beginning of 1946, proposing a new reconstruction plan for Fukuoka City in April of that year. As part of this plan, Fukuoka City authorities undertook a survey on housing supply and demand. The response was overwhelming: More than two thousand people registered for housing assistance in the first week.

Municipal housing in the immediate postwar era came under several categories, illustrating the variety of causes that had combined to create this housing crisis. The city lists four different types of municipal housing: working class housing (*shomin jūtaku*), emergency housing (*ōkyū jūtaku*), temporary housing (*tenyō jūtaku*), and municipal housing (*kōei jūtaku*). The highest demand was for working class housing, with nearly 150 applications for every house built.[30]

Aside from city-owned areas such as parks and recreation grounds, access to open land that could be built upon was limited. Much of the land formerly owned and used by the military had been requisitioned by the Allied occupation forces. By the end of 1946, emergency prefabricated housing could house only a fraction of those who had registered, with just 250 homes constructed in parks and former military parade grounds.[31] City data from 1947 showed that demand continued to outweigh supply.

Repatriate housing, constructed by the Welfare Ministry's Repatriation Office, was one of the earliest forms of emergency housing constructed in postwar Fukuoka. For officials working at the Hakata Repatriation Office, "when the paperwork at the port was finished, this was the real start of our work." In the initial months after the end of the war, repatriates were housed in four hastily constructed dormitories, eight schools, and eleven Buddhist temples spread across the city. The earliest of these facilities opened in March 1946, and in total they were capable of housing around 11,500 people.[32] The first repatriate dormitory to open was in the former stables building that had housed Korean repatriates in September 1945, which had apparently been improved to make it now fit for (Japanese) habitation.[33] After the Repatriation Office closed in 1947, the Fukuoka Repatriate Aid Group continued its work in offering aid and housing advice to repatriates.

Further dormitories were constructed on Fukuoka's military grounds and in the city's parks. One was built in 1946 in Ōhori Park, on a parade ground of the Imperial Army, whose Western Japan headquarters had been based in the Fukuoka Castle grounds nearby. By 1946 the park also contained rows of Quonset huts, constructed to house the US occupation forces, which were based in the former Imperial Army headquarters. After the Housing Corporation (Jūtaku Eidan) built 196 houses there in 1946, the Ōhori site developed into an area of permanent housing for repatriates known as Jōnai-machi, which still exists today.[34]

Such measures, however, were not enough to house all repatriates in the city. To supplement the construction of dormitories, the city government was forced to allow the building of temporary shacks, known as *barakku*, on cleared areas of land. These were meant to be temporary measures, to be replaced later with proper houses. As will be discussed more below, this often took much longer than anticipated.[35]

In the first two years after Japan's defeat and Korea's liberation, the stark differences between optimistic visions for the future and the reality of post-war reconstruction were joined by stark unevenness and inequality in the nature of that reconstruction. Both Pusan and Fukuoka, as key repatriation ports, were hampered in their efforts due to the influx of new populations, many of whom required assistance from the state. In their searches for solutions to these new problems, old plans reemerged, reusing marginal spaces in both cities.

Trade Links, Old and New

The end of Japan's empire and the aftermath of war resulted in a disentangling of imperial subjects, and the evacuation and repatriation of people through the cities of Pusan and Fukuoka, which led to new conflicts over urban space that often contained echoes of earlier times. After this hasty disentangling, however, there were other movements that continued to take place across the Tsushima Strait under occupation and, as will be discussed below, beyond the outbreak of another war.

In the immediate aftermath of Japan's surrender, although the imperial lifeline of the Tsushima Strait, which had been crucial in providing the Japanese home islands with food and raw goods from its colonies, was theoretically severed, it could not be disconnected entirely for fear of disrupting transport networks or leaving populations on both sides in serious danger of starvation. In the first few months after the end of the war, with the occupation of both Japan and Korea by Allied forces, demands came from both sides for the continued flow of food and fuel across the Tsushima Strait. In September 1945, the Supreme Commander for the Allied Powers (SCAP) issued a directive to the Japanese government ordering a monthly shipment of seventy thousand tons of coal to Pusan, to be consigned to the Commanding General of the US Forces in Korea "for use in operating the Korean Railways."[36] The date of this ordinance aligns with the beginning of the US-led repatriation efforts from Pusan, which, as discussed in chapter 6, relied on the smooth running of the Korean Railway link between Seoul and Pusan.

In the other direction, too, the severing of this lifeline was causing problems. Without access to its empire, Japan was in danger of running out of grain supplies. In the autumn of 1945 the former metropole's rice harvest was damaged by typhoons and floods that struck Western Japan in September and October. Projected yields were revised to some 80 percent of those originally expected.[37] A newspaper report from early 1946 describes the realization on the part of the Allied occupation that "Korea, which normally exported annually to Japan between 36,000,000 and 54,000,000 bushels of rice, this year would almost certainly be able to ship nothing." The Japanese Agriculture Ministry had "asked Allied permission some weeks ago to import 31,700,000 bushels of rice from [Korea] . . . [I]t also asked for 9,300,000 bushels of Formosan rice and rice wine, which is probably unavailable. About 2,200,000 bushels of Manchurian soybeans are in the same category."

Not only Japan but Korea, too, was affected by the decoupling of imperial Japan's food chains. The Soviet occupation of Manchuria had caused a disruption to colonial-era supply lines. Southern Korea, which during the colonial period had exported most of its own rice to the Japanese home islands and relied on "other grains from North Korea and Manchuria," was now eating "its own rice crop largely unsupplemented . . . a diet closely comparable to Japanese urban fare." Japan, previously at the top of an extractive imperial food chain—one in which it was seen as "urban" while Korea was "rural"— was in danger of starving once these links were severed. Allied occupation forces, which had previously hoped that any food shortage could be "quickly solved by emergency rice shipments across the 150-mile Tsushima Strait," were forced to face the problem of feeding a postimperial Japan without its colonial supply lines.[38]

Although rice no longer traveled from Korea to Japan via official routes, this is not to say that all shipments of rice stopped, or that people gave up on the idea of a return to colonial supply chains. The smuggling of Korean rice across the Tsushima Strait, reaching the shores of Western Japan from Hirado to Matsue, rose in response to the shortages faced in the home islands. In a strategy created to prevent the rice reaching the black market, SCAP ordered it to be seized and turned over to authorities, from where it was "expected to find its way into ordinary rationing channels."[39] Such actions must have only encouraged further smuggling, and as Japanese and Korean newspaper reports reveal, the Tsushima Strait continued to be a conduit for the flow of illicit goods and people between Japan and Korea throughout the 1940s, with trade increasing again during the Korean War.[40]

As former imperial links and flows were controlled and restricted, inhabitants of Pusan and Fukuoka reimagined and reoriented their overseas connections. Both Japan and South Korea were reopened for private international trade in 1947. Until then USAMGIK and SCAP had controlled government-to-government trade. In the years after liberation Pusan's trade links—both legal and otherwise—saw a shift to the Asian continent, with networks of trade linking it first to Hong Kong and Macau, then to the United States, and finally, with the limited reopening of private trade in 1947, back to Japan. In 1947 a report by a former settler in the magazine *Renrakusen* remarked on the startling inroads that "Chinese" were making in Pusan's economic world.[41] The *Kyŏnghyang Sinmun* also reported on the representative figure of these incursions: "the Chinese merchants" who "swagger along the street in their fancy clothes."[42] In South Korea these figures became known as "Macau gentlemen" (K: *mak'ao sinsa*), with Macau acting as synecdoche for various Chinese diaspora trading locations, including Hong Kong. The term referred especially to those who made their money under shady circumstances and who displayed their success via sartorial means. The first private foreign trade ship to arrive in postliberation South Korea was from Macau, carrying raw rubber, salt, woolen suit material, and newsprint, docking in Inch'ŏn in March 1947.[43] With postliberation Pusan home to a growing number of rubber factories, some existing since the colonial period, it is no wonder so many "Macau gentlemen" were present in its streets.[44]

In both Fukuoka and Pusan, in the aftermath of defeat and in the face of crippling food rationing, areas cleared for air defense purposes during the war very quickly became black or open-air (J: *aozora*) markets. In Pusan, one large area downtown near Yongdu-san, which had been cleared of houses during the war as an air defense tactic, became an open-air market. At first its stallholders sold various goods left by fleeing Japanese, and the products of the liberated city's fledgling metalworking and rubber companies. Later it became famous for black market and imported goods, taking on the name International Market (K: kukche sijang), as it is still referred to today. Products from Macau, Hong Kong, the United States, and elsewhere flowed into its stalls.

Zainichi (literally, "Japan-resident") Koreans in Fukuoka, similar to urban Zainichi communities elsewhere, had been active in networks of smuggling and black marketing in the immediate postwar period, but after a clampdown by GHQ in 1946, they were searching for legal ways to support small business owners.[45] In May 1947, around the same time that the Tsuruhashi International Market was set up in the Korean neighborhood of Ikaino in Osaka, reports in Fukuoka's Zainichi newspaper, *Seiki Shinbun,* announced the construction of a new "international" market just south of Watanabe-dōri itchōme, a crossroads that was a center of postwar reconstruction in Fukuoka.[46]

The new enterprise, also timed to coincide with the reopening of private international trade, was the work of the local Korea Commerce & Industry League, which was accepting applications for its fifty stores, each with residential space on the second floor.[47] Moon Yŏng-sil, vice president of the league, wrote that it was hoped the market would stimulate Japan's newly restarted overseas trade and provide the people of Fukuoka with quality products without resorting to black market brokers.[48] The construction was completed in October of 1947, but the market seems to have been destroyed in a fire only seven years later.[49] Such "international" markets in Japan tended to be made up predominantly of Korean and Japanese stallholders alongside a small group of Chinese or Taiwanese businessowners, whereas Pusan's reflected a different constellation of connections maintained and created in the postwar cities.[50]

Visions for future overseas trade in Fukuoka appeared to have rather narrow horizons, much like the backgrounds of stallholders in its "international" market. In the summer of 1947 the imminent reopening of private international trade prompted the *Seiki Shinbun* to hold a roundtable discussion on prospects for trade between Japan and Korea. While navigating this renegotiation of Japan and Korea's trade relationship, Zainichi Koreans in Fukuoka tried to position themselves as crucial go-betweens in the brokering of trade between the two countries.[51]

The port's recent history appeared to dictate future plans. Many of the talking points of the invited guests, both Japanese and Zainichi Korean (including Yoshikawa Yoshihiro, former board member of the Korean Chamber of Commerce), echoed complaints of prewar Fukuoka boosters: To them, Hakata still lagged behind the Kanmon ports in facilities and capacity, but with development, they could hope for increased trade with Korea, China, and the South Seas.[52]

Not only were the port of Hakata's desired trading partners similar to those from the days of Japan's empire, but the goods to be traded were too: There were "great hopes for rice from Korea." These desires to revert to former imperial trade networks were quashed by one guest at the roundtable, Tanaka

Sadame, an economics professor from Kyushu University, who was careful to remind those assembled that Korea was now an independent country and that one shouldn't expect import amounts similar to those in the colonial era.[53] It would take time for a new relationship between Japan and South Korea to emerge, especially when local plans for the future were being shaped by memories of the past.

THE KOREAN WAR AND ECHOES OF EMPIRE

In the early hours of the morning of October 4, 1951, Hakata Port police discovered a large-scale immigration attempt: A group of thirty-four Korean refugees, including women, were picked up just outside Hakata's harbor walls by the port patrol boat. According to a newspaper report, "Most of the stowaways were young men from twenty-five to thirty who had given up on their war-torn homeland and were attempting to make it to Japan for a new life." They included a graduate from a Japanese law school and an officer of the Korean police force who had lived in Japan. In the newspaper the officer was quoted describing how "after Korea's liberation I rushed back to my homeland, but after this tragic civil war that has broken out among my people, I've given up on them and left them to their fate."[54]

One of the three women aboard, twenty-three-year-old Song Kŭm-ju, who gave her Japanese name as Matsumoto Haruko, was a graduate of Tokyo Keiai Girls High School. She had recently married Kim T'ae-sŏn, a graduate of Kyoto University's Law School, who had begun work as a training officer at the Zainichi student volunteer corps in September of that year.[55] Song Kŭm-ju was hoping to join him. "After getting a letter from my husband to come and join him in Japan, my mind was made up to stow away. If I'd gone through the correct channels I would have had to wait for up to eight months. I couldn't bear it," she explained in tears.[56] These attempted evacuations across the Tsushima Strait—echoes of colonial-era crossings and reminders of the generations of Koreans who saw Japan as "home"—highlight the role of the Korean War in revealing the unfinished business of Japan and Korea's decolonization.

The Korean War broke out on June 25, 1950, when North Korean troops crossed the thirty-eighth parallel and began an offensive south, met with little resistance by South Korean (ROKA) forces. President Rhee fled Seoul almost immediately, and the Korean People's Army (KPA) had taken the city by June 28. Huge numbers of civilians and members of ROKA fled south as July saw the KPA forces advance down the peninsula. UN ground forces joined the war in support of South Korea by the end of June. On August 4 the Battle of the Pusan Perimeter began, with UN forces fighting the advance of KPA troops along a 140-mile-long line of defense. Between the outbreak of war and the beginning of the Battle of the Pusan Perimeter, refugees streamed toward Pusan, down main roads and following railroad tracks. On August 18, 1950, the city was declared South Korea's temporary capital.[57]

Fukuoka's proximity to the peninsula made it the obvious destination for evacuated officials connected to the US occupation and the United Nations Commission for Korea. In the days following the North Korean army's entry into Seoul, planes and ships carrying US evacuees arrived at Fukuoka's Itazuke Airport and Hakata Bay.[58] Itazuke Airport was the renamed Mushiroda Airfield, which had been completed with mobilized student labor at the end of the Second World War. From the end of June 1950, northern Kyushu, including Fukuoka, became the front line for US and UN forces, and the city's airport, harbor, and military facilities again became advance bases for a war in Asia.

These events reversed plans for Hakata Port's return to local control. Only weeks before the outbreak of war, SCAP and the Japanese government had put forward a new law devolving port administration to local government authorities.[59] The last repatriation ships had arrived into Hakata in 1947, and a few months later, with the restricted reopening of civilian trade between Korea and Japan on August 15, 1947, it was declared a new trade port. From July 1950, however, US and UN forces requisitioned ports across Japan, including Hakata, to act as military headquarters and supply bases for the war in Korea.[60]

The inhabitants of Fukuoka and the surrounding region experienced the Korean War far more viscerally than most in Japan. Although media at the time characterized the view of Japanese society toward the Korean War as "somebody else's problem" (J: *taigan no kaji*, literally, "a fire on the opposite shore"), this was not the case.[61] Japanese were involved in the war and were affected by it in many ways.[62] In Fukuoka, wounded soldiers were brought into Hakata Port on hospital ships and driven through the city on trucks to the US Army hospital, which had occupied the city's former insurance offices since 1945. LSTs (amphibious landing ships) and other naval vessels filled Hakata Bay, loading and unloading troops and munitions. Residents were afraid of the region's possible infiltration by North Korean guerrillas or its targeting by North Korean air strikes. One article on US bases in the city describes the "fresh red Korean mud" still clinging to the military equipment brought back to the city for repair.[63]

The author of the piece, Yata Fumio, connected these current events back to the region's historical role as an advance base for military activity in Asia, reminding readers that "thousands of years ago Empress Jingū sent her armies from here to Korea. . . . This spot has again become a mustering point for troops headed to the peninsula."[64] Although Yata didn't mention far more recent history here, the reality was that Hakata Port's involvement in repatriation after the collapse of Japan's empire had been a determining factor in the port being chosen for a key logistical role in the Korean War. Hakata's importance, first during repatriation and then as a troop and goods supply base during the Korean War, cemented the port's growing position in Japan; it was declared a Port of Importance (J: Jūyō kōwan) in January 1951.

Refugees

The outbreak of the Korean War increased unauthorized flows across the straits. In his 1951 Korean War reports from Pusan for the *Manchester Guardian*, French journalist Robert Guillain enumerated the licit and illicit flows in and out of the besieged city:

> Pusan is the sewer that carries off the foul waters of Korea's misery; it is the great refuse dump of the war. For a year the enormous influx of war material and the flood of men marching into battle have passed through Pusan to the shouts of the ragged urchins in the streets. . . . For a year too, the town has been the channel through which the wounded have poured back from the front, the hospital trains, the "rotations" troops returning to America, and the men on leave fleeing from Korea to spend a few days in the green paradise of Japan.

Guillain draws sharp contrasts between the flows of people into wartime Pusan with those few able to leave it, and how these controls led to smuggling of both goods and people in and out of the city:

> This town, crossed by so many men and so many consignments, the only "rear" in this war in the void, is the city of countless deals: wholesale deals carried out between Very Important Persons and innumerable deals of the small men. Cigarettes, chocolates, soap, pass in the twinkling of an eye from the Army canteens to the pavements of the adjoining streets, to be sold at

five times the purchase price. From America itself come a thousand articles, imported no one can say how, especially toilet or fashion goods, nylon bags, fabrics, lotions, fantastically incongruous here but sold at enormous prices. From Japan come cheap goods smuggled in by Japanese crews or taken over by professional smugglers at agreed meeting-places out at sea. There is the business of shipping Korean passengers across to the shores of Japan, where they are landed at night. There is the traffic in drugs and opium and in ginseng, the aphrodisiac root bought by the Chinese at exorbitant prices as far away as Singapore and Java. And the traffic in women.[65]

In Guillain's reports, entry across the straits into the "green paradise of Japan" was restricted to US soldiers and those who could pay brokers to ferry them across the straits, while refugees "camped in the streets, swarming together at night to keep warm, in heaps in ditches, doorways and the openings of alleys."[66] Human trafficking of women through Pusan was not new, either—as seen in the wartime shipping out of comfort women to Southeast Asia and the late nineteenth-century arrival of Japanese women and girls, many bought and sold into sex work to meet the demands of the port city's growing settler population.

Although Koreans with means and imperial-era connections were able to secure refuge in Japan for the duration of the hostilities, others had to make more dangerous attempts to escape the conflict.[67] As seen in the account of Song Kŭm-ju above, from the summer of 1950, newspapers in the northern Kyushu region began reporting on a new type of "stowaway" attempting to make their way across the Korean Straits: war refugees leaving southern Korea.

These new refugees joined the many other groups of people who had crossed the Tsushima Strait since the stowaways of the 1930s: Japanese troops upon the outbreak of war with China in 1937; the Korean laborers who were brought forcibly from the late 1930s to work in Kyushu's industrial belt; and, from 1945 to 1947, repatriates "returning" to homelands many of them had never seen before. What had been an imperial border was, by 1950, a militarized Cold War frontier—traversed in one direction by US fighter jets taking off from Fukuoka's Allied bases and in the other by a new wave of Korean refugees.[68]

Policy in occupied Japan with regards to Korean refugees was hard and unrelenting. After receiving intelligence that many Koreans were attempting to cross the Tsushima Strait, the Japanese coast guard put out a warning for its three headquarters on the Japan Sea coast at Moji, Maizuru, and Niigata to be on high alert, and it dispatched special patrols from Moji, Tsushima, and Nagasaki.[69] As Supreme Commander for the Allied Powers and commander in chief of the UN Command, Douglas MacArthur thought that allowing refugees from Korea into Japan would only deepen what he saw as the "problem" of Japan's Korean minority. He also believed that it would anger the Japanese due to the "past relations" between the two peoples.[70]

These "past relations," however, could not be avoided: They formed a part of the personal histories of those fleeing Korea. Many of the Korean refugees who made the journey across the straits upon the outbreak of war were in their twenties or thirties, born or educated in the colonial metropole. Some may have been fleeing conscription. Others were hoping to reach relatives who had been living in Japan since before the end of the war.[71] In the other direction, too, Korean men of a similar age left their homes in Japan to fight for South Korea. Most of the men who joined the Zainichi volunteer corps from Fukuoka were in their mid- to late twenties and came from urban regions, like Fukuoka or Kokura, or from villages among the Chikuhō coal fields. Half of them never returned.[72]

Throughout August 1950 the *NNS* reported on refugees escaping Pusan via the Tsushima Strait, who were discovered by authorities on the coasts of Tsushima and northern Kyushu. The tone of these reports vacillated between sympathy for and fear of these new arrivals, sometimes described as "refugees" and other times as "stowaways." On August 9 the *NNS* reported:

> Twenty-nine refugees, including three Japanese who left the refugee-flooded city of Pusan in three rowboats, were found off of Tsushima by the Izuhara Coast Guard on the eighth of August and are being held in custody at the Shimoagata police station. Due to local fears of there being North Korean guerrillas among the refugees, the police have been called on to investigate the situation thoroughly.[73]

The prewar newspaper accounts of provincial Koreans being duped out of extortionate sums of money by unscrupulous brokers, discussed in chapter 3, were in many ways more sympathetic toward the stowaways than these postwar reports.

While stories of Korean stowaways would have been familiar to residents of the region, the Cold War threat of North Korean guerrillas—an invisible enemy—was new. However, the Tsushima Strait had already borne witness to the violence of postliberation Korea, and to what fear of an invisible enemy could do: Mutilated bodies from the Cheju massacre of 1948–49 had been washed up on Tsushima and buried by the island's inhabitants.[74] The fear of

North Korean guerrillas infiltrating Pusan also motivated the attempts of many South Koreans to escape to Japan. Hwang In-am, a tradesman from Pusan's Wanwŏl neighborhood, was brought ashore in Tsushima in August 1950 and described the current situation in his city:

> Since the evacuation order was put out on the sixth of August, boats over fifteen tons in Pusan Harbor have been mobilized as evacuation ships.... It's said that a division of over three thousand North Korean guerrillas have managed to infiltrate Pusan and are wandering its streets. According to reliable sources... ten guerrillas disguised as evacuees have already made it to Japan.[75]

The outbreak of hostilities, the threat from the North Korean forces headed south to Pusan, and the panic over rumors of undercover North Korean guerrillas all played a role in the spread of rumors among South Koreans of an order to "flee to Japan." But behind all this lay deeper, long-term reasons. The movement of Koreans back across the Tsushima Strait after the outbreak of the Korean War was another example of "empire coming home." National boundaries that had "snapped back" into place on Japan's surrender five years earlier were easier to redraw on a map than to enforce in reality, especially when Korea's previously colonized population were faced with these extreme circumstances.[76] Since the end of the Second World War, people on either side of the Tsushima Strait had been affected by the creation of this new national border, and with the outbreak of another war only five years later, the decisions made by Korean refugees were animated by the numerous unsevered ties—whether familial, linguistic, historical, or simply geographic—that linked them to Japan.[77]

Human Reminders of Colonial Policy

The outbreak of the Korean War also shed light on the plight of Japanese who had chosen to remain in (or return to) Korea after 1945.[78] Like other Korean refugees, they had headed to Pusan after the outbreak of war. Many assumed it would be easy for them to reenter their home country when faced with the prospect of war in Korea, but the reality was more complicated. The Japanese who gathered in Pusan were from all over the peninsula, including some from North Korea. Most were women and children with Korean husbands or fathers.

Marriage between Japanese and Koreans (J: *naisen kekkon*; K: *naesŏn kyŏrhon*) had been encouraged by colonial authorities as part of the "Japan and Korea as one" policy from 1937 onward, but these families had faced difficult decisions after the end of empire.[79] An Associated Press report from 1951 described these women as "war widows ... whose husbands and fathers of Korean nationality were killed or reported missing since the beginning of the hostilities and who have been deprived of the means of livelihood."[80] Some of them had boarded ships with Korean refugees and made their way to Japan that way. Many others gathered in Pusan.

Morita Yoshio, who had worked for the Pusan Japanese Relief Society during the repatriation of settlers in 1945, was involved in this repatriation process too. He reported on the situation in 1951.[81] According to Morita, although these women and children had been living alongside Koreans until their flight to Pusan, upon arrival in the city and registering with authorities they were recategorized as Japanese. Just like Japanese repatriates had been five years before, most were housed separately in temples and empty warehouses. However, in a city with a population of over a million people, swollen with refugees, this was not always possible. Some of the Japanese women and children were housed alongside other Korean refugees in repurposed cattle sheds in the former Cattle Quarantine Station in Uam-ri (known as Akasaki in Japanese) or in rooms in a former brothel in the red-light district of Midori-machi. Others waited in boats moored in Pusan harbor.[82]

On May 29, 1951, fifty-nine of these "Japanese women with Korean nationality" and their dependents were repatriated to Moji.[83] In the following months a total of two hundred women and children were brought back from camps in Pusan. Some women stayed behind, wavering between remaining in Pusan in case their husbands returned and traveling to Japan without them.[84] On August 23 Inoue Takajirō, head of the Kyushu Liaison and Coordination Office in Fukuoka, sent a letter to Song Hak-nae, representative of the Fukuoka branch of the Korean Diplomatic Mission in Japan, who had asked for a report on the living conditions of the seventeen repatriates now living in Fukuoka.[85]

Inoue's report offered a bleak picture. Twenty-four-year-old Iwami Toshiko had been repatriated with her three children, aged five, four, and two. The youngest of these, Seito, "was taken to Kokura National Hospital right after landing at Shimonoseki Port on June 28, 1951, and died of undernourishment on July 9, 1951." The names of the three children, especially Toshiko's sons, Seito (Sŏng-in) and Seikan (Sŏng-kwan), use unusual Chinese character combinations that suggest their names were a way of bridging the gap between their Japanese and Korean parents. If the children's ages were accurate, all three of them would have been born after the end of Japanese colonial rule.[86] The family was now living with Toshiko's elder sister and aunt in Moji. Another repatriated family, thirty-two-year-old Akamatsu Fujiko and her four children, had returned to Fukuoka prefecture and were living with Fujiko's elder brother Sōshichi. Fujiko was unable to work and support herself or her children due to "tuberculosis of the spine" and was reliant on support from her brother and other siblings. Her eldest son, Shōichi, aged sixteen, had not been repatriated with them from Korea.[87]

As the Korean War continued and more Japanese refugees gathered in Pusan, they found that leaving the city was harder than they had imagined. Their plight came to the attention of Japanese involved in military transport.[88] In December 1952 one Shibasaki Tōyo, "Purser for Crew of the US Army LST-618," wrote a petition to the Japanese government on behalf of these women "stranded" in Pusan, sending a copy to the English-language *Nippon Times* newspaper:

> There are at present several hundred persons living in most dire circumstances. *These Japanese are WOMEN with CHILDREN.* Due to the cold weather and lack of work they are suffering beyond comprehension. They have no money and very little food and are only living from day to day. . . .
>
> You may recall that during the late war these women were encouraged to marry the Koreans. This plan was advanced to the people *under the name* of NAISEN KETTUKON [marriage between Japanese and Koreans]. Now most of these marriages have dissolved either by divorce or [desertion].
>
> In line with the democratic policies now endorsed by the Japanese Government it is felt that something should be done and very soon as *the hardship of winter* [has] already begun. It is also thought that transportation to Japan could easily be arranged. There are many ships plying their duties in Korean Waters under Japanese Flags.[89]

This letter illustrates the messy reality of decolonization across the straits, the unfinished and complex nature of which was thrown into stark relief by the outbreak of the Korean War. The war reconnected maritime links between Pusan and Hakata—as illustrated in the above letter's reference to the presence of Japanese nationals and ships in Korean waters. Now, in wartime, the Hakata–Pusan ferry route was also plied by hospital ships and other naval vessels, bringing soldiers back for "rest and recuperation leave" in the "green paradise of Japan."

The stranded Japanese women and children of Korean nationality, portrayed in the letter as victims of colonial-era policy of unity between Japan and Korea, were a problem close to home. Their presence in the port city of Pusan, some six years after the first *yamibune* (unofficial repatriation ships) left for Japan, acts as a reminder of the impossibility of drawing simple boundaries to the end of empire, whether temporal, national, or geographic.

EMERGENCY HOUSING AS AN "URBAN PROBLEM"

After 1945, and even after the outbreak of the Korean War, those who could come and go freely between Pusan and Fukuoka, between South Korea and Japan, were in the minority. As seen in the first half of this chapter, the two port cities became home to refugees, repatriates, the unhoused, and the unemployed—those with nowhere else to go. In both cities, responses to these groups hardened as authorities struggled to control the growth of informal housing and the dangers of fire and disease. Urban debates in the period from Japan's surrender in 1945 to the end of the Korean War in 1953 emerged first out of policies from wartime and earlier. However, how this discourse developed by the end of these eight years would set the postwar urban agenda on housing and unhoused people. National debates in both Japan and South Korea, evidenced by cases in both Fukuoka and Pusan, began over discussions on the informal housing of repatriates and other displaced persons at the end of empire, but they eventually came to reframe these people as "urban problems" rather than victims of war.

Pusan and P'anjach'on

As Pusan was the main port of entry for liberated repatriates, its urban spaces had been shaped dramatically by vast flows of people between 1945 and 1950. Following the outbreak of the Korean War, Pusan and Taegu were two of the only cities that remained unoccupied by Communist forces. Pusan's housing stock could not accommodate all these new and returning people, and informal housing sprang up on the city's margins, like bamboo shoots after rain. The language used to describe these new urban spaces and forms shifted from colonial terms to neologisms that would continue to be used long after their origins were forgotten.

In the initial months and years after liberation, the clusters of informal housing seen on Pusan's hillsides were mostly referred to as *purak* or *t'omak*—terms that had also been popular with the Japanese colonial authorities.[90]

One of the most famous and earliest informal settlements in postliberation Seoul, Haebangch'on (Liberation Village), settled by refugees fleeing from above the thirty-eighth parallel in 1946, was also described as a *purak* in news reports from the time.[91] Later, from 1952, references to "*parakk'ŭ*" (from the Japanese *barakku*) increased dramatically as well.[92]

After the outbreak of the Korean War, throughout the summer of 1950, thousands of refugees headed south to Pusan. Figures for the city's population in 1950 remain elusive, but the population nearly doubled between 1949 and 1951.[93] Pusan was already stretched beyond its prewar limits, with returning Koreans from the Japanese mainland causing the urban population to increase by over 150,000 between 1945 and 1947.[94] Most of the refugees arriving in Pusan were from Seoul and its surrounding areas, or from North Korea itself.[95] Just as in the colonial period, many of the city's new inhabitants lived in shantytowns on the city's margins, hillsides, and riverbeds.

In September 1951, just over a year into the war, journalist Robert Guillain described the wartime city of Pusan and its swollen population:

> The only thing that reflects any light is the estuary, which fits the bluish-grey mirror of the port waters like a wedge in this black hive embedded in mud. All the rest is just a thick urban paste the spread of which, broken up by a labyrinth of alleys, extends as far as it can in a mould hollowed out of the hills. Squeezed into the bottoms of the valleys, the town climbs ravines and splashes half-way up bare hillsides in a sort of foam made of hovels and shanties crowded together and piled one above another. A little higher up the roofs enter the low cloud that shuts in the whole scene.[96]

To Guillain, the expanding city had become a living organism, a "hive," "mould," or "foam" where individual inhabitants disappeared into the "urban paste." A more human perspective of these shantytowns exists in the watercolor study from 1950 by Yang Dalsuk, featured on this book's cover, where the warm glow of lights illuminates the silhouettes of inhabitants against the backdrop of ramshackle houses.[97]

These shantytowns developed, in both coverage and speed, at a scale far beyond that of their prewar counterparts, becoming an urban form that would feature in South Korean discourse on housing and the city for decades after the end of the Korean War. As the destination for so many refugees and the provisional capital of South Korea, Pusan, unsurprisingly, was where such housing was clustered and where new terms were coined. The fixing upon the term *p'anjajip* (wooden plank house) and the collective term *p'anjajip ch'on* (wooden plank house village, later shortened to *p'anjach'on*) to describe this housing occurred in the crucible of the Korean War. As Russell Burge describes, this period's "informal subsistence economy" was "reflected in the new lexicon of found objects—*t'omak* in the late 1940s became *sangjajip*, or 'box house,' and then, with the Korean War and arrival of UN surplus materials on the peninsula, *p'anjajip*." [98] Looking at newspaper articles on informal housing between 1945 and 1953, the earliest extant reference to a *p'anjajip ch'on* appears to be in an article on Pusan from January 1952. [99]

Debates over housing that emerged in wartime Pusan foreshadowed policy regarding *p'anjach'on* in the 1960s, when such areas were seen as an obstacle to development and a fire hazard and were the target of often brutal demolition campaigns. In July 1953, looking ahead to the return of the capital to Seoul (which occurred with the Armistice Agreement on July 27 that year), Pusan's mayor Son Yŏng-Su announced plans for the clearance of all informal housing in the city and warned against the purchase and selling of *p'anjajip*. [100]

Illegal and crowded housing had been blamed for two large fires that had broken out in January: one in the Uam-ri/Akasaki refugee camp, where people were housed in the colonial-era Cattle Quarantine Station, and the second in the crowded structures of the International Market. The latter fire spread almost to the door of the US embassy, housed temporarily in the former Japanese Oriental Development Offices at the base of Yongdu-san. Before Mayor Son's planned clearances could begin, however, another large fire in November left the center of the city devastated. [101]

By the ceasefire of 1953 Pusan had undergone dramatic changes as a result of wartime population movement. Unlike much of the Korean peninsula, the city had not been bombed during the Korean War, but images from the aftermath of the November fire show how the center of Pusan had been reduced to a burnt expanse reminiscent of Fukuoka after the air raid of June 1945. Figure 18 shows the blackened shells of the city's colonial-era buildings in the background, with families in the foreground moving new planks of wood to rebuild their burnt houses on the slopes overlooking Pusan Bay.

After the Korean War, Seoul again became South Korea's center of gravity for population movement. The city had attracted large numbers of repatriates and refugees from north of the thirty-eighth parallel in the first weeks and months after liberation, and it was occupied multiple times during the Korean War. In the war's aftermath, new arrivals to Seoul often lived on the city's margins and hillsides in shanty villages, what had become known by

FIGURE 18. Rebuilding begins in Pusan after a fire in November 1953. Courtesy of the National Archives, photo no. 80-G-632799.

then as *p'anjach'on*. By the 1960s, as crackdowns on these shantytowns began, the origins of this term in the "thick urban paste" of wartime Pusan went unremarked: In both Pusan and Fukuoka, these urban forms that had developed out of war and displacement soon came to be viewed simply as "urban problems" that were an obstacle to both cities' and countries' postwar development.

Fukuoka's Postimperial Margins

In 1951 Fukuoka was still dealing with the aftermath of imperial collapse and the emergency policies put in place to deal with the ensuing housing crisis. Unauthorized housing and unhoused populations were still unsolved problems. The prefecture's first five-year plan for reconstruction of housing began in 1950, but in 1951 more than twenty thousand repatriates in the city were still living in *barakku* or other temporary accommodation.[102] Despite the efforts of the Hakata Repatriation Office, which had overseen the creation of orphanages for the hundreds of children who arrived at Hakata without parents or guardians, unhoused children and other groups were still a common sight in the city.

In public discourse, where once there had been benevolence there was now consternation. In November 1951 the *NNS* published an article bemoaning the hundreds of unhoused people who were "evacuated" to parks or the waterfront in summer but gathered in Hakata station when the nights got colder, "turning it into a lumpen hotel."[103] According to the article, those spending the night in the waiting room were a mixed bunch: "lumpen, ragpickers, day laborers" who, when the whistle of the last train blew, moved into the empty waiting room, bringing burlap sacks and straw wrappings off charcoal packages with them. Their numbers could reach two hundred, "occupying the entire space with their presence but also with their body odor and smoke."[104] The unhoused people of Fukuoka were depicted as engaging in other antisocial activities, including the *oyabun* (bosses) among them preying on waifs and strays present in the station, "selling off" runaway girls to the city's red-light district.[105]

The "runaway girl" was common journalistic shorthand for women forced into sex work by their economic circumstances. The term had a specific historical resonance in 1950s Kyushu. As part of the occupation's labor reforms in 1947, women were banned from working underground in coal mines, leaving many women of Chikuhō's mining districts without employment. Large numbers of these women ended up moving from rural coal-mining villages into the city, and some entered into sex work in entertainment districts like Nakasu.[106]

Whereas in the prewar period Japan's colonies were seen as a release valve for Kyushu's poor or so-called "surplus" populations, postwar Fukuoka City was where many such marginal groups ended up after repatriation. Subsequent postwar migration from rural Kyushu regions was redirected to North and South America, as well as to Hawai'i.[107] There is evidence that some of these postwar migrants included repatriates from Japan's colonies, who had found it impossible to rebuild their lives upon returning to postwar Japan and chose to become "pioneers" yet again.[108]

The early 1950 saw a shift in discourse on the living conditions of repatriates, from emotive and sympathetic reports in the immediate postwar period to more technocratic discussions of hygiene and safety.[109] An article on housing policy in the *NNS* from 1951 shows the limits of the city's attempts to deal with the crisis and the continuing shortages it still faced. In the previous two years the prefecture had built some 929 houses for repatriates, but more were still needed, with plans to build another 973 in the prefecture by 1952.[110] Such limited construction barely made a dent in the numbers of repatriates living in what was described as dangerously overcrowded and unsafe accommodation.

City hall bemoaned the large number of "matchbox" houses that were thwarting their attempt to create fireproof zones in the center of Fukuoka.[111] These structures failed to comply with building codes: They had wooden shingle roofs and were built so tightly together that it was impossible for a fire truck to get through the narrow streets. Since they were packed so close together and were made from highly flammable building materials, sparks could quickly spread fire from one house to the next.

The 1951 newspaper report on the housing issue framed this as an "urban problem," one that needed to be dealt with in order to create an orderly and safe urban environment. Fukuoka City had begun *barakku* clearances as early as 1949, when it tore down nearly 150 houses that had developed in the central neighborhood of Tenjin-machi, begun as an open-air market on cleared land by repatriates and war victims. Although the city had helped to set up other shopping arcades for repatriates, it was less charitable when these developed into black markets or shantytowns, especially those on land needed for road-widening projects. Inhabitants reluctant to leave their homes without concrete plans for relocation were described as acting in an "uncivic" (J: *hishimin-teki*) manner.[112]

Repatriates were not the only people living in such dangerous and "unhygienic" accommodation. Clusters of *barakku* existed across the city, and those that were built along the banks of the Ishidō River in Chiyo-machi were for a long time the most visible reminder of the large Korean population that remained in the city after the repatriation of Koreans had officially ended.[113] These areas had developed out of *barakku* constructed by Koreans who had arrived at the port at the end of the war but who, for various reasons, had been unable or had chosen not to repatriate. The inhabitants of these neighborhoods made their living any way they could: on the black market, by brewing alcohol, or by raising pigs.[114] As Sayaka Chatani describes, these neighborhoods—*tongne* in Korean—became almost "autonomous territories" where "human interactions and relationships grew intimate and dense" due to external discrimination.[115]

By the early 1950s, although there was a shift in the overall policy toward informal housing, there was still a noticeable difference in the attitude of city

FIGURE 19. *Barakku* along the Ishidō River in Fukuoka, 1961. Courtesy of the Nishiyama Uzō Photography Archives.

government toward these two groups of *barakku* inhabitants. The pace of construction of formal housing for Japanese repatriates and Zainichi Koreans in Fukuoka was markedly different, and while the former was discussed in the newspapers, the latter rarely got any coverage at all. Indeed, the removal of Fukuoka's Zainichi Koreans from their *barakku* along the Ishidō River occurred almost two decades after repatriate Japanese had been rehoused. Despite the creation of new housing complexes for Zainichi Koreans beginning in the late 1950s, the *barakku* were present throughout the 1960s before the last area was finally torn down in 1976 (see figure 19).[116] By this juncture the postcolonial origins of the structures had been forgotten, and instead they became the subject of anecdotes presenting the area as a microcosm of the divided Korean peninsula itself; the *barakku* neighborhood was said to be divided between those whose loyalties lay with either Mindan (Republic of Korea) or Chongryŏn (North Korea) associations.

IMPERIAL PALIMPSESTS

At the ceasefire of the Korean War in 1953, Pusan and Fukuoka were two markedly different ends of empire. After the fire that had devastated Pusan's city center, new urban visions for the city emerged by the end of 1953. Announcing "A Port City Brought Back to Life," the *Tong-a Ilbo* discussed the reconstruction plan put forward for the city.[117] Pusan's new urban center would have wider roads and strict building codes to prevent such fires in future. Firebreaks would be constructed regularly in areas with wooden buildings. The plan was followed by an emergency meeting on the city's future between Korean and American officials. One of the main concerns raised was the rebuilding of *p'anjajip* by those who had lost their homes in the fire. The members of the meeting decided that these newly unhoused people, who had increased in number yet again, should be housed in the city's former prisoner-of-war camps.[118]

Postliberation Pusan's urban spaces contained a patchwork of camps that were repurposed to incarcerate different waves of interned peoples. From 1953, one group were Japanese fishermen, many from Kyushu, imprisoned in Pusan for crossing over and fishing within South Korea's new maritime border with Japan.[119] This was the so-called Peace Line delineated by Syngman Rhee before the former MacArthur Line was dissolved in April 1952, when the San Francisco Peace Treaty came into effect. By 1958, when they were finally released, more than nine hundred Japanese fishermen were being held in Pusan in an "alien internment camp" north of the refugee village of Amidong, which had previously been built to hold Japanese women attempting to leave Korea.[120]

As this suggests, land use and labor patterns that emerged during the Korean War were entrenched in the subsequent decades. Uam-dong (known in the colonial period as Uam-ri or Akasaki) had been a site of one of the official refugee camps during the war, and *p'anjach'on* grew up around it, with many residents working as day laborers in Pusan's nearby docks during the Korean War, unloading US aid supplies. As the city's economy recovered from the late 1950s into the '60s, these areas became sites of new light industry, as well as being close to the city's expanding port facilities. By the 1960s Uam-dong, site of the former colonial Cattle Quarantine Station and later home to successive waves of repatriates and refugees, was at the heart of a residential zone for the day laborers who powered Pusan's industrial development.[121]

By 1953, eight years of reconstruction in Fukuoka had created a city that was very different from the "burnt expanses" (J: *yakenohara*) that had greeted repatriates on their arrival into Hakata Bay in 1945. Housing was still in short supply, and the city's population was projected to keep growing as it continued to cement its position as Kyushu's center of commerce, local government, and education. At the end of 1952 the city council put forward plans to create an international airport at Itazuke after the US army decommissioned its base there. The following year the US military returned Hakata Port and its buildings to the city. In August 1953 Fukuoka Zoo opened in Minami Kōen (South Park), one of the "green spaces" originally planned as an evacuation zone during the war.

Alongside the cities' diverging paths, however, their histories remained connected, as displacement and war led to echoes of wartime and colonial policies in and across the urban spaces of Pusan and Fukuoka for many years after 1945. This chapter has demonstrated how, after a swift and incomplete "decolonizing" via repatriation across the straits, the two cities continued to be linked by regional visions, smuggling routes, divided families, and their new roles in the military and supply network of the United States.

Tessa Morris-Suzuki refers to this new network as "a regional space of movement . . . separate from the space of movement inhabited by most of the region's people."[122] While the geography of the US military may have existed parallel to that of the national borders that constrained the movements of most Japanese and Koreans, this "regional space of movement" was built upon military networks constructed only a few years before, during Japan's imperial and military expansion, which had emerged out of processes of urbanization, industrialization, and migration set in motion in the late nineteenth century. These networks and their geographies were constantly in flux but were "always-already imbricated" within what Stephanie Malia Hom calls "empire's Mobius strip." The sites discussed in this chapter, whether the margins of the city or newly built airfields, are examples of where, as Hom argues, "the imperial finds fixture in physical form," spanning past and present, "operat[ing] unevenly [and] built on mobility."[123]

The echoes and remnants of empire, brought into sharp relief by renewed war, were noted by those at the time. In the novelist Yuasa Katsue's 1952 work of literary journalism, *Tsushima*, he notes how, of goods being smuggled from Japan to Korea, the "majority were daily necessities that should be treated as normal trade, were diplomatic relations to be resumed." Yuasa put this down to incomplete decolonization: "It's only been six or seven years since what was once a single nation was dismantled. Even if you split a living tree with an axe, the fibers will still be connected somewhere."[124]

Similarly, Yata Fumio's report on occupation bases in Fukuoka, published in 1953, depicts a city where recent history was being rehearsed with new actors: "During the war, Japanese chasing the dream of the Greater East Asia Co-Prosperity Sphere went to and fro from Gannosu airfield. Now it's taken on a new name, Camp Brady, where small planes come and go, and large aircraft come to pick up fuel and other goods to carry to Korea." As a result of the Korean War, Yata argued, Fukuoka had been transformed once again into a military city, but one whose occupants were now the occupied:

> The city is surrounded on three sides by bases and is the playground [*ian no chi*] for the troops stationed in them, and also their political center. When anyone arrives in Hakata Station they are forced to listen to the poor English announcements coming from the speakers. There are Western-looking hotels, covered with a thin veneer of concrete, and beer halls full of American troops.[125]

While Japan may have been a "green paradise" for US and UN troops on R & R from Korea, the reality felt quite different for its Japanese inhabitants, and would continue to for many years.

The US Air Force bases in Fukuoka remained open until 1972. In 1956, a portion of the US base at Itazuke was returned to Fukuoka City and opened as a civilian airport. In 1967, its first international flight linked the city once again with Pusan. On September 3, JAL Flight 29 landed at Pusan's Suyŏng Airport, formerly known as Haeundae airfield, constructed for the Japanese military in 1940.[126] As this chapter has shown, the "regional spaces of movement" across the Tsushima Strait were continually reshaped and repurposed beyond the ends of empire.

Decolonization, liberation, war, and occupation altered not only the relationship of these two cities with each other, but also their roles within their newly (re)formed nations. During the Korean War, Pusan was South Korea's provisional capital for nearly three years, as well as the nation's key locus of trade and industry. This period strengthened the existing links between Pusan and Seoul as the "backbone" of South Korea.[127]

Postwar Fukuoka returned to a peripheral position within the new geography of a Japan constrained to its Meiji-era boundaries. The outbreak of the Korean War briefly returned it to its imperial role as the gateway to battlefields on the Asian continent, but in the aftermath of the conflict, the city was relegated to its now-secure position as the largest urban center and unofficial capital of Kyushu, as well as Fukuoka prefecture, while the national center of gravity returned to Honshū.[128]

In 1949 a publication from the recently founded Kyushu Economic Research Center highlighted the resurgent local fear of Kyushu succumbing once again to the colonizing presence of "central capital" from Tokyo. With the loss of Japan's actual colonies, the report's authors worried, would its peripheries, like Kyushu, take their place?[129] These fears of colonization were somewhat ironic considering the Kyushu Economic Research Center, founded in 1946, employed many repatriated members of the Manchurian Railways Research Unit.

The expansion of the Japanese empire had enmeshed cities into empire, and the empire into cities. After 1945, the many human histories and geographies connected to the growth of Fukuoka and Pusan—which, through the lens of empire, had been brought into focus as an imperial dyad at the heart of an urban region spanning the straits—lost their former coherence. The histories and imagined futures of these two cities would be rewritten through the lens of their new nation-states.

Conclusion

IN 1989, ON THE CENTENARY OF Hakata and Fukuoka's merger and the birth of the modern municipality of Fukuoka, the city held the Asian-Pacific Exposition (J: Ajia taiheiyō hakurankai), also known as Yokatopia. Yoka means "good" in the local Hakata dialect, and, as the name suggests, the visions of the future presented in the exposition were filled with the heady optimism and trust in technology of bubble-era Japan (1986–91). Commemorative tickets featured holograms, microchips, and maps of the Asia-Pacific region photo-etched into Yawata Steelworks steel.

The exposition, fittingly for a city promoting its history of maritime exchange, was held on reclaimed land in Momochi, at the edge of Hakata Bay. The grounds featured domestic pavilions from major companies such as Mitsubishi, Sumitomo, Fujitsu, and Mitsui-Toshiba, which shared much in common with earlier industrial expositions in the city. The pavilions at the heart of the expo, clustered around the new Fukuoka Tower, also hearkened back to earlier exposition displays of "exotic" native peoples. These included Midori Ethnic World and Tōkyū Tropical Village, containing the Micronesian, Melanesian, and Polynesian Pavilions, next to Flower Paradise and Bird Country. The exposition's exoticizing of the Asia-Pacific was further evidenced by its mascots, designed by manga artist Tezuka Osamu. Taihei-kun was a Japanese boy wearing a loincloth and headband, and Yōko-chan was drawn as a Pacific Islander with flowers in her hair. Continental Asia went unrepresented, leaving Taihei-kun alone with his imagined island sweetheart.[1]

As visitors entered the exposition from the south gate, the first building they would see was the Theme Pavilion. While the overall theme of Yokatopia was "seeking to meet new worlds," the Theme Pavilion's motto—*michi, deai*—was more abstract. "Roads [*michi*] lead to meetings [*deai*]," explained Fukuoka mayor Kuwahara in the Theme Pavilion's catalog: "All the exhibits in this pavilion are objects that tell stories of 'roads and meetings' between Japan and the countries of the Asia-Pacific." These exhibits included a scale model of a *kentōshi-sen* (the ships that carried Japanese envoys to Tang China via Hakata from the seventh to ninth centuries) and archaeological finds from the Kōrokan, the ninth-century guest house for envoys from Tang and Silla. These included blue glazed Islamic pottery that spoke to Fukuoka's position at the end of the Silk Road. At the pavilion's center was the *kin'in*, a gold seal from the first century CE, unearthed on an island in Hakata Bay. Described as a gift from the late Han court to the king of the local state of Na and the oldest material evidence of links between the continent and the Japanese archipelago, the gold seal was a powerful symbol of Fukuoka's ancient ties to the Asian continent.[2]

The exposition in 1989 was one manifestation of the city's 1987 master plan, "to aim towards becoming a hub [*kyoten*] city of Asia."[3] *Kyoten* was the term that Mayor Hatayama had also used in his 1943 speech describing Fukuoka's future as an "advance base" for the Greater East Asia Co-Prosperity Sphere. Fukuoka City's 1980s plan for reimagining itself as an Asian hub city replaced the wartime Greater East Asia Co-Prosperity Sphere with a new vision of connectivity, reworked for this moment of optimism and hope for the "Asia-Pacific."[4] Plans for the city's internationalization (J: *kokusaika*) involved redeveloping links with countries in Asia and Oceania toward the goal of once again becoming a "point of exchange" in the region. Promotional materials for the city from the 1980s onward feature maps with concentric rings emanating out from Fukuoka, showing its proximity to the Asian continent. The emergence of a new "Pacific community" from the late 1970s onward allowed for Fukuoka's location to once again be deployed as an argument for its centrality.[5]

As the crystallization of the city's plan for Fukuoka's Asian future, Yokatopia left a lasting cultural imprint: The Yokatopia Foundation was responsible for the organization and running of the annual Asian Month and the Fukuoka Prize, which still continues today. It also left a material imprint in the form of new urban landmarks such as the Fukuoka Tower and the beach at Seaside Momochi.[6] Most significantly, after closing its doors in September 1989, the expo's Theme Pavilion reopened the following year as Fukuoka's new city museum.

The new museum's first director was Shintō Kazuma (1904–92), formerly the city's longest-serving postwar mayor, from 1972 to 1986. Until its dissolution by the Allied occupation in 1946, Shintō had also been the tenth and final president of the Gen'yōsha. As head of the Gen'yōsha, Shintō had been jailed during the occupation in Sugamo prison as a Class A war criminal but was later released without charge. From 1958, receiving the backing of former Gen'yōsha members, Shintō served for fourteen years as the Liberal Democratic Party member for Fukuoka's first district in the House of Representatives.[7] As Fukuoka's mayor from 1972, Shintō had overseen the city's reestablishment of links with Communist China soon after Prime Minister Tanaka Kakuei made his first visit to the country; leading a visit by a group of the city's youth organizations in 1974; and signing a sister city agreement with Guangzhou, Fukuoka's first Asian sister city, in 1979.[8] Shintō's rhetoric around these reestablished ties drew on his and Fukuoka's shared history: Shintō's father had also been Gen'yōsha president and had hosted exiled Chinese revolutionary Sun Yat-sen in the city in 1913.[9]

The permanent exhibition of Fukuoka City Museum that I first saw in 2007 was unchanged from its opening in 1990 but has since been updated, in 2013. It was here that, in response to gaps in the exhibition, my questions about Fukuoka's modern history with Asia, discussed in the introduction, began. Many years after noticing these silences, I learned that they were a considered decision by the curator in charge of the new museum's modern history exhibit, Torisu Kyōichi. At the time of planning the permanent exhibition, although it was undeniable that Fukuoka's modern development was connected to Japan's imperial expansion, Torisu considered this "negative" (J: *fu*) history inappropriate for the overarching theme of the new museum's modern history display.[10] Instead, in keeping with the history behind the museum's own founding, Torisu emphasized the role of industrial expositions in the formation of the modern city. In this version of the city's history, Fukuoka's modernization was severed from Japan's imperialism in Asia. Ironically, however, the city's 1980s rhetoric and the figurehead of Shintō Kazuma himself were direct echoes of Fukuoka's imperial expansion.

In contrast to the silences I found in Fukuoka, the modern history on display in Pusan's museums does not—indeed, cannot—ignore the city's colonial past. Until recently the Pusan Modern History Museum was housed in the former offices of the Oriental Development Company (ODC) in the center of what had been the colonial city's overwhelmingly Japanese downtown. When I started my research I found the still extant former home of Fukuokan settler magnate Kashii Gentarō a stone's throw away from the museum. Over the course of my research for this book, the Pusan Modern

History Museum has moved and expanded, and Kashii's dilapidated former home has been demolished.

The newly relocated and renamed Pusan Modern and Contemporary History Museum's permanent exhibitions span two floors, one presenting displays on the period 1876–1945 and the other from 1945 onward. The museum also stages temporary exhibitions, often on spatial or material aspects of modern urban daily life such as tourism, schools, department stores, or bathhouses.[11] While Fukuoka City Museum's modern history displays focus on the local and domestic, obscuring the role that the city played in Japan's imperial history and vice versa, in Pusan's Modern and Contemporary History Museum there is the reverse impetus: Pusan is held up as a microcosm of Korea's national experience of Japanese colonialism. This was common in the rhetoric of some at the time; Kim Chang-t'ae, for example, in his 1938 radio speech portrayed the city's history as emblematic of Japan's imperial expansion. But this book has shown many reasons why Pusan's colonial history cannot stand in for all of Korea, and how it has a regional history and trajectory of its own.

One encounter in the old Pusan Modern History Museum brought home to me how a more local history has been flattened through the focus on national narratives.[12] In a display of colonial-era items representative of "modern lifestyles" restricted to Japanese settlers was a tin, simply labeled *kwaja sangja* (confectionery box). Although utilized by the museum to illustrate a simple national narrative of Japanese modern life in a colonial Korean city, this item revealed a far more local story. Beneath the rust covering the box were the Japanese words *"Hakata meibutsu—niwaka senpei."* Hakata Niwaka is a form of comedic storytelling local to Fukuoka, and the rice crackers (still sold as souvenirs in Fukuoka today) take their name and shape from the masks worn by actors while performing. I do not know how this box ended up in the museum collection, nor how it came to Pusan in the first place. It is easy to imagine, however, after reading about the various trips of Fukuokans across the straits that it could have been brought to Pusan as a reminder of home. Perhaps Tsurusaki and Naitō, the journalists from *The Fukuokan,* also brought *niwaka senpei* with them on their trip to Pusan in 1936.

The *niwaka senpei* box is no longer on display in the newly expanded museum, but an installation at the entrance to the first permanent exhibition continued the same emphasis on a national narrative over more local history: A video projected waves lapping at the shore onto the entrance floor. Borne by the waves, key dates for Pusan were washed ashore one after another. For the colonial period, these consisted of three dates: the founding of Pusan's municipal system, the independence movement in 1919, and liberation in 1945.

Museum displays are not academic historiographies, however, nor are they a full accounting of the ways in which local histories are being reckoned with by local communities. The histories of Fukuoka, Pusan, and the Tsushima Strait region covered in this book were initially inspired by what I saw as a "missing" history, but my research is indebted to the already rich accounts of these cities written by historians in Japan and Korea, and the archivists whose work preserves and shares crucial historical materials. The remainder of this conclusion summarizes the book's major findings before offering short accounts of recent histories of Fukuoka and Pusan in three other "space-times."[13] We begin with the cities' and their surrounding regions' reabsorption into postwar/postliberation national dynamics, then examine the reconnection and confronting of imperial histories that emerged in the 1990s, and finally consider how the two cities face each other now, in the early twenty-first century.

For the past decade or so, I have found the imperial dyad of Fukuoka and Pusan to be, as Jeff Wasserstrom puts it, "good to think."[14] What their interconnected history has shown is, first, the direct connection between urbanization and imperial expansion in both Korea *and* Japan. Just as urban histories of Korea cannot ignore colonization's impact, historians cannot write histories of Japan's urbanization without considering Japan's imperial expansion or the involvement of colonized peoples in this process. The emergence of local patriots like the Gen'yōsha, and their eventual coalition with Fukuoka's business elites, revealed how Japan's emergence as a nation-empire impelled the reorientation of its peripheralized regions. But many of the people whose lives are discussed within this book's chapters did not have such grand visions of their or their city's role within the Japanese empire. Those on the margins—of empire and its cities—including laborers, the unhoused, repatriates, and refugees, appear in the archive as targets for urban policies, not the makers of it.

As this book has shown, however, the movement of these people to the cities of the Tsushima Strait and the labor they undertook there shaped the region irrevocably. From the late nineteenth century, the laborers who powered Fukuoka prefecture's factories and mines were drawn from rural hinterlands that spanned the metropole-colony divide. In the case of Pusan in particular, migrant and refugee populations also shaped the city, through both their labor as part of colonial-era public works projects and the development of Pusan's hillside neighborhoods. The movement of people across the straits led to closer cooperation between regional authorities in the metropole and colony, and to urban policies that spanned both these waters and the 1945 divide. This book has shown that the role of these populations in shaping the region was just as crucial as the visions of its boosters and bureaucrats. These empire-wide movements of people, along with imperialist projections of power over space, created new scales of urbanization.

Second, viewing the Japanese empire from Fukuoka and Pusan also allowed me to write a local history of empire, and conversely an imperial history of one region. In many of this book's chapters, "empire" acts as an animating force, while one's hometown appears as a mediating vector. For some Korean elites, local development within empire was a source of pride and personal gain. For both Japanese and Koreans, regional connections acted as a way to shrink the distances between colony and metropole. Local settler networks spanned the empire, motivating and facilitating the actions of people in their adopted colonial "hometowns" and those "back home." The balancing act between the local, the imperial, and the global, however, was not easy to maintain. The second part of this book has shown how from the late 1930s the Tsushima Strait region became a crucial logistical and industrial zone within the Japanese state's expanded visions for Greater East Asia. This was a shift that replaced multiple animating visions of empire with a hegemonic singular vision, simultaneously making the region more central to empire and more vulnerable to attack.

The third part of this book, which traces the aftermath of empire and imperial urbanization in both Pusan and Fukuoka, shows how the very new dynamics of repatriation and occupation were built on and enacted using imperial networks and patterns. This leads to the third intervention this book has made, via its temporal framework. The histories of migration, regional visions, and urban growth contained within this book—from the late 1800s to the mid-twentieth century—begin before and end after formal empire, and as such they allow us to ask how this phenomenon— imperialism—affected and altered these longer-term changes. As I argued in the introduction, we could see Fukuoka's position as a city within the Japanese empire as only temporarily "puffing it up," while Pusan's growth was simultaneously restricted, first by the narrow desires of its colonial elite and then by the intraimperial focus of the Government General.[15]

However, the effects of imperialism as an amplifier of *scale*—of processes of migration, urbanization, violent displacement, accumulation of wealth, and extraction of natural resources—lasted long after its official end. In the case of the Tsushima Straits region, imperial structures and networks remained submerged under the surface, reemerging with the outbreak of the Korean War, reconnected via new air links, and later reencountered by the region's inhabitants under new historical, national, and global circumstances.

AFTER THE IMPERIAL REGION

This book's history of Pusan and Fukuoka, and the imperial region that developed between the cities and across the Tsushima Strait, ends in 1953. Even prior to this point, the two cities had developed into important centers in their own subnational regions: Pusan as part of Yŏngnam (today's North and South Kyŏngsang provinces, what had been the Chosŏn-era Kyŏngsang province) and Fukuoka as the key urban area on the island of Kyushu.

Yŏngnam was central to South Korea's economy and politics in the second half of the twentieth century. Somewhat similar to Yamaguchi prefecture in Japan, it has produced a majority of South Korea's presidents, and due to this it has been the beneficiary of uneven and unequal developmental policies throughout South Korea's authoritarian era. In South Korean politics and society, regionalism pitted conservative, industrialized Yŏngnam against the more left-wing, agricultural Honam (today's North and South Chŏlla provinces, what had been the Chosŏn-era Chŏlla province).[16]

During South Korea's era of export-driven growth in the 1960s, Pusan became the country's locomotive of industrialization, a key center of manufacturing that benefited from its location to import raw materials and export finished goods. At the start of Park Chung Hee's First Republic in 1963, Pusan was designated the nation's first Directly Governed City. In 1970, the completion of one of Park's flagship projects, the Kyŏngbu Expressway, tied Pusan's development even more tightly to the country's capital of Seoul. Both events further strengthened the Seoul-Pusan axis that acted as South Korea's transportation and economic backbone.[17]

By the late 1970s, regional support for Park's developmentalism could not outweigh rising opposition to his repressive authoritarianism. On October 16, 1979, students from Pusan University protested Park's Yusin regime and its recent acts of repression, including the expulsion of the head of the opposition party, Pusan-born Kim Young Sam, from the National Assembly. They marched on the city center and were joined by people from all walks of life, as well as other students from the centrally located Dong-A University. Protests quickly spread to nearby Masan.[18] The ready participation by laborers and others in the student protests was due to the recent and sudden economic downturn, which had affected Pusan and Masan, and its labor-intensive manufacturing industries, particularly badly.[19] The protests were the largest in South Korea since those against President Rhee in 1960, and Park feared their spread, declaring martial law in Pusan and censoring media reports. Residents of Pusan, however, were able to follow the reaction on Japanese television and radio, which reached the city from Tsushima.[20] In the wake of the protests and their violent repression, with divisions among government heads over the response, Park was assassinated by Kim Chae-gyu, head of the Korean CIA, on October 26, 1979.[21] Park's developmental authoritarianism, predicated on regionalized economic growth, contained within it the seeds of its own downfall.

Unlike Pusan in Yŏngnam, Fukuoka and Kyushu returned to a peripheral position within the new borders of the Japanese archipelago after the end of Japan's empire. Local fears of being an "internal colony," present throughout the prewar period, were now amplified. In the postwar period northern Kyushu saw many cases of industrial action, industrial pollution, and disease, including two that became symbolic of entire movements: Minamata disease and the connected movement for justice and recognition in the 1960s, and the Miike Coal Mine Strike of 1960.[22] Japan's energy transition from coal to oil began in the mid-1950s, and Kyushu's largest coal mines, including Tagawa in Chikuhō and Miike in Ōmuta, were both shut down in the 1960s.[23] At the Miike mine, news of layoffs in 1960 sparked a yearlong struggle between labor and management. While some have argued that the clustering of these incidents suggests postwar Kyushu became a "replacement" for Japan's lost colonies, the reality was more complex.[24] We must not ignore the fact that, as we have seen in this book, the early industrialization of the region had actually powered Japan's colonization efforts in East Asia before 1945.

In postwar Fukuoka several local writers attempted to understand these complex and contradictory processes. For many, Chikuhō became an emblematic site to interrogate where empire and industry intersected, a site that, in the postwar period, was in the process of being abandoned by the state. One response to the marginalization of Kyushu and its workers was to reimagine the whole island as a single village. In 1958 this was the vision of the founders of the journal *Sākuru Mura (Circle Village)*, which was based in Nakama, in the heart of the Chikuhō mining district.[25] Their imagined village's inhabitants were members of local interest groups or "circles" from across Kyushu. One of the editors of *Sākuru Mura*, poet and essayist Morisaki Kazue (1927–2022) had been born in Taegu, southern Korea, into a Japanese settler family. Her postwar writings dealt with the conflicting and overlapping identities she felt as a result of this colonial inheritance, and her work on women coal miners and on *karayuki-san* (rural Japanese women and girls trafficked overseas to work in brothels) also drew important connections between individual (female) lives and the expansion and exploitation inherent in Japan's modern history.[26] Morisaki expressed her struggle viscerally, writing of wanting "to open the graves and give [Koreans] voice . . . to disembowel myself intellectually, to plunge the dagger deep into the fact that my confusion is itself my reason for being."[27]

The region's intertwined issues of industrial pollution and the aftermath of empire also inspired the work of photographer, oral historian, and documentary journalist Hayashi Eidai (1933–2017). Born in the Chikuhō mining town of Tagawa, Hayashi's father had been a *kannushi* (priest) at a local Shinto shrine. In wartime, he had harbored runaway Korean workers from the region's mines, and he died after being questioned and beaten by the military police. Hayashi saw this incident as shaping his life's work.[28] Hayashi's first publications in the late 1960s exposed cases of industrial pollution in Kitakyūshū. However, his most famous works were his writings on forced labor, on which he began publishing in the late 1970s, interviewing many Koreans who had worked in Fukuoka's industries during the war.

Although the end of empire and later postwar energy transitions changed the nature of urban growth, northern Kyushu's urbanization, set in motion by imperial expansion and industrialization in the prewar era, continued into the 1950s and '60s. The five cities of Kitakyūshū—Moji, Kokura, Yahata, Wakamatsu, and Tobata—finally merged to become Kitakyūshū City in 1963. Ishikawa Hideaki, whom we met in chapter 5 at his keynote speech on regional planning in Keijō, had been involved in early postwar plans for the merger, although he died in 1955, before he could see the realization of his long-held vision. In the late 1960s these urban areas of Fukuoka prefecture were predicted to develop into the southernmost tip of a newly coined Taiheiyō "megalopolis" stretching south along the Pacific coastline from Tokyo to Osaka.[29] As this book has shown, however, in the first half of the century Fukuoka had already been part of an urban region that had extended across the Tsushima Strait and linked northern Kyushu with southern Korea.

In 1989, the same year in which Yokatopia was held in Fukuoka, the heady optimism of Japan's bubble era was punctuated by the death of Emperor Hirohito. After Hirohito's passing, along with a heightened awareness of their own mortality, which led many who had been involved in imperial aggression and war in the 1930s and '40s to begin writing memoirs or contributing to oral history projects, there was an increased openness to reflect on an era presided over by the late emperor.[30] In South Korea the late 1980s saw an even more momentous shift: In the decade since Park's assassination in 1979, students and activists had been protesting for an end to authoritarian rule, especially after the 1980 massacre of protesters in Kwangju. This culminated in the June Uprising of 1987, with mass protests forcing President Chun Doo Hwan to allow direct presidential elections.

New fields of study emerged in the movement for local autonomy after South Korea's democratization. In the 1990s, academic Kim Sŏng-kuk founded Pusanhak (Pusan Studies), laying out an alternative conception of Pusan's history, identity, and path for development. Kim saw Pusan's "pioneering spirit" as its unique identity, formed through its citizens' contact with Japan: "Pusan, from its historical roots to its modern birth right through to its present growth, has developed through a special relationship with Japan. It prospers when relations with Japan are normalized, continued, or strengthened and declines when those relations are severed or weakened."[31] It is unclear exactly what Kim envisaged by "prosperity" for Pusan in any of those time periods, and for whom. As we have seen in this book, the city's colonial growth, especially, came at a high cost for many of its inhabitants.

Kim's suggestion that Pusan "go out to the world through Japan" came when Japan was still at the height of its global power.[32] By the 2000s this "dangerous" proposition to cut Pusan's success adrift from that of the nation had become hamstrung by worsening bilateral relations over territorial issues such as Dokdo/Takeshima.[33] Although Kim was trying to chart a course for Pusan's development separate from the nation, by envisaging these ties with a monolithic "Japan," he could not prevent his vision from being affected by ongoing postcolonial and diplomatic debates.

In 1991 increased openness in South Korea following its democratization intersected with growing Japanese introspection regarding the country's imperial history when the first former Korean "comfort women" came forward publicly.[34] In December 1991 three Korean women visited Tokyo to protest their wartime treatment and lodge complaints with the Tokyo court. In Fukuoka in early 1992, citizen journalist Morikawa Machiko had been encouraged by the high attendance at a local screening of a documentary on the comfort women issue by Zainichi director Park Soonam the previous year. She wrote a letter to Yun Chung-ok, the head of the South Korean organization coordinating the women's claims, inviting former comfort women to come and speak to audiences in Fukuoka.[35] The woman who answered this call was Mun Ok Chu, in her late sixties at the time. When she arrived in Fukuoka in March 1992, it was not her first time in the prefecture. Some fifty years before Mun had been brought to work in a Korean "special restaurant" in the mining town of Ōmuta, where she worked in the kitchen and entertained the Korean and Japanese miners by singing Japanese and Korean songs.

Morikawa was part of a local citizens network that would go on to support Korean former comfort women and forced laborers with their claims against the Japanese government. Another Fukuoka couple, Hanafusa Emiko and her husband Toshio, became heavily involved in the Shimonoseki-Pusan court case, named after the location of the court (Shimonoseki) and the origins of the three claimants (Pusan).[36] The name in Japanese, Kampu saiban, contained within it another colonial echo, of the Kampu ferry, which had linked Japan and Korea since 1905. In the 1930s Mun Ok Chu had escaped back to Korea on this ferry, running away from Ōmuta when she realized she was soon going to be forced to have sex with customers in the "special restaurant."

These local networks of support for former colonized peoples offer an additional and important counterpoint to the narratives of division and denialism at the national level. In the case of Morikawa Machiko and Mun Ok Chu, their meeting resulted not just in support for Mun's claims against the Japanese government, but also in collaboration on a Japanese-language account of Mun's life, detailing her trafficking first to Manchuria, and then to Burma, out of the port of Pusan and into military comfort stations.[37] We can see Morikawa's writing as continuing the work of Morisaki Kazue and Hayashi Eidai, focusing on the human scale and effects of imperial violence and industrialization in this region between Japan and Korea.

NEW VISIONS, OLD GEOGRAPHIES

In 2025 Pusan remains South Korea's second city, with a population of some 3.25 million people, ten times its population in 1945. The city's growth,

however, has begun to stagnate, both in terms of its economy, due to deindus-
trialization, and in terms of population, with cities like Inch'ŏn and Taegu
catching up in size. Perhaps more remarkable than the city's urban growth
after the end of the Korean War is the growth of Pusan's port hinterland, or
foreland, depending on how one views it. Pusan Port is now the world's sixth
largest (by total number of shipping containers), surpassing even the former
imperial entrepôt of Hong Kong, which Pusan's colonial elites had once
hoped to rival.

As most regional cities in Japan continue to shrink in size, with people
drawn from the regions into the still-growing orbit of Tokyo's megalopolis,
Fukuoka's recent trajectory has bucked these trends, drawing national attention. In 2020, for the first time in the hundred years since the term entered
popular usage, Japan's Big Six Cities saw a change in their membership. With
its population reaching 1.6 million, Fukuoka overtook Kobe to become the
sixth largest city in Japan. Back in 1970 one would have predicted that
Kitakyūshū, then in seventh place, and not Fukuoka, down in tenth, would
have been the city to overtake Kobe. However, Kitakyūshū's postindustrial
hollowing out saw its population growth almost flatline from the 1980s
onward. Recent gloomy predictions suggest that outside of Tokyo, Fukuoka
may be the one bright spot in a future of rapid population decline and shrinking cities, and that Japan's urban center of gravity will again move west,
toward Fukuoka, and toward Asia.[38]

In the twenty-first century land reclamation is still central to both Pusan
and Fukuoka's urban visions, both building out space into their cities' harbors. In Fukuoka, the manmade Island City now fills the bay between
Hakozaki Shrine and Uminonakamichi, site of the former international
airfield. The island was constructed out of earth dredged from the bay to
deepen access to Hakata Port's new international container terminal. This
project began in 1994, the new container terminal opened in 2003, and the
final expressway linking the island to the city was completed in 2021. In
Pusan, the dramatic expansion of the city's urban area has reached outward
into its harbor areas via landfill and up onto its hillsides, as well as via high-
rise and high-density apartments. In 2022 Pusan Bay was designated as the
site for a new technology of extended urbanization—a prototype for a "resil-
ient and sustainable floating community" of twelve thousand people, constructed by the US-based company Oceanix in partnership with
UN-Habitat.[39] The waters linking Pusan and Fukuoka are once again the site
of new projections of power over ocean space and its urbanization, this time

in an attempt to provide new solutions to the global issue of rising sea levels.

Other recent visions also echo earlier trends. Pusan and Fukuoka became sister cities in 2007, and two years later the cities announced plans for a supraregional Pusan–Fukuoka cross-straits economic zone, with several projects listed to increase cooperation and interaction between the two cities.[40] Plans for a tunnel linking Japan and South Korea under the straits are also periodically revived. One of the main proponents of this idea in the postwar was Unification Church leader Moon Sun Myung, who set up a Japanese research institute to look into the topic. This was part of Moon's bigger vision for "an international highway ... stretching from Tokyo to London, bringing peace and happiness to all mankind."[41] Such language does not seem that different from Japan's wartime plans for an "anti-communist" railroad, and indeed the president of the International Highway Foundation, Kajiguri Masayoshi, is also the current head of the Unification Church–affiliated International Federation for Victory over Communism.[42] This maritime link across the straits still commands the attention of those with globe-spanning as well as local visions.

Tourism and consumption-led economic development, while pressuring cities like Fukuoka and Pusan to come up with attractive local identities, also offers a pragmatic reason not to cleave too tightly to nationalist narratives.[43] The growth of economic links across the region has the potential to act as a deterrent from the nationalistic grandstanding that often clouds state-level interactions between Japan and Korea—something Pusan Studies founder Kim Sŏng-kuk saw as an impediment to any attempts by his city to tie its future development to that of Japan.

In 2015 this region's intertwined industrial and imperial histories were yet again deployed—and distorted—to further Japan's international ambitions. Sites across Kyushu and Yamaguchi prefectures connected to Japan's Meiji Industrial Revolution were put forward as part of a Japanese bid for UNESCO World Heritage status. In Fukuoka these included Miike Coal Mine and the Yawata Imperial Steelworks. The bid came under fire from various parties in Japan and South Korea for its limited acknowledgment of the role of forced labor—by Chinese, Koreans, and Allied POWs—at the various historical sites.[44] It could be surmised that the Abe administration hoped to avoid the subject of forced labor by restricting the period under discussion to the Meiji period (1868–1912), despite original plans for the submission referring more generally to "Japan's modernization."

In a response to Japan's UNESCO bid, in 2017 two South Korean and Japanese NGOs published a joint guidebook to the sites, which included information about local efforts at commemorating their history and depicting it more accurately. This included Mugunghwa-dang (Flower of Sharon Pavilion), an ossuary and memorial for the Korean workers who died in the Chikuhō mining region, erected in 2000 by an organization led by Pae Nae Sŏn (1921–2008).[45] In 1943 Pae was brought to work in Kaijima mine in Fukuoka prefecture after his local village head (K: *myŏnjang*) in Korea threatened to stop rations to his family. He managed to escape and spent the rest of the war as a manual laborer. Pae continued living in Fukuoka after the war, and in 1986 he heard about plans to try and find the remains of those Korean laborers who did not survive their time in the region's mines. For those unknown Korean dead, their bones often discarded in temples in boxes labeled simply "peninsula," Pae thought it better to erect a monument in the Chikuhō region rather than in South Korea.[46] In 2000 Pae's organization laid these remains to rest in the Flower of Sharon Pavilion at the Iizuka cemetery in Chikuhō. Ceremonies paying respect to the dead take place every year at the harvest festival of *chusŏk*, attended by representatives from both Zainichi Korean organizations, Mindan and Chongryŏn.[47]

Many of the urban spaces and histories discussed in this book remain unmemorialized. Others have been repurposed, while some have been entirely erased from the urban fabric. The colorful houses of Kamch'ŏn Culture Village are a famous tourist spot in Pusan today, but the origins of the village lie in the removal of poor Korean laborers from the city center, discussed in chapters 2 and 3. Its inhabitants grew in number with the end of colonial rule, and later the outbreak of the Korean War. When the Japanese settlers left Pusan in 1945, the bones of their deceased were repatriated from the city's various temples, and today they are housed in Shōfukuji, a Zen temple in Hakata that had also housed a repatriate orphanage. In Kamch'ŏn's neighboring Ami-dong, site of one of these Japanese cemeteries, the gravestones they left behind were repurposed by refugees fleeing south in the Korean War and embedded within the urban fabric as stairs, walls, and cornerstones.

In contrast to Kamch'ŏn and Ami-dong, which are relatively preserved, Uam-dong, across the bay from Kamch'ŏn and another site of waves of removal for those on the margins of the city, has suffered a different fate. When I visited in the winter of 2019, the long roofs of cattle sheds that had housed several waves of refugees and repatriates in the 1940s and '50s were still visible from the hillside above. Empty houses were marked with red spray paint circles, and flyers warning against trespassing in houses or on land connected to the area's redevelopment project were pasted to their doors. From the hillside of Uam-dong I had a clear view across to the North Harbor of Pusan, where Japanese development of the harbor began in the late nineteenth century, and which was again under redevelopment as a candidate site for the 2030 World Expo. When I visited again in 2025, after an intervening global pandemic, Uam-dong had been completely cleared, and although the 2030 World Expo bid had been unsuccessful, redevelopment continued apace.[48]

Across the Strait in Fukuoka's Maizuru Park, the Jōnai-machi repatriate housing, built on former army land, is slated for "relocation" to make way for the city's ambitious Central Park development, also up for completion in 2030.[49] For years the neighborhood has been thought to be living on borrowed time: "Born in the postwar, [Jōnai-machi] is fated to someday vanish along with the postwar."[50] Unlike the nearby Fukuoka castle ruins, Jōnai-machi is considered "nonhistoric."[51] The uneven processes and politics of urbanization and its histories continue to play out across these postcolonial and postimperial spaces.

NOTES

INTRODUCTION

1. *Fukuoka Kenjin*, October 1932, 38.

2. Colonial-era Japanese documents refer to it as *mintai,* and Japanese settlers referred to the fish as *mentai*. See Imanishi and Nakatani 2008.

3. The above summary is based on Kawahara 2013, 26–45.

4. As the saying goes in Japanese, *shosetsu ari*. There are various theories regarding the earliest restaurants serving "Hakata rāmen," but all date to the late 1930s or 1940s.

5. On the ancient, medieval, and early modern histories of Hakata/Fukuoka in English, see Batten 2006; Cobbing 2009, 2013.

6. For a collection of essays explicitly on empire and metropolitan cities, see Driver and Gilbert 1999.

7. Cohn 1996, 4, cited in Schmid 2000, 953.

8. On urban space in Korea, see, for example, Hashiya 2004, 2005; Henry 2013; Kuroishi 2014; Oh 2023. On urban space in modern Japan, see Fujitani 1998; Maeda and Fujii 2004; Miller 2013; Grunow 2022. Sand (2014) offers a discussion of Tokyo as a "contact zone" for touring Taiwanese aborigines.

9. On English-language scholarship on cities in Japan and its empire, see, for example, Hanes 2002; Han 2014; O'Dwyer 2015; Sewell 2019; Dawley 2019. On modern urban life see Harootunian 2000; Silverberg 2006; Young 2013.

10. Oh 2023, 13.

11. On urban migration and industrialization in colonial Korea, see Son 1996; Park 1999; Barraclough 2012. On urban migration and industrialization in Japan, see, for example, Tsurumi 1990; Mosk 2001; Huffman 2018. Kawashima (2009) offers a rare case where the two fields overlap.

12. Howell 1995, 4, 7.

13. Shepherd 2018.

14. Harvey 1985, chap. 1.

15. One pioneer of this approach in Japanese scholarship was Komagome Takeshi and his 1996 volume *Shokuminchi Teikoku Nippon no Bunka Tōgō*. See also Eskildsen 2002 and a summary of this shift in Hein 2023, 10–35.

16. Wigen 1995, 296.

17. The common Japanese term for this national development, used at the time, was *fukoku kyōhei* (rich country strong army).

18. See Lewis 2005; O'Dwyer 2015.

19. On mobility across the Asia-Pacific, see, for example, Dusinberre 2012; Shiode 2015; Azuma 2019; Lu 2019; Jin 2021. On Asia more broadly, see Amrith 2011. On mobility (*idō*) over migration (*ijū/imin*), see, for example, Araragi 2008 and Yoneyama and Kawahara 2007, 2015.

20. For examples of this see Kimura 1989; Matsuda 2018.

21. For a case study of the long histories of regional mobility that became intertwined with Japan's imperial expansion, see Uchida 2023.

22. Gallagher and Robinson 1953. As is the case for the British Empire, "Japanese" informal imperialism across the Asia-Pacific needs to be studied alongside its formal imperialism and colonial rule in order to understand the true nature and scope of Japanese expansion.

23. Hanes 1993, 56–57, discusses the reception of Gottmann's term by Japanese scholars.

24. Doi 1968, 96.

25. Hanes 1993, 72.

26. See Meili in Brenner, ed. 2014, 105-106. On the three mutually constitutive "moments" of planetary urbanization, see Brenner and Schmid 2015, 166.

27. Brenner 2016, 125.

28. Lefebvre 2003, 1.

29. Lefebvre 2003, 14.

30. See Shindō and Matsumoto 2010.

31. See Young 2013, 104–15.

32. Galindez 2023, 6.

33. On Harvey's recent comments that imperialism is only a "sort of metaphor," see Mohandesi 2018 (cited in Galindez 2023).

34. Driver and Gilbert 1999, 5.

35. Harvey 1985, 159.

36. This is not to say that histories of what we now call planetary urbanization do not exist—the obvious case being William Cronon's *Nature's Metropolis*—but that such works exist as part of a "subterranean stream of research" on the city "beyond" the city. See Brenner, ed. 2014, chaps. 1 and 24, for further discussion of Cronon's work on historicizing "socio-natural processes." On operational landscapes, see Brenner 2016.

37. There have been a few key works that make connective analyses of colonial and imperial urban formations (Ross and Telkamp 1985; King 1990; Driver and Gilbert 1999), but there is a great deal of room for further investigations.

38. I date the beginning of Japan's modern empire to 1869, a year after the Meiji Restoration, as 1869 marked the founding of the Hokkaido colonial office by the new Meiji state.

39. Few of the key theoretical and comparative volumes that have shaped my work discuss any examples from the Japanese empire. More recent works such as Elkins and Pedersen (2005) include scholarship on Japan, but perhaps more representative is Cooper 2005. Although Cooper's work pays lip service to including Japanese empire, its longest engagement with Japanese imperial history is in a footnote (p. 297).

40. See, for example, Tonooka 2016.

41. This is a version of the argument raised by Gordon 1998. One recent approach has been the fruitful interrogation of the relationship between empire, race, and white supremacy as it has intersected with Japan's imperial expansion. See Morris-Suzuki 1998; Gallicchio 2000; Fujitani 2011; Onishi 2013; Taketani 2014; Jae Kyun Kim 2015. On Japanese involvement in U.S. settler colonialism, see Fujikane and Okamura 2008; Matsumura 2020.

42. For a brief discussion of this, see Matsuda 2016, 195. See also Hoffnung-Garskof 2010, 3.

43. Arendt 2017, 290–348; Karuka 2019, chap. 9; Donia 2015; Caprio 2011.

44. On the Irish Sea region as "industrial zone," see Burnett et al. 2012.

45. Scally 1995, 193.

46. Scally 1995, 191–94.

47. Scally 1995, 193; Belchem 2007, 10-12.

48. See Blais and Deprest 2012, 40–44.

49. Segrè 1974.

50. Calderwood 2018, 24.

51. See Clancy-Smith 2010; El Houssi 2012.

52. Borutta and Gekas 2012, 8. On Italian internal colonization and regional colonization, see Giglioli 2017.

53. Hom 2019.

54. The call to recognize the United States as an empire dates back to William Appleman Williams's 1959 *The Tragedy of American Imperialism*. However, Williams still viewed American empire as exceptional. For challenges to American imperial exceptionalism, see Go 2011 and Immerwahr 2019.

55. Stephanson 1995; Karuka (2019) calls this process "railroad colonialism." On overseas expansion, see LaFeber 1963.

56. Ferrer 2021; Greenberg 2022, 20; LaFeber 1963, 5.

57. See Dudden 2017.

58. North Korea's official name in Korean is Chosŏn Minjujuŭi Inmin Konghwaguk, whereas South Korea's is Taehan Minguk.

59. For more see Shepherd 2024.

60. Steinberg 2001, 23.

61. See Amino 1992, 131. Amino cites the pioneering works of Tanaka 1987; Murai 1988; and Fujimoto 1988. On fifteenth-century networks between Hakata, Tsushima, Korea, and Ningbo, see Saeki 2013, 2014.

62. See Shapinsky 2016.

63. Dudden 2017, 188.

64. See Lewis 2015.

65. Robinson 2015, 43. Imports to Japan included ginseng and furs, while exports to Korea included silver and copper.

66. See Lewis 2003.

67. See Kang 2024.

68. Hellyer 2009, 242, 245.

69. Allen et al. 1998, 2. On space-time, see Massey 1994, 3.

70. On the English Channel, see Morieux 2016. On the Mediterranean, especially as a "colonial sea," see the special edition of *European Review of History* 19, no. 1 (2012).

71. Miyano 1931. On Jintan see Hoi-eun Kim 2019.

72. Here I am adapting from Gluck 1985, 247.

CHAPTER 1

1. Fukuoka shi shi henshū iinkai 2015, shiryō kaisetsu, 79.

2. This account based on Fukuoka ken suisan shikenjo 1898 in Fukuoka shi shi henshū iinkai 2015, 843–97.

3. Fukuoka ken suisan shikenjo 1898 in Fukuoka shi shi henshū iinkai 2015, 845. On population figures see "Chōsen ni okeru nihon kyoryūchi," *Tōhōkyōkai kaihō* 1897, 38: 78–80, and Pusan chikhalsi sa p'yŏnch'anwiwŏnhoe 2: 868.

4. Fukuoka ken suisan shikenjo 1898 in Fukuoka shi shi henshū iinkai 2015, 847.

5. Fukuoka ken suisan shikenjo 1898 in Fukuoka shi shi henshū iinkai 2015, 890.

6. Fukuoka ken suisan shikenjo 1898 in Fukuoka shi shi henshū iinkai 2015, 848.

7. Fukuoka ken suisan shikenjo 1898 in Fukuoka shi shi henshū iinkai 2015, 882.

8. On the shift from Tokugawa to Meiji era diplomacy, see Yamamoto 2023, chap. 1.

9. Fukuoka shi shi henshū iinkai 2015, shiryō kaisetsu, 79.

10. "Kankai tsūgyo to Hakata," *Fukuoka Nichi Nichi Shinbun*, May 17, 1900, in Fukuoka shi shi henshū iinkai 2015, 920.

11. "Kankai tsūgyo to Hakata," in Fukuoka shi shi henshū iinkai 2015, 920.

12. Fukuoka shi shi henshū iinkai 2015, shiryō kaisetsu, 79.

13. See Kamiya 2018, 62.

14. The Nihon Chōsen ryōkoku tsūgyo kisoku, or Regulations between Japan and Korea Respecting Fisheries, was signed on November 12, 1889.

15. Udagawa and Uehara 2012, 21; Fukuoka shi shi henshū iinkai 2015, 896.

16. This dependency coupled with Japan's shaky position in Korea in the wake of the Kapsin Coup and the rise of Chinese influence led to the "bean controversy"

in 1889, when the provincial governor of Hamgyŏng stopped exports to Japan without due notice, for which the Japanese demanded compensation (Seth 2020, 26).

17. Udagawa and Uehara 2012, 25. The Enyō gyogyō shōrei hō was promulgated in 1897 and in force from 1898.

18. Sugiyama 1991, 216.

19. Norman 1944, 266, 268.

20. Nishihara 1975, 457.

21. Kang Chang Il, "Yi Chuhoe 1843–1895," August 2007, on e-donghak.or.kr. See also Kuzuu 1981.

22. See Hwansoo Kim 2010, 106–7.

23. Between 1901 and 1907 Kuzuu published one book (1903) and ten articles in *Kokuryū* (the Kokuryūkai journal) on fishing in Korea.

24. See Phipps 2015.

25. The term "Big Six" was in use by 1912, and the first Big Six Cities Committee Meeting was held in Tokyo in 1919.

26. See Yamamoto 2023; Kang 2012.

27. Wigen 1995, 296.

28. Hibino calls this "hatten no yokubō." See Fukuoka shi shi henshū iinkai 2015, shiryō kaisetsu, 85–86.

29. Maske 2011.

30. Kawazoe et al. 1997, 265.

31. Harvey 1985, 150, 154.

32. Key English-language works that discuss the Gen'yōsha include (in chronological order): Norman 1944; Sabey 1972; Saaler and Koschmann 2007; Siniawer 2008; Driscoll 2020. Norman's article should be treated as a historical document itself; his analysis and comparisons remain crucial insights into the opinions held by those at the time and informed postwar treatment of the Gen'yōsha by occupation forces.

33. It is not clear when Takaba's academy closed, but it appears to have been active into the mid-1880s.

34. See Ishitaki 1997, 328–69. Ishitaki's sources include members' lists published by the Gen'yōsha, documents held by the family of sixth Gen'yōsha president Kitajima Atsushi, the *Tōa sengaku shishi,* the Gen'yōsha newspaper *Genyō*, and the memorial in Sōfukuji, Fukuoka, erected by the Meidōkan in 1972.

35. See Wigen 2010, 14.

36. Gen'yōsha shashi hensankai 1966, 8–9.

37. Ishitaki 1997, 168.

38. Batten 2006.

39. Wilson 2015, 36–38.

40. See Hellyer 2009, 241–45; Kim Kyŏng-nam 2015b.

41. Lewis (2005) looks at a similar case, although much later in the process of Japanese expansion in Asia.

42. Ravina (2017, 193) discusses how former samurai often dominated early politics in southwest Japan. For statistics see Naikaku tōkei kyoku 1962, 715–17. In 1883,

the highest percentage of former samurai on prefectural assemblies in Kyushu was in Kagoshima (91 percent) and the lowest in Ōita (31 percent).

43. Suzuki 2002, 174; Basco and Tang 2020, 465.

44. For more on the role of government bonds in *shizoku* investment, see Yonekura 2015.

45. This is not to say that *shizoku* had a monopoly on these industries, but to account for some of their early successes and ability to invest. On the Seventeenth National Bank, see Ishitaki 1997, 268–72. On the involvement of other merchant capital, see Yamamura 1967.

46. Basco and Tang 2020, 460, 466–67.

47. See Huffman 1997, especially chapter 5.

48. Nishi Nippon shinbunsha 1978b, 77.

49. Nishi Nippon shinbunsha 1978b, 150.

50. Harvey 1985, 154–55.

51. On a similar process across the British Empire, see Lester 2002, 30–31.

52. For lists of those involved, see Ishitaki 1997, 328–68, and on Japanese newspapers in Korea, see Kim Tae Hyŏn 2011.

53. They started the *Chōsen Jihō* in Pusan, the *Heijō Shinpō* in Pyongyang, and the Korean-language *Hansŏng Sinbo (Kanjō Shinpō)* in Seoul. See Sassa 1977, 27–29.

54. Pae 2019.

55. For more on *shizoku* in Hokkaido, see Lu 2016.

56. *Kaikon* was another Tokugawa term used for land reclamation and cultivation. The new Meiji government set up a "cultivation bureau" in the Home Ministry in 1869. The Fukuoka group may have been inspired by Saigō's Yoshino Kaikonsha school. See Ravina 2004, 195.

57. See Lu 2016, 262, and Ishitaki 1997, 156.

58. On the *bakumatsu* conceptualization of *kaihatsu*, see Marcon 2015, chap. 13. The *Nihon kokugo daijiten* notes this new usage in the 1899 Commercial Code (Shōhō) referring to companies "pioneering new markets" (*shijō no kaitaku*) and "developing natural resources" (*shigen no kaihatsu*).

59. Harvey 1985, 156–57.

60. On the shift from Tokugawa to Meiji in the region, see Yamamoto 2023, chap. 1.

61. Phipps 2015, 38.

62. Phipps 2015, 40.

63. Phipps 2015, chap. 5 and pp. 245–46.

64. Arima 1985, 25–26.

65. "Nikkan bōeki torishirabe iin no hōkokusho," *Fukuryō shinpō,* March 28, 1893, in Fukuoka shi shi henshū iinkai 2015, 906.

66. Fukuoka shi shi henshū iinkai 2015, 906.

67. See "Fukuoka ken kaigai ryoken kangōbo," in Japanese Diplomatic Archives (hereafter GGS) 3-8-5: Tsūshō: teikoku shinmin idō: ryokan. On passports see Takahiro 2017.

68. See Hayashi 2021.

69. Kan 1982.

70. McKeown 2001, 84–86. The discussion of migration from Fukuoka in this chapter is based on Shepherd 2018.

71. GGS, "Meiji nijūshichi nendo shichi gatsu yori jūnigatsu ni itaru hankibun kaigai ryoken kafu ichiran hyō."

72. Irie 1902, 71.

73. Tōjō 2003, 920–39.

74. Duus 1995, 354.

75. See Shepherd 2018, 487.

76. Kimura 1989, 41, 58.

77. My thanks to Professor Miya Shichinohe-Suga for this observation.

78. GGS, "Meiji nijūhachi nen shichi gatsu kara kugatsu ni itaru kaigai ryoken kafu ichiran hyō, Fukuoka ken." Fukuoka prefecture was responsible for the applications of migrants from other prefectures in Kyushu without an open port. Nearly 30 percent of all applications to Fukuoka for travel permission came from people born outside the prefecture, and two-thirds of these were from Kumamoto. GGS, "Kaigai ryoken kangōbo mokuroku (1868–1945)."

79. Nagashima 2009.

80. Hwansoo Kim 2010, 106.

81. Kang 2022, 70–71.

82. Sastre 2016, 204.

83. See Hwansoo Kim 2010, 106–7, and Sastre 2016, chap. 4, for a detailed discussion of their movements.

84. Sastre 2016, 216–24.

85. Fukuoka shi 1959, 1558.

86. Fukuoka shi 1959, 1559.

87. This chapter's summary of Fukuoka's local politics in Meiji is based on Onjō 2013.

88. Before Hiraoka, Tsuda Morihiko, another Fukuoka domain *shizoku,* had held the seat for the first three elections.

89. On Hakata's medieval merchants, see Cobbing 2013.

90. See Arima 1990.

91. Arima 1990, 445.

92. Arima 1990, 444–45.

93. Hibino 2009, 14–15. The steelworks are spelled Yawata in English, but the town is Yahata.

94. Shimizu 2010, 8.

95. Jansen 1954, 35.

96. Tōjō 1996.

97. These had been reignited by the announcement of a joint development in 1893. Onjō 2013, 129–30.

98. This widened the countries that could be traded with but still only allowed trade to be undertaken by Japanese-owned boats. See Fukuoka shi kōwan kyoku 1970, 30–33.

99. Planning for the Hakata Bay Railway Company began in December 1897.

100. Onjō 2013, 139.

101. Fukuoka shi 1959, 1580 ("Tairo dōshi Kyūshū taikai," September 10, 1903) See also Onjō 2013, 142, although he locates the event at the Kyōshinkan.

102. GGS, "Meiji san jū shi nen shichi gatsu yori ku gatsu ni itaru gaikoku tokō ryoken kafu hyō."

103. Kang 2021, 115.

104. See Kamiya 2018, 100–106.

105. Sastre 2016, 285.

106. See *Hakata shōgyō kaigisho hōkoku*, dai 33 gō, 10.

107. See Fukuoka shi gikai 1971, 917.

108. See Fukuoka shi 1959, 328, and *Hakata shōgyō kaigisho hōkoku*, dai 33 gō, 33–34.

109. *Fuken haichi hōritsu an,* 1903, National Archives of Japan.

110. This would not be the last time such a proposal was made; in 1946, islanders on both Tsushima and Iki formed movements to push for a change in jurisdiction, again from Nagasaki to Fukuoka. The motion made its way to the National Assembly in 1948.

111. *Hakata shōgyō kaigisho hōkoku*, dai 33 gō, 33.

112. *Hakata shōgyō kaigisho hōkoku*, dai 33 gō, 10.

113. Fukuoka shi 1959, 1584–85.

114. See Shimazu 2009.

115. Siniawer 2008, 56–57.

116. Fukuoka shi 1959, 1584–85.

117. Hwansoo Kim 2010, 108–9; Moon 2013, 267–71.

118. *Hakata Shōgyō kaigisho hōkoku,* dai 34 gō (1904), 31

119. "Sensō to Fukuhaku shōgyōka," *Fukuoka Nichi Nichi Shinbun*, March 11, 1904, in Fukuoka shi shi henshū iinkai 2015, 929–31.

120. Fukuoka shi shi henshū iinkai 2015, 930.

121. Thanks to Kurihara Miwa for showing me this.

122. Item 21, "Kannai jōkyo hōkoku no ken," Correspondence from Pusan Consul Ariyoshi Akira to Seoul Consul Hagiwara Moriichi, April 26, 1905, in Kuksa p'yŏnch'anwiwŏnhoe 1998.

123. See Hunter 1977, 598, and "Kampu renraku kaikōshiki shōhō," *Kyūshū Nippō*, September 13, 1905, 2.

124. "Hikōwa daiensetsukai," *Kyūshū Nippō*, September 16, 1905, 2.

125. *Hakata shōgyō kaigisho hōkoku*, dai 36 gō (1905), 38–39.

126. Fukuoka shi 1959, 1586.

127. *Hakata shōgyō kaigisho hōkoku*, dai 36 gō (1905), 48.

128. Chōsen tōkanfu 1908, 14–20; see also Kimura 1989, 115–18.

129. Kamiya 2018, 40. "Kankoku enkai oyobi naikai kōgyō yakutei" (August 1905). This kind of migrant fishing village had also existed in the Tokugawa period; see Howell 1995, 15.

130. Kamiya 2018, 37–41, 132.

131. See Nagata 1935, 60–61, and Ichimata 1975, 288–89, 310–12.

132. Cwiertka 2006, 61–65.

133. Nagata 1935, 60–61, and Takahara 1935, 2–3.

134. Kim Tae Hyŏn 2011, 83–84.

135. "Kankoku Irisa-mura no gyojō," *Kyūshū Nippō,* August 18, 1910, in Fukuoka shi shi henshū iinkai 2015, 933–34.

136. Takagi shrine, now in Chikushino city, Fukuoka prefecture.

137. Japanese and Korean historians use the terms *jiba/chijang* and *chihō/chibang* to refer to both Korean and Japanese local capital in this period.

138. Harvey 1985, 150, 154.

139. English translation from "Imperial Japanese Rescript Attached to the Proclamation and Treaty of Annexation" 1910.

140. "Kankoku heigō shukakai," *Kyūshū Nippō,* September 3, 1910.

141. Fukuoka-shi gikai 1971, 635.

142. Lynn 2005, 30. See also Moskowitz 1974.

143. "Gyoken kakutoku no kengi," *Fukuoka Nichi Nichi Shinbun,* December 22, 1910.

144. Data from Chōsen tōkanfu 1908, 14–20, and *Tōhōkyōkai kaihō* 1897 (38), 78–80.

CHAPTER 2

1. On the Korean peddler (*pobusang*) network and their links, see Hoi-Eun Kim 2019, 949. For a case study from British India, see Bayly 1993.

2. "Chōsen de yūkaku no ganso wa Pusan Midori-machi Anraku-tei no rōshu—jō," *Pusan Nippō,* September 8, 1918.

3. "Chōsen de yūkaku no ganso wa Pusan Midori-machi Anraku-tei no rōshu—ka," *Pusan Nippō,* September 11, 1918.

4. Pusan shōgyōkaigisho 1912, 43.

5. Pusan shōgyōkaigisho 1912, appendix, 44–45

6. "Pusan karyūkai no onjin: Anrakutei Ueno Yasutarō shi iku," *Pusan Nippō,* November 21, 1925, 7.

7. "Pusan karyūkai no onjin: Anrakutei Ueno Yasutarō shi iku," *Pusan Nippō,* November 21, 1925.

8. On growth coalitions see Harvey 1985, chap. 6.

9. See Uchida 2011 and Henry 2014, 204.

10. Hong 2010, 279.

11. Trask 2000, 2.

12. See my forthcoming article in *Modern Asian Studies,* "Japan's Local Imperialists: Expansive Ideas of Hometown and Empire within the Asia Pacific World."

13. Lewis 2005, chap. 5; Dusinberre 2008; Dusinberre 2012, chaps. 6 and 7.

14. See Matsuda 2018 for a new perspective on locality and empire.

15. "Gabi-san yori Pusan no shigai wo nozomu no kei," in Pusan shōgyōkaigisho 1912, front matter (see image 2.2).

16. *Fuchō*—literally, municipal government offices—is translated as "city hall" for simplicity.

17. Park Chŏl-gyu 2008 in Hong 2008b, 290.

18. Hong 2008b, 24. The Japanese names for these groups all use literary or historic appellations for the areas in question.

19. Uchida 2011, 93.

20. Takahashi 1908, 7.

21. See Kimura 1989; Hong 2008; Uchida 2011.

22. See Chōsen sōtokufu 1937, 73.

23. Chōsen sōtokufu 1937, 74–75.

24. See Chōsen sōtokufu doboku kyoku, 1913; Chōsen sōtokufu 1937, chap. 3; *Chōsen sōtokufu kanpō* 422 (January 26, 1912).

25. Uchida 2011, 70.

26. For more on urban sanitation projects in Pusan, see Kang 2012; Kim Jeong-Ran 2010.

27. See Oh 2008.

28. The term *buraku* carries with it nuances not conveyed by "hamlet." In discourse on urban planning and hygiene, the word is used to denote a slum-like group of dwellings.

29. Pusan kyoryūmindan 1912.

30. See Fedman 2020, 52–53.

31. Pusan shōgyōkaigisho 1912, 43.

32. *Chōsen to Kenchiku,* February 1935, 65. Pusan's new city hall (*fuchō*) was finished in 1936.

33. On the built environment as the "crowning glory of past capitalist development," see Harvey 1985, 25.

34. Pusan fu 1917, 3–4.

35. On hot springs and Pusan, see Pusan kŭndae yŏksagwan 2015.

36. See Hong 2008a and Uchida 2011. On the Kōinkai, see Hong 2010, 32–35.

37. See Pak and Jang 2010, 253–62.

38. See Dong 2011, 223–24.

39. Hong 2010, 294.

40. Hong 2008b, 33.

41. See Dong 2011, 48–49; Hong 2010, 289–94

42. Hong 2010, 285–97.

43. Dong 2011, chap. 2. On the debates over continuity and change in local government, see Hwang 2016, 78–79.

44. Hong 2010, 352 n. 32.

45. Hong 2010, 357.

46. Son 1996, 235–38.

47. *Chōsen to Kenchiku*, April 1933, 56.

48. *Chōsen to Kenchiku*, May 1928, 59.

49. *Chōsen to Kenchiku*, May 1928, 60.

50. For data on Korean members of the Pusan Assembly, see Hong 2010, 428–29. On the rise of a commercial brewing industry in the Kyongsang region and its effects on regional society, see Itagaki, 2008, chap. 3.

51. Hong 2010, 395. An article in the new municipal assembly rules stated that the number of members of one ethnic group cannot fall below a quarter of the total members.

52. Hong 2010, 407.

53. Hong 2010, 425–27.

54. In 1939 only 4 percent of the population of Pusan, Japanese or Korean, could vote.

55. "Pusan denki fuei hantai wo kaku daijin ni chinjō," *Pusan Nippō*, August 9, 1929, 3.

56. Inoue 1931, foreword, 3.

57. Inoue 1931, 25–28.

58. "Suwŏnjinakyŏpchuptaga: pŏn'gyŏn sonyŏege kyosang," *Tong-a Ilbo*, December 19, 1933, 3. See coverage also on December 21, 1933, 2; December 22, 1933, 3.

59. "Yaban na fuhō seido — banken mondai de hinan, kōgeki," *Pusan Nippō*, March 29, 1934, 3; "Chōsen jin giin, renbei sōjishoku," March 31, 1934, 3.

60. Kim Kyŏng-nam 2015a, 284. Although Kim points to the failure of the assembly to attend properly to the issues in poor Korean urban areas, she does not discuss the guard dog incident, which in the *Tong-a Ilbo* is given as the main spark for the mass resignation.

61. "Suwŏllimet'ppŏn'gyŏnsayongjenŭn chosŏninbuminjŏnch'eŭi moyok," *Tong-a Ilbo*, March 30, 1934, 3.

62. Inoue 1931, 12, 37–38.

63. See Kim Kyŏng-nam 2015a, 313, and Pak and Jang 2010, 15–20.

64. "Mansenkō," *Fukuoka Kenjin*, October 1932, 25–26.

65. On similar publications for regional Chinese diasporas, see Hsu 2000.

66. Kashii was president of the newspaper for two years, after the death of its first president, Akutagawa Masashi, and the takeover by his nephew, Akutagawa Hiroshi (both from Kumamoto). See Kim Tae Hyŏn 2017, 83–84.

67. Nagashima 2009, 260–63.

68. "Fukuoka ni shikyoku secchi," *Pusan Nippō*, November 20, 1930, 7. *Pusan Nippō*'s Fukuoka branch chief, Nagano Tamijirō, continued publishing in postwar Fukuoka under the imprint of the Great Fukuoka Development Research Group.

69. "Fukuoka shikyoku rakusei," *Pusan Nippō*, June 8, 1933, 3.

70. "Henshū yoteki," *The Fusan*, July 1929, 38.

71. "Mansenkō," *The Fukuokan*, October 1932, 28.

72. Uchida 2011, 240–41.

73. Nagashima 2009, 261.

74. *Fukuoka Kenjin*, February 1935, 19.

75. The Japanese is "*iwayuru tokaichūshinshugi*" ("Dai-Pusan kensetsu," *Fukuoka Kenjin*, March 1935, 12).

76. Shinozaki, "Dai-Pusan kensetsu," *Fukuoka Kenjin*, April 1935, 26–27.

77. See Ishikawa 1943. This topic is discussed more in chapter 5.

78. *Fukuoka Kenjin*, March 1935, 13.

79. *Fukuoka Kenjin*, March 1935, 13; Harvey 1985, 161.

80. Sugiyama was involved in contract negotiations over Pusan's port development with the resident general, Itō Hirobumi, in 1906 and was listed as the assignee in the transfer of the contract in 1908. Investors in Hakata Port were similarly involved in development projects in colonial Korea. See Choson naekak 1908, Naebu naegŏan vol. 2, "Pusanjin haemyŏn maech'uk e kwanhan chŏngwonsŏ mit kwallyŏnsŏryul ŭl naebu e songbuham," January 21, 1908, via db.history.ko.kr.

81. Nagashima 2009, 267.

82. Hong 2010, 286.

83. "Mansenkō," *Fukuoka Kenjin*, October 1932, 24–43.

84. In her study of Shanghai's *huiguan / tongxiang hui*, Goodman (1995, 10) discusses how the size of a regional community affected the granularity of its native place groups.

85. "Suitengū chinzasai jūhachi, kyū no ryōjitsu," *Pusan Nippō*, June 17, 1932, 1.

86. See Namigata 2008, 97–99.

87. Chōsen sōtokufu 1933.

88. Hong 2010, 147. Hong uses the term *yukch'e nodong* (physical labor) quite expansively, including most manufacturing workers, as well as manual laborers, fishermen, hawkers, and so on.

89. Chōsen sōtokufu 1933, 198–217. Employed Japanese men made up 62 percent of all male Japanese in Pusan. These jobs correspond to census categories 264, *buppin hanbai gyōshu* (excluding grain, marine products, and miscellaneous foodstuffs counted separately); 268, *ten'in/uriko*; 322, *kanri*; 236, *daiku*; 28.1, *gyogyō rōmusha*; 314, *unyu ni jūji suru mono*; 346, *boki-gakari/suitō-gakari/kaikei-gakari*; 324, *kankō no koyōin*; 348, *shokiteki shokugyō*; 269, *shōgyō tedasuke*.

90. These ten jobs made up 46 percent of all male Japanese employment. They correspond to census categories 269 *shōgyō tedasuke*; 359 *shujin no setai ni aru kaji shiyōnin*; 285 *ryokan/geshukuya/ryōriten/inshokuten nado no jochū/kyūjinin*; 284 *shōgi*. A fifth of all female Japanese people in the city were classed as employed.

91. In 1932 there were about 23,665 Japanese women in Pusan (49 percent of the settler population). Hong 2010, 119 (data from *Chōsen sōtokufu tōkei nenpō*).

92. Hong 2010, 147.

93. For more qualitative assessments of the role of Japanese women in colonial Korea, see Brooks 2005 and Kweon 2014. On Korean women see, for example, Janice Kim 2009; Barraclough 2012; Suh 2019; Nam 2021.

94. While 20 percent of all female Japanese were employed, only 15 percent of female Koreans were.

95. These correspond to census categories 359, *shujin no setai ni aru kaji shiyōnin*; 285, *ryokan/geshukuya/ryōriten/inshokuten nado no jochū/kyūjinin*; 131, *kase kuri kō/itogaeshi kō*; 135.3, *men hataori kō*; 272, *roten shōnin/gyōshōnin/yobiurishōnin*.

96. Chōsen sōtokufu 1933, 166–71.

97. Kawashima 2009, 67.

98. These correspond to census categories 367, *hiyatoi (to tan ni shinkoku shitaru mono)*; 28, *gyogyō rōmusha*; 264, *buppin hanbai gyōshu* (excluding subcategories of vegetables and marine products, counted separately); 272, *roten shōnin/gyōshōnin/yobiurishōnin*; 366, *zatsuekifu*; 312, *nakashi/niatsukaifu/unpanfu*.

99. The neighborhoods are now known as Taech'ang-dong, Taechŏng-dong, and Kwangbok-dong.

100. Kim Kyŏng-nam 2015a, 282.

101. The neighborhoods are now T'osŏng-dong, Pubyŏng-dong, and Ch'oryang-dong.

102. The island of Yŏngdo was incorporated into Pusan-fu in 1914.

103. Yu Chi-hwan, "Nŏmuna nangmanjŏgin Pusan" (*Sindonga* 56, 1936), cited in Oh 2008, 195.

CHAPTER 3

1. Yi 2013, 277.

2. As Tonomura (2008, 74) points out, there was no law against Korean travel throughout the Japanese empire, so contemporary discussions of "illegal" immigration were inaccurate.

3. See Park 1999, 38; Michael Kim 2016.

4. Shin 1996, 68–69; Kawashima 2009, 47–49.

5. Park 1999, 15.

6. See Park 1999, 21–22; Kawashima 2009, 57–59.

7. Park 1999, 34–35.

8. Chatani 2016.

9. Hashiya 2005, 256. Hashiya uses the term *fukidamari*, which means "drift" (as in snowdrift) but can also mean a "haunt" or "hangout."

10. Takahama 1912 (translation my own), cited in Lee 2008, 603.

11. See Hashiya 2005, 258.

12. Pusan-fu 1927, 2-8.

13. *Fusan Ihō* 52 (January 1935), 42–44. In November 1934 there were 500 Koreans and 261 Japanese seeking work.

14. Pusan-fu 1927, 13.

15. Pusan-fu 1928, 34–35.

16. Pusan-fu 1928, 32.

17. Onjō 1995, 115.

18. Pusan fu 1927, 8–9; Fukuoka ken shakai fukushi kyōgikai 1982, 554–55.

19. Fukuoka chihō shokugyō shōkai jimukyoku 1929, 196.

20. Fukuoka chihō shokugyō shōkai jimukyoku 1929, 197.

21. "Naichi jūyō toshi shakai shisetsu shisatsu kanken," *The Fusan*, January–March 1927.

22. *The Fusan*, March 1930, 27–37.

23. Kimura 2017, 140.

24. "Pusan mushukusha nikki no issetsu," *The Fusan*, March 1927, 34–40.

25. On Yoshida's editorial work on *The Fusan*, see Sakamoto and Kimura 2007, 61, and Sakane 2021, chap. 5.

26. On this wave, see Ambaras 2010, esp. 189–90.

27. See Silverberg 2009, xv.

28. On urban reportage in colonial Seoul at this time, see Oh 2023, especially chapters 5 and 6.

29. "Pusan mushukusha nikki no issetsu," 37.

30. "Pusan mushukusha nikki no issetsu," 39.

31. The facility was run by the Australian Presbyterian Church, headed by missionary James Noble Mackenzie.

32. *The Fusan*, September 1927, 8. For more on the interaction between Pusan's city government, leprosy sufferers, and urban space, see Kim Jeong-Ran 2010.

33. *The Fusan*, October 1928, 36–37.

34. *The Fusan*, January 1929, 35. The neighborhood police branch offices would form the basis of the ward system in Korean cities, first in wartime Seoul and then, post-liberation, in Pusan and other cities.

35. *Pusan fu shigaizu nanbu.*

36. Kim Ki-chŏn, "Pusanŭi pinmin'gulgwa pumingul," *Kaebyŏk* 34 (special Kyŏngnam edition), April 1923, 66–68 (translation my own).

37. Kim Ki-chŏn, "Pusanŭi pinmin'gulgwa pumingul," 66–67, quoted in Oh 2008.

38. Inoue 1931, 34–35.

39. *Chōsen to Kenchiku*, March 1930, 42.

40. Shinba Kōhei, the head of the Government General public works division at the time of the poor relief public works projects, had previously been head of Pusan's public works department and had originally put forward the idea for the bridge. See *Chōsen to Kenchiku*, March 1930, 42, and Hirose 2018.

41. *Chōsen to Kenchiku*, March 1932, 74.

42. Kawashima 2009, 67.

43. Chōsen sōtokufu 1935, 633–35.

44. Chōsen sōtokufu 1935, 633–35.

45. Ko 2012.

46. Seo 2010, 47.

47. "Pusan de soshi no rōdōsha wo kōjiba ni furimuku," *Chōsen shakai jigyō* 5, no 5 (May 1927), 86.

48. See Seo 2010, 8–9, 47, 59.

49. "Chōsen rōdōsha naichi tokō oyobi soshi gaikyō," *The Fusan*, March 1928, 41. On the discourse of "protection," see Kawashima 2009, 155.

50. In other words, the number of those traveling to the metropole minus those returning. "Chōsen rōdōsha naichi tokō oyobi soshi gaikyō," *The Fusan*, March 1928, 41–44.

51. Tonomura 2008.

52. "Burōkā no te de mikkō suru senjin ga ōi," *Kyūshū Nippō*, April 17, 1923.

53. Ryu 2011, 51.

54. Tonomura 2008, 72.

55. *The Fusan*, March 1928, 42. Urata was also a Fukuoka native, originally from the port city of Wakamatsu.

56. *The Fusan*, March 1928, 43. See also Tonomura 2008, 70.

57. Ryu 2011, 42. Ryu cites Keishō nando keisatsubu 1928.

58. *The Fusan*, February 1927, 9–10.

59. See Michael Kim 2016, 19.

60. *The Fusan*, February 1927, 10–11.

61. See Park 1999, 17, 22. See also Son 1996, chap. 1.

62. *The Fusan*, March 1928, 44.

63. *The Fusan*, March 1928, 44.

64. *The Fusan*, March 1928, 44.

65. "Kanpū ni furuete senjin no mikkōdan," *Fukuoka Nichi Nichi Shinbun*, January 7, 1930.

66. "Naichi tokō wo nozomu senjin," *Fukuoka Nichi Nichi Shinbun*, January 8, 1930.

67. "Naichi tokō wo nozomu senjin," *Fukuoka Nichi Nichi Shinbun*, January 8, 1930.

68. "Ch'un'gunge chigŏpkuk'ojŏ Hyŏnhaet'an kŏnnŏnŭndongp'o," *Tong-a Ilbo*, February 26, 1934, 2.

69. "Mirhangjaŭi imyŏnaehwa," *Tong-a Ilbo*, January 10, 1940, 3.

70. See Kawashima 2009, 41, and, more broadly, Esselstrom 2009.

71. See "Matamata mikkōsenjin," *Fukuoka Nichi Nichi Shinbun*, August 15, 1935.

72. The *Ville d'Alger*, the biggest French packet ship of its kind when built in 1935, could manage the Marseille–Algiers crossing in twenty hours.

73. See Tonomura 2008, 69–77.

74. Shihōshō chōsabu 1939, 4. For more on this roundtable, see Kimura 2016 and 2017.

75. Shihōshō chōsabu 1939, 2–5.

76. Shihōshō chōsabu 1939, 13–14.

77. Gordon 1985, 82–107, 415.

78. Ōmori Rintaro, head of the labor division of the mining company Aso Shōten, in Shihōshō chōsabu 1939, 9.

79. "Kyuminkyusai to rōryoku no kyōkyū," *Chōsen to Kenchiku*, September 1931, 35.

80. Fukuoka chihō shokugyō shōkaijo 1929, 204–11.

81. See Ryu 2011.

82. Shihōshō chōsabu 1939, 10.

83. This term was used by Gotō Kichigorō, head of Fukuoka's special police. See Shihōshō chōsabu 1939, 2.

84. See Sugihara 1998, 74–75. The route became regular in 1923.

85. See *Fukuoka ken: shichōsonbetsu jinkō zōgenritsu zu* 1925.

86. See Sakamoto 1998, chart 5, pp. 190–91. In the 1920s and 1930s this number was higher, at around 80 percent, and it was lower by 1940, at just under 70 percent.

87. Sakamoto 1998, 134, citing Kajimura 1993, 6: 17–18. The Japanese phrase is *"kokkyō wo matagu seikatsuken."*

88. Miki 1933, 42. The original source is by a Japanese bureaucrat, but Sakamoto (1998, 134) cites it to suggest this was how Koreans themselves viewed the region.

89. This is vividly portrayed in Yŏm Sangsŏp's novella of 1924, *Mansejŏn*. See also Eckert 2016, 85.

90. Keishō nandō keisatsubu 1928, in Pak 1975, 567–80.

91. For an overview of government policies relating to the forced labor of Koreans, see Tonomura 2012.

92. In Japanese, *"shūdan idō / shūdan boshū rōdō."*

93. See, for example, Weiner 1994; Smith 1999; Kim Kwang Ryŏl 2004; Hayashi 1981.

94. Research for this section would not have been possible without historian Mizuno Naoki's database, Senzen nihon zaijū chōsenjin kankei shinbun kiji kensaku (which is no longer active), or the pioneering research of Sakamoto Yuichi and Kimura Kenji.

95. Sakamoto 1998, 135.

96. *Tōyō taimusu*, March 25, 1921, 7, in Nishi nihon bunka kyōkai 1984.

97. Fukuoka ken shakai fukushi kyōgikai 1982, 550.

98. *Tōyō taimusu*, March 25, 1921, 7.

99. Kawashima 2009, 122.

100. *Tōyō taimusu*, March 15, 1923, 6.

101. Sakamoto 1998, 136, 138.

102. "Kankoku ninpu raichō," *Yorozu Chōhō*, June 18, 1908.

103. The figures are collated from the national censuses of 1930, 1935, and 1940.

104. See "Senjin nimei shishō," *Kyūshū Nippō*, August 22, 1934; "Asano umetatechi kyojū no senjin o dō atsukau ka," *Ōsaka Mainichi Shinbun*, September 17, 1930.

105. See, for example, "Senjin nimei asshi," *Ōsaka Mainichi Shinbun*, November 11, 1928; "Ninpu rokumei dosha ni umeru," *Fukuoka Nichi Nichi Shinbun*, March 25, 1922.

106. See Oh 2023, 13.

107. The figures are from Sakamoto 1998, chart 11, pp. 200–201. The figures are: for 1920, 2,466 men, 155 women; for 1930, 8,214 men, 3,435 women; and for 1940, 25,894 men, 16,360 women.

108. See Ryang 1998, 3–15.

109. One hundred nine Korean women were registered as working as stevedores at the coaling port of Wakamatsu in 1928–29. See Fukuoka chihō shokugyō shōkaijo 1929, 52. Female stevedores, Japanese and Korean, were a feature of the region. See Fukuoka chihō shokugyō shōkaijo 1927, 4–5, and Hayashi 1983.

110. Sakamoto 1998, chart 22, pp. 220–21.

111. Kōrai hakubutsukan Chōsen joseishi kenkyūkai 2021.

112. See the statement of Taguchi Eizō (pseudonym) in Senda 1978, 31–36.

113. See "Tanzan ni okeru hantōjin no kinrō kanri" 1940, in Pak 1982, 225–27.

114. See Shihōshō chōsabu 1939, 33. Although figures for Fukuoka prefecture are not readily available, by 1930 those under fifteen counted for 22 percent of the Korean population in Japan. This rose to 37 percent by 1940. See Tonomura 2004, 90.

115. "Senjin tōhyō dashin," *Fukuoka Nichi Nichi Shinbun*, January 29, 1932.

116. "Chōsen moji de kaita tōhyō mo yūkō to kettei," *Fukuoka Nichi Nichi Shinbun*, February 1, 1930.

117. Sakamoto 1998, 158–61.

118. Sakamoto 1998, 160. By 1945 Fukuoka ranked second next to Osaka for the number of elected Koreans in local government. See Matsuda 1995, 82.

119. Shihōshō chōsabu 1939, front matter.

120. The series was designed to allow regional courts to address topics of importance to their specific locality, such as traditional mutual support groups (*moai*) in Okinawa, snow in Yamagata, and horse racing in Yokohama.

121. Shihōshō chōsabu 1939, 49.

122. Shihōshō chōsabu 1939, 49-50.

123. See Sakamoto1998, chart 5, pp. 190–91.

124. Shihōshō chōsabu 1939, 50-51, 53.

125. On Pak's Sōaikai activities and his role as a Diet member, see Kawashima 2009, chap. 5.

126. Shihōshō chōsabu 1939, 37.

127. "Yuiitsu no Chōsenjin kōho," *Ōsaka Mainichi Shinbun* (Kitakyūshū edition), May 22, 1934.

128. "Tōgarashi motte, hantō senshi imon," *Ōsaka Mainichi Shinbun* (Kitakyūshū edition), January 29, 1944.

129. Shihōshō chōsabu 1939, 51.

130. Matsuda 1995, 92.

131. "Hantō gi'in no takumina shojo shitsumon," *Ōsaka Mainichi Shinbun* (Kitakyūshū edition), March 13, 1937.

132. Kawashima 2009, 19.

CHAPTER 4

1. In this book, and especially in this chapter, the term "citizen" is used as a reference to, or direct translation of, the Japanese and Korean terms *shimin/simin*, and it reflects their common usage in sources from the time to refer to residents of cities in both Japan and colonial Korea.

2. For an overview of recent port city literature, see Heerten 2021.

3. See Choi et al. 2007.

4. Fritzsche 1992, 176 and note 153.

5. The first designated shipping routes began in the 1870s. Ferries run on government-chosen routes (domestic, imperial, and international), they were supported by the Communications Ministry (Teishinshō). Local and colonial governments also decreed and supported routes. The Hakata–Pusan route was never funded by the central government. See Terashima 1924, 251–56.

6. In documents the company is called Tsushima Unyu Kaisha, and after 1920 as either Tsushima Shōsen, Tsushima Kisen Kaisha, or Tsushima Unyu Kisen Kaisha. The ships and routes remained consistent. See Kyūshū Yūsen 2010; Izuharamachi shi hensan iinkai 1997, 1019–20.

7. Fukuoka shi gikai 1971, 665.

8. Fukuoka shi sanjokai 1910, 57.

9. Fukuoka shi sōmuka 1912.

10. Kyūshū Yūsen 2010, 4.

11. "Kyūshū, Chōsen o renraku suru Haku—Fu kan shin kōro," *Pusan Nippō*, June 26, 1925, 2.

12. "Chōsen kyōankai Tōahaku kankeisha shōtai," *Pusan Nippō*, April 6, 1927, 2.

13. "Nijūyonichi nichiyōbi o riyō suru," *Pusan Nippō*, April 16, 1927, 7.

14. *Pusan Nippō*, April 9, 1927, 2; *Kōwan* 5, no. 6 (June 1927): 51–66.

15. Ariyoshi 1929, 29–31.

16. Ariyoshi 1929, 29.

17. "Pusan Hakata kan meirei kōrō jitsugen" and "Chosen Hakata kōrō ga meirei kōrō to naru yō," *Pusan Nippō*, August 28, 1929, 3.

18. "Ryōchi kyōdō no mondai," *Pusan shōkōkaigisho geppō*, June 1930, 1.

19. "Pu-Haku kan no missetsu na korai no kankei fukkatsu wo," *Pusan Nippō*, September 20, 1930, 2.

20. *Pusan fusei yōran* 1930, 180.

21. Pusan fu 1930, 180.

22. Chōsen sōtokufu teishin kyoku 1932, 133.

23. "Shōwa roku nen do meirei kōro kaihai," *Pusan Nippō*, January 15, 1931, 3.

24. *Pusan fusei yōran* 1933, 163.

25. *Pusan fusei yōran* 1934, 153.

26. Kyūshū Yūsen 2010.

27. Yoshida, *Kyūshū Yūsen kōro keisho kōtsu chōkanzu*, 1936.

28. Nishi nihon inshokuryō shinbunsha 1936, entry 18.

29. "Kyūshū keiki dashin zadankai (6)," *Ōsaka Mainichi Shinbun*, July 1, 1936.

30. Kumabe 1935, 58.

31. "Yŏnmal yŏnsiūi yŏgaek wanhwa," *Tong-a Ilbo*, December 12, 1939, 2.

32. On wartime links to the empire, see Inayoshi 2014, 290-96, 323.

33. "Chosŏn haehyŏp unsong," *Tong-a Ilbo*, August 9, 1940, 4; "Naisen shin renrakukō ni Hakatakō," *Kōwan*, October 1940, 88.

34. "Hakata Pusan renrakusen kōro kaisetsu," *Kōwan*, August 1943, 38.

35. "Shojo kōkai no sōto e," *Keijō Nippō*, July 16, 1943, 3; on the exhibition, see "Yakushin dai Fukuoka ten," *Keijō Nippō*, August 5, 1943, 1.

36. Furukawa 1988, 98.

37. "Pusan wa Hakata no tonarigumi," *Nishi Nippon Shinbun*, July 17, 1943, 2; "Dōzo yoroshiku," *Keijō Nippō*, July 18, 1943 (evening edition), 2.

38. "Kokka no tame ni ōi ni yarō," *Nishi Nippon Shinbun*, August 7, 1943, 4.

39. "Hakata Pusan renrakusen kōro kaisetsu," *Kōwan*, August 1943, 38.

40. As of 2025 the jetfoil route is no longer operating. See conclusion, note 48.

41. Fukuoka shiyakusho sangyō ka 1940, 12, 28–30.

42. *Pusan fusei yōran* 1939, 129–31.

43. *The Fusan*, November 1926 (*kaikō gojunen kinen gō*), 119.

44. Pusan Nippō sha 1926, 5–6.

45. Pusan Nippō sha 1926, 1.

46. Pusan Nippō sha 1926, 34.

47. Inayoshi 2014, 231–36.

48. Pusan Nippō sha 1926, 33.

49. *The Fusan*, November 1926, 54.

50. "Pusanchin umetate kaiketsu to kikōshiki," *Chōsen to Kenchiku*, December 1926, 20; *The Fusan*, November 1926, 94.

51. See Chōsen sōtokufu 1937.

52. "Kōji nyūsatsu wa jimoto gyōsha e," *Chōsen to Kenchiku*, April 1929, 92.

53. Chōsen sōtokufu 1937, 75–76.

54. Inayoshi 2014, 187–88. See also Nagao 1991.

55. "Pusanchin umetate kōji," *Chōsen to Kenchiku*, September 1925, 51.

56. "Pusanchin maichiku jigyō," *Chōsen to Kenchiku*, January 1926, 80.

57. "Pusanchin umetatekaisha no setsuritsu," *Chōsen to Kenchiku*, September 1926, 38; "Pusanchin umetate sōritsu sōkai," *Pusan Nippō*, October 24, 1926, 2.

58. "Pusanchin maichiku Sakaemachi ni honsha secchi," *Pusan Nippō*, October 30, 1926, 2.

59. "Pusanjin umetate kaiketsu to kikoshiki," *Chōsen to Kenchiku*, December 1926.

60. "Pusan nankō dai maichiku no jitsugen," *The Fusan*, July 1929, 31.

61. "Pusanchin maichiku to shina kūrī," *Chōsen to Kenchiku*, April 1927, 56.

62. See Chōsen sōtokufu 1937, 70. In 1922 over seventeen thousand days of work were logged by Chinese *ninpu* laborers, shrinking to under nine hundred by 1927.

63. "Dai Pusan kensetsu," *Chōsen to Kenchiku*, November 1929, 34.

64. "Pusan no kaya torishimari rei kaisei," *Chōsen to Kenchiku*, July 1931, 46.

65. "Pusan no kenchiku rei seitei yōsei," *Chōsen to Kenchiku*, September 1931, 34.

66. Young 1998; Eckert 1991; Han 2024.

67. McDonald 2017, 115.

68. Chōsen sōtokufu tetsudō kyoku 1936, 1.

69. "Pusan gaden chokuei yokuba keikaku," *Chōsen to Kenchiku*, September 1934, 42; "Kaiundai Shōtōen ryokan rakusei," *Chōsen to Kenchiku*, October 1934, 54.

70. "Kampu renraku wo kaizen suru Shimonoseki gawa no zōchiku kōji," *Chōsen to Kenchiku*, July 1936, 34.

71. "Pusan sanbashi no nikaishiki kaizō," *Chōsen to Kenchiku*, July 1929, 40.

72. "Pusan daiichi sanbashi daikaizō kōji," *Chōsen to Kenchiku*, May 1934, 44.

73. "Chōsen, Manshū ni kōjō shinsetsu keikaku," *Chōsen to Kenchiku*, January 1937, 48.

74. "Dai-Pusan kensetsu," *Fukuoka Kenjin*, March 1935, 12.

75. *Pusan Shōgyōkaigaisho Geppō* 107, March 1934, 1–4.

76. *Pusan Shōgyōkaigaisho Geppō* 111, July 1934, 15; *Pusan Shōgyōkaigaisho Geppō* 112, August 1934, 1–3.

77. "Samdaehang hwakchang kongsa," *Tong-a Ilbo*, April 29, 1936, 2.

78. *Pusan Bōeki Gairan*, 1927–35 editions, section 2, *bukka*.

79. "Kukche kyot'ongno 'Pusanhang,'" *Tong-a Ilbo*, May 4, 1936, 3; "Simnyŏn huŭi Pusanŭn tongyang yusuŭi tosi," *Tong-a Ilbo*, June 10, 1936, 4.

80. "Pu-Haku kan no missetsu na korai no kankei fukkatsu wo," *Pusan Nippō*, September 20, 1930, 1.

81. Batten 2005.

82. Phipps 2015, 25.

83. See *Saishin jissoku Fukuoka shigai zenzu* 1908.

84. See Murase 1961, 307. The three businessmen were Kawauchi Uhee, Watanabe Yohachirō, and Tani Hikoichi.

85. Fukuoka shi kōwan kyoku 2000, 46.

86. See Sankyū hyakunen no ayumi hensan iinkai 2019, 61–63; Katō 2019.

87. Sakamoto 1972, 3, 73.

88. Sakamoto 1972, 3

89. Ichimata 1975, 63–72.

90. For more on colonial Jilong's port, see Dawley 2019, 45–54.

91. Fukuoka shi kōwan kyoku 2000, 47.

92. See Hanes 2002, 173, 200; Inayoshi 2014, 187–88.

93. See "Hakatawan chikkō to beijin no tōshi," *Kōwan* 2, no. 4 (1924): 113.

94. "Hakatawan chikkō to beijin no tōshi," *Kōwan* 2, no. 4 (1924), 113; "Yellow River: Reclamation Successful," *Singapore Free Press and Mercantile Advisor*, January 3, 1924.

95. "Americans Win Japan Bid," *New York Times*, June 8, 1924.

96. "Engineering Topics of the Week," *Times of India Engineering Supplement*, October 31, 1924, 1.

97. Inayoshi 2014, 229–30.

98. *Kōwan* 3, no. 2 (1925): 136–37. These tours were part of the Port Association's mission to influence public opinion. See Inayoshi 2014, 230.

99. *Fukuoka Nichi Nichi Shinbun*, January 10, 1925, cited in Fukuoka shi kōwan kyoku 2000, 51.

100. Torisu 1987, 14.

101. The rank of the port dictated the ratio of funding from central and local government. See Terashima 1924, 378–79.

102. Fukuoka shi kōwan kyoku 2000, 58.

103. Baba 2013, 57.

104. Fukuoka shi kōwan kyoku 2000, 60; *Saishin Fukuoka shi chizu* (Fukuoka Kyōwakai, 1942). The area was renamed Higashi-hama in 1974.

105. "Chikkō chūshin no hatten," *Fukuoka Nichi Nichi Shinbun*, March 25, 1936, 14.

106. "Toshi keikaku dōro Hakataeki chikkō sen," *Kanpō* 3927 (February 10, 1940): 437.

107. See Tsutsui 1936, 1937, 1942; Fukuoka shiyakusho sangyō ka 1938a, 1938b, 1939a, 1939b, 1940; and Fukuoka shiyakusho shōkō ka 1941a, 1941b, 1942, 1943a, 1943b, 1944.

108. Nagashima 1941, 28.

109. Tsuruta 1993, 50–53. "Official nursing" of civil aviation was not unique to Japan. See Hudson and Pettifer 1979, 23.

110. "Airways Will Link Japan to Mainland," *Washington Post*, March 24, 1929, 11.

111. See Van Riper 2004, 84, and Hudson and Pettifer 1979, 37.

112. Nihon kōtsū kyōkai 1929, 80.

113. "Kōku nihon no genzai narabi ni shōrai," *Kōtsū kenkyū shiryō* 34 (August 1935): 15.

114. Nihon kōku yusō 1938b, 23, 31; Dai Nippon Kōkū shashi kankōkai 1975, 82.

115. Tachiarai machi kyōdoshi hensan iinkai 1981, 324.

116. "Fukuoka hikōjō shikichi kimaru, kokusai kōkūro no," *Kōbe Shinbun*, December 16, 1927.

117. Although the Najima aerodrome is no longer extant, a road near the original site has been renamed Lindbergh Avenue (Rindobāgu dōri) in honor of the visit.

118. "Lindberghs to Fly to Nanking Today," *New York Times*, September 18, 1931, 14; "Rindē ki ni hisonde shōnen mikkō," *Fukuoka Nichi Nichi Shinbun*, September 18, 1931, 2.

119. Nihon kōkū yusō 1938a, 87.

120. "Lindberghs to Fly to Nanking Today," *New York Times*, September 18, 1931.

121. "Important Airlink Foreseen in Japan," *New York Times*, August 16, 1931.

122. "Important Airlink Foreseen in Japan," *New York Times*, August 16, 1931.

123. See Fritzsche 1992, 186–87, and Van Riper 2004, 30.

124. "Rindē ki tobisaru," *Kyūshū Nippō*, September 19, 1931, *dai ni gōgai*.

125. The test flight via floatplane took place on October 4, 1931, and took nine and a half hours to fly eight hundred miles. Nihon kōku yusō 1938b, 13.

126. Nihon kōku yusō 1938b, 31.

127. Nihon kōku yusō 1938b, 33.

128. Nagashima 1941, 30.

129. Fukuoka ken 1936, 29; Fritzsche 1992, 151. The comment refers to Brecht's radio play about Lindbergh, *Der Ozeanflug*.

130. An official estimated some 90 percent of British Imperial Airways customers in the 1930s were part of the colonial or metropolitan bureaucracy. Hudson and Pettifer 1979, 79.

131. The prices are from Senkōkai 1986, 1032. The plane specifications are from Nihon kōku yusō 1938, 35.

132. Statistics on this vary. See *Kōtsū kenkyū shiryō* 39 (September 1936): 124; Nihon kōku yusō 1938, 40; Senkōkai 1986, 1032.

133. Fukuoka ken 1936, 39–40.

134. The Chinkai Fortified Defense Command became the Pusan-Chinkai Fortified Defense Command during the Pacific War as Pusan developed its own military installations.

135. See Senkōkai 1986, 1030–40; "Kukche hanggong no chosŏnch'ŭk sisŏl," *Tong-a Ilbo*, May 19, 1928, 1.

136. *Chōsen* 164 (January 1929): 176–77.

137. "Taikyū hikōjō menseki," *Ōsaka Asahi Shinbun*, October 27, 1936; Nihon kōku yusō 1938b, 23–24.

138. Fritzsche 1992, 176.

139. "Kampu renraku ryokyaku hikō," *Pusan Nippō*, January 23, 1934, 1.

140. "Kameura Mukōjima ni jūman tsubo," *Pusan Nippō*, June 29, 1933, 1. In 1945 the site was eventually developed as an airfield for the Japanese naval flying corps.

141. "Chōsen tōbu ni arata ni kōkūro kaisetsu," *Pusan Nippō*, November 11, 1934, 2.

142. "Hikōjō iten ni Urusan yūmin funki," *Pusan Nippō*, August 24, 1935, 1.

143. Fritzsche 1992, 179.

144. See *Fukuoka Kenjin*, November 1936, 56, and *Pusan Nippō*, September 26, 1936, 3.

145. *Kyūshū Nippō*, September 15, 1936, 7. Prince Nashimoto may have been selected for symbolic reasons. His daughter Masako had married Korean Crown Prince Yi Un in 1920.

146. *Kyūshū Nippō*, September 30, 1936, evening edition, 1, and October 1, 1936, 7.

147. "Mamore warera ga sora no seimeisen," *Pusan Nippō*, September 30, 1936, 1.

148. Nihon kōku yusō 1938b, 9.

149. Nihon kōku yusō 1938b, 32.

150. Van Vleck 2013, 113.

151. Van Riper 2004, 30; Fritzsche 1992, 183.

152. "Fukuoka hikōjō no kakuchō" *Fukuoka Nichi Nichi Shinbun*, December 26, 1938, 5.

153. "Dai fukuoka shi kensetsu e," *Kyūshū Nippō*, January 14, 1939, 3.

154. See Goswami 2012, 1463.

CHAPTER 5

1. In Japanese, Keijō fumin kan, and in Korean, Kyŏngsŏngbumin'gwan.

2. Keijō toshi keikaku kenkyū kai 1936.

3. Keijō toshi keikaku kenkyū kai 1936, 234-35.

4. Ishikawa became one of the most influential planners in postwar Japan. He worked on the reconstruction of Tokyo into the 1950s and was involved in early plans for the merger of the five cities of Kitakyūshū. See Tokumoto 1988.

5. Keijō toshi keikaku kenkyū kai 1936, 236-42.

6. Keijō toshi keikaku kenkyū kai 1936, 242–43.

7. Keijō toshi keikaku kenkyū kai 1936, 236.

8. Office of Population Research 1943, 75.

9. For an overview of the change in Japanese policy, see Eckert 1991, 40–45.

10. On the development of plans for Rajin, Chongjin, and Unggi, see Inayoshi 2014, 262–68. On this period (1931–40), see Son 1996, 184–226.

11. Homei 2020, 139; Mimura 2011, 191; Moore 2013, 136.

12. Kawakami 2008, 1.

13. Kawakami cites Ishikawa 1941, which also gives 1937 as the date for the Toyama conference, and therefore the first discussion of national land planning (*kokudo keikaku*). Conference publications and journals confirm, however, that it was held in May 1936, only weeks after the Keijō conference.

14. Nishimura 1936, 8.

15. Tōgo 1935, 173–81.

16. Zenkoku toshi keikaku kyōgikai 1935, 1.

17. "Kitakyūshū tenbōdai" *Fukuoka Kenjin*, November 1932.

18. "Kitakyūshū no renkei toshi, "*Fukuoka Kenjin*, November 1932, 2.

19. "Dai fukuoka kensetsu," *Fukuoka Kenjin* , November 1932, 40.

20. "Dai fukuoka kensetsu," *Fukuoka Kenjin*, November 1932, 40–41.

21. See Mori Kazuo, "Rokko sankei no kaihatsu keikaku," *Toshi Kōron* 13, no. 7 (July 1930): 77–95.

22. The Japanese term *taiheiyō beruto* was first used in Prime Minister Ikeda's 1960 Income Doubling Plan in reference to industrializing the corridor from Tohoku to Kyushu.

23. "Dai fukuoka kensetsu," *Fukuoka Kenjin*, November 1932, 41.

24. Tōgo 1934, 1935.

25. Shinozaki, "Dai–Pusan kensetsu (2)," *Fukuoka Kenjin,* March 1935, 13. See also chapter 2.

26. "Kitakyūshū goshi no fūchi chiku wo kettei," *Fukuoka Nichi Nichi Shinbun*, April 26, 1936, 5.

27. Tokumoto 1983, 280.

28. Keijō toshi keikaku kenkyū kai 1936, 296–308.

29. The first air defense drill was held in 1928. In 1936 there were forty-three drills held across thirty-four prefectures and municipalities. Jōhōji 1981, 138.

30. Fukuyama 1936, 44–66.

31. Fukuyama 1936, 46.

32. "Japanese Shocked: New Attackers Heading for a Key Island—Navy Base," *New York Times*, February 24, 1938, 1; Naikaku jōhōbu, "Kaikūgun no senka kagay-aku," *Shūhō* 73 (March 9, 1938): 22.

33. Chinese accounts—reported in British and US newspapers—stated that the planes reached their targets of Fukuoka and Nagasaki Cities. See "Two Chinese Bombers Fly over Japan," *Daily Telegraph*, May 21, 1938, 13. However, eyewitness reports from Japan suggest their path was further south, over Kyushu's sparsely populated mountainous southern regions of Miyazaki and Kumamoto. See Iechika 2012, 163–71.

34. Chongqing was bombed from 1938 to 1943. The initial two strikes of Operation 100 in May 1939 killed approximately 4,400 people. See Maeda 2009, 148.

35. Chikuzen machi 2009.

36. For more on radio listeners in colonial Korea, see Kim Yŏng Hŭi 2015.

37. Kim Chang-t'ae 1939, 1.

38. Kim Chang-t'ae 1939, 3–4.

39. Kim Chang-t'ae 1939, 6

40. See Eckert 1991, chap. 8. This placing of "class over nation," or even region over nation, was not complete, as Eckert has since discussed. See the new e-book introduction to his book *Offspring of Empire*, March 2014.

41. Only a year after the tunnel opened, it was plagued with construction issues. See, for example, "Haejŏdoro ilbup'aswae," *Tong-a Ilbo*, August 7, 1933, 1.

42. Fukuyama 1936, 53–54.

43. Wada 1939.

44. Wada 1939, 102.

45. Onoda 2014, 202.

46. On the nostalgia for this original "bullet train" in postwar Japan, see Abel 2022, 161–69.

47. "Tokkyū Shōnan yuki," *Shashin Shūhō* 252 (October 1942): 12–13.

48. Onoda 2014, 200. For more on the "anti-communist" railroad, see Yumoto 1939.

49. See Fritzsche 1992, 176–77.

50. UK National Archives, FO 262/1976, Aviation—Civil (1938), 12, 29.

51. See "Meiho dokki mo kuru Berurin-Tokyo kan ōfuku hikō," *Ōsaka Asahi Shinbun*, November 19, 1938, and "Doitsu hōnichi shinzenki," *Ōsaka Asahi Shinbun*, November 23, 1938, 2. See also Fukuoka shi 1966, 812–13.

52. See Onoda 2014, 199, and Nakano 2007, 179.

53. This was the subtitle of Yumoto's 1939 work on the Central Asian railway.

54. The postwar Tōkaidō and Sanyō *shinkansen* plans were based on the prewar routes and made use of some tunnels already constructed. The English name for the postwar plan, the bullet train, is a legacy of its prewar name, *dangan ressha*.

55. Colegrove 1941.

56. Mimura 2011, 191.

57. Akaiwa 1940, 178.

58. *Fukuoka Kenjin*, November 1932, 23.

59. "Tōa kokudo keikaku yōmoku oyobi nihon kokudo keikaku kikan secchi yōmō," reproduced in *Toshi Mondai* 32, no. 2 (February 1941): 44.

60. A National Diet Library digital search for materials containing the phrase "*kokudo keikaku*" produces four entries in 1938, ten entries in 1939, and 121 in 1940.

61. See, for example, Suzuki 1941.

62. On the mobilizing of ideology, see Yellen 2019, 94–99.

63. Akaiwa 1943, 83.

64. Hatayama 1943.

65. Hatayama 1943, 76.

66. Hatayama 1943, 78.

67. Hatayama 1943, 78.

68. Hatayama 1943, 78.

69. "Fukuteki no seizō shita Fukuoka shimin taikai: bōshiyōchō no iki chūten," *Kyūshū Nippō*, July 22, 1937 (evening edition), 2.

70. "Pusan eki mae ni akari ni umaru," *Pusan Nippō*, December 14, 1937 (evening edition), 2.

71. See Fukuoka shi 1966, 805; "Hantō shusshinsha ni mo retsu retsu taru kono sekisei," *Fukuoka Nichi Nichi Shinbun*, September 13, 1937, 5; "Yūwa jigyō dantai soshiki hakkai shiki," *Kyūshū Nippō*, September 25, 1937, 3.

72. See, for example, "Pusan shusshin 2 yūshi 22 nisseki mugon no gaisen," *Pusan Nippō*, December 21, 1937, 2, and "Yūshi mugon no gaisen," *Pusan Nippō*, December 23, 1937, 2.

73. Hedinger 2017, 2000.

74. "Kangei Fukuoka ken min taikai," *Fukuoka Nichi Nichi Shinbun*, April 23, 1938 (evening edition), 1.

75. *Italia Giaponne Manciucuo 1938* (Rome: Istituto Nazionale Luce, 1938), Imperial War Museum, COI 42.

76. Nagashima 1941, 533–35.

77. See Imperial War Museum oral histories of Robert Peaty (4841, Reel 1), Henley T. A. Wade (22673, Reel 6), Douglas Parker Hanson (4986, Reel 2), and Jack Roberts (6058, Reel 5). See also "Pusan jōriku no Eihei horyo funai ni kōshin," *Pusan Nippō*, September 24, 1942, 2. The holiday was the autumnal *kōreisai*, a day of remembrance for past emperors.

78. See "Fukuoka toshi keikaku kōen kettei no ken" (1941), cited in Yoshino et al. 2007.

79. This type of transwar continuity was seen in many Japanese cities. See Sorensen 2002, 146.

80. Sorensen 2002, 146.

81. Yoshino et al. 2007, 175.

82. United States Strategic Bombing Survey (hereafter USSBS), Fukuoka (consisting of 3 envelopes): Interviews, Report no. 58b(3)(b), interview with K. Kuwabara, November 20, 1945.

83. See Kim Kyŏng-nam 2011.

84. Kim Kyŏng-nam 2011, 101; Nagaki Junkichi, "Chōsen dai 7420 butai shiryō: zai Pusan kōshaho rentai," National Institute for Defense Studies (Bōeikenkyūjo senshi kenkyū sentā), Chōsen 85, n.d., 28.

85. For an overview of labor mobilization and control during the war, see Park 1999, chap. 3.

86. Figures from Kim Dae-Rae et al. 2005, 301–3.

87. "Jigyō no jicchi o hitsuyō to suru riyu," 1942, in *Pusan-fu kakyū rōmusha shūyōchi zōsei jigyō hi kisai no ken,* Korean National Archives, CJA0003666, p. 0783.

88. The term *domaku* (*t'omak* in Korean) described informal housing inhabited by Koreans. Researchers from Keijō Imperial University undertook a survey of *t'omak* in the same year as Yamashita's petition. See Keijō teikoku daigaku eisei chōsabu 1942.

89. "Jigyō no jicchi o hitsuyō to suru riyu," 1942, in *Pusan-fu kakyū rōmusha shūyōchi zōsei jigyō hi kisai no ken,* Korean National Archives.

90. "Jigyō no jicchi o hitsuyō to suru riyu," 1942, in *Pusan-fu kakyū rōmusha shūyōchi zōsei jigyō hi kisai no ken,* Korean National Archives.

91. *Pusan-fu kakyū rōmusha shūyōchi zōsei jigyō hi kisai no ken*, Korean National Archives; see the figure on p. 0811.

92. *Pusan (Fusan) Kyongsang namdo (Keisho-nando) Korea*, 1946, United States Army Map Service.

93. Office of the Chief of Naval Operations 1944, 6.

94. For an overview see Kratoska 2005 and Park 1999.

95. See Shihōshō chōsabu 1939.

96. "Chōsenjin rōdōsha no naichi rōryoku busoku ōen," *Pusan Nippō*, August 24, 1939.

97. "Nansen chihō kara hachi man mei wo okuru," *Pusan Nippō*, September 2, 1939.

98. Pusan shokugyō shōkaijo 1940b.

99. Pusan shokugyō shōkaijo 1940b, 2.

100. Although it has been suggested that official mediation (J: *kan assen*) was not begun by authorities in Korea until after the start of the Pacific War, it appears that after the labor conscription ordinance (*chōyō rei*) of 1939, a complex system involving both official and private forms of mediation was employed, at least in the catchment area of the Pusan employment center.

101. Pusan shokugyō shōkaijo 1940b, 2–3.

102. Pusan shokugyō shōkaijo 1940b, 15.

103. Pusan shokugyō shōkaijo 1940b, 16.

104. Pusan shokugyō shōkaijo 1940b, 19.

105. See "Tokōsha no shidōkikan keishōnandō naisen kyōkai wo setsuritsu" *Ōsaka Mainichi Shinbun*, February 1, 1940, 5, and "Keinan naisen kyōkai," *Pusan Nippō*, March 21, 1940.

106. Pusan shokugyō shōkaijo 1940b, 21.

107. Pusan shokugyō shōkaijo 1940b, 22.

108. Pusan shokugyō shōkaijo 1940b, 50.

109. Pusan shokugyō shōkaijo 1940b, 54.

110. On this topic the classic work is Hayashi 1981. See also Yamada 1987; Ōkubo 1996; Smith 1999.

111. See Pak and Jang 2010, 162–73; "Mokuzō sen kaijō e," *Pusan Nippō*, December 29, 1943, 2.

112. See Kratoska 2005, 19.

113. Pusan shokugyō shōkaijo 1940a.

114. Pusan shokugyō shōkaijo 1940a.

115. Pusan shokugyō shōkaijo 1941.

116. Morikawa 2015, 46–47.

117. Kankoku teishintai mondai taisaku kyōgikai 1993, 1: 287–98; Noguchi 2007, 76, 83.

118. The year 1944 also saw the conscription of Korean men into the Imperial Army. See Uchida 2011, 378, and Janice Kim 2005, 142.

119. USSBS, Fukuoka(consisting of 3 envelopes): Interviews. Report no. 58b(3)(b), Interview S-17 with Fujii Takeo and Koga Katsutaka.

120. USSBS, Fukuoka (consisting of 3 envelopes): Report on city, Report no. 58b(3)(a), Table 12, "Industrial Labor in Fukuoka City."

121. USSBS, Fukuoka (consisting of 3 envelopes): Interviews, Report no. 58b(3)(b), interview S-14 with Ōuchi Kakunosuke, November 23, 1945, 3.

122. USSBS, Fukuoka (consisting of 3 envelopes): Interviews, Report no. 58b(3)(b), interview S-14 with Ōuchi Kakunosuke, November 23, 1945, 4.

123. United States Strategic Bombing Survey 1975, Report no. 1, "Summary Report: Pacific War," 8.

124. United States Strategic Bombing Survey 1975, Report no. 78, "The Offensive Mine Laying Campaign against Japan," 1.

125. Senkōkai 1986, 1035.

126. United States Strategic Bombing Survey 1975, Report no. 78, "The Offensive Mine Laying Campaign against Japan," 9.

127. United States Strategic Bombing Survey 1975, Report no. 78, "The Offensive Mine Laying Campaign against Japan," 14.

128. "Daiseikyō no Bōkūgoten," *Pusan Nippō*, April 1, 1941, 2; "Bōkūgoten nyūjō 70 man," *Pusan Nippō*, October 14, 1941, 2.

129. "Zensen ichi no bōkūgo," *Pusan Nippō*, October 5, 1941.

130. Nagaki Junkichi, "Chōsen dai 7420 butai shiryō: zai Pusan kōshaho rentai," National Institute for Defense Studies (Bōeikenkyūjo senshi kenkyū sentā), Chōsen 85, section 3.3.

131. Nagaki Junkichi, "Chōsen dai 7420 butai shiryō: zai Pusan kōshaho rentai," National Institute for Defense Studies (Bōeikenkyūjo senshi kenkyū sentā), Chōsen 85, section 3.3.

132. P'ohang and Kosŏng are referred to as "targets of opportunity" in the official account of the mission. See Craven and Cate 1953, 101.

133. Nagaki Junkichi, "Chōsen dai 7420 butai shiryō: zai Pusan kōshaho rentai," National Institute for Defense Studies (Bōeikenkyūjo senshi kenkyū sentā), Chōsen 85, section 3.3.

134. Nagaki Junkichi, "Chōsen dai 7420 butai shiryō: zai Pusan kōshaho rentai," National Institute for Defense Studies (Bōeikenkyūjo senshi kenkyū sentā), Chōsen 85, section 3.3.

135. Nagaki Junkichi, "Chōsen dai 7420 butai shiryō: zai Pusan kōshaho rentai," National Institute for Defense Studies (Bōeikenkyūjo senshi kenkyū sentā), Chōsen 85, section 3.3.

136. USSBS, Fukuoka (consisting of 3 envelopes): Air-raid casualties, Report no. 58b(3)(d), US Bomber Command, "Target Information Sheet," 3.

137. Karacas and Fedman 2012, 320.

138. USSBS, Fukuoka (consisting of 3 envelopes): Air-raid casualties, Report no. 58b(3)(d), US Bomber Command, "Target Information Sheet," 1–2.

139. According to data from the 1940 census, the ten most populous cities in the empire were: Tokyo (6,778,804), Osaka (3,252,340), Nagoya (1,328,084), Kyoto (1,089,726), Yokohama (968,091), Kobe (967,234), Keijō (935,000), Hiroshima (343,968), Taipei (326,407), and Fukuoka (324,217).

140. USSBS, Fukuoka (consisting of 3 envelopes): Report on city, Report no. 58b(3)(a), 2.

141. The army air raid warning "net" had previously alerted the city every time aircraft neared the prefecture's borders. See USSBS, Fukuoka (consisting of 3 envelopes): Report on city, Report no. 58b(3)(a), Part II: Air Attacks.

142. USSBS, Fukuoka (consisting of 3 envelopes): Report on city, Report no. 58b(3)(a), 2.

143. USSBS, Fukuoka (consisting of 3 envelopes): Report on city, Report no. 58b(3)(a), 2.

144. USSBS, Fukuoka (consisting of 3 envelopes): Air-raid casualties, Report no. 58b(3)(d), "Target Information Sheet," 3.

145. Exact figures for the number killed in the raid differ: The United States Strategic Bombing Survey gives a total of 1,044 dead, whereas *Fukuoka dai kūshū* gives 902, with another 244 missing. See Nishi Nippon shinbunsha 1978a, 40.

146. USSBS, Fukuoka (consisting of 3 envelopes): Interviews, Report no. 58b(3)(b), Interrogation S-15.

147. USSBS, Fukuoka: Background Report (part Japanese), Report no. 14(f)4(b), 6.

148. USSBS, Fukuoka (consisting of 3 envelopes): Report on city, Report no. 58b(3)(a), Part II: Air Attacks, 13. The Jūtaku Eidan had been set up in 1941 to build houses for laborers in key industrial areas.

149. Prideaux 1945, 53.

150. Prideaux 1945, 53, and USSBS, Fukuoka (consisting of 3 envelopes): Interviews, Report no. 58b(3)(b), Interrogation S-15, 2.

151. Oguma and Kang 2008, 22.

152. The flight log of Commander Ashworth, weaponeer on *Bockscar*, noted "heavy ground haze and smoke" (Ramsey 1982, 35). See also interviews with Russell E. Gackenbach and Robert Krauss at manhattanvoices.org.

153. See "B-29's Bomb Again," *New York Times,* August 14, 1945.

154. Craven and Cate 1953, 733.

155. See MacIsaac 1976, 117.

156. Scholarly work on Allied raids on occupied territories remains limited. On air defense in colonial Korea, see Cho 2011, 81–116. On Singapore, see Toh 2020, 109–25.

157. United States Strategic Bombing Survey 1975, Report no. 78, 15.

158. United States Strategic Bombing Survey 1975, Report no. 78, 15.

CHAPTER 6

1. Uchida 2011, 3.

2. For a discussion of the varying estimates of Koreans present in Japan at the end of the war, see Suzuki 2010, 189–98, and Watt 2009, 91, note 93.

3. Schmid 2018, 3.

4. This is based on about 1,890,000 people through Hakata and about 1,495,000 people through Pusan.

5. See the account of Matsuzaki Naoko, who repatriated from Yŏngwol in Kangwon-do in southern Korea, in Hikiagekō hakata o kangaeru tsudoi 2017, 82–84.

6. See Watt 2009, 99.

7. See Augustine 2023, the first book in English on this topic. See also Izumi 1993. Other recent works include Suzuki 2017.

8. Tanabe 1980, 284–85.

9. Tanabe 1980, 282.

10. Tanabe 1980, 283.

11. Tanabe 1980, 283.

12. Watt (2015) somewhat flattens this complexity and unevenness of experiences in wartime Korea, even among Japanese settlers.

13. "Major Freedoms Restored in Korea," *New York Times*, September 20, 1945, 2.

14. Nagaki Junkichi, "Chōsen dai 7420 butai shiryō: zai Pusan kōshaho rentai," National Institute for Defense Studies (Bōeikenkyūjo senshi kenkyū sentā), Chōsen 85, n.d., 36.

15. See Nagaki Junkichi, "Chōsen dai 7420 butai shiryō: zai Pusan kōshaho rentai," National Institute for Defense Studies (Bōeikenkyūjo senshi kenkyū sentā), Chōsen 85, n.d., 37; Bullitt 1946, 1.

16. Tanabe 1980, 287.

17. For more on *Minju Jungbo* and newspapers in postliberation Pusan, see Ch'oe 1997 and Chae 2009. The newspaper had briefly been called just *Jungbo* before changing to *Minju Jungbo* on September 17 (Chae 2009, 175).

18. "Irin'gongjang kyŏngyŏngŭn kunjŏngbuŭi chŭngmyŏng p'iryo," *Minju Jungbo*, October 4, 1945, 1.

19. "Kwihwandongp'orŭl udae sŏilbon'gisŏndo chigwŏni kwalli," *Minju Jungbo*, October 7, 1945, 2.

20. "Irin ŏŏpkwŏn'gwa ŏgu hoesu," *Minju Jungbo*, October 11, 1945, 2.

21. See, for example, advertisements in *Minju Jungbo* on December 3, 14, 19, 23, and 26, 1945.

22. *Minju Jungbo*, December 10, 1945, 2.

23. "Undesirables" included Shinto priests, geisha and other women involved in the entertainment business, and former Japanese police. Gane 1946, 44.

24. Tanabe 1980, 293.

25. Tanabe 1980, 298.

26. Youth and church associations were some of the many groups that were involved on the Korean side with repatriation from Japan. See Gane 1946, 53–80.

27. Tanabe 1980, 290.

28. Tanabe (1980, 291) describes the Japanese as giving orders with the borrowed authority of the US Army by using a Japanese proverb that describes "a fox borrowing the authority of a tiger."

29. Gayn 1981, 395. See also Kuksa p'yŏnch'anwiwŏnhoe 2014, vol. 3, chap. 3.

30. Tanabe 1980, 292.

31. In Hakata hikiage engo kyoku 2002 [1947], 176, the order is said to have come from SCAJAP, the Shipping Control Authority for the Japanese Merchant Marine, set up by the occupation forces in order to control shipping in Japan and provide ships for the repatriation of civilians and military personnel overseas. However, this wasn't active until October 1945. See Hikiage engo chō 1950, 31.

32. Hakata hikiage engo kyoku 2002 [1947], 177.

33. "Nansen tairyū hojin hikiage ni tsuki kinkyū haisen," in Japanese Diplomatic Archives, Taiheiyō sensō shūketsu ni yoru zaigai hōjin hogo hikiage kankei zakken: Zaigai kakuchi jōkyō oyobi zengo sochikankei—nansen no jōkyō (K'.7.1.0.1-2-2), 34–41.

34. Nagaki Junkichi, "Chōsen dai 7420 butai shiryō: zai Pusan kōshaho rentai," National Institute for Defense Studies (Bōeikenkyūjo senshi kenkyū sentā), Chōsen 85, n.d., 35.

35. These figures are from Kim Dae-Rae et al. 2005, 301–3.

36. See Gane 1946, 8, and Maruyama 1980, 392. It is unclear if the figure for the end of December includes those left waiting to be repatriated or just refers to those originally based in Pusan, but it is most likely the latter. Gane (1946, 27) offers a different number—closer to 3,500.

37. Maruyama 1980, 391.

38. "Ilboninyuryŏkchaga chip'yeppurok'a iyong," *Minju Jungbo*, October 17, 1945, 2.

39. "Puduŭi susong yŏkhae irin ppurok'a amyak," *Minju Jungbo*, October 10, 1945, 2.

40. Gane 1946, 50.

41. Gane 1946, 50–51.

42. Gane 1946, 50.

43. Account of prefectural *shakai-ka* employee Yoshitake (first name unknown), in Hakata hikiage engo kyoku 2002 [1947], 201.

44. Hakata hikiage engo kyoku 2002 [1947], 178.

45. Hakata hikiage engo kyoku 2002 [1947], 179.

46. Account of Yoshitake in Hakata hikiage engo kyoku 2002 [1947], 179.

47. Hakata hikiage engo kyoku 2002 [1947], 202.

48. Hakata hikiage engo kyoku 2002 [1947], front matter.

49. On September 28, 1945, the Japanese government ordered the Kōseikai, at the prefectural level, to take control of coordinating the repatriation of Koreans. See Augustine 2023, 42–43.

50. For more on the Kyōwakai, see Higuchi 1986.

51. Suzuki 2017, 79. The division was part of the Ministry of Welfare and began on September 27, 1944—the same month an association (Zaidan hōjin Chōsenjin kinrō dōin engokai) was set up to help "mobilized Korean workers."

52. "Hanba chōyō no yō na katachi de," Hakata hikiage engo kyoku 2002 [1947], 184. See Tonomura 2012, Ryaku nenpyō (appendix), 7.

53. Account of prefectural office bureaucrat Utsunomiya Ichū, formerly of the *sōshutsu* (departures) section of the Hakata Repatriation Office, in Hakata hikiage engo kyoku 2002 [1947], 183.

54. See Suzuki 2017, 109.

55. Izumi 1993, 97, note 13.

56. Smith 1999, 267, 343.

57. Smith 1999, 335–37.

58. Figures for 1945 are from Sakamoto 1998, 119. Figures for Koreans in Fukuoka in November 1945 suggest there were 20,000 in Hakata and 190,000 in the prefecture overall. Whether these included Koreans who had arrived from other prefectures or not, and how often the figures were updated to reflect repatriation, is unclear. See Gane 1946, 14.

59. The Japanese was "*bakeijō sono mama no sugata.*" Hakata hikiage engo kyoku 2002 [1947], 185.

60. Hakata hikiage engo kyoku 2002 [1947], 185.

61. Hikiage engo chō 1950, 55. The term used was "*kyū dōhō.*"

62. Hikiage engo chō 1950, 56.

63. The term *joshi kinrō teishintai* (girls' volunteer corps) developed a meaning in postwar South Korea that conflated the group's members with the comfort women (*wianbu* in Korean) who were recruited, tricked, or forced into sexual slavery for the Japanese military.

64. "Yume mita Chōsen hantō: kikoku inochigake," *Nishi Nippon Shinbun*, December 4, 2014.

65. Nagaki Junkichi, "Chōsen dai 7420 butai shiryō: zai Pusan kōshaho rentai," National Institute for Defense Studies (Bōeikenkyūjo senshi kenkyū sentā), Chōsen 85, n.d., 40.

66. Gane 1946, 69.

67. Gane 1946, 70.

68. Bullitt 1946, 30.

69. Gane 1946, 69. On the Occupation use of DDT in Japan and Korea, see Igarashi 2000, 67–69, and DiMoia 2013, chap. 2.

70. Gane 1946, 75–77.

71. Gane 1946, 50.

72. Watt 2009, 93. The total number of Koreans reported as having been "deported" by 1950 was 1,014,541.

73. Gane 1946, 68. Shimonoseki and Ozuki reception centers were used to prepare groups of Koreans before sending them via train to Senzaki, which did not have the capacity to hold large numbers of people on site.

74. Gane 1946, 68 and Appendix E, figures 7–9.

75. Cumings 1981, 316–18.

76. Cumings 1981, 318.

77. Nishizaki 2016 focuses mainly on "occupational transitions" but offers significant demographic information on repatriates and their movement within postwar Japan.

78. Account of the city government's port section head Shinomura in Hakata hikiage engo kyoku 2002 [1947], 196.

79. Hakata hikiage engo kyoku 2002 [1947], 199.

80. "Minato ni hiraku ukiyo no shukuzu," *Seiki Shinbun* 47 (April 10, 1947): 2. See also Fukuoka ken keisatsushi iinkai 1980, 521–22, cited in Izumi 1993. The aid group's links to Chōren may account for the disparaging terms that Hakata Port's "lawless" period is referred to in Mindan's history of its Fukuoka branch.

81. Zai Nihon Daikan minkoku mindan, Fukuoka ken chihō honbu 2016, 285.

82. Hakata hikiage engo kyoku 2002 [1947], 98.

83. Oguma and Kang 2008, 230.

84. Hakata hikiage engo kyoku 2002 [1947], 199–200. On Korean involvement in open air markets, see Ko 2014.

85. Hakata hikiage engo kyoku 2002 [1947], 203.

86. As Eiji Takemae (2003, 448) describes, resident Koreans' "ambiguous status" also led to occupation policy "treating Koreans alternately as Japanese nationals and as aliens, as was convenient."

87. Hakata hikiage engo kyoku 2002 [1947], 192.

88. Hakata hikiage engo kyoku 2002 [1947], 193. There is nothing of this nature in the Potsdam Declaration. Kawafuji appears to be echoing Home Minister Horikiri Zenjirō, who argued that "Koreans and Taiwanese had lost their Japanese nationality with Japan's acceptance of the Potsdam Declaration" (quoted in Watt 2009, 95).

89. Hakata hikiage engo kyoku 2002 [1947], 195.

90. The newspaper went by *Seiki Shinpō* in its early days. Its name was also romanized as *Seiki Sinmun*. See Ŏm and Lee 2018, 3–18.

91. "Sokoku ni kikan shita dōhō no jissō," *Seiki Shinbun*, May 16, 1946, 2.

92. As reported in the *Keijō Nihonjin Sewakai kaihō* 19 (September 25, 1945) in Japanese Diplomatic Archives, Taiheiyō sensō shūketsu ni yoru zaigai hōjin hogo hikiage kankei zakken: Zaigai kakuchi jōkyō oyobi zengo sochikankei—nansen no jōkyō, Keijō nihonjin sewakai kaihō susuri (K'.7.1.0.1-2-2-1).

93. Hakata hikiage engo kyoku 2002 [1947], 202.

94. "Bōeki saikai ni Chōsen shōnin mo kappatsuka," *Seiki Shinbun*, August 16, 1947.

95. "Kokusai bōeki o mezashite Chōsen shōkō renmei handai ni hassoku," *Seiki Shinbun*, November 30, 1946, 1.

96. "Sirŏpcha taech'aege manjŏn: chigŏp sogaeso kigu ilssin," *Minju Jungbo*, January 29, 1946, 2.

97. *Seiki Shinbun* 2 (May 2, 1946). In February 1947 a representative of the Liaison Office also took part in a roundtable on the future of Japan and Korea.

98. See "Chaeildongp'obakhaeirigusim 60 mandongp'och'ukch'urŭmmo yŏksŏnjŏnŭro yŏllaksamusodo p'yeji," *Tong-a Ilbo*, April 13, 1947, 1; "Chaeildongp'oege pakhaeusim irŭmmoro saengjon'gwŏndo hyŏbwi," *Kyŏnghyang Sinmun*, April 13, 1947, 3. For more on the liaison offices, see Augustine 2023, 80–81.

99. Goto (ca. 1901–85), not to be confused with Baron Gotō Shinpei, worked for the University of Hawai'i both before and after his time in Japan and was involved in US-Asia relations, including agricultural exchange between Hawai'i and Okinawa. See Koikari 2015, 115–24.

100. This was a survey undertaken from 1944 to offer impartial findings on the effects of strategic bombing, first in the European and then the Pacific theaters. The interviews and notes by Goto mentioned here formed part of a report on "the effects of strategic bombing on Japanese Morale."

101. United States Strategic Bombing Survey (hereafter USSBS), Fukuoka: Special interviews (part Japanese), Report no. 14(f)4(a), item 14.

102. USSBS, Fukuoka: Special interviews (part Japanese), Report no. 14(f)4(a), item 17. For more on the occupation role of Japanese American nisei, see Azuma 2009, 183–211.

103. "M'Arthur Planes Shift to Okinawa to Attack Japan," *New York Times*, July 6, 1945, 1.

104. For a detailed study of Okinawan refugees and their postwar repatriation, see Augustine 2023.

105. USSBS, Fukuoka: Special interviews (part Japanese), Report no. 14(f)4(a), 2, "Repatriating Okinawans," Special Interview by Kochi at Fukuoka, November 25, 1945 (translation by Sargeant Baron Goto).

106. Account of Gushiken Itoku, who acted as secretary of the Okinawa Office, in Naha-shi kikaku bu henshū shitsu 1981, 403–5.

107. Yoshida 1976, 23, and Urasaki 1965, 269.

108. Urasaki 1965, 268.

109. Augustine 2015 and Urasaki 1965, 276–77.

110. Hakata hikiage engo kyoku 2002 [1947], 193.

111. USSBS, Fukuoka: Special interviews (part Japanese), Report no. 14(f)4(a), 2, "Repatriating Okinawans," 1.

112. Augustine 2015, 217.

113. One story mentioned by several of the officials involved the "sacrificial efforts" (*giseiteki doryoku*) made by office head Kido, who took it upon himself to clean up "after all of the pier became a toilet for those Koreans." Hakata hikiage engo kyoku 2002 [1947], 197.

114. For more on this see Oguma 2002.

115. Hakata hikiage engo kyoku 2002 [1947], 41.

116. Maruyama 1980, 391.

117. Adachi is referring to the *Minju Jungbo*.

118. "Pusan to Fukuoka no jōkyō," *Keijō nihonjin sewakai kaihō* 19 (September 25, 1945), in Japanese Diplomatic Archives, *Keijō nihonjin sewakai kaihō susuri*.

119. "Hakata no jōkyō," *Keijō nihonjin sewakai kaihō* 79 (December 7, 1945), in Japanese Diplomatic Archives, *Keijō nihonjin sewakai kaihō susuri*.

120. "Kŭmhu irin chosŏnipkuk kŭmji," *Tong-a Ilbo*, December 24, 1945, 2.

121. "Nissenkan no shiji ryokō wa kinshi," *Keijō nihonjin sewakai kaihō* 102 (January 8, 1946), in Japanese Diplomatic Archives, *Keijō nihonjin sewakai kaihō susuri*.

122. "Kurisumasu no okurimono wo itashimashō," *Keijō nihonjin sewakai kaihō* 86 (December 15, 1945), in Japanese Diplomatic Archives, *Keijō nihonjin sewakai kaihō susuri*.

123. "Pusan nihonjin sewakai ni kansuru ken," letter from Gaimushō Shimonoseki renraku jimusho addressed to Gaimushō kanrikyokuchō Morishige Chifu, January 31, 1946, in Japanese Diplomatic Archives, *Zaigai kakuchi jōkyo oyobi zengo sochikankei—nansen no jōkyo* (K'.7.1.0.1-2-2).

124. "Kaitakumin no kokoro de kikoku subekida," *Keijō nihonjin sewakai kaihō* 67 (November 22, 1945), in Japanese Diplomatic Archives, *Keijō nihonjin sewakai kaihō susuri*.

125. On Yamada, see Fukuoka Asian Art Museum 2015, 373, and Asahi 1976, 39.

126. Its full title was *Renrakusen: Chōsen hikiagesha shōsoku zasshi*.

127. The original title in Japanese is *futōgen* (port word), a play on *kantōgen* (foreword).

128. *Renrakusen* 1, no. 1, 1.

129. "Kitakyūshū tenbyō," *Renrakusen* 1, no. 4, 8.

130. *Renrakusen* 1, no. 3, 18.

131. "Chōsen no miryoku," *Renrakusen* 2, no. 2, 5.

132. These numbers are from Hakata hikiage engo kyoku 2002 [1947]. As well as the estimated one hundred thousand Koreans who left Japan between August 1945 and the end of 1946 via official repatriation routes, it is estimated another four hundred thousand used *yamibune* to cross the straits. See Suzuki 2010, 191.

133. Hakata hikiage engo kyoku 2002 [1947], 90, 97, and Watt 2009, 93.

134. Gane 1946, 7, 28.

CHAPTER 7

1. In 1943 *Nishi Nippon Shinbun* replaced all other local newspapers, including the *Fukuoka Nichi Nichi Shinbun*, which had already merged with the *Kyūshū Nippō* the previous year.

2. "Kyūsoku ni minju seisan e" *Nishi Nippon Shinbun*, August 17, 1945.

3. "Senzai toshi no saiken keikaku," *Nishi Nippon Shinbun*, August 28, 1945; "Gunto wo kōgyō, gakuen toshi e," *Nishi Nippon Shinbun*, September 27, 1945; and "Sangyō toshi saiken e," *Nishi Nippon Shinbun*, October 8, 1945.

4. On wartime planning see Yoshino et al. 2007, 174.

5. "Hoken toshi no kensetsu e," *Nishi Nippon Shinbun*, August 23, 1945.

6. "Dōro no kakuchō nijūten," *Nishi Nippon Shinbun*, December 2, 1945; "Entotsu no machi ni midori no hayashi," *Nishi Nippon Shinbun*, December 12, 1945; and "Musū no ryokuen ga shutsugen," *Nishi Nippon Shinbun*, December 19, 1945.

7. "Fūtō sōji ni shukkin," *Nishi Nippon Shinbun*, November 1, 1945.

8. "Saejosŏnŭi kiji: Pusanŭi ch'oegŭn p'yŏnmo," *Kyŏnghyang Sinmun*, April 5, 1947.

9. Emergency restrictions were put in place in March 1946 (Chokurei 126: Tokaichi ten'nyū yokusei kinkyū sochi rei), made official in December 1947 (Hōritsu 221), and not completely removed until 1949. The 1947 act was applied to thirteen cities and Tokyo's twenty-three special wards. In Fukuoka prefecture, the restrictions applied to Fukuoka and Yahata City. The law made several exceptions, including for those repatriating from "colonies" (*gaichi*) or overseas.

10. United States Army Fortieth Division, 1945.

11. Cumings 1981, 316–18.

12. Gayn (1981, 401–3) offers an illustrative vignette of a "rightist" who failed to be elected in provincial elections being chosen to replace a county magistrate considered a "leftist" by the US authorities.

13. Gane 1946, 61. See Suzuki 2017, chap. 6. Chŏng T'ae Hŭi had previously been working as communications officer for the Overseas Korean War Victims Aid Association.

14. "Chŏksanjut'aek munjee taehae," *Tong-a Ilbo*, August 27, 1948. Also see Chang 2012.

15. Chang 2012, 365. On housing projects by USAMGIK, see Kwak 2015 and Augustine 2023, 110–14.

16. "Pindong kuje wŏlgan hangdoŭi haro," *Minju Jungbo*, December 22, 1946, 2.

17. Kim and Choi 2016, 23–38.

18. "Kŭkpinja jut'aegŭl taeryanggŏnch'uk," *Kyŏnghyang Sinmun*, November 6, 1947.

19. "Ilje t'oegehan ch'oegŭn busanhangŭi p'yŏnmo," *Kyŏnghyang Sinmun*, November 11, 1947.

20. See, for example, Kamitsubo 1979 or the often-reproduced *Asahi Shinbun* photograph from December 1946 of a twelve-year-old repatriate arriving at Shinagawa station from Manchuria carrying the ashes of her parents.

21. "Saejosŏnŭi kiji: Pusanŭi ch'oegŭn p'yŏnmo," *Kyŏnghyang Sinmun*, April 5, 1947. *Naniwabushi* is a type of Japanese song, usually with a tragic narrative and often accompanied by the shamisen.

22. "Saejosŏnŭi kiji: Pusanŭi ch'oegŭn p'yŏnmo," *Kyŏnghyang Sinmun*, April 5, 1947. The Korean Liberator (Chosŏn haebangja-ho) was the name of the express train between Seoul and Pusan from May 1946 until the Korean War.

23. Fukuoka ken jūtaku kensetsu hokushin kyōgi kai 1959, 16.

24. "Hoken toshi no kensetsu e," *Nishi Nippon Shinbun*, August 23, 1945.

25. Fukuoka shi 1948, 17. By 1947, however, the number of deaths had dropped back to pre-1944 levels, with just over six thousand deaths registered.

26. Shibata 1948, 95–96.

27. Fukuoka ken jūtaku kensetsu hokushin kyōgi kai 1959, 59. Out of 30,977 units, 18,369 were for mine workers.

28. United States Army, Fukuoka Military Government, Semi-Monthly Activities Report, Period ending December 31, 1946, 41–42; Monthly Activities Report, Period ending January 15, 1947, 69.

29. "Dekita no wa kanrakuba dake: jūtakugai wa kusa bōbō," *Nishi Nippon Shinbun*, June 19, 1946, 2.

30. Fukuoka shi 1948, 83.

31. Fukuoka shi 1978, 730.

32. Hakata hikiage engo kyoku 2002 [1947], 104, 110.

33. Hakata hikiage engo kyoku 2002 [1947], 105.

34. See Shimamura 2013, 37–39.

35. The term *barakku* first came into common parlance after the 1923 Great Kantō Earthquake and almost always refers to informal rather than planned temporary housing. See Weisenfeld 2012, 191. *Barakku* housing was not included in the first postwar housing survey of 1948.

36. SCAPIN-60: Provision of coal at Fusan, Korea, for use of CG, US Forces in Korea 1945/09/25, Supreme Commander for the Allied Powers Directives to the Japanese Government, United States National Archives (NARA) RG-331

37. General Headquarters Supreme Commander for the Allied Powers 1945, 44.

38. "Allies in Dilemma on Feeding Japan," *New York Times*, January 10, 1946, 6.

39. "Smuggling of Rice Attacked in Japan," *New York Times*, January 30, 1946, 4.

40. See "Chōsen kara no mitsuyu," *Nishi Nippon Shinbun*, January 30, 1946; "Pinbŏnhan taeil milssu," *Kyŏnghyang Sinmun*, February 4, 1947; "Hyŏnhaedan'gŏnnŭnŭn milmuyŏksat'ae han'guginmilssuch'uri t'aeban," *Kyŏnghyang Sinmun*, December 12, 1948. For more on smuggling between Korea and Japan in the immediate postwar period, see Augustine 2023, chaps. 4 and 5.

41. "Pusan yori ryūyōsha kaeru," *Renrakusen* 2, no. 3–4: 4.

42. "Ilje t'oegehan ch'oegŭn busanhangŭi p'yŏnmo," *Kyŏnghyang Sinmun*, November 11, 1947.

43. See "Cho-magan muyŏngno gaech'ŏk!," *Tong-a Ilbo*, March 18, 1947, 1. On the "Macau trade" and Pusan, see Kim and Chŏng 2010, 121, 130.

44. On Pusan's central position in South Korea's postliberation rubber industry, see Pak 2010, 34.

45. See Murakami 2013 and 2018.

46. *Seiki Shinbun*, May 23, 1947, 2.

47. The league may have been associated with the national Korean Industry Association, on which see Ko 2014, 115–17.

48. "'Kokusai shōtengai' kōsetsu no igi ni tsuite," *Seiki Shinbun*, June 4, 1947, 2.

49. Fukuoka ken 2011, "Fukuoka shi kokon daikasai kiroku," 135.

50. See Imsisudoginyŏmgwan 2012.

51. "Chōsen to Nihon no bōeki wo kataru (2)," *Seiki Shinbun*, July 20, 1947, 2.

52. "Chōsen to Nihon no bōeki wo kataru (5)," *Seiki Shinbun*, July 25, 1947, 2.

53. "Chōsen to Nihon no bōeki wo kataru (4)," *Seiki Shinbun*, July 24, 1947, 2.

54. "Hakata kōgai de mikkō 34 mei agaru," *Nishi Nippon Shinbun*, October 4, 1951.

55. Some 642 Korean youth joined the Zainichi gakuto giyū gun. On the eighty who joined from Fukuoka prefecture, see Zai Nihon Daikan minkoku mindan 2016, 70–73.

56. "Hakata kōgai de mikkō 34 mei agaru," *Nishi Nippon Shinbun*, October 4, 1951.

57. See Cumings 2010, 16–23; Janice Kim 2017.

58. "Street Fighting On; South Korean Capital Is Entered by Communist Forces," *New York Times*, June 27, 1950, 1.

59. The new Port and Harbor Act (Kōwan hō) had been promulgated on May 31, 1950. Fukuoka shi kōwan kyoku 2000, 76.

60. Ishimaru 2013, 54.

61. Ishimaru 2013, 67. See also Hayashi 2006, 11.

62. For recent scholarship that problematizes this stance, see Morris-Suzuki 2018.

63. See Ishimaru 2013, 62, and Yata 1953, 188.

64. Yata 1953, 188.

65. Robert Guillain "The Korean Purgatory III—The Sewer of Pusan," *Manchester Guardian*, September 22, 1951.

66. Robert Guillain "The Korean Purgatory III—The Sewer of Pusan," *Manchester Guardian*, September 22, 1951.

67. As a child, video artist Nam June Paik and his family fled to Tokyo via Hong Kong. I have been told by Tsushima residents that other wealthy Koreans, including officials from Pusan, went to Tsushima. See also Cumings 2010, 19.

68. See Morris-Suzuki 2010, 28–32, on the redrawing of this border as part of the MacArthur Line, then later the Rhee Line.

69. "Senran no Nansen kara hi'nanmin sendan," *Nishi Nippon Shinbun*, August 8, 1950.

70. Top-secret telegram from S. J. Sebald, GHQ-SCAP Records, Box AG-12 (16), Entry and Departure, January 1951–March 1951, quoted in Morris-Suzuki 2010, 88, note 92.

71. Morris-Suzuki 2010, 81–82, cited in Yoon 1979.

72. Zai Nihon Daikan minkoku mindan 2016, 70–73.

73. "Mata 29 mei Tsushima ni hinan," *Nishi Nippon Shinbun*, August 9, 1950.

74. Tsushima islanders discussed this with me on a research trip in November 2015. Because of media restrictions on coverage of the massacre at the time, it seems the islanders did not know where these bodies—including those of women and children—came from, but they buried them all the same. See also Morris–Suzuki 2007, 54–55.

75. "Mata 29 mei Tsushima ni hinan," *Nishi Nippon Shinbun*, August 9, 1950.

76. Watt 2009, 4, 35.

77. See Schmid 2018, esp. 3-4.

78. On Japanese women who "returned" to Korea after 1945, see Kamisaki 1982.

79. On representations of *naisen kekkon*, see Su Yun Kim 2020. On earlier repatriation attempts, see Utsunomiya 2016.

80. "Japanese 'War Widows' Shortly to Be Repatriated from Korea," AFP Pusan, May 19, in Japanese Diplomatic Archives, Kankoku zanryūsha hikiage kankei 1 (K'.7.1.0.15), 85.

81. "Chōsen yori no Nihonjin fujoshi hikiage ni kansuru hōkoku," in Japanese Diplomatic Archives, Kankoku zanryūsha hikiage kankei 1 (K'.7.1.0.15), 93–115.

82. "Chōsen yori no Nihonjin fujoshi hikiage ni kansuru hōkoku," in Japanese Diplomatic Archives, Kankoku zanryūsha hikiage kankei 1 (K'.7.1.0.15), 103.

83. The Japanese term is *Kankoku seki Nihon fujoshi*.

84. "Chōsen yori no hikiage fujoshi ni kansuru jōhō ni tsuite," in Japanese Diplomatic Archives, Kankoku zanryūsha hikiage kankei 1 (K'.7.1.0.15), 251–56.

85. This office (Kyūshū renraku chōsei jimukyoku) was one of eleven branch offices set up by the Ministry of Foreign Affairs Liaison Bureau in 1949 to work with the occupation. All regional branches were shut down at the end of March 1952, when the San Francisco Peace Treaty came into effect.

86. Letter from Takajiro Inoue to Song Hak Nai [*sic*], August 23, 1951, in Japanese Diplomatic Archives, Kankoku zanryūsha hikiage kankei 1 (K'.7.1.0.15), 289.

87. Letter from Takajiro Inoue to Song Hak Nai [*sic*], August 23, 1951, in Japanese Diplomatic Archives, Kankoku zanryūsha hikiage kankei 1 (K'.7.1.0.15), 288.

88. On Japanese crew in the Korean War, see Morris-Suzuki 2012, 18–22.

89. Letter from Thoyo Shiba Saki [*sic*] to Okazaki Katsuo, Minister of Foreign Affairs, "Japanese Nationals Stranded in Pusan, Korea," December 8, 1952, in Japanese Diplomatic Archives, Kankoku zanryūsha hikiage kankei 4 (K'.7.1.0.15), 51–52.

90. The Japanese terms are *buraku* and *domaku*.

91. See, for example, "Pinjaŭi ildŭng: haebangch'onjumindŭl manch'ŏnyŏwŏnhŏnnap," *Kyŏnghyang Sinmun*, November 12, 1949, 2, where Haebangch'on is described as a "village for war refugees" (*chŏnjaemin purak*).

92. There is some indication that the term shifted in meaning in postwar South Korea to suggest regulated temporary housing, in contrast to the unregulated *p'anjajip*.

93. A 79 percent increase—from 470,750 to 844,134. Data from Pusan chikhalsi sa p'yŏnch'anwiwŏnhoe 1989, 2: 1127.

94. Pusan chikhalsi sa p'yŏnch'anwiwŏnhoe 1989, 2: 1127.

95. Imsisudoginyŏmgwan 2012, 224.

96. Robert Guillain "The Korean Purgatory III—The Sewer of Pusan," *Manchester Guardian*, September 22, 1951.

97. Yang Dalsuk (1908–84) was born on the island of Kŏje in South Kyŏngsang province. In 1932 his work was featured in the Chōsen Art Exhibition, after which he studied for a while at Tokyo's Imperial School of Art but did not graduate. Yang later returned to Korea, and in 1937 he became part of a Pusan artists' group called the Ch'un'gwanghoe. During the Korean War he worked as a war artist. Unlike his

1950 watercolor *P'anjach'on*, on this book's cover, most of Yang's work features rural landscapes.

98. Burge 2016, 7. Over time, *p'anjatchip* has become the accepted orthography, but documents from the early 1950s commonly spell it *p'anjajip*, which I have followed.

99. "Hwando hŭimanggwa Pusan p'yojŏng," *Kyŏnghyang Sinmun*, January 31, 1952.

100. "Wanjŏn hwandohu ch'ŏlgŏdanhaeng Son Pusansijang p'anja maemae e kyŏnggo," *Tong-a Ilbo*, July 14, 1953.

101. This fire, on November 27, 1953, is known as the Pusanyŏk taehwajae (Pusan Station Fire), as the areas most badly affected were in front of the station.

102. "Hikiagesha ni 'ie'," *Nishi Nippon Shinbun*, October 3, 1951.

103. The Japanese use of the term "lumpen" refers back to the German usage as a pejorative term denoting the bottom rung of society.

104. "Hakata eki wa runpen hoteru," *Nishi Nippon Shinbun*, November 9, 1951.

105. "Hakata eki wa runpen hoteru," *Nishi Nippon Shinbun*, November 9, 1951.

106. Arizono 2008, 108.

107. For example, Fukuoka Prefectural Clubs for overseas migrants from Fukuoka were set up in San Francisco in 1950, Mexico in 1952, and Hawai'i in 1957, replacing prewar *kenjinkai*.

108. See Araragi 2017, 78. On the connections between pre- and postwar migration to the Americas, see Lu 2019 and Iacobelli 2017. Iacobelli notes that 40 percent of the postwar community of Japanese migrants in San Juan, Bolivia, were former repatriates (47).

109. Motooka 2015, 48–49, and Fukuoka shi 1948, 82.

110. "Hikiagesha ni 'ie'," *Nishi Nippon Shinbun*, October 3, 1951.

111. "Maru de macchibako: ōi barakku kensetsu ihan," *Nishi Nippon Shinbun*, October 8, 1951.

112. Yamada Tadaaki, "Fukuoka Tenjinmachi ichiba 144 to no kyōsei jokyo ni tsuite," *Shin Toshi*, July 1949, 9–12; *Shin Toshi*, August 1949, 24–26.

113. Nishiyama 2007, 92–93. The images show Fukuoka's Ishidō River *barakku* in 1961.

114. See Shimamura 2010 and Chatani 2021.

115. Chatani 2021, 12.

116. Shimamura 2010, 69.

117. "Yŏgijŏgip'anjajip!," *Tong-a Ilbo*, December 1, 1953.

118. "T'e janggun hwajaejigu kuhogyehoekpalp'yo," *Tong-a Ilbo*, December 3, 1953.

119. The first boat and crew captured, with one fisherman killed by the Korean coast guard, was a Fukuokan fishing vessel, the *Daiichi Daihō Maru*, in January 1953.

120. See Hyun 2020 and Choi 2017.

121. Imsisudoginyŏmgwan 2014, 43–48.

122. Morris-Suzuki 2010, 128.

123. Hom 2019, 6–7.

124. Yuasa 1952, 21.

125. Yata 1953, 188–89.

126. "JAL 29 myŏng t'aeugo Pusan~Pokkang ch'ŏtch'wihang," *Tong-a Ilbo*, September 4, 1967.

127. Kim and Chŏng 2010.

128. Sekai bunkasha 1954, 18. See also Otao 1949, 8, which refers to Fukuoka as the sun (*taiyō toshi*) of Kyushu's urban "solar system."

129. Kyūshū keizai chōsa kyōkai 1949, 144.

CONCLUSION

1. Ajia taiheiyō hakurankai kyōkai 1989a.

2. Ajia taiheiyō hakurankai kyōkai 1989b. For more on the gold seal and its colorful history and historiography, see Fogel 2013.

3. Fukuoka ajia toshi kenkyūjo 2009, 11.

4. On the Asia-Pacific idea, the classic text is Dirlik et al. 1998.

5. Santa-Cruz 2005.

6. The above is based on work in Shepherd 2009.

7. "Shintō Kazumashi ga shikyo: Fukuoka shichō o 4 ki 14 nen," *Asahi Shimbun*, November 28, 1992 (evening edition).

8. Fukuoka shi hakubutsukan 2015, 8 (Hino shiryō).

9. Arima, Ishitaki, and Konishi 2021, 300–301.

10. Personal communication from a professor, who as a doctoral student had worked for the preparation committee of the museum between 1988 and 1989. There may also have been a practical element to this decision. As former museum director and historian Arima Manabu discussed with me, posters and ephemera connected to expositions make for good exhibition displays. Koga (2016, 21) cites the term "negative inheritance" (J: *fu no isan*) when discussing Japanese tourism in Chinese cities with postcolonial heritage.

11. See, for example, Pusan kŭndae yŏksagwan 2004, 2010, 2011, 2013, 2015.

12. For a critique of the Pusan Modern History Museum regarding local communities and memory, see Chang 2012.

13. Massey 1994, 3.

14. Wasserstrom 2007.

15. Thanks to Kären Wigen for this phrase.

16. Yu 2009, 63–88.

17. Kim and Chŏng 2010.

18. Choi 2010.

19. Lee 1980, 66–69.

20. Telegram 79 Seoul 015909 from American Embassy Seoul to Secretary of State Washington DC, 5, in Kwangju Incident Records (MS 1766) Manuscripts and Archives, Yale University Library.

21. Chang 2015, 201–3.

22. On Minamata and environmental activism, see, for example, George 2001.

23. Lim 2017, 175.

24. Mori 2020, chap. 3

25. Tanigawa Gan, editor's introduction, *Sākuru Mura* 1, no. 1 (September 1958): 2.

26. Goodman, preface to Morisaki 1978, 12.

27. Morisaki 1978, 13.

28. "Hayashi Eidai-san shikyo: 'Shōgai jānarisuto' soshiki ni zokusazu furī tsuranuku," *Mainichi Shimbun* (Chikuhō edition), September 2, 2017.

29. Hanes 1993 and Doi 1968.

30. See Field 1991 and Ruoff 2001, 126.

31. Kim Sŏng Kuk cited in Kim, Hwang, and Im 2012, 709.

32. Kim, Hwang, and Im 2012, 710.

33. Kim, Hwang, and Im 2012, 710.

34. On this shift in Japan, see Lee 2014 and Field 1991.

35. *Kusa no ne Tsūshin* 234 (May 5, 1992).

36. Hanafusa and Hanafusa 2021.

37. Morikawa 2015.

38. Mori and Murakami 2024, 3, 33–34.

39. Stas Margaronis "Can Oceanix Busan's Floating City Defend Against Sea Level Rise?," *American Journal of Transportation*, July 26, 2024, www.ajot.com /insights/full/ai-can-oceanix-busans-floating-city-defend-against-sea-level-rise.

40. Takaki and Lim 2011.

41. Ippan zaidan hōjin Kokusai Highway Zaidan, "Zaidan gaiyō," https://ihf .jp/overview/plan/.

42. IFVOC Official Website, "Kaichō go aisatsu," www.ifvoc.org /chairman2024/.

43. See Koga 2016, chap. 4, for a study of Dalian's "political economy of redemption."

44. See, for example, "Battleship Island: A Symbol of Japan's Progress or Reminder of Its Dark History?," *The Guardian,* July 3, 2015.

45. Center for Historical Truth and Justice (South Korea) and Network for Fact Finding on Wartime Mobilization and Forced Labor (Japan), *Sites of Japan's Meiji Industrial Revolution and Forced Labor: Korea-Japan NGO Guidebook,* 2017, https://ksyc.jp/sinsou-net/201711_unesco_guidebook_EN.pdf.

46. Oguma and Kang 2008, 109–19.

47. Chō Misaki, "Chōsenjin rōdōsha wo tsuitō: Iizuka-shi no mukyūkadō, 30 nin sanka," *Nishi Nippon Shinbun,* October 23, 2021.

48. On this trip in January 2025, however, instead of the high-speed jetfoil *Beetle* run by JR Kyushu, which had linked Hakata and Pusan in under three hours, I had to take the much slower overnight Kampu ferry, as many of my historical actors had done a century before. After a scandal over a safety issue cover-up with its new trimaran *Queen Beetle*, the jetfoil route has been suspended. What this means for the future of high-speed sea links between Fukuoka and Pusan is unclear, especially as

the jetfoil route had already been losing out to low-cost air travel. In April of 2025, the *Queen Beetle* was sold by JR Kyushu to the Pusan-based PanStar Line ferry company on the condition it would not be used on the Hakata–Pusan route, as "repairs to make it strong enough to withstand the Genkainada waves would be difficult." Fukami Kazuto, "Munashisa tadayō 'kuīnbītoru' no saigo," *Norimono Nyūsu*, April 27, 2025, https://trafficnews.jp/post/542184/3.

49. Fukuoka shi 2014, 25; Fukuoka shi 2019.

50. Hattori and Honda 2006, 111.

51. Fukuoka shi 2019, 21.

REFERENCES

ARCHIVES

Colonial Archives, Busan Metropolitan Simin Municipal Library
Hitotsubashi University Institute of Economic Research, Tokyo
Hoover Institution Library and Archives, Stanford
Imperial War Museum, London
Japanese Diplomatic Archives (GGS), Tokyo
Korean National Archives (KNA)
Kyushu Historical Museum Archives, Fukuoka
Manuscripts and Archives, Yale University Library
National Archives of Japan (Kokuritsu kōbunshokan), Tokyo
National Institute for Defense Studies (Bōeikenkyūjo senshi kenkyū sentā), Tokyo
UK National Archives, London
United States National Archives (NARA)
United States Strategic Bombing Survey (USSBS): Entry 41, Pacific Survey Reports and Supporting Records 1928–1947

NEWSPAPERS AND PERIODICALS

Asahi Shimbun
Chōsen Jihō
Chōsen Shakai Jigyō
Chōsen Sōtokufu Kanpō
Chōsen Sōtokufu Tōkei Nenpō
Chōsen to Kenchiku
Daily Telegraph
Fukuoka Kenjin (The Fukuokan)
Fukuoka Nichi Nichi Shinbun
The Fusan

Fusan Ihō
The Guardian (formerly The Manchester Guardian)
Hakata Shōgyō Kaigisho Hōkoku
Hakkō
Kaebyŏk
Kanpō
Keijō Nippō
Kōbe Shinbun
Kōgyō Kokusaku
Kōtsū Kenykyū Shiryō
Kōwan
Kusa no ne Tsūshin
Kyŏnghyang Sinmun
Kyūshū Nippō
Mainichi Shimbun
Minju Jungbo
New York Times
Nishi Nippon Shinbun
Ōsaka Asahi Shinbun
Ōsaka Mainichi Shinbun
Pusan Fusei Yōran
Pusankō Bōeki Gairan
Pusan Nippō
Pusan Shōgyō/Shōkō kaigisho Geppō
Renrakusen
Sākuru Mura
Seiki Shinbun
Shashin Shūhō
Shin Toshi
Shūhō
Tōhōkyōkai kaihō
Tong-a Ilbo
Toshi Kōron
Toshi Mondai
Washington Post
Yorozu Chōhō

MAPS AND IMAGES

Fuken haichi hōritsu an fuzu. Naikaku, 1903.
Fukuoka ken: shichōsonbetsu jinkō zōgenritsu zu. Fukuoka, publisher unknown, 1925.
Pusan fu shigaizu nanbu. Takeda Kōbundō, 1933.
Saishin Fukuoka shi chizu. Fukuoka Kyōwakai, 1942.

Saishin jissoku Fukuoka shigai zenzu. Chiri kenkyūkai, 1908.

Teiki kōkū annai. Nihon kōkū yusō kabushikigaisha, 1935.

Yoshida Hatsusaburō. *Kyūshū Yūsen kōro keishō kōtsū chōkanzu*, 1936 cover of Kyūshū Yūsen, "Keiei kōro" (pamphlet).

PUBLICATIONS

Abel, Jessamyn R. 2022. *Dream Super-Express: A Cultural History of the World's First Bullet Train.* Stanford University Press.

Ajia taiheiyō hakurankai kyōkai, ed. 1989a. *Ajia taiheiyō hakurankai Fukuoka '89 kōshiki gaidobukku.* Ajia taiheiyō hakurankai kyōkai.

———. 1989b. *Michi, deai: ajia taiheiyō hakurankai Fukuoka 89 tēmakan tenjizuroku.* Ajia taiheiyō hakurankai kyōkai

Akaiwa Katsumi. 1940. "Kitakyūshū toshi no rekishiteki hatten ni tsuite." In *Honpō toshi hattatsu no dōkō to sono shomondai*, 161–83. Zenkoku toshimondai kaigi.

———. 1943. "Kitakyūshū chihō keikakujo no shomondai." *Kokudo keikaku* 2, no. 4: 82–105.

Allen, John, Allan Cochrane, and Doreen B. Massey, eds. 1998. *Rethinking the Region.* Routledge.

Ambaras, David. 2010. "Topographies of Distress: Tokyo c. 1930." In *Noir Urbanisms: Dystopic Images of the Modern City*, edited by Gyan Prakash, 187–217. Princeton University Press.

Amino, Yoshihiko. 1992. "Deconstructing Japan." *East Asian History* 3: 121–42.

Amrith, Sunil S. 2011. *Migration and Diaspora in Modern Asia.* Cambridge University Press.

Araragi Shinzō, ed. 2008. *Nihon teikoku wo meguru jinkōidō no kokusaishakaigaku.* Fuji shuppan.

———. 2017. "The Collapse of the Japanese Empire and the Great Migrations." In *The Dismantling of Japan's Empire in East Asia: Deimperialization, Postwar Legitimation, and Imperial Afterlife*, edited by Barak Kushner and Sherzod Muminov, 66–83. Routledge.

Arendt, Hannah. 2017. *The Origins of Totalitarianism.* Penguin Random House.

Arima Manabu. 1985. "Nisshin bōeki kenkyūsho to Fukuoka." *Museum Kyushu* 5, no. 2.

———. 1990. "Meiji-ki ni okeru chihō shihonka to taigai katsudō." In *Kinsei kindai shi ronshū*, 437–56. Yoshikawa kōbunkan.

———, ed. 2009. *Kindai Nihon no kigyōka to seiji: Yasukawa Keiichirō to sono jidai.* Yoshikawa Kōbunkan.

Arima Manabu, Ishitaki Toyomi, and Konishi Hidetaka. 2021. *Fukuoka ken no kingendai.* Yamakawashuppansha.

Ariyoshi Kenshō. 1929. "Hakata yori Pusan e no chokkōki." *Fukuoka*, June, 29–31.

Arizono Masayo. 2006. "Fukuoka shi ni okeru kanrakugai no keisei to henyō: Yanagi machi kara Nakasu e." In *Shishi kenkyū Fukuoka* 1 (March): 103–110

Armitage, David, Alison Bashford, and Sujit Sivasundaram, eds. 2017. *Oceanic Histories*. Cambridge University Press.

Asahi Akira. 1976. "Yamada Shinichi: Aru seishun tono saikai." *Sansai* 334 (April): 35–39.

Augustine, Matthew R. 2015. "Dividing Islanders: The Repatriation of 'Ryūkyūans' from Occupied Japan." In *Japan as the Occupier and Occupied*, ed. Christine de Matos and Mark E. Caprio. Palgrave Macmillan.

———. 2017. "The Limits of Decolonization—American Occupiers and the 'Korean Problem' in Japan, 1945–1948." *International Journal of Korean History* 22, no. 1: 43–75.

———. 2023. *From Japanese Empire to American Hegemony: Koreans and Okinawans in the Resettlement of Northeast Asia*. University of Hawai'i Press.

Azuma, Eiichirō. 2009. "Brokering Race, Culture, and Citizenship: Japanese Americans in Occupied Japan and Postwar National Inclusion." *Journal of American-East Asian Relations* 16, no. 3.

———. 2019. *In Search of Our Frontier: Japanese America and Settler Colonialism in the Construction of Japan's Borderless Empire*. University of California Press.

Baba Hiroe. 2013. "Keiyakusho ni miru Sugiyama Shigemaru no kōdō: Taiwan ginkō, Tōkyō chikkō, Hakatawan chikkō, mittsu no keiyakusho wo chūshin ni." *Yumeno Kyūsaku to Sugiyama san dai kenkyūkai* 1.

Barraclough, Ruth. 2012. *Factory Girl Literature: Sexuality, Violence, and Representation in Industrializing Korea*. University of California Press.

Basco, Sergi, and Tang, John P. 2020. "The Samurai Bond: Credit Supply, Market Access, and Structural Transformation in Pre-War Japan." *Journal of Economic History* 80, no. 2.

Batten, Bruce. 2006. *Gateway to Japan: Hakata in War and Peace, 500–1300*. University of Hawai'i Press.

Bayly, Christopher. 1993. "Knowing the Country: Empire and Information in India." *Modern Asian Studies* 27, no. 1.

Belchem, John. 2007. *Irish, Catholic and Scouse: The History of the Liverpool-Irish, 1800–1939*. Oxford University Press.

Blais, Hélène, and Florence Deprest. 2012. "The Mediterranean, a Territory between France and Colonial Algeria: Imperial Constructions." In *European Review of History / Revue européenne d'histoire* 19, no. 1: 33–57.

Borutta, Manuel, and Sakis Gekas. 2012. "A Colonial Sea: The Mediterranean, 1798–1956." *European Review of History / Revue européenne d'histoire* 19, no. 1.

Brenner, Neil. 1998. "Global Cities, Glocal States: Global City Formation and State Territorial Restructuring in Contemporary Europe." *Review of International Political Economy* 5, no. 1: 1–37.

———, ed. 2014. *Implosions/Explosions: Towards a Study of Planetary Urbanization*. JOVIS.

———. 2016. "The Hinterland, Urbanized?" *Architectural Design*, July/August.

Brenner, Neil, and Christian Schmid. 2015. "Towards a New Epistemology of the Urban?" *City* 19, nos. 2–3: 151–82.

Brooks, Barbara. 2005. "Reading the Japanese Colonial Archive: Gender and Bourgeois Civility in Korea and Manchuria before 1932." In *Gendering Modern Japanese History*, ed. Barbara Molony and Kathleen Uno, 296–325. Harvard University Asia Center.

Bullitt, John M. 1946. *History of Evacuation and Repatriation through the Port of Pusan, Korea 28th Sept 1945 – 15th Nov 45*. United States Army, 40th Infantry Division.

Burge, Russell. 2016. "License to Build: Seoul and the Politics of the Shantytown 1961–1971." Paper delivered at the annual conference of the Urban History Association in Chicago, October.

Burnett, John A., et al. 2012. "Scottish Migrants in the Northern 'Irish Sea Industrial Zone,' 1841–1911: Preliminary Patterns and Perspectives." *Northern History* 49, no. 1 (March).

Calderwood, Eric. 2018. *Colonial al-Andalus: Spain and the Making of Modern Moroccan Culture*. Harvard University Press.

Caprio, Mark. 2011. *Japanese Assimilation Policies in Colonial Korea, 1910–1945*. University of Washington Press.

Chae Baek. 2009. "Min'gunjŏnggi minjujungboŭi inyŏmjŏk sŏnghyang." *Han'gugŏllonjŏngbo hakpo* 48 (Winter).

Chang, Paul. 2015. *Protest Dialectics: State Repression and South Korea's Democracy Movement 1970–1979*. Stanford University Press.

Chang Kyung-Jun. 2012. "Kiŏgŭi chŏngch'iwa sŭt'orit'elling; kŭnhyŏndae yŏksae taehan kiŏgŭi pojŏn'gwa kongyu—Pusan'gŭndaeyŏksagwan unyŏng saryerŭl chungsimŭro." *Taegu sahak*, 106.

Chang Sŏk Hong, ed. 2012. *Haebang hu hanin kwihwan ŭi yŏksajŏk kwaje*. Yŏksa konggan.

Chatani, Sayaka. 2016. "The Ruralist Paradigm: Social Work Bureaucrats in Colonial Korea and Japan's Assimilationism in the Interwar Period." *Comparative Studies in Society and History* 58, no. 4.

———. 2021. "Revisiting Korean Slums in Postwar Japan: Tongne and Hakkyo in the Zainichi Memoryscape." *Journal of Asian Studies* 80, no. 3: 587–610.

Chikuzen machi. 2009. *Chikuzen chōritsu Tachiarai Heiwa Kinenkan: Jōsetsu tenji annai*. Chikuzen machi.

Cho Geon. 2011. "Chŏnsich'ejegi chosŏn chudun ilbon'gunŭi panggongjojikkwa hwaldong" *Sungsil sahak* 27: 81–116.

Ch'oe Hae Gun. 1997. *Pusan chiljŏnnyŏn kŭ yŏngyogŭi paljach'wi 3 haebangbuttŏ hyŏndaekkaji*. Pusanŭl kakkunŭn moim.

Choi, Hye Eun. 2010. "Untold Narratives and Inchoate Histories: Remembering the Pusan and Masan Uprising of 1979." MA thesis, University of Texas, Austin.

Choi Youngho. 2017. "1957 nyŏn hanil ŏngnyuja sanghosŏkpang kaksŏŭi kyŏngwiwa kyŏlgwa." In *Hanil minjok munje yŏn'gu* 32: 151–86.

Choi Youngho, Pak Jin-woo, Ryu Kyo-yŏl, and Hong Yŏn-jin. 2007. *Pugwan yŏllaksŏn'gwa pusan: singminjidosi pusan'gwa minjogidong*. Nonhyŏng.

Chokin kyoku, ed. 1935. "Kaigai zairyū honpōjin sōkin kaku fuken betsu hikaku." In *Sekai chizu*. Chokin kyoku.

Chōsen sōtokufu. 1933. *Chōsen kokusei chōsa hōkoku, Shōwa 5 nen, dōhen dai 7 kan: Keishō nandō*. Chōsen sōtokufu.

———. 1935. *Shisei nijūgonen shi*. Chōsen sōtokufu.

———. 1937. *Pusan chikkō no ryakushi*. Chōsen sōtokufu.

Chōsen sōtokufu doboku kyoku. 1913. *Pusan sakuhei kōji hōkoku*. N.p.

Chōsen sōtokufu teishin kyoku, ed. 1932. *Chōsen sōtokufu teishin nenpō: Shōwa 6 nen do*. Chōsen sōtokufu teishin kyoku.

Chōsen sōtokufu tetsudō kyoku, ed. 1936. *Hantō no kin'ei*. Ōsaka: Nihon hanga insatsu.

Chōsen tōkanfu, ed. 1908. *Tōkanfu tōkei nenpō daiichiji*. Tōkan kanbō bunshoka.

Clancy-Smith, Julia. 2010. *Mediterraneans: North Africa and Europe in an Age of Migration, c. 1800–1900*. University of California Press.

Cobbing, Andrew. 2009. *Kyushu. Gateway to Japan: A Concise History*. Global Oriental.

———. 2013. "The Hakata Merchant's World: Cultural Networks in a Centre of Maritime Trade." In *Hakata: The Cultural Worlds of Northern Kyushu*, ed. Andrew Cobbing. Brill.

Cohn, Bernard. 1996. *Colonialism and Its Forms of Knowledge: The British in India*. Princeton University Press.

Colegrove, Kenneth. 1941. "The New Order in East Asia." *Far Eastern Quarterly* 1, no. 1 (November): 5–24.

Cooper, Frederick, and Ann Laura Stoler, eds. 1997. *Tensions of Empire: Colonial Cultures in a Bourgeois World*. University of California Press.

———. 2005. *Colonialism in Question: Theory, Knowledge, History*. University of California Press.

Craven, Wesley Frank, and James Lea Cate, eds. 1953. *The Army Air Forces in World War II. Volume V, The Pacific: Matterhorn to Nagasaki, June 1944 to August 1945*. University of Chicago Press.

Cronon, William. 1991. *Nature's Metropolis: Chicago and the Great West*. Norton.

Cumings, Bruce. 1981. *The Origins of the Korean War: Liberation and the Emergence of Separate Regimes, 1945–1947*. Princeton University Press.

———. 2010. *The Korean War: A History*. Modern Library.

Cwiertka, Katarzyna. 2006. *Modern Japanese Cuisine: Food, Power, and National Identity*. London: Reaktion Books.

Dai Nippon Kōkū shashi kankōkai, ed. 1975. *Kōkū yusō no ayumi*. Nipponkōkū kyōkai.

Dawley, Evan. 2019. *Becoming Taiwanese: Ethnogenesis in a Colonial City, 1880s–1950s*. Harvard University Press.

De Matos, Christine, and Mark E. Caprio, eds. 2015. *Japan as the Occupier and Occupied*. Palgrave Macmillan.

Department of Railways. 1920. *An Official Guide to Eastern Asia Vol. 1: Chosen & Manchuria, Siberia*, 2nd ed. Tetsudōshō.

DiMoia, John. 2013. *Reconstructing Bodies: Biomedicine, Health, and Nation-Building in South Korea*. Stanford University Press.

Dirlik, Arif, et al. 1998. *What Is in a Rim? Critical Perspectives on the Pacific Region Idea*. Rowman & Littlefield.

Doi, Takashi. 1968. "Japan Megalopolis: Another Approach." *Ekistics* 26, no. 152.

Dong Sŏn–hŭi. 2011. *Singmin'gwŏllyŏkkwa chosŏnin chiyŏk yuryŏkcha*. Sŏn'in.

Donia, Robert. 2015. "The Proximate Colony: Bosnia-Herzegovina under Austro-Hungarian Rule." In *WechselWirkungen: Austria-Hungary, Bosnia-Herzegovina, and the Western Balkans, 1878–1918*, ed. Clemens Ruthner, Diana Reynolds-Cordileone, Ursula Reber, and Raymond Detrez. Peter Lang.

Dower, John. 1999. *Embracing Defeat: Japan in the Wake of World War Two*. W. W. Norton.

Driscoll, Mark. 2020. *The Whites Are Enemies of Heaven: Climate Caucasianism and Asian Ecological Protection*. Duke University Press.

Driver, Felix, and David Gilbert, eds. 1999. *Imperial Cities: Landscape, Display and Identity*. Manchester University Press.

Dudden, Alexis. 2017. "The Sea of Japan / Korea's East Sea." In *Oceanic Histories*, ed. David Armitage, Alison Bashford, and Sujit Sivasundaram. Cambridge University Press.

Dusinberre, Martin. 2008. "Unread Relics of a Transnational Hometown in Rural Western Japan." *Japan Forum* 20, no. 3: 305–35.

———. 2012. *Hard Times in the Hometown: A History of Community Survival in Modern Japan*. Hawai'i University Press.

Duus, Peter. 1995. *The Abacus and the Sword: The Japanese Penetration of Korea, 1895–1910*. University of California Press.

Duus, Peter, Ramon Myers, and Mark Peattie, eds. 1989. *The Japanese Informal Empire in China, 1895–1937*. Princeton University Press.

———. 1996. *The Japanese Wartime Empire, 1931–1945*. Princeton University Press.

Eckert, Carter J. 1991. *Offspring of Empire: The Koch'ang Kims and the Colonial Origins of Korean Capitalism, 1876–1945*. Seattle: University of Washington Press.

———. 1999. "Exorcising Hegel's Ghosts: Towards a Postnationalist Historiography of Korea." In *Colonial Modernity in Korea*, ed. Gi-Wook Shin and Michael Robinson. Harvard University Asia Center.

———. 2016. *Park Chung Hee and Modern Korea: The Roots of Militarism, 1866–1945*. The Belknap Press of Harvard University Press.

El Houssi, Leila. 2012. "Italians in Tunisia: Between Regional Organisation, Cultural Adaptation and Political Division, 1860s–1940." *European Review of History / Revue européenne d'histoire* 19, no. 1.

Elkins, Caroline, and Susan Pedersen, eds. 2005. *Settler Colonialism in the Twentieth Century: Projects, Practices, Legacies*. Routledge.

Eskildsen, Robert. 2002. "Of Civilization and Savages: The Mimetic Imperialism of Japan's 1874 Expedition to Taiwan." *American Historical Review* 107, no. 2 (April): 388–418.

Esselstrom, Erik. 2009. *Crossing Empire's Edge: Foreign Ministry Police and Japanese Expansionism in Northeast Asia.* University of Hawai'i Press.

Fedman, David. 2020. *Seeds of Control: Japan's Empire of Forestry in Colonial Korea.* University of Washington Press.

Ferrer, Ada. 2021. *Cuba: An American History.* Scribner.

Field, Norma. 1991. *In the Realm of a Dying Emperor.* Pantheon Books.

Fogel, Joshua A. 2013. *Japanese Historiography and the Gold Seal of 57 C.E: Relic, Text, Object, Fake.* Brill.

Fritzsche, Peter. 1992. *A Nation of Fliers: German Aviation and the Popular Imagination.* Harvard University Press.

Fujikane, Candace, and Jonathan Y. Okamura. 2008. *Asian Settler Colonialism: From Local Governance to the Habits of Everyday Life in Hawai'i.* University of Hawai'i Press.

Fujimoto Tsuyoshi. 1988. *Mō futatsu no Nihon bunka.* Tokyo Daigaku shuppankai.

Fujitani, Takashi. 1998. *Splendid Monarchy: Power and Pageantry in Modern Japan.* University of California Press.

———. 2011. *Race for Empire: Koreans as Japanese and Japanese as Americans during World War II.* University of California Press.

Fukuoka ajia toshi kenkyūjo. 2009. *Fukuokashi ni okeru ajia seisaku no kako, genzai, mirai* 1. Fukuoka ajia toshi kenkyūjo.

Fukuoka Asian Art Museum, ed. 2015. *Nikkan kindai bijutsuka no manazashi: "Chōsen" de kaku.* Fukuoka Asian Art Museum.

Fukuoka chihō shokugyō shōkai jimukyoku. 1927. *Kannai nakashi rōdō jijō.* Fukuoka chihō shokugyō shōkai jimukyoku.

———. 1929. *Kannai zaijū chōsenjin no rōdō jijō.* Fukuoka chihō shokugyō shōkai jimukyoku.

Fukuoka ken. 1888. *Fukuoka ken tōkeisho meiji nijūnen.* Fukuoka ken.

———. 1936. *Fukuoka hikōjō kōji gaiyō.* Fukuoka ken.

———. 2011. *Shōbō nenpō Heisei 23 nen.* Fukuoka ken.

Fukuoka ken jūtaku kensetsu hokushin kyōgi kai. 1959. *Fukuoka ken jūtaku fukkō shi.* Fukuoka ken jūtaku kensetsu hokushin kyōgi kai.

Fukuoka ken keisatsu shi hensaniinkai, eds. 1980. *Fukuoka ken keisatsushi: Shōwa zenhen.* Fukuoka ken keisatsu honbu.

Fukuoka kenritsu yanagawa kōtō jogakkō dōsōkai. 1925a. *Yanagi no kage* 16. Fukuoka kenritsu yanagawa kōtō jogakkō dōsōkai.

———. 1925b. *Yanagi no kage: kaikō nijūgonen gō* 17. Fukuoka kenritsu yanagawa kōtō jogakkō dōsōkai.

———. 1926. *Yanagi no kage* 18. Fukuoka kenritsu yanagawa kōtō jogakkō dōsōkai.

———. 1927. *Yanagi no kage* 19. Fukuoka kenritsu yanagawa kōtō jogakkō dōsōkai.

Fukuoka ken shakai fukushi kyōgikai, ed. 1982. *Fukuokaken shakai fukushi jigyō shi* (jō kan). Fukuoka ken shakai fukushi kyōgikai.

Fukuoka shi. 1948. *Fukuoka shisei yōran, Shōwa 22 nen ban (sai kan dai ichi gō).* Fukuoka shi.

———. 1959. *Fukuoka shi shi: Meiji hen.* Fukuoka shi.

———. 1963. *Fukuoka shi shi: Taishō hen*. Fukuoka shi.

———. 1965. *Fukuoka shi shi: Shōwa zen hen (jō)*. Fukuoka shi.

———. 1966. *Fukuoka shi shi: Shōwa zen hen (ka)*. Fukuoka shi.

———. 1978. *Fukuoka shi shi: Shōwa hen kōhen (4)*. Fukuoka shi.

———. 2014. *Sentoraru Park kōsō*. Fukuoka shi.

———. 2019. *Sentoraru Park kihon keikaku (an) honpen*. Fukuoka shi.

Fukuoka shi gikai. 1971. *Fukuoka-shi gikaishi dai ikkan: meiji hen*. Fukuoka shi gikai.

Fukuoka shi hakubutsukan, ed. 2015. *Shūzōhin mokuroku 30: Heisei 24 nendo shūshū*. Fukuoka shi hakubutsukan.

Fukuoka shi kōwan kyoku. 1970. *Hakatakō no ayumi*. Fukuoka shi yakusho.

———. 2000. *Hakatakō shi: kaikō hyaku shū nen kinen*. Fukuoka shi kōwan kyoku.

Fukuoka shi sanjokai. 1910. *Fukuoka shi annai*. Fukuoka shi sanjokai.

Fukuoka shi shi henshū iinkai, eds. 2015. *Shin shū Fukuoka shi shi shiryō hen kingendai 2*. Fukuoka shi.

Fukuoka shi sōmuka. 1912. *Fukuoka shisei ippan*. Fukuoka shi sōmuka.

Fukuoka shiyakusho sangyō ka, ed. 1938a. *Hakatakō to Iki, Tsushima narabi ni Misumikō, Kagoshimakō*. Fukuoka shiyakusho sangyō ka

———. 1938b. *Hakatakō yushutsuhin no gaikyō*. Fukuoka shiyakusho sangyō ka.

———. 1939a. *Hakatakō to hokushi narabi ni Manshūkoku kinshu nekka ryōshō*. Fukuoka shiyakusho sangyō ka.

———. 1939b. *Haku-rei kōro kaisetsu ni tsuki*. Fukuoka shiyakusho sangyō ka.

———. 1940. *Hakatakō to Taiwan*. Fukuoka shiyakusho sangyō ka.

Fukuoka shiyakusho shōkō ka, ed. 1941a. *Hakatakō to Chūshi narabi ni Ōita, Miyazaki ryō ken*. Fukuoka shiyakusho shōkō ka.

———. 1941b. *Ren'unkō kaikō to Hakatakō*. Fukuoka shiyakusho shōkō ka.

———. 1942. *Kanmon kaikyō tetsudō suidō kaitsū to Hakata*. Fukuoka shiyakusho shōkō ka.

———. 1943a. *Hakatakō to sōko*. Fukuoka shiyakusho shōkō ka.

———. 1943b. *Hakatakō to Tōbu Manshū*. Fukuoka shiyakusho shōkō ka.

———. 1944. *Hakatakō*. Fukuoka shiyakusho shōkō ka.

Fukuyama Kanpō. 1936. *Waga kokubō no genjō to kyōdo bōei*. Fukuoka ken kokubōkai.

Furukawa Tatsuō. 1988. *Tetsudō renrakusen hyakunen no kōseki*. Seizandō shoten.

Galindez, Kyle. 2023. "Planetary Urbanization and Imperialism: A View from Guåhan/Guam." *International Journal of Urban and Regional Research* 47, no. 1: 5–21.

Gallagher, John, and Ronald Robinson. 1953. "The Imperialism of Free Trade." *Economic History Review* 6, no. 1: 1–15.

Gallicchio, Marc S. 2000. *The African American Encounter with Japan and China: Black Internationalism in Asia, 1895–1945*. University of North Carolina Press.

Gane, William J. 1946. "Repatriation from 25 September 1945 to 31 December 1945." United States Army Military Government in Korea.

Gayn, Mark. 1981. *Japan Diary*. Tuttle.

General Headquarters Supreme Commander for the Allied Powers. 1945. "Summation No. 1: Non-Military Activities in Japan and Korea for the Months of September–October 1945." War Department.

Gen'yōsha shashi hensankai. 1966. *Gen'yōsha shashi*. Meiji bunken.

George, Timothy S. 2001. *Minamata: Pollution and the Struggle for Democracy in Postwar Japan*. Harvard University Press.

Giglioli, Ilaria. 2017. "Producing Sicily as Europe: Migration, Colonialism and the Making of the Mediterranean Border between Italy and Tunisia." *Geopolitics* 22, no. 2.

Gluck, Carol. 1985. *Japan's Modern Myths: Ideology in the Late Meiji Period*. Princeton University Press.

Go, Julian. 2011. *Patterns of Empire: The British and American Empires, 1688 to the Present*. Cambridge University Press.

Goodman, Bryna. 1995. *Native Place, City, and Nation: Regional Networks and Identities in Shanghai, 1853–1937*. University of California Press.

Gordon, Andrew. 1985. *The Evolution of Labor Relations in Japan: Heavy Industry, 1853–1955*. Harvard University Press.

———. 1998. "Taking Japanese Studies Seriously." In *The Postwar Development of Japanese Studies in the United States*, ed. Helen Hardacre. Brill.

Goswami, Manu. 2012. "Imaginary Futures and Colonial Internationalisms." *American Historical Review* 117, no. 5 (December): 1461–85.

Gragert, Edwin H. 1994. *Landownership under Colonial Rule: Korea's Japanese Experience, 1900–1935*. University of Hawai'i Press.

Greenberg, Amy S. 2022. "Cuba and the Failure of Manifest Destiny." *Journal of the Early Republic* 42, no. 1.

Grunow, Tristan. 2020. "Cultivating Settler Colonial Space in Korea: Public Works and the Urban Environment under Japanese Rule." *International Journal of Korean History* 25, no. 1: 85–119.

———. 2022. "Pebbles of Progress: Streets and Urban Modernity in Early Meiji Tokyo." *Japan Forum* 34, no. 1: 53–78.

Hakata hikiage engo kyoku. 2002 [1947]. *Kyokushi*. Reproduced in *Kaigai hikiage kankei shiryō shūsei: kokunai-hen* 9. Yumani shobō.

Han, Eric C. 2014. *Rise of a Japanese Chinatown: Yokohama, 1894–1972*. Harvard University Asia Center.

Han, Suk-Jung. 2024. *The Origin of the 1960s Korean Developmental Regime: Manchurian Modern*. Lexington Books.

Hanafusa Toshio and Hanafusa Emiko. 2021. *Kampu saiban ga mezashita mono: kankoku no obaasan tachi ni yorisotte*. Hakutakusha.

Hanes, Jeffrey. 1993. "From Megalopolis to Megaroporisu." *Journal of Urban History* 19, no. 2.

———. 2002. *The City as Subject: Seki Hajime and the Reinvention of Modern Osaka*. University of California Press.

Harada Katsumasa. 1966. "Gen'yōsha shashi kaisetsu." In *Gen'yōsha shashi*. Meiji bunken.

Harootunian, Harry D. 2000. *History's Disquiet: Modernity, Cultural Practice, and the Question of Everyday Life*. Columbia University Press.

Harvey, David. 1985. *The Urbanization of Capital: Studies in the History and Theory of Capitalist Urbanization*. Johns Hopkins University Press.

Hashiya Hiroshi. 2004. *Teikoku Nihon no shokuminchi toshi*. Yoshikawa kōbunkan.

———. 2005. "Pusan, Jinsen no keisei." In *Kindai Nihon to shokuminchi*, vol. 3, *Shokumichika to sangyōka*, ed. Ōe Shinobu et al., 243–62. Iwanami shoten.

Hatayama Shiomi. 1943. "Dai tōa kyōeiken zenshin kyoten taru Fukuoka shi." *Toshi Kōron* 26, no. 1 (January): 75–78.

Hattori Hideo and Honda Kana. 2006. "Jōnai jūtaku shi sono 1: sōron to zenshi." *Hikaku shakai bunka gaku* 12.

Hayashi Eidai. 1981. *Kyōsei renkō, kyōsei rōdō: Chikuhō chōsenjin kōfu no kiroku*. Tokuma shoten.

———. 1983. *Kaikyō no onnatachi: Kanmonkō okinakashi no shakaishi*. Ashi shobō.

Hayashi Reiko. 2021. "Senzen no zaigai hōjinsū tōkei." *Jinkō mondai kenkyū* 77, no. 3.

Hayashi Yoshinaga. 2006. "Chōsen sensō to Nihon: Nikkan kankeishi no shiten kara." *Senshi kenkyū nenpō* 9.

Hedinger, Daniel. 2017. "The Spectacle of Global Fascism: The Italian Blackshirt Mission to Japan's Asian Empire." *Modern Asian Studies* 51, no. 6: 1999–2034.

Heerten, Lasse. 2021. "Mooring Mobilities, Fixing Flows: Towards a Global Urban History of Port Cities in the Age of Steam." *Journal of Historical Sociology* 34, no. 2.

Hein, Laura, ed. 2023. *The New Cambridge History of Japan: Volume 3, The Modern Japanese Nation and Empire, c. 1868 to the Twenty-First Century*. Cambridge University Press.

Hellyer, Robert. 2009. *Defining Engagement: Japan and Global Contexts, 1640–1868*. Harvard University Press.

Henry, Todd A. 2014. *Assimilating Seoul: Japanese Rule and the Politics of Public Space in Colonial Korea, 1910–1945*. University of California Press.

Hibino Toshinobu. 2009. "Nisshin nichiro senkanki no Yasukawa Keiichiro." In *Kindai Nihon no kigyōka to seiji: Yasukawa Keiichirō to sono jidai*, ed. Arima Manabu, 12–39. Yoshikawa Kōbunkan.

Higuchi Yūichi. 1986. *Kyōwakai: Senjika chōsenjin tōsei sōshiki no kenkyū*. Shakai hyōron sha.

Hikiage engo chō, ed. 1950. *Hikiage engo no kiroku*. Hikiage engo chō.

Hikiagekō Hakata o kangaeru tsudoi, ed. 2017. *Are kara nanajū nen: Hakatakō hikiage wo kangaeru*. Tosho shuppan nobu kōbō.

Hirose Teizō. 2018. "Chōsen sōtokufu nihonjin doboku kanryō no shakai kōji ninshiki." *Fukuoka daigaku jinbun ronsō* 50.

Hoffnung-Garskof, Jesse. 2010. *A Tale of Two Cities: Santo Domingo and New York after 1950*. Princeton University Press.

Hom, Stephanie Malia. 2019. *Empire's Mobius Strip: Historical Echoes in Italy's Crisis of Migration and Detention*. Cornell University Press.

Homei, Aya. 2020. *Science for Governing Japan's Population*. Cambridge University Press.

Hong Sun-kwŏn. 2008a. "1910–1920 nendai Pusan fu kyōgikai no kōsei to chihō seiji" (1). *Seisakukagaku* 16, no. 1 (October): 103–11.

———, ed. 2008b. *Pusan ui tosi hyŏngsŏng kwa ilbonindŭl*. Sŏn'in.

———. 2009. "1910–1920 nendai Pusan fu kyōgikai no kōsei to chihō seiji" (2). *Seisakukagaku* 16, no. 2 (February): 145–56.

———, ed. 2010. *Kŭndaedosiwa chibanggwŏllyŏk: hanmal ilcheha pusanŭi tosi paljŏn'gwa chibangseryŏgŭi hyŏngsŏng*. Sŏn'in.

Howell, David L. 1995. *Capitalism from Within: Economy, Society and the State in a Japanese Fishery*. University of California Press.

Hsu, Madeline Y. 2000. "Migration and Native Place: Qiaokan and the Imagined Community of Taishan County, Guangdong, 1893–1993." *Journal of Asian Studies* 59, no. 2.

Hudson, Kenneth, and Julian Pettifer. 1979. *Diamonds in the Sky: A Social History of Air Travel*. Bodley Head.

Huebner, Stefan, Nadin Hée, Ian J. Miller, and William Tsutsui, eds. 2024. *Oceanic Japan: The Archipelago in Pacific and Global History*. University of Hawai'i Press.

Huffman, James. 1997. *Creating a Public: People and Press in Meiji Japan*. University of Hawai'i Press.

———. 2018. *Down and Out in Late Meiji Japan*. University of Hawai'i Press.

Hunter, Janet. 1977. "Japanese Government Policy, Business Opinion and the Seoul—Pusan Railway, 1894–1906." *Modern Asian Studies* 11, no. 4: 573–99.

Hwang, Kyung Moon. 2015. *Rationalizing Korea: The Rise of the Modern State, 1894–1945*. University of California Press.

Hyun, Mooam. 2020. "Japanese Women in Korea in the Postwar: Between Repatriation and Returning Home." In *New Frontiers in Japanese Studies*, ed. Akihiro Ogawa and Philip Seaton. Routledge.

Iacobelli, Pedro. 2017. *Postwar Emigration to South America from Japan and the Ryukyu Islands*. Bloomsbury.

Ichimata Masao. 1975. *Sugiyama Shigemaru: Meiji tairiku seisaku no genryū*. Hara shobō.

Iechika Ryōko. 2012. *Shō Kaiseki no Gaikō Senryaku to Nitchū Sensō*. Iwanami shoten.

Igarashi, Yoshikuni. 2000. *Bodies of Memory: Narratives of War in Postwar Japanese Culture, 1945–1970*. Princeton University Press.

Imanishi Hajime and Nakatani Mitsuo. 2008. *Mentaiko Kaihatsushi: sono rūtsū o saguru*. Seizandō shoten.

Immerwahr, Daniel. 2019. *How to Hide an Empire: A History of the Greater United States*. Random House.

"Imperial Japanese Rescript Attached to the Proclamation and Treaty of Annexation." 1910. *American Journal of International Law* 4, no. 4 (October), Supplement: Official Documents, 283–84.

Imsisudoginyŏmgwan. 2012. *Imsisudoginyŏmgwan: chŏnsigwan kaegwan kinyŏmdorok*. Imsisudoginyŏmgwan.

———. 2014. *Uamdong: saramdŭrŭi konggan'gwa sam*. Imsisudoginyŏmgwan.

Inayoshi Akira. 2014. *Kaikō no seijishi: Meiji kara sengo e*. Nagoya daigaku shuppankai.

Inomata Kōzō, ed. 1953. *Kichi nihon*. Wakōsha.

Inoue Kiyomaro. 1931. *Pusan wo katsugu mono*. Kanmon hōchi shinbunsha.

Irie Masanori, ed. 1902. *Fukuoka ken annai*. Shūbunkan.

Ishikawa Hideaki. 1941. *Nihon kokudo keikaku ron*. Hachigensha.

——. 1943. *Daitō-a kokudo keikaku*. Dōmei tsūshinsha.

Ishimaru Yasuzō. 2013. "Chōsen sensō to Nihon no kōwan." *NIDS Senshi tokushū*, 53–67.

Ishitaki Toyomi. 1997. *Gen'yōsha hakkutsu: mō hitotsu no jiyū minken*. Nishi Nippon shinbunsha.

Itagaki Ryūta. 2008. *Chōsen kindai no rekishi minzokushi: Kyonbuku Sanju no sho-kuminchi keiken*. Akashi shoten.

Izuhara machi shi hensan iinkai. 1997. *Izuhara machi shi*. Izuhara machi.

Izumi Kaoru. 1993. "Haisen go no Hakatakō ni okeru Chōsenjin kikoku ni tsuite." *Hōsei kenkyū* 60, no. 1: 71–101.

Jansen, Marius. 1954. "Yawata, Hanyehping, and the Twenty-One Demands." *Pacific Historical Review*, 23, no. 1.

Jin, Michael R. 2021. *Citizens, Immigrants, and the Stateless: A Japanese American Diaspora in the Pacific*. Stanford University Press.

Jōhōji Asami. 1981. *Nihon bōkūshi: gun, kanchō, toshi, kōkyō kigyō, kojō, minbōkū no zenbō to kūshū higai*. Hara Shobō.

Kajimura Hideki. 1993. "Zainichi Chōsenjin ron." In *Kajimura Hideki chosakushū* 6. Akashi shoten.

Kamisaki Fuyuko. 1982. *Keishū Nazare'en*. Chuokōronsha.

Kamitsubo Takashi. 1979. *Mizuko no uta: hikiage koji to okasareta onnatachi no kiroku*. Gendai shi shuppankai.

Kamiya Niji. 2018. *Kindai nihon gyomin no Chōsen shutsuryō: Chōsen nanbu no gyogyō konkyochi Changsŭngpo, Narodo, Bangōjin wo chūshin ni*. Shinkansha.

Kan Hideki. 1982. "Fukuoka ken kara no Hawai, hokubei imin no shakai / keizaishiteki kōsatsu: Meiji shoki ~ Taishō jūsan nen." *Kitakyūshū Daigaku Gaikokugo gakubu kiyō* 47 (September): 95–163.

Kang Chang-il. 2022. *Kindai Nihon no Chōsen shinryaku to dai Ajia shugi: uyoku rōnin no kōdō to shisō*. Akashi shoten.

Kang Hyeok Hweon. 2024. "Kingpins at Court: Contraband Diplomacy between Korea, Japan, and Tsushima, 1607–71." *Journal of Asian Studies* 83, no. 1: 116–39.

Kang, Sungwoo. 2012. "Colonizing the Port City Pusan in Korea: A Study of the Process of Japanese Domination in the Urban Space of Pusan during the Open-Port Period 1876–1910." PhD diss., Oxford University.

——. 2021. "'Same Bed, Different Dreams': The Dynamics of Competition and Cooperation in Constructing the Seoul–Pusan Railway." *Acta Koreana* 24, no. 2: 93–121.

Kankoku teishintai mondai taisaku kyōgikai, eds. 1993. *Shōgen: Kyōseirenkō sareta Chōsenjin gunianfutachi*. Akashi shoten.

Karacas, Cary, and David Fedman. 2012. "A Cartographic Fade to Black: Mapping the Destruction of Urban Japan during World War II." *Journal of Historical Geography* 38: 306–28.

Karuka, Manu. 2019. *Empire's Tracks: Indigenous Nations, Chinese Workers, and the Transcontinental Railroad*. University of California Press.

Katō Tetsuya. 2019. "Ningen kikō: Nakamura Seishichirō" (jō, ge) *Zaikai Kyūshū* vol. 1142, 1143.

Kawahara Takeshi. 2013. *Mentaiko o tsukutta otoko: Fukuya sōgyōsha Kawahara Toshio no jinsei to keiei*. Kaichōsha.

Kawakami Yukio. 2008. *Kokudo keikaku no hensen: Koritsu to kohei no keikaku shiso*. Kajima shuppankai.

Kawashima, Ken. 2009. *The Proletarian Gamble: Korean Workers in Interwar Japan*. Duke University Press.

Kawashima Yoshishige, ed. 1934. *Shin Pusan taikan*. Pusan shuppan kyōkai.

Kawazoe Shōji et al. 1997. *Fukuoka ken no rekishi*. Kōbunkan.

Keijō-fu, ed. 1937. "Zenkoku toshi mondai kaigi sōkai narabi naichi toshi gyōsei shisatsu hōkokusho." Keijō iho dai 190 gō furoku.

Keijō teikoku daigaku eisei chōsabu. 1942. *Domakumin no seikatsu, eisei*. Iwanami shoten.

Keijō toshi keikaku kenkyū kai, ed. 1936. *Chōsen toshi mondai kaigi kaigi roku: Shōwa 11 nen*. Keijō toshi keikaku kenkyū kai.

Keishō nandō keisatsubu. 1928. *Naichi dekasegi senjin rōdōsha jōtai chōsa*. Keishō nandō keisatsubu.

Kim Chang-t'ae. 1939. *Fusan no konjaku*. Kyōdō insatsu gōshi kaisha.

Kim Dae Oh and Choi Mack Joong. 2016. "Han'gugŭi ap'at'ŭ konggŭpkwa suyoŭi yŏksajŏk yŏnwŏne kwanhan yŏn'gu: haebang ihu chut'aegŭi sujikchŏk chipchŏkhwa kwajŏngŭl chungsimŭro." *Journal of Korea Planning Association* 51, no. 6: 23–38.

Kim Dae-Rae and Chŏng I-gŭn, eds. 2010. *Han'guk chŏnjaeng kwa Pusan kyŏngje: Kyŏngbu sŏngjangch'uk ŭi kanghwa*. Haenam.

Kim Dae-Rae, Kim Ho-Beom, Jang Ji-Yong, and Jeong Ee-Kyen. 2005. "Ilche gangjŏmgi Pusan jiyŏk in'gu t'onggyeŭi chŏngbiwa punsŏk." *Hanguk minjok munhwa* 26: 289–319.

Kim, Hoi-Eun. 2019. "Adulterated Intermediaries: Peddlers, Pharmacists, and the Patent Medicine Industry in Colonial Korea (1910–1945)." *Enterprise & Society* 20, no. 4: 939–77.

Kim, Hwansoo. 2010. "'The Future of Korean Buddhism Lies in My Hands': Takeda Hanshi as a Sōtō Missionary." *Japanese Journal of Religious Studies* 37, no. 1.

Kim Hyun Suk, Hwang Kap-Jin, and Im Ho. 2012. "Anak'isŭt'ŭ chiyŏgyŏn'guŭi chŏn'gaewa kwaje: Pusanhagesŏ tongasiagongdongch'eronkkaji." *Sahoewa iron* 21, no. 2.

Kim, Jae Kyun. 2015. "Yellow over Black: History of Race in Korea and the New Study of Race and Empire." *Critical Sociology* 41, no. 2.

Kim, Janice. 2009. *To Live to Work: Factory Women in Colonial Korea, 1910–1945*. Stanford University Press.

———. 2017. "Pusan at War: Refuge, Relief, and Resettlement in the Temporary Capital, 1950–1953." *Journal of American-East Asian Relations* 24, no.2/3.

Kim Jeong-Ran. 2010. "Shokuminchiki ni okeru Pusan no 'raibyō' ni taisuru seisaku." *Chōsenshi kenkyūkai ronbunshū* 48.

Kim Kwang Ryŏl. 2004. *Ashi de mita Chikuhō: Chōsenjin tankō rōdō no kiroku.* Akashi shoten.

Kim Kyŏng-nam. 2011. "Senji taisei ki ni okeru kindai toshi Pusan kaihatsu no shokuminchiteki tokusei." *Keiei keizai ronshū* 18, no. 1: 75–109.

———. 2015a. *Ilcheŭi singmindosigŏnsŏlgwa chabon'ga.* Sŏn'in.

———. 2015b. "Kyōkai chiiki ni okeru rokaritei kōryū kūkan no keisei to henkei: Tsushima to Pusan wo chūshin ni." *Ōhara shakai mondai kenkyūjo zasshi* 679 (May): 2–20.

Kim, Kyu Hyun. 2004. "Reflections on the Problems of Colonial Modernity and 'Collaboration' in Modern Korean History." *Journal of International and Area Studies* 11, no. 3: 95–111.

Kim, Michael. 2016. "Re-Conceptualizing the Boundaries of Empire: The Imperial Politics of Chinese Labor Migration to Manchuria and Colonial Korea." *Sungkyun Journal of East Asian Studies* 16.

Kim, Su Yun. 2020. *Imperial Romance: Fictions of Colonial Intimacy in Korea, 1905–1945.* Cornell University Press.

Kim Tae Hyŏn. 2011. "Chōsen ni okeru zairyū nihonjin shakai to nihonjin keiei shinbun." PhD diss., Kōbe University.

———. 2017. "Shokuminchi Chōsen no Nihonjin shinbun 'Pusan nippō' to shokuminchi toshi 'Pusan.'" *Global-Local Studies* 10.

Kim Yŏng Hŭi. 2015. "Shokuminchi jiki Chōsen ni okeru rajio hōsō no shutsugen to chōshusha." In *Sensō Rajio Kioku (zōho kaitei),* ed. Kishi Toshihiko, Kawashima Shin, and Son An Suk. Bensei shuppan.

Kimura Hideaki. 1999. *Beigun ga utsushita shūsen chokugo no Fukuoka ken.* Hikiagekō Hakata o kangaeru tsudoi.

Kimura Kenji. 1989. *Zaichō nihonjin no shakaishi.* Miraisha.

———. 2016. "'Zadankai: Fukuoka ken shita zaijū chōsenjin no dōkō ni tsuite' ni miru Chōsenjin kan." *Shimonoseki shiritsu daigaku chiiki kyōzō sentā nenpō* 9, 43–56.

———. 2017. *Senkyūhyakusanjūkyūnen no zainichi Chōsenjinkan.* Yumani shobō.

King, Anthony. 1990. *Urbanism, Colonialism, and the World-Economy.* Routledge.

Ko T'ae-woo. 2012. "1930 nyŏndae chosŏnch'ongdokpuŭi kungmin'gujet'omoksaŏpkwa chiyŏkkaebal." *Yŏksa wa hyŏnsil* 86.

Ko U-I. 2014. *Zainichi Korian no sengoshi: Kōbe no yamiichi wo kakenuketa Mun Dongon no mihatenu yume.* Akashi shoten.

Koga, Yukiko. 2016. *Inheritance of Loss: China, Japan and the Political Economy of Redemption After Empire.* University of Chicago Press.

Koikari, Mire. 2015. *Cold War Encounters in US-Occupied Okinawa.* Cambridge University Press.

Kōrai hakubutsukan Chōsen joseishi kenkyūkai, eds. 2021. *Chōsen ryōriten sangyō ianjo to Chōsen no joseitachi.* Shakai hyōronsha.

Kuroishi, Izumi, ed. 2014. *Constructing the Colonized Land: Entwined Perspectives of East Asia around WWII*. Ashgate.

Kratoska, Paul, ed. 2005. *Asian Labor in the Wartime Japanese Empire: Unknown Histories*. M. E. Sharpe.

Kuksa p'yŏnch'anwiwŏnhoe, ed. 1998. *Chuhanilbon'gongsagwan'girok*, vol. 26. Kuksa p'yŏnch'anwiwŏnhoe.

——, ed. 2014. *Chuhan migunsa / History of the United States Army Forces in Korea*, vol. 3. Sŏnin.

Kumabe Shimei. 1935. *Fukuhaku no jinbutsu*. Fukuoka shuppan kyōkai.

Kuzuu Yoshihisa. 1903. *Kankai tsūgyo shishin*. Kokuryūkai.

——. 1981. *Tō-A senkaku shishi kiden*. Hara shobo.

Kwak, Nancy. 2015. *A World of Homeowners: American Power and the Politics of Housing Aid*. University of Chicago Press.

Kweon, Sug-in. 2014. "Japanese Female Settlers in Colonial Korea: Between the 'Benefits' and 'Constraints' of Colonial Society." *Social Science Japan Journal* 17, no. 2: 169–88.

Kyūshū keizai chōsa kyōkai, ed. 1949. *Kyushū no shakai to keizai*. Kyūshū keizai chōsa kyōkai.

Kyūshū Yūsen. 2010. "Kaisha nenpyō" and "Kyūshū Yūsen kabushikigaisha no rekishi." N.p.

LaFeber, Walter. 1963. *The New Empire: An Interpretation of American Expansion, 1860–1898*. Cornell University Press.

Lee, Chong-Sik. 1980. "South Korea 1979: Confrontation, Assassination, and Transition." *Asian Survey* 20, no. 1.

Lee Chung Sup. 2017. "Ilche kangjŏmgi tosihwawa in'guidong: 1930 nyŏn puwa chijŏngmyŏn chiyŏgŭl chungsimŭro." *Taehanjirihakhoeji* 52, no. 1.

Lee, Helen J. S. 2008. "Writing Colonial Relations of Everyday Life in Senryū." *positions: east asia cultures critique* 16, no. 3: 601–28.

Lee, Misook. 2014. "The Japan-Korea Solidarity Movement in the 1970s and 1980s: From Solidarity to Reflexive Democracy." *Asia-Pacific Journal* 12, issue 38, no. 1 (September 22).

Lefebvre, Henri. 1991. *The Production of Space*, trans. Donald Nicholson Smith. Blackwell.

——. 2003. The Urban Revolution, trans. Robert Bononno. University of Minnesota Press.

Lester, Alan. 2002. "British Settler Discourse and the Circuits of Empire." *History Workshop Journal* 54, no. 1.

Lewis, James B. 2003. *Frontier Contact between Choson Korea and Tokugawa Japan*. Routledge Curzon.

——, ed. 2015. *The East Asian War 1592–1598: International Relations, Violence, and Memory*. Routledge.

Lewis, Michael. 2005. *Becoming Apart: National Power and Local Politics in Toyama: 1868–1945*. Harvard University Press.

Lim, Tai-Wei. 2017. *Energy Transitions in Japan and China: Mine Closures, Rail Developments, and Energy Narratives*. Springer Singapore.

Lu, Sidney Xu. 2016. "Colonizing Hokkaido and the Origin of Japanese Trans-Pacific Expansion, 1869–1894." *Japanese Studies* 36, no. 2: 251–74.

———. 2019. *The Making of Japanese Settler Colonialism*. Cambridge University Press.

Lynn, Hyung Gu. 2005. "Malthusian Dreams, Colonial Imaginary: The Oriental Development Company and Japanese Emigration to Korea." In *Settler Colonialism in the Twentieth Century: Projects, Practices, Legacies*, ed. Caroline Elkins and Susan Pedersen. Routledge.

MacIsaac, David. 1976. *Strategic Bombing in World War Two: The Story of the United States Strategic Bombing Survey*. Garland Publishing.

Maeda, Ai, and James A. Fujii. 2004. *Text and the City: Essays on Japanese Modernity*. Duke University Press.

Maeda, Tetsuo. 2009. "Strategic Bombing of Chongqing by Imperial Japanese Army and Naval Forces." In *Bombing Civilians: A Twentieth-Century History*, ed. Yuki Tanaka and Marilyn B. Young. New Press.

Marcon, Federico. 2015. *The Knowledge of Nature and the Nature of Knowledge*. University of Chicago Press.

Maruyama Hyōichi. 1980. "Pusan nihonjin sewakai no katsudō." In *Chōsen shūsen no kiroku: shiryōhen dai 2 kan—minami Chōsen chiiki no hikiage to nihonjin sewakai no katsudō*, ed. Morita Yoshio and Osada Kanako, 390–96. Gannando shoten.

Maske, Andrew L. 2011. *Potters and Patrons in Edo Period Japan: Takatori Ware and the Kuroda Domain*. Ashgate.

Massey, Doreen. 1994. *Space, Place, and Gender*. University of Minnesota Press.

Matsuda Hiroko. 2016. "Japanese 'New Imperial History' in Comparative Perspective: The Case of Okinawan and Taiwanese Migrations." *Journal of History for the Public* 13.

———. 2018. *Liminality of the Japanese Empire: Border Crossings from Okinawa to Colonial Taiwan*. University of Hawai'i Press.

Matsuda Toshihiko. 1995. *Senzenki no zainichi Chōsenjin to sanseiken*. Akashi shoten.

Matsumura, Wendy. 2020. Review: *In Search of Our Frontier: Japanese America and Settler Colonialism in the Construction of Japan's Borderless Empire*, by Eiichiro Azuma; *Liminality of the Japanese Empire: Border Crossings from Okinawa to Colonial Taiwan*, by Hiroko Matsuda; *The Making of Japanese Settler Colonialism: Malthusianism and Trans-Pacific Migration, 1868–1961*, by Sidney Xu Lu; *Unsustainable Empire: Alternative Histories of Hawai'i Statehood*, by Dean Itsuji Saranillio. *Pacific Historical Review* 89, no. 3.

McDonald, Kate. 2017. *Placing Empire: Travel and the Social Imagination in Imperial Japan*. University of California Press.

McKeown, Adam. 2001. *Chinese Migrant Networks and Cultural Change: Peru, Chicago, Hawaii 1900–1936*. University of Chicago Press.

Miki Imaji. 1933. "Naichi ni okeru Chōsenjin to sono hanzai ni tsuite." *Shihō kenkyū* 17 (March).

Miller, Ian Jared. 2013. *The Nature of the Beasts: Empire and Exhibition at the Tokyo Imperial Zoo*. University of California Press.

Mimura, Janis. 2011. *Planning for Empire: Reform Bureaucrats and the Japanese Wartime State*. Cornell University Press.

Miyano Hanafumi. 1931. "Genkainada mandan." *Umi* 28 (March): 32–33.

Mohandesi, Salar. 2018. "The Specificity of Imperialism." *Viewpoint Magazine*. https://viewpointmag.com/2018/02/01/the-specificity-of-imperialism/.

Molony, Kathleen, and Barbara Uno, eds. 2005. *Gendering Modern Japanese History*. Harvard University Asia Center.

Moon, Yumi. 2013. *Populist Collaborators: The Ilchinhoe and the Japanese Colonization of Korea, 1896–1910*. Cornell University Press.

Moore, Aaron S. 2013. *Constructing East Asia: Technology, Ideology, and Empire in Japan's Wartime Era, 1931–1945*. Stanford University Press.

Mori Motonao. 2020. *Kokudō sangōsen: teikō no minshūshi*. Kyōwakoku shuppan.

Mori Tomoya and Murakami Daisuke. 2024. "The Rise and Fall of Cities under Declining Population and Diminishing Distance Frictions: The Case of Japan." Research Institute of Economy, Trade and Industry (RIETI) Discussion Papers, no. 24028.

Morieux, Renaud. 2016. *The Channel: England, France and the Construction of a Maritime Border in the Eighteenth Century*. Cambridge University Press.

Morikawa Machiko. 2015. *Mun Okuchu : Biruma sensen tate shidan no "ianfu" datta watakushi*. Nashinokisha.

Morisaki Kazue. 1978. "Two Languages, Two Souls." *Bulletin of Concerned Asian Scholars* 10, no. 3.

Morita Yoshio and Osada Kanako, eds. 1980. *Chōsen shūsen no kiroku: shiryōhen dai 2 kan—minami chōsen chiiki no hikiage to nihonjin sewakai no katsudō*. Gannando shoten.

Morris-Suzuki, Tessa. 1998. "Debating Racial Science in Wartime Japan." *Osiris* 13.

———. 2007. *Exodus to North Korea: Shadows from Japan's Cold War*. Rowman & Littlefield.

———. 2010. *Borderline Japan: Foreigners and Frontier Controls in the Postwar Era*. Cambridge University Press.

———. 2012. "Post-War Warriors: Japanese Combatants in the Korean War." *Asia Pacific Journal: Japan Focus* 10, no. 31.

———, ed. 2018. *The Korean War in Asia: A Hidden History*. Rowman & Littlefield.

Mosk, Carl. 2001. *Japanese Industrial History: Technology, Urbanization, and Economic Growth*. M. E. Sharpe.

Moskowitz, Karl. 1974. "The Creation of the Oriental Development Company: Japanese Illusions Meet Korean Reality." *Occasional Papers on Korea* 2 (March 1974): 73–121.

Motooka Takuya. 2015. "Toshi no jiseiteki shūraku to shite no barakku gai." *Toshi o senkyo suru: yamiichi, barakku gai kara mita toshi kūkan no "sengo."* *Jinbunken bukkuretto v. 50*. Dōshisha University Humanities Research Centre.

Murai Shōsuke. 1988. *Ajia no naka no chūsei Nihon*. Azekura shobō.

Murakami Shihori. 2013. "Sannomiya higashi chiku 'Sannnomiya kokusai māketto' no keisei to henyō katei ni tsuite." *Nihon kenchiku gakkai keikakukei ronbunshū* 78, no. 693.

———. 2018. *Kōbe yamiichi kara no fukkō: Senryō-ka ni semegi au toshi kūkan*. Keio University Press.

Murase Tokio. 1961. *Hakata ni sen nen*. Ibunsha.

Myers, Ramon, and Mark Peattie, eds. 1984. *The Japanese Colonial Empire, 1895–1945*. Princeton University Press.

Nagao Yoshimi. 1991. "Wagakuni no umetate shi." *Tsuchi to Kiso* 39, no. 1.

Nagashima Hiroki. 2009. "Kō-A no jissen kyoten toshite no Pusankō to Genyōsha/Kokuryūkai." In *Kindai Nihon no kigyōka to seiji: Yasukawa Keiichirō to sono jidai*, ed. Arima Manabu. Yoshikawa Kōbunkan.

Nagashima Yoshirō. 1941. *Hakata shōkōkaigisho gojūnenshi*. Hakata shōkōkaigisho.

Nagata Mutsuharu, ed. 1935. *Pusan meishi roku shōwa jū nen*. Pusan meishi roku kankōkai.

Naha-shi kikaku bu henshū shitsu. 1981. *Naha-shi shi shiryō hen 3*, vol. 8. Naha-shi kikaku bu henshū shitsu.

Naikaku tōkei kyoku, ed. 1962 [1883]. *Dainihon teikoku tōkei nenkan dai 2 kai*. Tōkyō repurinto shuppansha.

Nakano, Yoichi. 2007. "Negotiating Modern Landscapes: The Politics of Infrastructure Development in Modern Japan." PhD diss., Harvard University.

Nam, Hwasook. 2021. *Women in the Sky: Gender and Labor in the Making of Modern Korea*. Cornell University Press.

Namigata Tsuyoshi. 2008. "*Shumi no Hakata, Fukuoka kenjin*, soshite *Fukuoka*." *Shishi kenkyū Fukuoka* 3 (February): 97–99.

Nihon kōku yusō kabushikigaisha. 1938a. *Kōkū eikaiwa*. Nihon kōkū yusō.

———, ed. 1938b. *Nihon kōkū yusō kabushikigaisha jūnenshi*. Nihon kōkū yusō.

Nihon kōtsū kyōkai, ed. 1929. *Sōritsu kinen kōtsū kōenshū dai ichi gō*. Nihon kōtsū kyōkai.

Nishihara Kazumi. 1975. *Yumeno Kyūsaku no sekai*. Hirakawa Shuppan.

Nishimura Kiichi. 1936. "Kokudo keikaku ni kan suru seido yōkō ni tsuite." *Toshi Kōron* 19, no. 8 (August): 8–24.

Nishi nihon bunka kyōkai, ed. 1984. *Fukuoka ken shi kindai shiryō hen (4) Tōyō taimusu 1*. Nishi nihon bunka kyōkai.

———, ed. 1996. *Fukuoka ken shi: kindai kenkyū hen kaku ron (2)*. Nishi nihon bunka kyōkai.

———, ed. 2000. *Fukuoka ken shi: tsūshi hen kindai (2) Sangyō keizai (1)*. Nishi nihon bunka kyōkai.

Nishi nihon inshokuryō shinbunsha, ed. 1936. *Gurabikku gurēto Fukuoka: Fukuoka kaisha shōten annai*. Nishi nihon inshokuryō shinbunsha.

Nishi Nippon shinbunsha, ed. 1978a. *Kaitei Fukuoka dai kūshū*. Nishi Nippon shinbunsha.

———, ed. 1978b. *Nishi Nippon shinbun hyakunenshi*. Nishi nippon shinbunsha.

Nishiyama Uzo. 2007. *Shōwa no Nihon no sumai*. Sōgensha.

Nishizaki, Sumiyo. 2016. "After Empire Comes Home: Economic Experiences of Japanese Repatriates, 1945–1956." PhD diss., London School of Economics.

Noguchi Uneme. 2007. *Taiheiyō sensō urabanashi: ichi heisotsu no jitsuroku to sono omoi*. Tōkyō tosho shuppankai.

Norman, E. Herbert. 1944. "The Gen'yōsha: A Study in the Origins of Japanese Imperialism." *Pacific Affairs* 17, no. 3: 261–84.

O'Dwyer, Emer. 2015. *Significant Soil: Settler Colonialism and Japan's Urban Empire in Manchuria*. Harvard University Asia Center.

Office of Population Research. 1943. "Population Redistribution and Urbanization in Japan." *Population Index* 9, no. 2 (April): 73–77.

Office of the Chief of Naval Operations. 1944. *Port of Fusan (Addenda No 1) OP-16-FE 64–44*. Office of the Chief of Naval Operations, Division of Naval Intelligence, Navy Department, December.

Oguma, Eiji. 2002. *A Genealogy of Japanese Self Images*. Translated by David Askew. Trans-Pacific Press.

Oguma Eiji and Kang Sang-jung. 2008. *Zainichi issei no kioku*. Shūeisha.

Oh, Mi-il. 2008. "The Spatial Arrangement and Residential Space of a Colonial City: The Spatio-Temporality of Hill Villages in Busan." *Korea Journal* 48, no. 3: 173–203.

Oh, Se-Mi. 2023. *City of Sediments: A History of Seoul in the Age of Colonialism*. Stanford University Press.

Ōkubo Yuri. 1996. "Senjika no Fukuoka ken Yame chihō ni okeru zainichi Chōsenjin." *Zainichi Chōsenjin shi kenkyū* 26.

Ŏm Ki Kwŏn and Lee Kyŏng Kyu. 2018. "Chŏnhu chibangŭi chaeiljosŏnin midiŏ yŏn'gu—segisinmun ŭl saryero." *Ilbonŏ munhak* 78.

Onishi, Yuichiro. 2013. *Transpacific Antiracism*. New York University Press.

Onjō Akio. 1995. "Kindai toshi kūkan ni kansuru chirigakuteki kenkyū." PhD diss., Kyushu University.

———. 2013. "Meijiki no chihō toshi ni okeru senkyo to chiiki shakai: Fukuokashi no chihō seiji jōtai ni kan suru oboegaki." *Shien* 150.

Onoda Shigeru. 2014. "Chōsen kaikyō tonneru keikaku to sono keii." *Doboku shi kenkyū kōenshū* 34: 199–207.

Otao Kōji. 1949. *Dai Fukuoka shi no kōsō ni tsuite*. Fukuoka shōkōkaigisho.

Pae Pyŏng-uk. 2019. "Kaehanggi kumamot'ogukkwŏndang ŭi 'chosŏnŏhaksaeng p'agyŏnsaŏp'." *Chiyŏkkwa Yŏksa* 44.

Pak Kyŏng-sik, ed. 1975. *Zainichi chōsenjin kankei shiryō shūsei v. 1*. San'ichi shobō.

———, ed. 1982. *Chōsen Mondai Shiryō sōsho v. 2: Senji kyōsei renkō, rōmu kanri seisaku*. Ajia mondai kenkyūjo.

Pak Sŏp and Jang Ji-Yong, eds. 2010. *Pusanŭi kiŏpkwa kiŏpkadanch'e*. Haenam.

Pak Yong-gu. 2010. "Pusanŭi chejoŏp: ch'unggyŏkkwa taeŭng." In *Han'guk chŏnjaeng kwa Pusan kyŏngje: Kyŏngbu sŏngjangch'uk ŭi kanghwa*, ed. Kim Dae-rae and Chŏng I-gŭn. Haenam.

Park Chŏl-gyu. 2008. "1914 nyŏn chŏnhusigi pusanjiyŏk yulyŏk ilbonin." In *Pusan ui tosi hyŏngsŏng kwa ilbonindŭl*, ed. Hong Sun-kwŏn. Sŏn'in.

Park, Soon-Won. 1999. *Colonial Industrialization and Labor in Korea: The Onoda Cement Factory*. Harvard University Asia Center.

Phipps, Catherine. 2015. *Empires on the Waterfront: Japan's Ports and Power, 1858–1899*. Harvard University Press.

Prideaux, Tom. 1945. "The B-29ers." *Impact: Air Victory over Japan* 3, no. 9: 53–58.

Pusan chikhalsi sa p'yŏnch'anwiwŏnhoe, ed. 1989. *Pusan si sa*. 4 vols. Pusan si.

Pusan fu. 1917. *Pusan fusei ippan*. Pusan fu.

———. 1927. *Pusan fu shakai shisetsu gaiyō*. Pusan fu.

———. 1928. *Pusan fu shokugyō shōkaijo jigyō yōran*. Pusan fu.

Pusan kŭndae yŏksagwan. 2004. *Kwanggo kŭrigo ilsang: kwanggo no ponŭn kŭndae ŭi sam kwa munhwa 1876–1945*. Pusan kŭndae yŏksagwan.

———. 2010. *Kŭndae kwan'gwangŭl sijakhada*. Minsogwŏn.

———. 2011. *Kŭndaeŭi kiŏk hakkyoe kada: 2011 pusan'gŭndaeyŏksagwan t'ŭkpyŏlgihoekchŏn*. Pusan kŭndae yŏksagwan.

———. 2013. *Paekhwajŏm, kŭndae ŭi pyŏlch'ŏnji*. Pusan kŭndae yŏksagwan.

———. 2015. *Kŭndaeŭi mogyokt'ang tongnaeonch'ŏn*. Pusan kŭndae yŏksagwan.

Pusan kyoryūmindan. 1912. *Pusan kyoryūmindan shokurinshi*. Pusan kyoryūmindan yakusho.

Pusan Nippō sha. 1926. *Pusan*. Pusan Nippō sha.

Pusan shōgyōkaigisho. 1912. *Pusan yōran*. Pusan shōgyōkaigisho.

Pusan shokugyō shōkaijo, ed. 1940a. *Kaki shokugyō jisshū sei kansō bunshū*. Pusan shokugyō shōkaijo.

———. 1940b. *Naichi e no hantō rōmusha kyōshutsu gaikyō*. Pusan shokugyō shōkaijo.

———. 1941. *Jikyoku to shokugyō fujin*. Pusan shokugyō shōkaijo.

Ramsey, Norman F. 1982. "August 1945: The B-29 Flight Logs." *Bulletin of the Atomic Scientists* 38, no. 10: 33–35.

Ravina, Mark. 2004. *The Last Samurai: The Life and Battles of Saigō Takamori*. John Wiley & Sons.

———. 2017. *To Stand with the Nations of the World: Japan's Meiji Restoration in World History*. Oxford University Press.

Robinson, Kenneth R. 2015. "Violence, Trade, and Imposters in Korean-Japanese Relations, 1510–1609." In *The East Asian War, 1592–1598: International Relations, Violence, and Memory*, ed. James B. Lewis. Routledge.

Ross, Robert, and Gerard J. Telkamp, eds. 1985. *Colonial Cities: Essays on Urbanism in a Colonial Context*. Leiden University Press.

Rozman, Gilbert. 1999. "Backdoor Japan: The Search for a Way Out via Regionalism and Decentralization." *Journal of Japanese Studies* 25.

Ruoff, Kenneth James. 2001. *The People's Emperor: Democracy and the Japanese Monarchy, 1945–1995*. Harvard University Asia Center.

———. 2010. *Imperial Japan at Its Zenith: The Wartime Celebration of the Empire's 2600th Anniversary*. Cornell University Press.

Ryang, Sonia. 1998. "Inscribed (Men's) Bodies, Silent (Women's) Words: Rethinking Colonial Displacement of Koreans in Japan." *Bulletin of Concerned Asian Scholar* 30, no. 4.

Ryu Kyo-yŏl. 2011. "Teikoku to shokuminchi no rōdō idō to kanri: Kampu renrakusen wo chūshin ni." *Kyūshū Kokusai Daigaku keiei keizai ronshū* 13, no. 1: 31–53.

Saaler, Sven, and Victor Koschmann, eds. 2007. *Pan-Asianism in Modern Japanese History: Colonialism, Regionalism and Borders.* Routledge.

Sabey, John Wayne. 1972. "The Gen'yōsha, the Kokuryūkai, and Japanese Expansionism." PhD diss., University of Michigan.

Saeki Kōji. 2013. "Muromachi jidai no Hakata shōnin sōkin to Kyoto, Kanyō, Pekin." In *Neiha to Hakata*, ed. Itō Kōji and Nakajima Gakushō. Kyūko shoin.

———, ed. 2014. *Chūsei no Tsushima: hito, mono, bunka no kakidasu Nicchō kōryūshi.* Bensei shuppan.

Sakamoto Toshihiko. 1972. *Shiryō hakatawan chikkō shi.* Hakatakō shinkō kyōkai.

Sakamoto Yūichi. 1998. "Fukuokaken ni okeru Chōsenjin imin shakai no seiritsu: senkanki no Kitakyūshū kōgyōchitai o chūshin toshite." *Seikyū gakujutsu ronshū* 13: 131–224.

———. 1999a. "Kyūshū zaijū Chōsenjin kankei shinbun kiji mokuroku sono ichi: Moji Shinpō 1917–1937." *Shakaibunka kenkyūsho kiyō* 43: 39–75.

———. 1999b. "Kyūshū zaijū Chōsenjin kankei shinbun kiji mokuroku sono ni: Fukuoka Nichi Nichi Shinbun (jō) 1917–1926." *Shakaibunka kenkyūsho kiyō* 44: 1–32.

———. 1999c. "Kyūshū zaijū Chōsenjin kankei shinbun kiji mokuroku sono san: Fukuoka Nichi Nichi Shinbun (ge) 1927–1939." *Shakaibunka kenkyūsho kiyō* 45: 1–38.

———. 2000. "Kyūshū zaijū Chōsenjin kankei shinbun kiji mokuroku sono yon: Kyūshū Nippō 1917–1939." *Shakaibunka kenkyūsho kiyō* 47: 75–106.

Sakamoto Yūichi and Kimura Kenji. 2007. *Kindai shokuminchi toshi Pusan.* Sakurai shoten.

Sakane Yoshihiro. 2021. *Hyōden: Chōsen sōtokufu kanri Yoshida Masahiro to sono jidai.* Seibundō shuppan.

Sand, Jordan. 2013. *Tokyo Vernacular: Common Spaces, Local Histories, Found Objects.* University of California Press.

———. 2014. "Imperial Tokyo as a Contact Zone: The Metropolitan Tours of Taiwanese Aborigines, 1897–1941." *Asia-Pacific Journal* 12, issue 10, no. 4.

Sankyū hyakunen no ayumi hensan iinkai, eds. 2019. *Sankyū hyakunen no ayumi.* Sankyū.

Santa-Cruz, Arturo. 2005. "Out of the Blue: The Pacific Rim as a Region." *Portal: Journal of Multidisciplinary International Studies* 2, no. 2: 1–18.

Sassa Hirō. 1977. "Kumamoto kokkentō to Chōsen ni okeru shinbun jigyō." *Kokushikan daigaku bungakubu jinbungakkai kiyō* 9: 21–38.

Sastre, Gregoire. 2016. "Le phénomène des agents d'influence Japonais en Asie 1880–1915." PhD diss., Université Sorbonne Paris Cité.

Scally, Robert James. 1995. *The End of Hidden Ireland: Rebellion, Famine, and Emigration*. Oxford University Press.

Schmid, Andre. 2000. "Colonialism and the 'Korea Problem' in the Historiography of Modern Japan: A Review Article." *Journal of Asian Studies* 59, no. 4: 951–76.

———. 2018. "Historicizing North Korea: State Socialism, Population Mobility, and Cold War Historiography." *American Historical Review* 123, no. 2: 1–24.

Segrè, Claudio G. 1974. *Fourth Shore: The Italian Colonization of Libya*. University of Chicago Press.

Sekai bunkasha. 1954. *Nihon taikan dai ichi gō*. Sekai bunka sha.

Senda Kakō. 1978. *Jūgun Ianfu, Seihen*. Sanichi Shobō.

Senkōkai, ed. 1986. *Chōsen kōtsū shi honpen*. Senkōkai.

Seo Il-soo. 2010. "1930 nyŏndae chŏnban kungmin'gujet'omoksaŏbŭi taedosi saryewa sŏnggyŏk: Kyŏngsŏng·Pusan·P'yŏngyangŭl chungsimŭro." Master's diss., Chungang University.

Seth, Michael J. 2020. *A Concise History of Modern Korea: From the Late Nineteenth Century to the Present*. Rowman & Littlefield.

Sewell, Bill. 2019. *Constructing Empire: The Japanese in Changchun, 1905–45*. UBC Press.

Shapinsky, Peter. 2016. "Envoys and Escorts: Representation and Performance among Koxinga's Japanese Pirate Ancestors." In *Sea Rovers, Silver, and Samurai: Maritime East Asia in Global History, 1550–1700*, ed. Tonio Andrade, Xing Hang, et al. University of Hawai'i Press.

Shepherd, Hannah. 2009. "Fukuoka: The Making of an 'Asian' City." Master's thesis, SOAS, University of London.

———. 2018. "Fukuoka's Meiji Migrants and the Making of an Imperial Region." *Japan Forum* 30, no. 4.

———. 2024. "An Urbanizing Ocean: Constructions of the Tsushima Strait, 1876–1945." In *Oceanic Japan: The Archipelago in Pacific and Global History*, ed. Stefan Huebner, Nadin Hée, et al. University of Hawai'i Press.

Shibata Masafumi. 1948. "Waga toshi no jūtaku fukkō o kataru: Fukuoka." *Shin jūtaku* 19: 95–96.

Shihōshō chōsabu. 1939. "Fukuoka ken shita zaiju Chōsenjin no dōkō ni tsuite." *Setai chōsa shiryō* 26 (September).

Shimamura Takanori, ed. 2013. *Hikiagesha no sengo*. Shinyōsha.

Shimamura Yasunori. 2010. *Ikiru hōhō no minzokushi: Chōsenkei jūmin shūjū chiiki no minzokugakuteki kenkyū*. Osaka: Kwansei gakuin daigaku shuppan kai.

Shimazu, Naoko. 2009. *Japanese Society at War: Death, Memory and the Russo-Japanese War*. Cambridge University Press.

Shimizu Norikazu. 2010. "Kan'ei Yahata seitetsusho no sōritsu: kōhatsu kōgyōka wo jitsugen shita senkō ikkan seitetsusho no kakuritsu." *KIU Journal of Economics & Business Studies* 17, no. 1.

Shin, Gi-Wook. 1996. *Peasant Protest and Social Change in Colonial Korea*. University of Washington Press.

Shin, Gi-Wook, and Michael Robinson, eds. 1999. *Colonial Modernity in Korea.* Harvard University Press.

Shin, Gi-Wook, and Do-Hyun Han. 1999. "Colonial Corporatism: The Rural Revitalization Campaign, 1932–1940." In *Colonial Modernity in Korea,* ed. Gi-Wook Shin and Michael Robinson. Harvard University Asia Center.

Shindō Muneyuki and Matsumoto Yoshio, eds. 2010. *Zasshi "Toshi mondai" ni miru toshi mondai, 1925–1945.* Iwanami shoten.

Shiode Hiroyuki. 2015. *Ekkyōsha no seijishi: Ajia taiheiyō ni okeru nihon no imin to shokumin.* Nagoya daigaku shuppan kai.

Silverberg, Miriam. 2006. *Erotic Grotesque Nonsense: The Mass Culture of Japanese Modern Times.* University of California Press.

Siniawer, Eiko Maruko. 2008. *Ruffians, Yakuza, Nationalists: The Violent Politics of Modern Japan, 1860–1960.* Cornell University Press.

Smith, William Donald. 1999. "Ethnicity, Class, and Gender in the Mines: Korean Workers in Japan's Chikuhō Coal Field, 1917–1945." PhD diss., University of Washington.

Son Chŏng-mok. 1996. *Ilche kangjŏm'gi tosi kwajŏng yon'gu.* Iljisa.

Sorensen, André. 2002. *The Making of Urban Japan: Cities and Planning from Edo to the Twenty-First Century.* Routledge.

Steinberg, Philip E. 2001. *The Social Construction of the Ocean.* Cambridge University Press.

Stephanson, Anders. 1996. *Manifest Destiny: American Expansion and the Empire of Right.* Hill and Wang.

Sugihara Kaoru and Tamai Kingo, eds. 1996. *Taishō—Ōsaka—Suramu: mō hitotsu no nihonkindai shi.* Rev. edition. Shinyōron.

Sugihara Tōru. 1998. *Ekkyō suru tami: kindai Ōsaka no Chōsenjinshi kenkyū.* Shinkansha.

Sugiyama Tatsumaru. 1991. "Yumeno Kyūsaku no shōgai." In *Yumeno Kyūsaku no sekai,* ed. Nishihara Kazumi. Chusekisha.

Suh, Jiyoung. 2019. "The Gaze on the Threshold: Korean Housemaids of Japanese Families in Colonial Korea." *positions: asia critique* 27, no. 3.

Suzuki Jun. 2002. *Ishin no kōsō to tenkai.* Kōdansha gakujutsu bunko.

Suzuki Kumi. 2010. "Kaihō go no Chōsenjin kikanshasū ni kansuru saikentō." *Zainichi Chōsenjin shi kenkyū* 40.

———. 2017. *Zainichi Chōsenjin no "kikoku" seisaku 1945–1946.* Ryokuin shobō.

Suzuki Takeo. 1941. "Kokudo keikaku to Chōsen toshi." *Toshi Mondai* 32, no. 1: 245–46.

Tachiarai machi kyōdoshi hensan iinkai. 1981. *Tachiarai machi shi.* Tachiarai machi.

Takahama Kyoshi. 1912. *Chōsen.* Jitsugyō no nihon sha.

Takahara Mokuji. 1935. *Kyojin Kashii ō no henrin.* Self-published.

Takahashi Tōsen. 1908. *Zaikan seikō no Kyūshūjin.* Torayogō shoten.

Takaki Naoto and Jung Duk Lim. 2011. "Building an Integrated Trans-border Economic Region between Busan and Fukuoka." *Seoul Journal of Economics* 24, no. 2: 197–220.

Takemae, Eiji. 2003. *The Allied Occupation of Japan*. Continuum.

Taketani, Etsuko. 2014. *The Black Pacific Narrative: Geographic Imaginings of Race and Empire Between the World Wars*. Dartmouth College Press.

Takezawa Shōichiro. 2018. "Jinruigaku wo hiraku: *Bunka wo kaku* kara *Sākuru mura* e." *Bunka jinrui gaku* 83, no. 2.

Tanabe Tamon. 1980. "Shūsen zengo no Pusan chihō kōtsū kyoku." In *Chōsen shūsen no kiroku: shiryōhen dai 2 kan—minami chōsen chiiki no hikiage to nihonjin sewakai no katsudō*, ed. Morita Yasuo and Osada Kanako, 280–99. Gannandō shoten.

Tanaka Yasuo. 1987. "Wakō to higashi ajia tsūkō ken." In *Nihon no shakaishi 1: rettō naigai no kōtsū to kokka*, edited by Asao Naohiro. Iwanami shoten.

Terashima Shigenobu. 1924. *Teikoku kaiun seisaku ron*. Ganshōdō shoten.

Tōgo Takusaburō. 1934. "Kitakyūshū chihō keikaku." *Toshi Mondai* 18, no. 4: 123–31.

———. 1935. "Toshi keikaku yori mitaru Kitakyūshū goshi gappei mondai." *Toshi Kōron* 18, no. 6: 173–81.

Toh, Boon Kwan. 2020. "Black and Silver: Perceptions and Memories of the B-29 Bomber, American Strategic Bombing and the Longest Bombing Missions of the Second World War on Singapore." *War & Society* 39, no. 2.

Tōjō Nobumasa. 1996. "Nisshin sengo no chikugo ni okeru Chōsenjin tankō rōdōsha boshū keikaku." In *Fukuoka ken shi: kindai kenkyū hen kaku ron (2)*, edited by Nishi nihon bunka kyōkai, 55–68. Fukuoka ken.

Tōjō Tadashi. 2003. "Meiji zenki ni okeru kogata ryokyaku kisen no teiki unkō." In *Fukuoka ken shi: tsūshihen kindai sangyō keizai (1) 66*, edited by Nishi nihon bunka kyōkai. Fukuoka ken.

Tokumoto Masahiko. 1983. "Daiichiji Kitakyūshū goshi gappei undō no kōsatsu." *Hōsei kenkyū* 49, nos.1–3: 233–85.

———. 1988. "Sengoshoki no Kitakyūshū goshi gappei ron." *Hōsei kenkyū* 54: 245–76.

Tonomura Masaru. 2004. *Zainichi Chōsenjin shakai no rekishigakuteki kenkyū*. Ryokuin shobō.

———. 2008. "Chōsen rōdōsha no 'Nihon naichitokō' saikō: hijunbikataidō, seikatsusenryakuteki idō to rōdōryoku tōsei." *Kankoku chōsen no bunka to shakai* 7.

———. 2012. *Chōsenjin kyōsei renkō*. Iwanami shoten.

Tonooka, Chika. 2016. "Reverse Emulation and the Cult of Japanese Efficiency in Edwardian Britain." *Historical Journal* 60, no. 1.

Torisu Kyoichi. 1987. "Kindai toshi Fukuoka no keisei to hakurankai, kyoshinkai." *Museum Kyūshū: Bunmei no kurosurōdo* 25: 9–15.

Tōyō takushoku kabushiki kaisha, ed. 1922. *Ijūmin nenbo*. Tōyō takushoku kabushiki kaisha.

Trask, Haunani-Kay. 2000. "Settlers of Color and "Immigrant" Hegemony: 'Locals' in Hawai'i." *Amerasia Journal* 26, no. 2: 1–26.

Tsurumi, E. Patricia. 1990. *Factory Girls: Women in the Thread Mills of Meiji Japan*. Princeton University Press.

Tsuruta Masaaki. 1993. "Nihon kōkū yusō kabushikigaisha no setsuritsu to sono haikei: Shōwa shoki no minkan kōkū seisaku." *Kōtsū shi kenkyū* 29.

Tsutsui Chūgo, ed. 1936. *Hakatakō taikan*. Fukuoka shiyakusho sangyō ka.

———. 1937. *Hakatakō to Manshūkoku*. Fukuoka shiyakusho sangyō ka.

———. 1942. *Hakatakō to Chōsen*. Fukuoka shiyakusho shōkō ka.

Uchida, Jun. 2011. *Brokers of Empire: Japanese Settler Colonialism in Korea 1876–1945*. Harvard University Press.

———. 2016. "From Island Nation to Oceanic Empire: A Vision of Japanese Expansion from the Periphery." *Journal of Japanese Studies* 42, no. 1: 57–90.

———. 2023. *Provincializing Empire: Ōmi Merchants in the Japanese Transpacific Diaspora*. University of California Press.

Udagawa Masaharu and Uehara Yukihiko. 2012. *A History of a Hundred Years of Nippon Suisan Kaisha*. Nippon Suisan Kaisha.

United States Army 40th Division and Maxwell Barach, eds. Ca. 1945. *Evacuation*. US Army.

United States Army, Fukuoka Military Government. 1946–47. *Semi-Monthly Activities Reports, Fukuoka Military Government Team*. US Army.

———. 1947–1948. *Monthly Military Government Activities Reports, Fukuoka Military Government Team*. US Army.

United States Strategic Bombing Survey. 1975. *Final Reports of the United States Strategic Bombing Survey 1945–1947*. National Archives.

Urasaki Jun. 1965. *Kieta Okinawa ken*. Okinawa jijishuppan sha.

Utsunomiya Megumi. 2016. "Nihonjin josei no Chōsen hikiage to "Naisen kekkon." *Nihon gakuhō* 35.

Van Riper, A. B. 2004. *Imagining Flight: Aviation and Popular Culture*. Texas A&M University Press.

Van Vleck, Jenifer. 2013. *Empire of the Air: Aviation and the American Ascendancy*. Harvard University Press.

Wada Shigetatsu. 1939. "Tokyo-Fukuoka kan kokuei jidōsha dōro to sono kokusakuteki igi." *Kōgyō kokusaku* 2, no. 2: 101–3.

Wasserstrom, Jeffrey N. 2007. "Is Global Shanghai 'Good to Think'? Thoughts on Comparative History and Post-Socialist Cities." *Journal of World History* 18, no. 2: 199–234.

Watt, Lori. 2009. *When Empire Comes Home: Repatriation and Reintegration in Postwar Japan*. Harvard University Asia Center.

———. 2015. "Embracing Defeat in Seoul: Rethinking Decolonization in Korea, 1945." *Journal of Asian Studies* 74: 153–74.

Weiner, Michael. 1994. *Race and Migration in Imperial Japan*. Routledge.

Weisenfeld, Gennifer. 2012. *Imaging Disaster: Tokyo and the Visual Culture of Japan's Great Earthquake of 1923*. University of California Press.

Wigen, Kären. 1995. *The Making of a Japanese Periphery, 1750–1920*. University of California Press.

———. 2010. *A Malleable Map: Geographies of Restoration in Central Japan, 1600–1912*. University of California Press.

Wilson, Noell. 2015. *Defensive Positions: The Politics of Maritime Security in Toku-gawa Japan*. Harvard University Asia Center.

Yamada Shōji. 1987. "Chōsenjin kyōsei rōdō no rekishiteki zentei: Chikuhō tanden wo omo na jirei toshite." *Zainichi Chōsenjin shi kenkyū* 17.

Yamamoto, Takahiro. 2017. "Japan's Passport System and the Opening of Borders, 1866–1878." *Historical Journal* [online] 60, no. 4.

———. 2023. *Demarcating Japan: Imperialism, Islanders, and Mobility, 1855–1884*. Harvard University Asia Center.

Yamamura, Kozo. 1967. "The Role of the Samurai in the Development of Modern Banking in Japan." *Journal of Economic History* 27, no. 2.

Yata Fumio. 1953. "Fukuoka shi: Itazuke kūgun kichi." In *Kichi nihon*, ed. Inomata Kōzō. Wakōsha.

Yellen, Jeremy. 2019. *The Greater East Asia Co-Prosperity Sphere: When Total Empire Met Total War*. Cornell University Press.

Yi Nam-wŏn. 2013 [1935]. "Pusan." English translation in *Rat Fire: Korean Stories from the Japanese Empire*, ed. Theodore Hughes, Jae-Yong Kim, Jin-kyung Lee, and Sang-Kyung Lee. Cornell University Press.

Yŏm Sangsŏp. 2010. "On the Eve of the Uprising [Mansejŏn]." English translation in Sunyoung Park and Jefferson J. A. Gatrall, translators, *On the Eve of the Uprising and Other Stories from Colonial Korea*. University of Hawai'i Press.

Yonekura, Seiichiro. 2015. "The Samurai Company: Double Creative Response in Meiji Japan." *Hitotsubashi Journal of Commerce and Management* 49, no. 1: 1–23.

Yoneyama Yutaka and Kawahara Norifumi, eds. 2007. *Nikkeijin no keiken to kokusai idō: zaigai nihonjin imin no kingendaishi*. Jinbun shoin.

———, eds. 2015. *Nikkeijin no kokusai idō to taiheiyō sekai*. Bunrikaku.

Yoon Hak-jun. 1979. "Waga mikkōki." *Chōsen kenkyū* 190: 4–15.

Yoshida Shien. 1976. *Chiisana tatakai no hibi: Okinawa fukki no urabanashi*. Bunkyō shōji.

Yoshino Hiroaki, Kajita Yoshitaka, and Akimoto Fukuo. 2007. "Toshikeikakuhō seitei go kara shūsenji made (1920 nen~1945 nen) no Fukuoka toshikeikaku ni kansuru kenkyū—Daifukuokashi ron ni chakumoku shite." *Doboku shi kenkyū kōen shu* 27: 169–76.

Young, Louise. 1998. *Japan's Total Empire: Manchuria and the Culture of Wartime Imperialism*. University of California Press.

———. 2013. *Beyond the Metropolis: Second Cities and Modern Life in Interwar Japan*. University of California Press.

———. 2014. "Japan's New International History." *American Historical Review* 119: 1117–28.

Yu, Eui-Young. 2009. "Regionalism in Korea." In *Korea Confronts Globalization*, ed. Yun-shik Chang, Hyun-ho Seok, and Donald Baker. Routledge.

Yuasa Katsue. 1952. *Tsushima*. Shuppan Tokyo.

Yūki, Masami Raker. 2009. "New Life, New Language: Ecological Identity in the Work of Morisaki Kazue." *Gengo bunka ronsō* 13.

Yumoto Noboru. 1939. *Chūō ajia ōdan tetsudō kensetsu ron: sekai heiwa e no ōdō*. Tōa kōtsū sha.

Zai Nihon Daikan minkoku mindan, ed. 2016. *Fukuoka Kankoku Mindan 70 nen shi*. Zai Nihon Daikan minkoku mindan, Fukuoka ken chihō honbu.

Zenkoku toshi keikaku kyōgikai, ed. 1935. *Dai ni kai zenkoku toshi keikaku kyōgikai kyōgai jikō*. Zenkoku toshi keikaku kyōgikai.

INDEX

Founded in 1893,
UNIVERSITY OF CALIFORNIA PRESS
publishes bold, progressive books and journals
on topics in the arts, humanities, social sciences,
and natural sciences—with a focus on social
justice issues—that inspire thought and action
among readers worldwide.

The UC PRESS FOUNDATION
raises funds to uphold the press's vital role
as an independent, nonprofit publisher, and
receives philanthropic support from a wide
range of individuals and institutions—and from
committed readers like you. To learn more, visit
ucpress.edu/supportus.